PICTURING FAITH

PICTURING FAITH

photography and the great depression

COLLEEN MCDANNELL

Yale University Press

New Haven and London

Frontispiece: John Vachon, truck of an itinerant preacher parked in front of the U.S. Capitol. Washington, D.C., July 1939 (LC-USF34-060110-D).

Publication of this book is supported in part by a grant from the Nancy Batson Nisbet Rash Publication Fund.

Designed by Sonia L. Shannon.
Set in Bulmer type with Futura display by Tseng Information Systems, Inc.
Printed in the United States of America by Edwards Brothers, Inc.

Library of Congress Cataloging-in-Publication Data
McDannell, Colleen.
Picturing faith : photography and the Great Depression /
Colleen McDannell.
    p.   cm.
Includes bibliographical references and index.
ISBN 0-300-10430-8 (hardcover : alk. paper)
1. United States — Religion — 1901–1945 — Pictorial works.   2. United States — Religious life and customs — Pictorial works.   3. Documentary photography — United States — History — 20th century.   I. Title.
BL2525.M395 2005
200'.973'09043 — dc22
2004007820

A catalogue record for this book is available from the British Library.

The paper in this book meets the guidelines for permanence and durability of the Committee on Production Guidelines for Book Longevity of the Council on Library Resources.

10 9 8 7 6 5 4 3 2 1

To my parents,
Kenneth A. McDannell and Margaret Mary McDannell,
who were there.

Contents

PICTURING FAITH

1.1   Dorothea Lange, *Revival Mother,* woman praying at Victory Through Christ Society Sunday morning worship service in a garage. Dos Palos, California, June 1938 (LC-USF34-018216-E)

1
Introducing Americans to America

saw and approached the hungry and desperate mother, as if drawn by a magnet," Dorothea Lange remembered years later. "I do not remember how I explained my presence or
my camera to her, but I do remember she asked me no questions. I made five exposures,
working closer and closer from the same direction. I did not ask her name or her history.
She told me her age, that she was 32. She said that they had been living on frozen vegetables from the surrounding fields, and birds that the children killed. She had just sold
the tires from her car to buy food. There she sat in that lean-to tent with her children huddled
around her, and seemed to know that my pictures might help her, and so she helped me. There
was a sort of equality about it." Dorothea Lange took many pictures that chilly spring of 1936.
She was concluding a monthlong trip photographing migratory farm labor in California for
the Historical Section of the Resettlement Administration. In the short term, Lange's photographs did aid the migrant workers. Lange took the pictures to an editor she knew at the *San*

1.2   Dorothea Lange, *Migrant Mother,* destitute pea picker with
three of her seven children. Nipomo, California, March 1936
(LC-USF34-009058-C)

Francisco News, he contacted local relief agencies, and food was dispatched to the starving
pea pickers. He also agreed to print several of the photographs in the newspaper: "What Does
the 'New Deal' Mean to This Mother and Her Children?" read the headline on one article.[1]

One of the photographs that Dorothea Lange took of the California pea pickers has become an icon of the Great Depression (fig. 1.2). Called *Migrant Mother,* it has been reproduced
countless times in newspapers, magazines, scholarly monographs, photography books, and
college textbooks. Like the *Mona Lisa,* it is a classic portrait; it has been used to summarize both the reality of human tragedy and the imprecise nature of visual images. Certainly
Migrant Mother appears whenever the discussion turns to how the federal government sent
out photographers to document the suffering of innocent people during the Great Depression. The picture is used to introduce the artistry of Dorothea Lange and the other talented
photographers who worked to establish documentary photography in the United States.[2]

In June 1938 Dorothea Lange took more pictures of migrants in California. Two were of a
prayer service of the Victory Through Christ Society. Lange did not merely make the photographs, she took the time to describe what she saw. Her captions explain that the "Sunday

morning revival" met in a garage in Dos Palos, California (see fig. 1.1). In one photograph a woman is prominent in the picture and stands with her hands outstretched. Lange quotes her as testifying, "He's such a wonderful savior, Glory to God. I'm so glad I came to home. Praise God. His love is so wonderful. He's coming soon. I want to praise the Lord for what he is to me. He saved me one time and filled me with the Holy Ghost. Hallalulah! He will fill your heart today with overflowing. Bless His Holy name."[3] The care in which Lange preserved the woman's image and testimony indicates that the photographer was struck by the intensity of spirit she found in a California garage. Lange had happened on a Sunday prayer service led by a Pentecostal woman preacher. She may have been leading the prayers of women in a separate area, or she may have organized her own small congregation of which we see only the women.

Lange had been photographing refugees from Oklahoma and Texas who had come west for the harvest. Her primary photographic goal was to document migrant suffering: crowds waiting for relief checks, families traveling in overpacked cars, tent camps, and the strenuous work of picking vegetables and fruit. While backbreaking labor certainly dominated migrant life, Lange also managed to photograph another life in California: a couple singing hymns inside their tent, a group of children attending an outdoor Sunday school, a wooden church, and a bus with a "Jesus Saves" sign. These photographs of Dorothea Lange do not have the classic status of *Migrant Mother,* and they have seldom been seen. They, and other photographs of religious practices, are not part of our mental image of the Depression.

Migrant Mother was initially distributed in order to elicit sympathy for the California migrants and thus gain popular support for New Deal agricultural reforms. Eventually through sheer visual repetition, it came to summarize the insecurities of the Great Depression and the power of documentary photography. Lange's other photograph, which we can call *Revival Mother,* presents a different perspective on the era. Unlike *Migrant Mother,* the strength and independence of *Revival Mother* does not stimulate pity. Lange photographed *Revival Mother* wearing her Sunday best, hat and all, and appearing confident in her religious rapture. *Revival Mother* is experiencing something that separates her from other mothers; her ecstasy connects her to something fundamentally different from Dust Bowl poverty. She stands apart from her community, rather than being tightly framed by her children. *Revival Mother* may not even be a mother. Calling upon biblical imagery to help interpret the photograph, she looks more like the independent New Testament women of Corinth condemned for speaking in church rather than the humble Virgin Mary (see 1 Cor 14:34–37). *Revival Mother*'s full attention is directed toward her God; not out toward an uncertain future or inward toward her children. What could the New Deal add to what this woman is already receiving?

These two photographs by Dorothea Lange, one a familiar icon and the other unknown, are among the approximately 164,000 black-and-white negatives now preserved by the Library of Congress. Between 1935 and 1943 the federal government spent almost one million dollars creating such pictures. Under the auspices first of the Resettlement Administration, then of the Farm Security Administration (FSA), and finally of the Office of War Information (OWI), "Historical Section" photographers traveled across the country making a visual record of the impact on the American people of the Depression, and eventually the Second World War. The director of the project, Roy E. Stryker, hired (and sometimes fired) more than twenty photographers. Many of those photographers—Dorothea Lange, Walker Evans, Carl Mydans,

Arthur Rothstein, Russell Lee, Jack Delano, Edwin Rosskam, Marion Post Wolcott, John Collier, Jr., John Vachon, Gordon Parks—continued to shape documentary photography after their government service was over. Filing cabinets in the Prints and Photographs Division of the Library of Congress store 107,000 prints made from their original negatives, as well as reels of the microfilmed lots of the photographs. Almost all of the images are also available online.[4]

Some of the images are well-known: photographs of a woman's gnarled hands, of a man and boy running in a dust storm, of a girl with a vacant stare—these have become a part of our mental image of the Depression. The coffee table books of recent years continue to present a set of familiar images: Americans struggle to earn a living on inhospitable land, they enjoy modern entertainments, they have families, they build, they reform. What we have not seen are pictures like *Revival Mother*. Occasionally a few wooden churches are reproduced to evoke nostalgia for the past, but these speak more to the beauty of vernacular architecture than to the faith commitments of their builders. When the rare religious practice is included, no explanation accompanies it, as the picture is assumed to "speak for itself." The visual image built from the photographic file presents America as decidedly secular.

It is my intention to challenge the legitimacy of that conclusion and to insist that photographs like *Revival Mother* were an integral aspect of the documentary project undertaken by the Farm Security Administration and later by the Office of War Information. Roy Stryker told his photographers to include pictures of religious life, and they complied. They photographed women singing hymns before meetings, the shrines of Mexican farm workers, and African-American children dressed in choir robes. The everyday lives of Utah Mormons and Pennsylvania Mennonites are portrayed, along with praying New York Catholics and Texas Methodists. The FSA/OWI file includes photographs of "God Bless Our Home" prints and Jewish religious goods stores. It illustrates how Americans went to outdoor baptisms, built adobe churches, sent their boys and girls to Hebrew School, and traveled in "Gospel cars." *Revival Mother* is only one of hundreds of photographs that give us an unprecedented glimpse into the religious world of everyday people.

While many Americans of the thirties and forties were religious, others were not. The thirties were also a profoundly secular period of American history. Roy Stryker and his photographers were among the "unchurched" of America. Raised as Protestants, Catholics, and Jews, as adults they criticized organized religion and did not participate in its rituals. Stryker and his photographers understood themselves to be modern, progressive people who valued open inquiry, freedom, flexibility, democracy, change, and individuality. They were humanists who demanded social and economic justice. From their perspective, religious communities frequently worked against those goals. The richness of the file indicates, however, that in spite of their secular orientation they were drawn to religious expressions. Stryker had been raised in a Protestant family, and he understood the importance of religion for many Americans. People expressed their creativity and innovation, as well as their faith, in their sacred spaces and rituals. As artists, the photographers recognized the beauty of religious buildings and the drama of pious practices. As reformers, Stryker and his team respected the ways that congregations flourished within a context of overwhelming economic crisis and social change. As propagandists, they acknowledged that "freedom of religion" was something that people were willing to fight a war over. And yet their correspondence reminds us that they also understood religious people to be unpredictable, patronizing, and authoritarian. *Picturing Faith* tells the story of how a set of photographers — who were not themselves religious — saw religion in the United States.

Picturing Faith is thus more than a visual story of religion in America. Stryker and the photographers focused on certain aspects of faith and ignored others. Their "eyes" were shaped by their own personal biographies, their understanding of the project's mission, the reigning standards of art, and the changing American political environment. Photographers filtered religion through the aesthetic lenses of abstract modernism and American regionalism. Local, ordinary piety was photographed rather than national organizations or unusual, heroic expressions of faith. By the late thirties, the demands of war caused a shift in their mission. Neither Stryker nor the photographers wanted to be remembered as propaganda makers, and yet much of the file celebrated the strength of the nation, not its weaknesses. In these later years, photographers used religious communities as ways to assert the cohesiveness of American society.

The Documentary Impulse

The photographic project of the Farm Security Administration was undertaken with the same spirit as many of Roosevelt's "alphabet" agencies established within one hundred days of his election in 1934. These agencies were to examine America's national economic problems and then to implement specific solutions. By 1935 the Resettlement Administration — the forerunner to the Farm Security Administration — was established. Roosevelt appointed a Columbia University economics professor, Rexford Tugwell, as its director. Tugwell had been undersecretary of agriculture, but now he was to oversee efforts to improve the conditions of American farmers. The Resettlement Administration was to coordinate land-use planning, run migrant labor camps, support semicooperative farm projects, and fund various loan and grant programs and tenant-purchase plans (fig. 1.3). Between 1935 and 1937 the Resettlement Administration (RA) educated farmers about soil erosion and environmental pollution, established flood control and reforestation programs, and pressed for recognition of the plight of rural laborers. In 1937 its programs were taken over by the Farm Security Administration. Tugwell had used pictures in his economics textbooks and thought that by making pictures of real rural people suffering, he could gain support for the projects of the RA. Tugwell hired Roy Stryker to direct a group of photographers who were asked to provide an accurate, visible description of the government's efforts to improve America's social conditions. These men and women eventually made up the Historical Section of the Division of Information of the Farm Security Administration.

Tugwell, Stryker, and the photographers all shared the assumption that pictures put specific faces on the problems of rural life. Statistics and reports were important, but few Americans would be moved by a set of dry facts. If Americans *saw* the lives of the poor, they would be more concerned about poverty in the United States. Stryker and most of the photographers saw their mission as bringing together social scientific investigation, government reform policy, and artistic expression. The stated aim of the photographic project was to educate,

1.3   Russell Lee, kitchen of farm home built under FSA tenant purchase program.
Hidalgo County, Texas, February 1939 (LC-US34-032145-D)

persuade, and convince. Several years before photojournalism became standard in magazines, government photographers had — in the words of Roy Stryker — "introduced Americans to America."[5] From Stryker's perspective, there was nothing sentimental about their depictions of rural life. Photographers employed the camera, the technological medium of the twentieth century, to document in a realistic and rigorous way the problems confronting American society.

The Historical Section was part of a documentary movement that flourished during the thirties and early forties. Americans collected information about the human dimension of the nation and presented their findings to a curious public. Some of this information was statistical and could fit easily into almanacs or encyclopedias. Artists looked at the regional American landscape and made paintings that stressed the unique character of the United States. Case studies, once considered mere scientific texts produced by social workers, were compiled into popular books. Private publishers developed picture magazines like *Life* (1936) and *Look* (1937) that used photographs to stress the documentary nature of their reporting. Such texts emphasized the universality of the human condition and conveyed the details of everyday life in ways that acknowledged the drama of feeling and emotion. People read documentary books, saw documentary movies, and looked at documentary pictures not merely because they wanted to be amused and entertained but because they wanted to know and understand. Depression miseries had forced them to take a closer look at the country in which they lived.[6]

During the thirties, photography was also used to illustrate what it was like to exist on the edge of society. The Photo League, which split off from the Film and Photo League in 1936, believed that photography was an "expressive medium that could mirror social problems and promote social change."[7] Many of the Photo League's associates, members, and teachers came from immigrant Jewish families, especially from eastern Europe.[8] In their preference for the streets of New York's East Side, members of the Photo League did not make simple reform photographs but rather complicated representations of the social and cultural ethos in which they lived. Their photographs explored the raw character of their neighborhoods and families rather than promoting photography as a genteel art of beauty and technical skill. The Photo League's commitment to "honest" photography (rather than art photography) created a standard for street photography. With the onset of the Depression, members were hired by government agencies, and they continued to shape documentary photography as it evolved during the New Deal years.

What was particularly new and important about the documentary impulse of the thirties was that the federal government funded much of this movement. During a period of massive unemployment and economic turmoil, the documentary impulse flourished because the government paid people to work. The FSA/OWI photographic project may have been the most extensive and easily accessible of those sponsored by the federal government, but it was by no means the only one. Foremost among those New Deal agencies that produced documentary works was the Works Program Administration (WPA). The WPA was begun in 1935, renamed the Works Projects Administration in 1939, and dismantled in 1943. It was under the WPA's auspices that most art, theater, film, history, and photography projects were funded. From supporting Aaron Copland to write *Appalachian Spring*, to decorating post offices with historical murals, to preserving the words of former ex-slaves, WPA projects were absolutely essential to the thirties documentary spirit. Although only 7 percent of the WPA's total budget, the federal arts and history projects convinced many Americans that they *had* an important culture.[9]

The WPA funded photography as a part of its humanities projects and also through a specific Photographic Division within the Federal Art Project. As with other New Deal agencies, pictures were taken of the various WPA divisions. The National Archives, for instance, houses 25,092 images depicting Federal Theater Project productions and 2,500 images made for the American Guide series organized by the Federal Writer's Project.[10] Within the WPA's Federal Art Project, the Photographic Division funded specific creative projects. Rather than depicting the nuts and bolts of WPA humanities-oriented projects, these photographs were to be examples of art themselves. WPA photographers who worked for the Federal Art Projects designed and controlled their own projects. They made studies of urban poverty, children, Jewish rituals, Harlem, and Coney Island. While images of New York City dominated federal creative photography, some photographers did work in Louisiana, Florida, Oregon, and California.

Stryker's Team

Given the flurry of documentary projects going on in the interwar years, it is not surprising that Stryker could employ a steady and talented pool of photographers. For the most part the photographers Stryker hired were young men and women beginning their professional lives. They were not seasoned photographers recognized for their documentary expertise. Those who were familiar with cameras and photography were still developing their skills, although many had been trained as artists. At any one time, there would be only between three and six photographers employed by the Historical Section, but freelance photographers also sent Stryker pictures. Some of the men traveled with their wives, but most were single men and women who had no family ties. Their adventurous spirit was closely aligned to a curiosity about and a respect for humanity. Many had traveled to Europe in the twenties and thirties and then watched with awe as the brutal arm of fascism swept across the continent. The photographers were outsiders—Jews, women, an African American, an Irish Catholic—who had learned as children the fragility of social class and to be wary of the privileges of wealth. Most agreed that their job was to educate and reform through making pictures. There are, of course, exceptions to these generalizations. Not all of the photographers were educated, well traveled, and reform oriented. John Collier, Jr., traveled around the Horn of Africa but was dyslexic and never went to high school. John Vachon, who had majored in English in college, was originally hired as a filing clerk. Arthur Rothstein had never ventured outside of New York City before joining the Historical Section. Walker Evans showed little interest in the reforming possibilities of the photograph. Dorothea Lange had two children herself and married a man with three children. The length of time individuals worked for Stryker also varied, although all remember their experiences as formative.

What they experienced on the road knitted together all but the most independent-minded photographers into "Stryker's team." Photographers were given five dollars a day for living expenses and three cents a mile for gas. Stryker sent them informal scripts and letters describing various projects he wanted them to pursue. He also sent them lists of books and articles, expecting them to be intellectually prepared for their assignments. Cars were packed with at least two, usually three cameras, film, developing chemicals, replacement parts, lenses, flash bulbs, tripods, and enough clothes to get the photographer through weeks of sleeping in bare-bones hotels. When the photographers arrived in an area, they had to contact various governmental agencies whose representatives pointed out the appropriate places and people to photograph. Once in the field, the photographers had to persuade the skeptical to let them "shoot" their homes, families, fields, animals, and leisure activities. The women photographers had to convince the moralistic that a single woman on the road was not a prostitute. Arthur Rothstein remembered being asked about being a Jew, and Gordon Parks experienced the racism of a segregated Washington, D.C.

After a long day of photography, some developed the film in the hotel bathroom and sent the negatives back to Washington, where prints were made. Most, however, mailed the film to Washington, where Stryker's darkroom staff made contact sheets. These were sent back to the photographers, who wrote captions for the acceptable photographs. If they could stay awake a few hours more, they would write of their adventures to Stryker or merely ask for more film. Life on the road was exciting but tough. All of the FSA/OWI photographers remember the experience as intensely educational, professionally stimulating, and personally challenging. Most made little more than $35 per week in salary, but they did not complain. What could have been better than being paid to travel around the country photographing when millions of people were waiting in breadlines and worrying about how to feed their children?

While the photographers were busy traveling the country, Stryker and his Washington staff spent most of their time trying to get the pictures out to the public. The FSA/OWI photographs appeared in major newspapers and magazines throughout the country, from the *Washington Post* to the *African American,* from *Architectural Forum* to *Junior Scholastic.* Stryker argued that publishing the photographs reduced social distances between classes, races, and regions and helped promote New Deal reforms. In addition to newspapers and magazines, FSA/OWI photographs appeared in commercial books. Archibald MacLeish used them to illustrate his epic poem *Land of the Free* (1938), Sherwood Anderson published them in *Home Town* (1940), and Richard Wright scattered them throughout *12 Million Black Voices* (1941). Publishers paid nothing for the rights to reproduce the government's photographs. The Historical Section assembled pictures of poor white and black farmers into small traveling exhibitions that went to camera clubs, universities, church groups, conventions, and state fairs. When a selection of FSA photographs was shown at the 1938 First International Photographic Exposition in Grand Central Palace in New York City, 540 responses were dropped in a comment box. While the majority of respondents felt the pictures were "moving and dramatic," some called them "subversive propaganda." Others warned the government, "Don't spend taxpayers' money on film." In 1939 and 1940 the Photo League in New York City used FSA photographs in exhibitions on rural America. Baptists displayed FSA exhibitions on sharecropping at their adult summer camps. Even the American Historical Association hosted an exhibition of FSA pictures at its national meeting in 1940.[11]

Larger collections of pictures were sent to prominent art museums. In 1938 the Museum of Modern Art in New York coordinated a traveling exhibition of fifty of the FSA photographs. Its press release boasted, "After the usual diet of the art world — cream puffs, éclairs and such — the hard, bitter reality of these photographs is the tonic the soul needs." Stryker mailed the pictures to whomever asked for them. He asked only for a shipping fee and set no restrictions on how the pictures should be used. The photographers had no control over the meanings ascribed to their pictures or their use. Newspapers cropped the photographs, laid them out at odd angles, and created their own narratives about what they meant. Museums mounted FSA photographs without the photographers' names near the prints. Baptists used them in 1941 to promote missionary work among the Dust Bowl migrants to California, ignoring entirely their original captions.[12] Since their deposit in 1944 at the Library of Congress, the photographs have been widely reprinted in every conceivable medium and now are even more available in digitized form. The project that Stryker began in 1935 continues to shape how we understand the thirties and forties, and to define the role of the visual in culture.

Cowpunchers Don't Need Toothbrushes or Religion

In January 1939 Roy Stryker wrote a letter to one of his three photographers, Marion Post. Post had been traveling in Florida, and Stryker wanted her to meet with "a Miss Lowry" from the "Federal Council of Churches, Home Missions Board." Stryker explained that Miss Lowry was promoting a "little book" called *They Starve That We May Eat* and that "she and her crowd are trying to stir the church groups up on the whole migrant, displaced agricultural labor problem." Stryker seemed unusually curious about Miss Lowry. He asked Post to find out what Lowry thought about the failure of the La Follette hearings to go forward on their examination of New Deal violations of labor rights, and, perhaps more important, how other church groups were reacting to it. "Easy on this," Stryker wrote in another letter. "I would hate to see Miss Lowry stampede her groups into any mass action. As you know, I have certain qualms about church groups anyway—you never know whether their ammunition is going to come out the proper end of the barrel, or whether it is going to come back and hit you in the face." [13]

Marion Post attempted to accommodate her boss's wishes but had a difficult time trying to connect with Lowry. Finally, the two women met in Belle Glade, Florida. Post wrote Stryker that she had taken Lowry and two other women to visit several families and to talk with workers in the field—doctors, nurses, and community leaders. The exchanges between Lowry, her associates, Post, and the other field contacts must not have gone well. "Maybe I'm intolerant in my own way," Post wrote Stryker, "and I suppose these women are at least aware of a few more things and interested and active, but god damn it I can't stand their approach to problems or their unrealistic and sentimental way of handling it. After a whole day of that crap and listening to them playing Jesus I could just plain puke!" Post had no sympathy for the churchwomen's charitable solutions as she perceived them: "Just a little daily bible reading for the kiddies and a service on Sunday for all the folks." She informed Stryker that she had told everyone that there was no connection between the FSA photographic project and that of the churchwomen, and that she would help out but that Lowry could not count on traveling with her. Post acknowledged that she would have to continue to meet with Lowry, but she assured her boss, "I won't let her mess my plans up." [14]

Stryker enjoyed the feisty letter from Post. "The description of the encounter with God's Chosen delighted me no end," he wrote back. "It just goes to prove my theory that once you get in the services of God, you seldom [are] ever able to free yourself of these damnable traits. Some do it, but not many." He then thanked Post for her efforts and reassured her that she did not have to go out of her way to help Lowry make contacts in Florida. "I think this will cure me," Stryker concluded, "of ever imposing any more people on you photographers." [15] Stryker and Post came to an understanding in their correspondence: religious people were difficult; their methods were sanctimonious, patronizing, and ineffective; and there was no reason why a government photographer whose goal it was to improve rural living conditions should have to interact with "God's Chosen."

Given Roy Stryker's sarcasm about "God's Chosen," we might be surprised to find out that he was raised in a Christian household and influenced by the Social Gospel movement. Like many twentieth-century reformers, Stryker learned as a child the values, practices, and languages of a religious community. As adults, however, both he and his photographers found the world outside of religion more hospitable to their efforts of social change. Stryker and his team had an intense interest in America's people but were skeptical of organized religion. Churches and synagogues were not initiating changes in society and appeared only to support bigotry and otherworldliness. Stryker's biography not only provides a sense of the leader of the Historical Section, it also is an example of how the men and women of the thirties moved through and then out of religious communities.

Roy Emerson Stryker (1893–1975) was the quintessential "beyond-the-Beltway" government outsider, and his biography and personality shaped how the photographic project would develop. Born in Great Bend, Kansas, Stryker moved with his family to Montrose, Colorado, when he was three. In 1896 Montrose was a sleepy Colorado town barely fourteen years old. This frontier community on the western slope of the Rockies, however, was quickly developing the marks of culture. A high school and opera house were built, along with a series of churches—Methodist (1884), Congregational (1885), Baptist (1898), and Episcopal (1912). By 1912 even the Catholics, in "one of the most impressive ceremonies Montrose has ever had," had laid the cornerstone for their church.[16]

Stryker's father, George, was a farmer who has been called a "radical Populist." He dabbled in politics and pursued small-business ventures in the growing town. George and his wife, Ellen, had seven children, and Roy was the youngest boy. According to Roy, at some point George "got religion from a circuit-riding preacher." Stryker remembered that his father "always tried new things and he tried them harder than anybody else." Family worship became a part of their daily activities: "We all had to get down on our knees in the evening and pray good and loud and nobody prayed louder than he did." The elder Stryker combined his faith with his concern for radical politics. According to his son, the prayers became especially loud "at the end of one day when he had been stumping for Populism. He started out all right, but all at once his convictions got hold of him, and at the top of his voice he prayed: 'Please God, damn the bankers of Wall Street, damn the railroads, and double damn the Standard Oil Company!'"[17]

Roy Stryker frequently told this story in order to illustrate his long-term commitment to social activism, something he had learned at his father's knee. Stryker also used the tale for its humorous ironic twist. After he left the federal government, he actually joined Standard Oil, setting up the company's photographic department. Stryker also probably thought that the combination of praying and damning shed some light on the unpredictable character of religion. His father, however, might have been puzzled by his son's sentiments, because George Stryker probably perceived a continuity between Populism and evangelical Protestantism. Social reform movements—from abolition to women's rights to temperance to civil rights—have been fueled by the religious convictions of their leaders and supporters. Populism and evangelism share a pragmatic concern for reform, an anti–big business orientation, and the belief that Americans can successfully improve their society because of their Christian commitments. While churches in the cities certainly could be bastions of wealth and privilege, rural churches like those in Montrose often had closer ties with grassroots needs and experiences. Farmers met in churches and used biblical language to articulate their concerns. Even if Stryker's father never set foot in a Methodist or Baptist church, it would not be unusual that his own Christian beliefs energized his politics and his politics deepened his religious convictions. Although the humor of Roy Stryker's story is based on the opposition of praying and damning, the two acts often have been joined in religious history. "Getting religion" for many Americans has been a politically radicalizing experience.

There is no question that Stryker's time in rural Colorado gave him an insight into American life that was different from many of the government bureaucrats in the Roosevelt administration. His self-confidence, salty tongue, pointed sense of humor, and belief that there was more to America than the East Coast may have been cultivated on the rugged western landscape (fig. 1.4). His experiences in Montrose may also have given him a realistic perspective on the precarious position of rural Americans in the national economy during the early decades of the twentieth century. Life on the High Plains could be brutal and capricious. Ranchers were as dependent on the vicissitudes of livestock trends determined by urban markets as they were on the weather and the land. Stryker may also have felt somewhat out of place in the physically demanding rural West. A small man with weak eyes, he was at home with books as well as with horses. He served, for instance, as the manager of the high school football team, not as one of the players. The death of Stryker's father when he was sixteen must also have heightened his sense of vulnerability. His family's support of his desire for learning and education gave Stryker an alternative to a life of hard and frequently boring rural labor. Like many youngest sons, Stryker could not find a place for himself on the farm, so in 1920 he moved permanently to the city—initially to the small town of Golden, located near Denver, Colorado. There he pursued a science degree at the Colorado School of Mines.

Stryker might have stayed in Denver and had a career in chemistry if he had not made the acquaintance of George Collins, a young minister. Stryker remembers meeting several socially committed ministers during his time in Golden who understood his desire to experience the world outside of Colorado. These ministers ran a "kind of crazy workshop" where young people would work in industry and then meet—sometimes as many as four nights a week— to discuss issues "with all kinds of people." Stryker credited one of the ministers, George Collins, with facilitating his move to New York City. In a 1967 interview Stryker recalled that he "read the *New Republic*, and I saw the *Nation*, and I read a lot of Rauschenbusch. I read a lot of things and my life was changing rapidly." [18]

Through this "crazy workshop" Stryker had been introduced to the Social Gospel movement, a group of theologians, teachers, and ministers who encouraged political progressivism and social action by the churches. These liberal Protestants were well aware of the negative consequences of the Industrial Revolution—the concentration of economic power in the hands of a few, the poverty of the workers, the squalor of urban centers. They argued that Christians must not be satisfied with individual piety or simple-minded charity. Instead, Christian charity needed to be brought into the modern era. Biblical and theological insights should be accompanied by scientific analysis of the causes of poverty. Saving souls was not enough. Christians ought to attend to the nation's ills and work toward creating a just and righteous social order.

Stryker remembered that the writings of Walter Rauschenbusch had influenced his social awareness. Walter Rauschenbusch was a Baptist minister who spent the first ten years of his career as pastor of a slum church in New York City. He later became a professor at Rochester Seminary, and his books *Christianity and the Social Crisis* (1907), *Christianizing the Social Order* (1917), and *A Theology of the Social Gospel* (1917) were best sellers. In 1916 he published *The Social Principles of Jesus,* a study book for college students just like Roy Stryker. Rauschenbusch was a part of the radical wing of the Social Gospel movement, and his writings

1.4   Roy Stryker as a young man in western Colorado. From Jack Hurley, *Portrait of a Decade:*
Roy Stryker and the Development of Documentary Photography in the Thirties
(Baton Rouge: Louisiana State University Press, 1972), 7.

leveled sharp criticisms at American capitalism. He argued that "the church is both a partial realization of the new society in which God's will is done and also the appointed instrument for the further realization of that new society in the world about it."[19] To be converted to the path of Jesus meant turning from profit motives and cultural prejudices and toward brotherhood, sharing, and cooperation. Under Collins's guidance Stryker gained an awareness of America's social problems and began to volunteer at boys' clubs in Denver. It was through a Protestant minister that Roy Stryker moved from being a bookworm cattle herder to being a socially conscious twenty-seven-year-old.

The experience of studying with George Collins and working with the poor of Denver convinced Stryker that a degree in chemistry was not what he wanted. Stryker discussed with Collins his interest in leaving Colorado to pursue a degree at Columbia University in New York City. Collins had contacts in New York and knew people at Union Theological Seminary, a center of progressive Protestantism. He eventually arranged for Roy and his new bride, Alice, to be hired as workers at a settlement house run by Union. In September 1921 the newlyweds headed east. Once in New York, the Strykers learned that in order to be eligible for permanent employment and lodging at the settlement house, one of them had to be registered as a student at Union Theological Seminary. Since Union was a graduate institution, the student had already to have completed an undergraduate degree. Consequently Alice, who had been a teacher in Colorado, enrolled as a theology student at Union while Roy signed up for classes a block away at Columbia. For the next year the couple worked for room and partial board at Union's settlement house on 105th Street, ten blocks from Columbia. At the end of the year the Strykers moved to an apartment and ended their ties with Union. At Columbia, meanwhile, Roy met and impressed his economics professor, Rexford Tugwell. In 1934 President Roosevelt appointed Tugwell to be undersecretary of agriculture, and a year later Tugwell hired Stryker to head a photographic department (fig. 1.5).

Roy and Alice Stryker were able to move from Colorado to New York because of the support of a minister. And yet in his later years, Stryker was known to say, "Cowpunchers don't need toothbrushes or religion."[20] Neither his daughter nor his professional acquaintances remember Stryker as having any religious commitments. Alice and Roy did not make their daughter go to church. After leaving Colorado, Stryker never reconnected with a religious community even though the family continued their friendship with George Collins.

Roy and Alice Stryker maintained an interest in religion into their young adulthood because they found a minister who connected faith to social reform. Just as the Social Gospel had initially excited their spiritual commitments, its failure to catch hold in grassroots Protestantism may have motivated their absence from church. Christian socialism in Europe and the Social Gospel movement in the United States had offered the most sophisticated analysis of Western economic problems ever attempted by theologians. Hopes had been raised, but the Christian churches were unable to rise to the occasion. The vast majority of their members did not support the exchange of capitalism for socialism. Middle-class Protestants had established a style of church life that was segregated, snobbish, hierarchical, and isolated from social ills. Liberal Protestantism was still too steeped in middle-class notions of propriety, charity, and piety to fulfill the hopes of the Social Gospel movement. Seminary professors may have been writing books about social change, but not much was changing. Worship in

1.5   John Collier, Jr., portrait of Roy E. Stryker. Washington, D.C.,
January 1942 (LC-USF34-082105-C)

New York probably lacked the intimacy and conviction of Stryker's small, home-based Social
Gospel community in Denver. As Stryker later explained, "I was basically a radical. I was basically from a socialist home."[21] The Social Gospel movement had raised the expectations of
men like Stryker, but by 1921 it was obvious that large-scale progressive social change was not
going to come from religious communities. Stryker may have found in the settlement house
work of Union Seminary exactly the same sanctimonious naïveté that Marion Post saw in Miss
Lowry. When Stryker moved to Washington, D.C., serious social reform was coming from
people working in government service and not in the church.

The "Churched" and the "Unchurched"

No one knows exactly why Roy and Alice Stryker or the other photographers stopped going
to church and synagogue. We can only speculate in general about possible causes for their
loss of interest. For Protestants, one reason may have been that by the end of the twenties,
religious culture no longer commanded the attention it once had. In late-nineteenth-century

America, Methodists, Presbyterians, Baptists, Episcopalians, and Congregationalists dominated American life. Their members sat in Congress and on the Supreme Court. They staffed the major research universities. They ran America's industries. In 1898 President William McKinley, a Methodist, sent American troops to the Philippines to uplift, civilize, and "Christianize" the mostly Catholic Filipinos. Progressive-era reforms—everything from improving prisons to supporting public education to demanding an end to drinking—had close associations with mainline Protestantism.

At the same time, various internal and external forces were undermining the cultural and social position of Protestantism. By the twentieth century, conservative movements within mainline denominations had begun to force Protestant theologians to articulate more clearly where they stood on such issues as biblical literalism, biological evolution, and the reality of heaven and hell. Populist politicians like William Jennings Bryan argued for the farmer and laborer while condemning theological modernism. Protestants were leaving churches they thought of as too liberal and joining fundamentalist groups that preached individual salvation, personal morality, and political disengagement. Others became Latter-day Saints, Seventh-day Adventists, and Jehovah's Witnesses. These smaller religious communities grew quickly in the interwar years. Those who remained in mainstream Protestant congregations were more and more willing to let nonreligious organizations take over the nation's social service organizations. Hospitals, orphanages, schools, and charity groups severed their ties with Protestant denominations and presented themselves as independent, secular institutions.

By the thirties whatever Protestant consensus had earlier existed in America was gone. Immigration from southern and eastern Europe brought more Catholics and Jews to the nation's shores. Cities filled with people who did not speak English and did not go to a Protestant church. For many Catholics, ethnic parishes became places where newcomers not only received spiritual and physical sustenance but organized to promote their own interests. Catholics built churches, schools, and seminaries that transformed the look of the urban landscape and spoke to their increasing social prominence. Irish Catholics in particular became involved with local politics and threatened the hold that Protestants had over East Coast cities. Linking with labor organizers and northern intellectuals, they agitated against Prohibition. The Democrats in 1928 nominated Alfred E. Smith, a Catholic and prorepealer, for president. Although Smith lost the election, it was clear that the cities no longer were in Protestant hands. Roosevelt secured the ascendancy of Catholics by rewarding their political loyalty with government jobs.

Jews also were moving into traditionally Protestant circles. The FSA/OWI photographers Jack Delano, Ben Shahn, Edwin Rosskam, Esther Bubley, Carl Mydans, Arthur Rothstein, Charles Fenno Jacobs, Arthur Siegel, Edwin and Louise Rosskam, and Howard Liberman all came from Jewish families, though their biographers do not define them as "religious" Jews.[22] These photographers may have continued their families' commitment to humanitarian causes or even to socialism, but they did not become involved in Jewish ritual life in the thirties and early forties. For many eastern European Jews who came to America in the late nineteenth century, *Yiddishkeit* was based more on ethnic associations than on religious beliefs. Ritual observance was only one of many ways that people could understand their Jewishness in the New World. Some Jews who came to America had little religious training and even less religious interest. Others, who had chafed under the restrictions of Jewish village life or the suffocation of the immigrant home, welcomed the openness of the city streets. Socialists, communists, labor organizers, and intellectuals could turn away from traditional Judaism without turning away from being Jewish. Ideologies other than religious ones linked people from diverse European regions with native-born Americans.

Even religious Jews had flexibility in the expression of their faith commitments. Synagogue life was diverse both ritually and socially, but to the consternation of American rabbis, Jews could participate in religious life at home without supporting synagogue culture. Following the trend in Protestant America to connect piety with domesticity, women became critical players in defining what was religiously "Jewish." Jews could get involved in humanitarian movements such as the Ethical Cultural Society, which promoted a nonreligious orientation to reform but was run by acculturated Jews. Its founder, Felix Adler, the son of a reformed rabbi, stressed the importance of creating proper relationships among all people rather than promoting religious doctrines. But the Ethical Society also provided Sunday morning services with addresses by teachers, songs, "festivals of humanity," and rites of passage. The father of the photographer Margaret Bourke-White, though raised in an Orthodox Jewish household, married his Irish-American bride Minnie at the Ethical Culture Society in New York. Felix Adler developed a workable ideology of secular humanism, but he also provided Jews a place where they could be married and buried without recourse to rabbis or ministers.[23]

Success in the United States may not have included converting to Christianity, but it often meant downplaying or erasing one's "Jewishness." Rather than losing social status by assimilating, during the twenties and thirties Jews actually gained cultural and economic advantages by not associating with their religious communities. The anti-Semitism of the period limited the movement of Jews in education and the professions by questioning Judaism's legitimacy as a religion appropriate to modern democracy. Assimilation into American culture often entailed a reworking of one's ethnicity to eliminate names that were difficult to pronounce or that sent the wrong "signals." The FSA/OWI photographer Jacob Ovcharov—Jack Delano—remembers that his parents approved of his new American name. The dropping of certain religious practices and beliefs was not merely a voluntary turn toward the "dis-enchanted" world; it also was the recognition that participation in certain religions restricted one's movement in America.

The fragmentation of Protestantism and Judaism in the early twentieth century both diversified religious observance and opened up a space for quiet absence from religious practices. Some Americans did not merely switch churches; they stopped going to church entirely. While it had always been acceptable for men of certain classes, especially young men, not to be involved in a religious organization, by the twenties many more Americans could count themselves among the unchurched. The rise of mass entertainment, the legitimization of leisure activities on Sunday, the establishment of an anticlerical Marxian socialism, the popularization of Freud, and the public acceptance of agnostic intellectuals all contributed to the social acceptance of skipping church on Sunday or forgoing prayers on Sabbath. Americans may have still said that they were Methodist or Presbyterian, but this said more about their parents then about themselves. Roy Stryker and his photographers were typical of many of the cultural trendsetters of the interwar years who no longer looked to institutional religion as a source for cultural innovation or social influence. Many upper-echelon New Deal workers, artists, writers, and even liberal theologians no longer put much stock in weekly attendance at church or participation in Jewish ritual observances. The religion of their parents may have stimulated their social conscience, but a faith community did not sustain them.

Hopeless People with Hope

Religious behaviors were photographed because they were understood to be a part of American culture, not because the photographers were religious. If the photographers were to produce *real* pictures of America rather than propaganda, they needed to include religion. Stryker acknowledged the importance of religion in the lives of Americans and explicitly asked the photographers to look for religious practices. After a lunch with the sociologist Robert Lynd in 1936, he sent a list of "things which should be photographed as American background." The list included:

> Attending church
> Follow through a set of pictures showing people on their way from their home to
>   church
> Getting out of church,
> Visiting and talking
> Returning from church to home,
> visiting and talking in the vestibule.[24]

Another list of "stories of culture of the U.S." featured: "American roadside, American interiors, mantle pieces — wall paper . . . 'God Bless our Home' [mottoes] bibles . . . movies . . . churches — missions — tabernacles — itinerant preachers — gospel cars — hymn singing — religious signs, posters — religious statues, shrines, exhortations — going to church — talking after church."[25] Roy Stryker told his photographers not merely to photograph poverty and New Deal reforms but to capture the human side of the people who were living through difficult times. Most of the FSA/OWI photographs illustrate religion as a local, ordinary phenomenon that is fundamental to the daily life of average people. This stress on the ordinary resulted from the humanistic orientation of New Deal ideology as well as from the progressive principles of Stryker and his team. While the importance of illustrating "American Background" became more pressing with the war buildup, from the very beginning Stryker hoped to create a broad-based photographic file of life in the United States for present and future use.

During the first years of the project the photographers spent their time in rural America, which limited the religious communities with which they would come into contact. Protestant and Catholic practices make up the bulk of the religious images produced in the thirties. The FSA was, however, interested in experimental ways of improving agriculture, so in 1935 and 1936 photographers did visit a Jewish cooperative farm in New Jersey. After war broke out in Europe, the FSA photographed a Jewish community in rural Connecticut and, in the forties,

Jews living in New York City. On the other hand, Native American religion or the religions of Asia are never pictured in the file. Stryker steered his photographers clear of native peoples, who had been extensively photographed and whose images were finally being protected both by their leaders and by the government. While there were Buddhists, Hindus, and Muslims in the country in the thirties and forties their numbers were quite small. Strict immigration quotas and outright exclusions had restricted non-European populations. Photographers sought out certain tight-knit communal groups, such as the Amish and the Mormons, but these communities failed to challenge the assumption that religion in rural America was Christian. Still, the image that emerges from the FSA/OWI file demonstrates the tremendous vitality, breadth, and persistence of religious expressions during the interwar years.

At times photographers did criticize religious practices. This was particularly the case when religious people behaved in ways that challenged the New Deal model of state-based social reform. Stryker and his photographers preferred religion to be about rituals and sacred spaces, not welfare policy. There are few examples of religious organizations trying to cope with the demands of the Depression on their congregations. Direct visual disapproval, however, was rare. More often than not, photographers merely focused on those elements of religion to which they were attracted. Given the widespread and diverse character of religious life in the United States, it was not difficult for Marion Post to ignore Protestant charity workers in Florida and instead to photograph an itinerate preacher. Post took several photographs of this evangelist talking with African Americans along the roadside (fig. 1.6). She quoted him as saying, "Before I knew our Lord I used to be a terrible sinner. I'd get so drunk I couldn't stand up." City clergy and national organizations were disregarded, while local devotions and congregational leaders were presented as the religion of the "common man." [26]

Roy Stryker was charged with documenting the impact of the Depression on the "common man," but that was not as easy as simply showing poor Americans as "the most friendless, hopeless people in the whole country, [whom] nobody wanted to see." [27] If people were represented as totally worn out physically and spiritually, like the land and the economic order, then what good would it be to enact New Deal reforms? Pictures of deserted farms, decaying homes, and desiccated people would only intensify the notion that rural life had lost its vitality and was vanishing into the natural environment. A harsh portrayal of rural poverty might motivate lawmakers and citizens to assume that the situation was hopeless and that agricultural problems were so massive that nothing could be done to solve them. The visual image would paralyze viewers rather than spur them on to change.

At the same time, showing the poor as having hope and retaining a sense of their humanity in the face of economic disaster had its own set of problems. Presenting the poor as individuals with dignity and spirit tended to romanticize their lives. In pursuit of the strength of the poor, photographers could end up with "beautifying" poverty. The thirties documentary filmmaker Paul Rotha explained that "beauty is one of the greatest dangers of documentation." [28] If the photograph was too artistic, the viewer would not see the reality of economic decay and instead would be captivated by the feel of the image. The picture then would become a symbol of timeless sorrow rather than a reflection of a situation created by people—a situation that might also be ended by people.

1.6   Marion Post [Wolcott], wandering preacher talking with two African Americans and children. Belle Glade, Florida, January 1939 (LC-USF34-050927-D)

Stryker and his photographers were also concerned about the propagandistic nature of their project. Americans did not want to see propaganda. Fascists and communists produced art, movies, and photographs that were overly dramatic, that omitted critical information, and that enhanced the power of the government. With World War I over, the U.S. government had no business making propaganda. Even in the forties, when the Historical Section was asked to help mobilize people for war, Stryker and the photographers resisted making sentimental propaganda. Stryker believed that *real* pictures of Americans who displayed authentic spirit and vitality would convince citizens to fight for freedom. If the photographs were too simplistic, or too dramatic, or too romantic, or too preachy, Americans would not take the images seriously. While from our contemporary perspective all the FSA/OWI photographs might be considered propaganda, from Stryker's perspective none of them should be.

The Historical Section thus had complicated tasks to accomplish. Stryker and his team were reformers, but they did not want to make propaganda. The photographers were asked to portray the nightmare of poverty but not to represent it as so horrible that people would turn their faces away from the images. The pictures had to show the inhumanity of economic hardship without destroying the humanity of the poor or directly attacking capitalism. Likewise, the photographers were to have eyes for art, but they were not to make pictures so beautiful such that the viewers missed the point of the photograph. Meeting these goals was difficult.

Within the FSA/OWI file there are examples of success and failures, as well as every expression in between. Photographing religious practices, spaces, and objects helped the photographers achieve their goals by presenting faith as an integral but circumscribed part of the culture of average Americans. But the religious world is not so easily controlled. Stryker was well aware that sometimes the "ammunition" did not always come out of the "proper end of the barrel."

2.1   Dorothea Lange, gospel bus on Sunday morning. Kern County, California, November 1938
(LC-USF34-018372-E)

2
Enduring Faith

We have a grave problem in this state of California," Dorothea Lange wrote to Roy Stryker in 1937, "with these tens of thousands of drought people." Lange had been traveling with her husband, the economist Paul Taylor, throughout California, taking pictures for the FSA. "They keep on arriving, and the [rain] is coming. The newspapers are playing headlines and no one has the solution. This is no longer a publicity campaign for migratory agricultural labor camps. This is a migration of people, and a rotten mess."[1] Lange and Taylor were witnessing the living conditions of poor, mostly white workers who had come from the Dust Bowl states to labor in the fields. The life of nonnative migrant workers in California had always been exceedingly hard. California landowners, however, were hiring native-born Americans to pick their crops since many Mexicans had been forced to return to

Mexico. The sight of so many young, white American men, along with their wives and children, struggling to find work shocked middle-class Americans like Dorothea Lange and Paul Taylor. Lange and Taylor's main goal was to document migrant life: crowds waiting for relief checks, families traveling in overpacked and decrepit cars, tent camps, and the strenuous work of picking cotton, vegetables, and fruit. Like many New Deal reformers, they believed that their collection of facts about the situation, both economic data and visual evidence, would provide the scientific basis for the state to take action.

That spring of 1937 Lange photographed a camp of potato pickers in Kern County, California. An agricultural center, Kern County had attracted migrants from Oklahoma, Texas, Arkansas, and Missouri with the hope of work. Lange's photographs show families living in lean-tos fastened to their cars, with no water and poor sanitary conditions. Her captions explained that after the potatoes were dug by machines and strewn on the ground, pickers put the potatoes into sacks suspended from their waist between their knees. When full, the sacks were loaded onto field trucks and taken to sheds for sorting and grading. Potato pickers earned forty cents an hour that year. With the exception of four photographs, all of Lange's pictures of the Kern potato pickers show the workers, their living conditions, or their labor.[2]

The four photographs that do not show work are of a couple singing hymns and migrant children attending Sunday school. Lange had been at the makeshift camp on a Sunday when she took the photographs of religious activities. During her travels in California, Lange made several other photographs of the Protestant piety of the migrants. That August she photographed a wooden church built near Blythe that sat on a barren lot. The church had signs proclaiming, "Jesus Saves," "Apostolic Faith," and "Tabernacle." In November 1938, Lange again photographed Sunday in Kern County. This time she took two pictures of a "Gospel bus" with a "Jesus Saves" sign and several pictures of women praying and singing hymns before the opening of a meeting of the Mothers' Club at Arvin FSA camp for migrants. A few months later, in June, Lange took a pair of photographs of the Victory Through Christ Society. In 1939 she photographed the exteriors of a Pentecostal Church of God in Salinas, a Church of Christ in Tranquillity, and a church "for colored people" in Bakersfield.[3]

Dorothea Lange's photographs of Dust Bowl migrants in California have become emblematic of the poverty of Depression-era farmers, but the pictures tell only part of the story of rural misery in the thirties. Other lesser-known FSA photographs of rural poverty reveal a country that was an economic failure for many more of its residents. Miners, lumberjacks, and Mexicans, as well as white migrants and black sharecroppers, experienced the deteriorating quality of rural life. Nor was Lange alone in photographing the religious practices of the nation's rural poor. In documenting submarginal housing and presenting the decaying rural landscape, other FSA photographers unintentionally recorded the religious practices of many poor Americans. The photographs show us how people used Christian material culture to visually open up their materially constricted world to a much larger religious world of beliefs and rituals. They also help us understand how the government photographers picked certain aspects of religious behavior to emphasize while ignoring others.

One Third of a Nation

On January 20, 1937, President Franklin Delano Roosevelt delivered his second inaugural address to the American people. Following a landslide election, he felt confident that his New Deal was responding to the needs of the country. Although the nation had been blessed with a "great wealth of natural resources" and the people were "at peace among themselves," Roosevelt asked, "have we found our happy valley?" The answer was no. "I see millions of families," Roosevelt told the nation, "trying to live on incomes so meager that the pall of family disaster hangs over them day by day. . . . I see millions denied education, recreation, and the opportunity to better their lot and the lot of their children. I see millions lacking the means to buy the products of farm and factory and by their poverty denying work and productiveness to many other millions." Roosevelt expressed what many Americans already knew: in spite of the New Deal, each day was a struggle for survival. "I see one-third of a nation," Roosevelt concluded, "ill-housed, ill-clad, ill-nourished." Roosevelt explained that he was painting a picture not in despair but in the hopes that once the country saw and understood the injustice of poverty, the nation would "paint it out." Americans had both the spirit and the ability to raise the standard of living in the United States. As president, Roosevelt assured the people that the government would use democratic methods to "spread the volume of human comforts." He concluded: "The test of our progress is not whether we add more to the abundance of those who have much; it is whether we provide enough for those who have too little."[4]

Roosevelt's promise to continue to address the economic problems of the nation must have been particularly encouraging to FSA photographers such as Dorothea Lange, who had seen firsthand the devastating effect of the collapse of Great Plains farming. Before 1931 the southern plains contained the most prosperous farmland in the country. Spread out over more than one hundred million acres, it included parts of Kansas, Colorado, New Mexico, Oklahoma, and Texas. In spite of a cycle of rain and drought, green fields and chocolate soil gave the nation abundant crops of wheat, corn, and other grains. World War I had brought high prices for crops and a vigorous demand for wheat. Farmers throughout the country prospered because they were not only feeding America's troops but also sending food to embattled Europeans. In the twenties, some farmers bought more land and received loans to begin to mechanize their harvesting. Where a strong man could plow three acres with a horse, a good farmer could plow fifty acres with a tractor. Days and nights they plowed up the soil, paying little attention to the region's ecology.

After the war was over and the troops returned home, farm prices plummeted across the country. The decline in agricultural prices was the sharpest ever. Farmers who owned land and used tenants or croppers to work it found they could no longer afford to work the land. They stopped paying their workers and forced them off the land. Other farmers realized that they could survive only by investing in tractors rather than people, and again workers were forced off the land. Farmers who had taken out loans to buy new equipment or expand their acreage could not repay their loans. As early as the twenties, farm families were already migrating westward in hope of finding work. In 1929 fully 40 percent of all Americans still lived in rural places, and agriculture created 25 percent of the nation's jobs. The postwar farming crisis could not be ignored.[5]

Then the rain stopped. The summer of 1930 brought the first drought; Arkansas was hit the hardest. The next summer the drought continued, and the wheat withered in the sun. In 1933 farm prices hit rock bottom. The summer of 1936 was the hottest ever. The natural disaster of the drought aggravated the ecological disaster caused by overfarming. Winds blew the topsoil away. The dust storms filled the air with stinging, blinding dirt that darkened the days and made it difficult for people to breathe. A violent dust storm that began on April 14, 1935, continued for twenty-seven days and nights. People struggled to plant and to stay in their homes, but some ended up shooting their cattle because there was no grain. Many more packed up a few possessions and moved.

Eventually four million people — 23 percent of those born in Oklahoma, Texas, Arkansas, and Missouri — left their homes and settled in the West. A quarter of those migrants settled permanently in California, while others remained in Arizona, New Mexico, Oregon, and Washington. Close-knit rural communities fell apart as people abandoned their farms to the dust and sun. Some moved to larger towns in their regions, but the farm crisis rippled across the land. Regional economies were tied to farming, and since the health of the nation was failing, there was little respite in the cities. People who had struggled for years, refusing help from the government, ended up on relief rolls. Others were reduced to living off the scraps of once prosperous communities. Franklin Roosevelt had replaced Herbert Hoover as president in 1933, but the crisis continued. In 1939 the photographer Russell Lee wrote a caption describing "May's Avenue camp, an agricultural workers shack town," and aptly summarizing the condition of many farmers during the thirties: "This family had been farmers until four years ago. Since then they have lived in a community camp getting some food from the vegetable dumps, doing 'trashing' and going on the road as migrant workers. They have also been to Arizona to pick cotton. Here they are picking over ripe fruit that they picked up at vegetable packing places (fig. 2.2)."

Farm Security Administration photographs of migrant laborers brought the plight of rural agriculture into the newspapers and magazines of the country. In the same spirit as Roosevelt's inaugural address, the photographers were painting a picture in the hopes of "painting it out." While the FSA pictures were new, the camera had been used to "paint a picture" ever since the advent of urban reform. In 1851 Henry Mayhew illustrated his *London Labor and the London Poor* with engravings based on daguerreotypes, and in 1877 *Street Life in London* used photographs by John Thomson. Part exposé and part catalog of urban outcasts for the titillation of the middle classes, *Street Life in London* was intended to "draw attention to poverty at a time of expanding national wealth."[6] Initially reformers were limited to street photography because early cameras needed natural light. By the turn of the century, however, improvements in lenses and lighting made photography a more important aspect of social reform because it recorded how people lived indoors.

Key in the shift from street to interior photography was the work of Jacob Riis (1848–1914). Riis had come to the United States in 1870 from Denmark. The young man had difficulty supporting himself and moved from job to job in New York City, thus seeing American poverty close up. In 1877 he started to follow the police as a reporter, and it was then he realized the potential of images to corroborate sociological data and official statistics. In 1888 he published in the *New York Sun* a set of engravings — "Flashes from the Slums" — based on

2.2   Russell Lee, a family who lives in an agricultural workers' shack town picking overripe fruit that they get from vegetable packing factories. Oklahoma City, Oklahoma, July 1939 (LC-USF34-33845-D)

his photographs. Two years later he printed a collection of his photographs in *How the Other Half Lives*, the first book to publish reform-oriented photographs along with a text. Like many Progressive-era reformers, Riis hoped his work would prove that the evils of drink and the perils of heredity were not the major causes of poverty. The poor did not merely need to learn the moral lessons of abstinence, thrift, persistence, and humility, as Victorian reformers had preached. Rather, poverty was the consequence of a larger moral breakdown that allowed the rich to exploit the poor while offering them no security.

Jacob Riis intended his pictures to move middle-class viewers "from voyeurism to horror to enlightenment and finally to direct activism."[7] He gave his first illustrated lecture at the Broadway Tabernacle City Mission Society and eventually was supported by the Social Gospel proponents Charles Parkhust and Josiah Strong. One of the reasons that Riis's lantern-slide lectures were shocking was that they included many interior pictures. While the streets were assumed to be places of danger and deprivation by middle-class viewers, to see the homes of the poor was to experience the inner world of poverty. Homes, typically understood as places of safety and love, were revealed to be devoid of any markings of domesticity. Taken with an exploding flash, Riis's interior photographs exaggerated the squalor of tenement apartments, dingy cellars, and lodging rooms. The harsh flash inflated surface irregularities, heightened variations in texture and sheen, and embellished blemishes. Cluttered rooms were made to look even more chaotic and dirty. The photographs overstated the wretched conditions of the poor, even as they looked natural and generalized. For instance, Riis caught "parts" of people inside the frame of the photograph so that the picture looked casual and spontaneous, not like a portrait designed by a photographer. He did not call attention to any one particular element in the photograph. Riis was talented at making pictures that conveyed the impression that the photographer was disengaged from the scene and absolutely objective in his representation.

Lewis Hine (1874–1940) also used a large-format camera with its exploding flash as an educational tool. Hine photographed immigrants coming through Ellis Island between 1904 and 1909 and again in 1926. In 1907 he was invited to join the Pittsburgh Survey, an effort to document the problems of an industrial city. Unlike Jacob Riis, who did not work for any particular organization and who frequently lectured to Protestant church groups, Hine was hired by unions and private organizations that were not connected with established religious associations or denominations. His work better parallels that of the FSA photographers who had no connection to religious communities, the traditional providers of charity in America.

More than Jacob Riis, Hine was intent on presenting the poor not as objects of charity but as candidates for deserved justice. His images countered stereotypes about the depraved nature of "new" immigrants by showing them as individuals rather than as members of generic groups. Hine photographed immigrants, workers, and children looking directly at the camera, indicating that they knew they were being photographed. Hine's pictures gave "the impression of a direct, polite social encounter between individuals who are relatively equal."[8] The success of Riis's and Hine's photographs motivated other photographers to try to picture the urban world. Settlement house reformers, as well as commercial photographic houses like the Detroit Photographic Company, popularized images of immigrant life in the city. By the time of the FSA photographic project, interior images of tenement poverty had become a standard trope in both commercial and reform photography. "Painting" pictures on film— pictures that represented both the reality of poverty and the attitudes of the photographers toward that poverty—was critical to solving the problem of "one-third of a nation."

Ordinary Religion

Dorothea Lange (1895–1965) did not begin her career as a photographer hoping to make pictures to motivate reform. Like many young Americans, she had moved to the West Coast to find adventure and to leave her troubled family. In 1919, after first training as a photographic technician in San Francisco, she opened up her own studio, where she made careful and sensitive portraits of the city's wealthy. A year later she married the painter Maynard Dixon, and throughout the twenties she explored both commercial and art photography. By the early thirties, however, the economic crisis of the nation was drying up the money of the rich, and Lange was drawn more and more to the world of breadlines and waterfront strikes. In 1934 one of her photographs of an unemployed worker caught the attention of Paul Taylor, a professor of economics at the University of California, Berkeley. The two began a collaboration that was to result in their employment by the California State Relief Administration and, eventually, their marriage. Their report on migrant labor made its way to Washington, where it caught the attention of Rex Tugwell and Roy Stryker. Stryker was moved by the power of the report's photographs. He contacted Lange, and in 1935 she began to provide pictures for the Historical Section. Lange's artistic independence, not to mention the section's continual budgetary crises, was a constant challenge to Stryker, who fired and rehired her several times. Nonetheless, she set the standard for FSA/OWI photography.

Lange's photographs depict the ordinary character of religious life among California's migrant laborers. In March 1937 Lange was in Kern County, California. The FSA had established a temporary tent camp near the potato fields, and Lange was probably photographing workers resting on Sunday. In one tent she took two pictures of a neatly dressed couple (fig. 2.3). "This couple," Lange observed in her caption, "are Oklahoma potato pickers." Explaining that they were singing hymns on a Sunday afternoon, Lange even included the title of one of the more relevant songs: "The Great Reaping Day." Lange also reported that "the woman had been 'saved' the week before." The two people calmly sing in their tent. Unlike in other photographs, where household goods are shoddy and packed onto trucks, this couple had set up a bed, a dresser, a nightstand, and chairs in their tent. The man's shirt is clean; the woman's dress has lace down the front.

Probably on that same day, Lange took two photographs of children gathering for Sunday school (fig. 2.4). A wooden bench is set up outside of the tents under the trees, and the children have assembled to listen to their teachers. These two photographs were shot from a distance, and in one Lange snapped the shutter as the children said their prayers. A year later, in November, Lange photographed a Gospel bus picking up children on a Sunday morning outside of another Kern County migrant camp (see fig. 2.1). "Many Texans, Oklahomans, and Arkansans are settling in this country," she notes in her caption. "Their cultures and forms of religious expression are being transferred with them." And it was not merely children who were singing and praying. That same November, Lange photographed the opening of the meeting of the Mothers' Club at the Arvin camp run by the Farm Security Administration. According to Lange's captions, the discussion of the evening centered on the possibility of buying kerosene in large quantities and distributing it cooperatively in order to cut costs. Before the women got down to the business of running the camp, they sang a series of hymns (fig. 2.5).

Singing hymns before discussing the importance of kerosene might have seemed odd to Lange. Although Lange had been baptized at St. Matthew's Trinity Lutheran church in Hoboken, New Jersey, her parents were not churchgoers. She was not exposed to Sunday school or to the routine of daily prayer. Lange's father had abandoned his family when she was twelve, and there is no evidence that her mother felt strongly about any faith. When Lange married her first husband, Maynard Dixon, the ceremony was conducted in her photographic studio and performed by a minister from the People's Liberal Church.[9] While Christianity held no importance in Lange's life, there is evidence that Judaism shaped the photographer's eye.

Lange's mother worked as a librarian on New York's Lower East Side, and she sent her daughter to the nearby elementary school. Mother and daughter commuted by ferry from Hoboken to Manhattan early each morning. Lange later remembered, "I was the only Gentile among 3,000 Jews, the only one." School life was difficult for her because the other children had a great hunger for knowledge and achievement; they were "fighting their way up." "To an outsider," she recalled, "it was a savage group because of this overwhelming ambition." And yet she "saw a very great deal." Lange looked at Jewish life around her and watched what she would call "a race alien to myself." She told an interviewer that "never a September comes that I don't stop and remember what I used to see in those tenements when they had the Jewish

2.3   Dorothea Lange, Oklahoma potato pickers singing hymns on a Sunday afternoon.
Kern County, California, March 1937 (LC-USF34-016324-E)

2.4   Dorothea Lange, Sunday school for migrant children in a
potato picker's camp. Kern County, California, March 1937
(LC-USF34-016432-E)

holidays, the religious holidays. In those days all the women wore *sheytls,* you know the black wigs, and the men wore beards and little black hats, *yarmulke.* . . . I'm aware that I just *looked* at everything. I can remember the smell of the cooking too, the way they lived. Oh, I had good looks at that, but never set foot myself. Something like a photographic observer. I can see it."[10] Lange watched religion as a child, but she did not participate in it. She knew that religion was more than merely a set of ideas. Religion included practices that involved the senses. People wore special clothes; they ate special foods. Lange was personally detached from beliefs and rituals, but at a formative age the sights and smells of faith engaged her.

Lange's experiences as a child prepared her to recognize that deeply rooted religious sentiments can survive physical and social displacement. Migrants — Jews or Oklahomans — might have left their places of worship behind them, but they continued to teach their children religious principles, sing familiar songs, and hold religious services. The southwesterners who fled the drought and the dust were deeply religious people who belonged to a wide array of Protestant churches. They certainly participated in the activities Lange photographed, but they also enjoyed spirit-filled church services with loud music and excited praise, healed with oil-anointed handkerchiefs, and beat their children because the Bible said, "Spare the rod and spoil the child." Their faith was certainly integrated into their everyday lives, but it also brought them far out of bounds of the normal. They participated in many different forms of religious expression, only a very few of which Lange recorded on film. Large num-

2.5   Dorothea Lange, hymn singing before the opening of the meeting of the Mothers' Club at Arvin FSA migrant camp. Kern County, California, November 1938 (LC-USF34-018534-E)

bers settled in Los Angeles and other towns, challenging the rural images promoted by Lange and John Steinbeck. There they attended Baptist and Methodist churches connected to larger, national organizations. They used prayer books and hymnals published at denominational headquarters and belonged to associations that linked them with other Americans. Migrants not only joined existing faith communities, they built their own churches. They belonged to such Pentecostal denominations as the Church of the Nazarene or the Assemblies of God. Still others were members of small nondenominational Pentecostal or Holiness congregations. Migrants also joined "new" religions like the Seventh-day Adventist church or the Jehovah's Witnesses. Believers experienced their faith within specific communities, not merely as a "generic" Christianity.

Newcomers had many denominational affiliations, which served to separate the migrants into distinct groups, but they also shared elements of a particular religious style. Evangelical culture of the Dust Bowl focused on the language of the Bible, emphasized personal piety, and assumed the intensity of prayer. Congregations that permitted music in church enjoyed lively services with contemporary religious tunes. Even those migrants who were not church-goers were still steeped in the "rhythm of sin and repentance."[11] Young men, for instance, might reject the strong personal piety of conservative Protestantism, but they carried with them the language, sensibilities, and awareness of that faith. They were "unchurched" in a way significantly different from that of Dorothea Lange, Marion Post, or Roy Stryker.

Protestant churches in the Central Valley did not sufficiently serve migrant religious needs. In 1912 Baptists had agreed that California would reside in the territory of the Northern rather than the Southern Baptist Convention. Northern Baptists, who held more liberal beliefs and whose preaching was emotionally restrained and intellectual, did not welcome the religious style of the strangers. The migrants stood out from the established Baptists of the agricultural towns with their stress on the literal truth of the Bible, their pious language, and their unfashionable clothes. Theology and religious style, as well as class and cultural differences, separated the native Californians from the newcomers.

Smaller denominations had an easier time responding to the influx of newcomers. Holiness and Pentecostal churches sprang up quickly because their worship styles and belief systems suited migrant needs. Such churches counted on the migrants themselves to provide leadership. It was common in Oklahoma, Arkansas, and Missouri for men—and even women—to be part-time preachers and full-time farmers. These ministers migrated to California along with their flocks. Few gave up on Christianity, as had Jim Casy, the preacher from John Steinbeck's *Grapes of Wrath* (1939). "I ain't preachin' no more much," Casy informs Tom Joad even before they both head west. "The sperit ain't in the people much no more; and worse'n that, the sperit ain't in me no more." [12] While Casy agonized over the future of American society, most migrant preachers set up prayer circles and devised plans for building churches. Just as in Oklahoma, Arkansas, Texas, and Missouri, religion and music were the key ways for poor people to describe their current plight and express their hopes for the future.

Lange ignored both the enthusiastic worship style of poor agricultural workers and the conflicts between the locals and the newcomers. Religion entered her photographic field of vision only for brief moments and only when it served to support her perspective that the migrants were able to continue their "cultures and forms of religion" in a new region. To have made more pictures of religious behavior would have distracted from the central goal she and Paul Taylor shared: to show that "These people are not hand-picked failures. They are the human materials cruelly dislocated by the processes of human erosion." [13] Lange made pictures of the most acceptable and uncontroversial elements of Protestant religious life in America. She photographed commonplace practices that would have been difficult to ignore. There are no pictures that lead us to think that religion breaks through and breaks apart normal life. Women offer a prayer and sing a hymn or two before beginning a business meeting; they are not shown healing through the power of Jesus and holy oil. Just as the FSA/OWI file does not contain pictures depicting the inflamed passions of labor meetings, it does not show religious practices that provoke extreme emotional responses. Praying, like the other activities of the poor, is pictured as intense but never inflammatory. From the perspective of the file, religion does not call people to do unusual things. Faith is pictured as present but not threatening.

Dorothea Lange's photographs stylistically emphasize the ordinary character of faith. Lange held the camera at eye level. She photographed either straight on, squarely in front of the person or church, or directly from behind. Usually, the people do not look into the camera but continue what they are doing as if no one were there. By avoiding dramatic angles, extreme close-ups, and special lighting, Lange created pictures that minimize the photographer's presence. Like Jacob Riis's work, her religious photographs stress the casual and the spontaneous in order to convey the impression that there is objectivity in the representation. It is as if we—the photographer and the viewers of the photograph—are quietly being taken behind the scenes to see how things *really* are. We are not influencing the events. Lange constructs a visually neutral space in which, we are led to conclude, normal things happen. These are not special Sundays. The internal structure of the photograph underscores its content. What we are seeing is Lange's construction of the everyday religious life of the community.

Lange's photographs are unmarked by denominational differences and represent faith as part of the culture of the poor. During the twenties and thirties, "culture" was no longer considered to be possessed only by the educated and the wealthy. Social scientists insisted that all people had culture, comprising simply the ways that they lived in the world. Picturing religious behaviors communicated the idea that the lives of the migrants were richer than the ramshackle collections of old cars, mattresses, and tents indicated. Including religion made the photographs look "real" because religion introduced a dimension of life beyond that of hard work. These were not merely laboring animals living in squalid conditions; these were people — like us — who had a recognizable way of life.

Using religion as evidence that migrants had an enduring faith and thus an enduring culture was particularly important before the establishment of FSA migrant camps. When the migrants first arrived in California, they lived out of their cars and tents. They spent their days either looking for work, waiting to work, or working. Praying and singing were activities that required few if any material possessions. Once permanent government-sponsored camps were set up, photographers were no longer limited by the cultural thinness of migrant life. In such camps the FSA provided tent housing, sanitary facilities, running water, basic health care, and even libraries and meeting rooms. Sometimes complete housing complexes were built. The cultural life of the camp served the same purpose for the photographer as religious practice. Photographs of baseball fields and community gardens demonstrated what the government was funding as well as showing the poor with a recognizable culture.[14]

The FSA photographers assumed that religious practices could be exchanged with any other aspect of culture. Lange was profoundly secular in her attitude that praying and singing were no different from other leisure pastimes. If migrant workers were playing baseball or gardening, it was not necessary to photograph their children attending Sunday school. Indeed, photographing religious behaviors actually undermined the purpose of photographing federally sponsored migrant camps because such cultural activities did not illustrate the ability of the government to provide for the poor. It is doubtful, however, that migrants stopped sending their children to Sunday school when they had running water or camp libraries. For them, religion was not interchangeable with other cultural activities. Religion was a special aspect of life that had no substitute. As is clear from Lange's photographs of the Arvin FSA camp, migrants sang hymns *and* read in their library.[15]

Poverty, Catholicism, and Men

The same year that Dorothea Lange was photographing potato pickers in Kern County, California, another FSA photographer was discovering rural life in the eastern United States. In the winter of 1937 Arthur Rothstein photographed people living on submarginal farms in western New York. The Farm Security Administration wanted to convince Americans that rural poverty was not merely the result of the Dust Bowl or the exploitation of southern sharecroppers. While the plight of the "Okies" may have dominated the newspapers, and the predicament of the sharecropper the social science literature, rural people throughout the country made up a part of "one-third of the nation." As the FSA photographers traveled throughout the country, they saw poverty in a variety of forms. They also were exposed to the enduring faith of Catholic Americans.

Arthur Rothstein (1915–1985) was the first photographer hired by Stryker, joining the team in 1935 straight from finishing his undergraduate work at Columbia University. The son of a Jewish storeowner from Brooklyn who sold tires, Rothstein had met Stryker at Columbia. Stryker and Rex Tugwell had hired the student camera buff to make illustrations for their project on the history of American agriculture. In later years, Rothstein remembered himself as a "provincial New Yorker" who was given "a wonderful opportunity" to be able to see what the rest of the country looked like. He also explained that there was a "great excitement in Washington in those days—a feeling that you were in on something new and exciting." Like the others on the team, Rothstein felt "a missionary sense of dedication to this project—of making the world a better place in which to live."[16] At twenty-two, Rothstein was seeing a world distinctly unfamiliar to a young Jew from Brooklyn.

The December 1937 snow kept people of Allegany County indoors, and so Rothstein was limited in what he could film. At one point he photographed a collection of religious prints that John Dudeck, an "old bachelor," had arranged over a table (fig. 2.6). Two were framed and a third tacked to the wall. Next to two of them Dudeck had placed blessed palms that are given to Catholics on the Sunday before Easter to commemorate Christ's entry into Jerusalem. One of the prints is faded beyond recognition. The other two are standard Catholic images: the Holy Family of Jesus, Mary, and Joseph, with the Holy Ghost as a dove in the background, and Christ at the Last Supper with St. John, the beloved disciple. Dudeck stands below the prints, lighting a kerosene lamp on a cluttered table. Books are piled on the floor, and thick, heavy ones tower on one side of the table.

Had it not been for Dudeck's arrangement of his religious prints, Rothstein's photograph would have been a conventional reform photograph documenting the disorganization of poor households. Rothstein has set up his photograph, however, to call attention to Dudeck's piety. He centers the prints in the photograph and places Dudeck off to the side. Visually balanced with Dudeck are the piles of books, which also challenge the stereotype that the poor lack education. The books and the religious prints contrast with the clutter, making it more difficult to construct easy conclusions about the lives of the poor. By putting the print of the Holy Family in the center of his picture, Rothstein "deneutralized" the photograph, moving the viewer's attention to a specific point on the wall. The prints are not just accidental images appearing in the background. If Rothstein had omitted the prints, John Dudeck's gestures would have made the photograph look spontaneous and not posed. We, the viewers, might have forgotten that a photographer with his flashbulbs was in a dark house. But the prints dominate the photograph and make us look closer at what is going on in the picture. Their placement in the photograph, in addition to their religious content, break the feel that we are merely seeing a poor farmer lighting his lamp.

Objects were the focus of FSA photographs not merely because they caught the eye of the photographer. As Russell Lee, one of Stryker's most prolific photographers, explained, "The things people kept around them could tell you an awful lot about the antecedents of these

people."[17] Objects were included in pictures to connect people to specific class, ethnicity, religion, and region. Just as the prints of Jesus and the saints broke the visual monotony of the living space, their content broke the "work monotony" of the person's life by connecting the poor with the wider world of religious beliefs, myths, rituals, and customs. The Holy Family print found in Dudeck's home was distributed throughout the Catholic world from the beginning of the twentieth century. Its publication followed the apostolic brief *Neminem Fugit* (1892) of Pope Leo XIII that urged families to pray daily before an image of the Holy Family. Catholic bishops also asked their flocks to enroll in the Association of Christian Families Consecrated to the Holy Family, a society that distributed such prints.[18] Devotion to the Holy Family was particularly encouraged in the working class because of the appropriate models it presented: St. Joseph's steadfast support of his household and the Virgin Mary's selfless domesticity. Dudeck or a relative may have been a member of a Holy Family Association, he may have received the print as a gift, or he may have merely picked it up at church. By the thirties, such prints could be found throughout the country and were not restricted to any one ethnic group. The mass printing and distribution of Catholic material culture made images available to even the poorest of farmers.

Later that year, another FSA photographer took a picture of a different Catholic farmer (fig. 2.7). Russell Lee (1903–1986) took five photographs of John Bastia, who lived in Iron County, Michigan. According to Lee's caption, Bastia was a former lumberjack and coal miner who spoke only Italian and who was deaf. As with many residents of the area, when the mines and mills shut down, Bastia was forced to eke out a living through farming. Darning a sock, the Italian is surrounded by symbols of his faith. Above his gun rack and behind a shelf that holds three glasses Bastia keeps a print of the Immaculate Heart of Mary. Unlike John Dudeck's house, where the symmetry of the prints contrasts with the disorderly piles of books and messy table, John Bastia's religious prints parallel his orderly and tidy cabin. He has carefully tacked up some prints and framed others, setting up his space in a way that displays his personal devotion and respect for the Catholic tradition. Bastia, like many poor Catholics, displays pictures of holy people in layers, repeating the same image of a favorite saint over and over.

In both Rothstein's and Lee's photographs, old men are surrounded by sacred figures that link the men to worlds beyond their everyday working lives. The Catholic Church has a long history of encouraging its members to use devotional images. Statues and prints, sometimes assembled into domestic altars, traditionally were meant to enable people to construct and maintain personal relationships with Jesus, Mary, and the saints. Through the image the worshiper conversed intimately and personally with the divine. Such communication encouraged the person to live a better life, pray more devoutly, or experience healing comfort. Catholics handled, cherished, prayed to, and even ate images in order to arouse affection and evoke tears. Through the image, believers felt the guidance and protection, as well as the judgment and silence, of the saints. Images were points of conversation, perhaps experienced even

2.6 (facing page)   Arthur Rothstein, John Dudeck lighting a lamp in front of religious prints. Dalton, New York, December 1937 (LC-USF34-026119-D)

2.7   Russell Lee, John Bastia, a former lumberjack and coal miner, darning his socks while
surrounded by his religious prints. Iron County, Michigan, May 1937 (LC-USF34-010907-D)

more intensely by single, elderly men, who may have been isolated from the larger Catholic community.

Rothstein's and Lee's photographs continued the convention in reform photography of picturing only "innocents" as living in poverty. Women, children, and the elderly were shown in squalid surroundings because it was assumed that they could not be expected to earn a reasonable wage and thus remove themselves from poverty. Innocents were at the mercy of a larger industrial order. Rothstein and Lee may have focused on the religious prints of these men in order to help "feminize" the scene. Women and children, not men, typically are associated with domestic piety. In Christian households, women organize domestic rituals (even if they might not preside over them). They display in their homes the symbols of their faith. While men might also pray at home and look at religious images (as these two men obviously do), the stereotype is that family religion falls under the aegis of women. Since women and children were not expected to work, men constructed as women were also not expected to work. Including the religious prints in the photographs helped reiterate a key assumption of Stryker and the photographers that the poor were not responsible for their own poverty.

To picture healthy men in photographs designed to illustrate poverty was risky. Even during the Depression, with its massive unemployment, Americans felt that there was something wrong with a single man who did not work. Unemployed men were typically photographed in public spaces, not at home. Shown standing by their cars on the road west, waiting for relief, or picking through garbage, the men in such photographs were active "doers"; they were not passively sitting at home waiting for something to happen. To photograph an unemployed man inside of his home, without his family, raised too many questions about his character.

I have found only one FSA photograph that shows middle-aged men and domestic religious objects not also accompanied by women or children. It was taken by Sheldon Dick (1906–1950), one of the lesser-known FSA photographers. Born into a wealthy family, Dick was willing to photograph for Stryker for a dollar a year, but even at that he worked only on and off between 1937 and 1938. Dick was typical of those photographers who were not government employees but who sent Stryker pictures for his file.[19] Dick's photographs are not well known, and we can know little about why he was photographing in a particular place. Sheldon Dick's most serious photographs were those he shot inside the General Motors Fisher Body plant in Flint, Michigan, during the 1937 auto industry strike. Dick was the most infamous of the FSA photographers; in 1950 he murdered his third wife and then killed himself.[20]

At some point, probably in 1938, Dick took pictures of life in coal mining towns. All but one of Dick's photographs of coal mining are straightforward examples of the hardworking, hard-drinking life of miners. One picture, however, may be used as an example to show how in certain contexts religious images can be disruptive. Sheldon Dick took a series of photographs inside the house of Marcella Urban in Gilberton, Pennsylvania. Two of the photographs merely show places where plaster is falling off the walls in Urban's home. In the third, Dick photographed two unnamed men standing next to the decaying wall (fig. 2.8). From other captions we learn that the man on the left is a friend of Urban's and the one on the right may be a local bar owner. They stand in front of two framed religious prints and a sideboard holding blessed palms. One print shows the dead body of the Christ resting in the sepulcher, attended by two angels. On the ground are the instruments of the Passion, and above the grave floats a chalice and host. Such a print would have been given out as a token to those who joined a Happy Death association, which encouraged Catholics to be spiritually ready to die. Like the chromolithograph of the Holy Family, it was widely distributed beginning at the turn of the century. The other print is partially obscured but is probably a New Testament biblical scene.

Dick's photograph is unusual in many ways, all of which contribute to the unease it communicates to viewers. The direct gaze of the men sets the photograph up as a portrait or a family snapshot, rather than a spontaneous illustration of decaying housing. The men's neat clothes contrast with the exposed laths and bare lightbulb. With his hands in his pockets, his hat at a jaunty angle, and a bandage on his ear, the dark-eyed man on the right looks like a character from a thirties crime movie. Unlike Rothstein's and Lee's photographs of Dudeck and Bastia with their religious images, Dick does not explain in the caption the connection of these men to the house. Nor is there correspondence hinting at why he took their picture. Are they Marcella Urban's borders? Visitors? Relatives? Why didn't Dick photograph Marcella Urban in front of her prints? While we cannot recoup the reasons for the photograph, there is something about the picture that raises questions and confuses its ability to directly

2.8   Sheldon Dick, Marcella Urban's house with two unidentified men.
Gilberton, Pennsylvania, 1938 (?) (LC-USF34-040404-D)

show submarginal housing. The healthy men do not fit together with the pious print or the deteriorating home. The Catholic images, rather than reinforce the innocence of the poor or stress the endurance of their faith, introduce unanswered questions about the men.

During the first four years of the Historical Section, religious practices and objects were primarily photographed when they supported New Deal assumptions about the poor. Photographers expected a certain amount of religious expression in the homes of the poor. Hymn singing and Sunday schools, prints of the Holy Family, blessed Easter palms, these fit with couples, children, women, and old men. Sheldon Dick's photograph, however, provides us an example of a "bad" reform photograph. Dick, who probably was less interested in making photographs that supported the goals of the Historical Section than were Lange or Rothstein, made a picture that probably spoke to his own sense of visual irony. Here, in a dilapidated house, were elaborately framed pious prints, blessed palms, and a weighty Victorian-style dresser. Situate two men among the dresser, prints, and bare lightbulb and you have a complicated, challenging composition. The sentimental piety, perhaps even the exotic piety, of the print heightens the ambiguity of the men, who do not seem quite "innocent." Sheldon Dick uses religious images and practices to break visual reform conventions. The prints "stick out" because of the other objects in the photograph. The composition is unrepresentative of those initially taken by the other photographers because it transgresses common assumptions about men and religion and therefore appears to be less "documentary."

Mexican Migrants

During the early spring of 1939, Russell Lee photographed the living conditions of Mexicans living in borderland towns. The towns spanned from San Antonio in the north, to Corpus Christi in the east, to the tip of Texas in the south.[21] During the boom years of American agriculture, Mexicans had been actively recruited to work on farms and in rural businesses. When white and black laborers were unavailable, Mexicans traveled freely across the borders to pick cotton and vegetables. At the start of the Depression, hundreds of thousands of Mexicans working in the United States lost their jobs. Federal and local authorities both encouraged and coerced them to return to Mexico. In 1932 as many as two hundred thousand Mexicans, including some who were American citizens, were sent back across the border. Other Mexicans remained in the United States and clustered in shantytowns near the agricultural fields or in barrios in larger towns (fig. 2.9). In Texas it is estimated that there were four hundred thousand migrant laborers looking to pick cotton or harvest other crops during the thirties. Most Mexicans lived in incredible poverty.

While sympathy for "Okies" was being generated by the press and through popular novels like *The Grapes of Wrath,* in 1939 few Americans knew or cared about the plight of Mexican workers. Poverty was thought to come in two colors: black and white. Federal relief was available only to migrants who qualified for state relief, and Mexican citizens were not eli-

2.9   Russell Lee, the house and yard of a Mexican family. San Antonio,
Texas, March 1939 (LC-USF34-032552-D)

gible. Residency requirements made it difficult even for those who *were* citizens to qualify for aid. Crop restrictions promoted by federal agricultural authorities to prop up farm prices also served to force even more Mexican migrant laborers out of work. Ethnic prejudice, already present in the borderlands, was intensified by the competition for jobs during the Depression. Signs warned, "Only White Labor Employed" and "No Niggers, Mexicans, or Dogs Allowed."[22] Russell Lee, who had training in engineering as well as art, had developed a system of flashes to facilitate interior photography. Stryker may have sent him to Texas because he knew Lee could produce compelling photographs that documented the grueling field labor of Mexicans, as well as the interiors of filthy privies, dilapidated shacks, and primitive cooking facilities.

The timing of Lee's visit also coincided with the height of labor unrest in the borderlands. Although Mexican labor agitation was the exception rather than the rule, in 1933 in California there had been thirty-seven strikes of mostly Mexican migrant workers. Another round of strikes had begun in 1937 and lasted through 1938. For three months in 1938 in San Antonio, Texas, five thousand pecan shellers led by Emma Tenayuca walked off their jobs in 137 plants. After a series of confrontations with owners and city officials that garnered national attention, the workers were granted a small increase in wages and the right to unionize. By the time Lee photographed union and nonunion factories a year later, the Fair Labor Standards Act (1938) had raised their wages to twenty-five cents an hour. Agricultural labor, however, had been exempted from New Deal legislation. Mexican and other farm workers were excluded from unemployment and industrial accident insurance, as well as from Social Security compensation. For Mexican workers, there was not much of a "deal" in the New Deal.

Russell Lee must have known how difficult it would be to convince the nation that living conditions on the border were brutal while at the same time illustrating the enduring dignity of poor Mexicans. In Crystal City, Texas, a "vegetable town" made up almost exclusively of Mexican migrant laborers, Lee photographed their deplorable living conditions. At times he was accompanying a health care worker, who pointed out the severe health problems in the migrant community. Lee's captions described babies suffering from malnutrition and skin diseases. Photographs showed men with tuberculosis and women with severe arthritis and gonorrhea.[23] More than any of the other series in the file, the Crystal City photographs come close to transgressing the unspoken rule that pictures should not show people whose physical or emotional states make them look undignified. All Lee's borderland pictures of Mexican life depict unrelenting misery, but those of Crystal City are particularly poignant.

Russell Lee's borderland photographs represent Mexican farm laborers living in a world tightly defined by backbreaking work and domestic poverty. He does not document community activities or attempts by individuals to break out of the tedium of everyday life. There are no photographs of Saturday dances, birthday parties, or saints' fiestas, although he does include one photograph of a man holding his prized fighting cocks.[24] Children do not smile or sing. Men and women do not flirt or tease each other. There are no FSA camps for Mexican workers. The pictures of Mexican life are strictly in the reformist mode of Jacob Riis, who hoped his photographs would show a material world so devoid of normal comforts as to shock middle-class viewers into immediate action.

The notable exceptions to this crushing portrayal are Lee's photographs of Mexican home altars and graveyards.[25] Lee ignored the community's churches and the religious activities of its men, focusing instead on domestic piety. In the United States, Mexicans continued a tradition of making and maintaining a shelf on which they placed pictures and statues of Jesus, Mary, and the saints. Next to the images they set votive candles, rosaries, and miscellaneous household items. Family photographs were assembled nearby, connecting the family on earth, the ancestors in heaven, and Jesus and the saints. Typically the altar was built in a corner of a room just above eye level, where children and animals could not disturb it. These home shrines contained images of sacred characters popular in Mexican communities — El Niño de Atocha, San Ramón, or Nuestra Señora de Guadalupe, for example — as well as those recognized throughout the Catholic world, like the Sacred Heart of Jesus, the Good Shepherd, and Our Lady of Perpetual Help. One mother from San Antonio displayed a print of the Holy Family not unlike the one that John Dudeck put up in his home (fig. 2.10; see fig. 2.6). Home altars were the creative and pious expressions of Mexican women who assembled physical symbols of their personal history and their religious commitments. Poor Catholics used cheap and available religious material culture to thicken their homes against the thinning of their lives by the material deprivation of poverty.

Lee's compositions of domestic piety remind us of those taken by Lewis Hine rather than those of Jacob Riis. Like Hine, Lee composes his photographs to show people as individuals and not simply members of generic groups. He arranges the most vulnerable members of the migrant family, the women and children, next to the most visually creative aspect of migrant culture, the altar. As with Hine's pictures of immigrant workers, the photographs are posed portraits in which the camera is pointed directly at the subject. The pictures are tightly composed so that only the sitters and the shrines are pictured. Bedsheets are smoothed out. No extraneous magazine advertisements are tacked onto the bare wooden walls to distract from the pairing of child and shrine, woman and altar. The photographs lead me to conclude that Lee wants us to understand the centrality of the shrine for the family. He uses the altar to help those outside the Mexican community to better understand the migrant character. The women and children are not merely workers in the fields; they produce and maintain a creative link to a supernatural world.

Lee's photographs stress the dignity of the "innocents" who live with hunger and illness. In one picture a young girl's oval face is balanced by the image of Jesus in an oval frame (fig. 2.11). In this photograph of a young Crystal City resident, disease is not the subject. The girl's direct gaze breaks any appearance of spontaneity or informality in Lee's composition. We know the picture was not quickly snapped while life was "proceeding as normal." The religious picture does not just "happen" to appear in the background. The girl looks right at the camera, with her arms folded and a gaze of sadness and determination in her eyes. Lee composes his portrait by including other portraits. The "portrait" of Jesus is framed both by wood and by a ring of smaller snapshots and advertisements. A portrait of a woman in a stylish dress, perhaps a dead family member, balances it. The bed headboard frames the girl herself.

The subject of Lee's photographs is not the devotional life of the family. Lee does not show us women and children praying near the altars or placing objects on their shrines. We do

2.11   Russell Lee, girl on bed with print of Jesus surrounded by pictures.
Crystal City, Texas, March 1939 (LC-USF34-032348-D)

2.10 (facing page)   Russell Lee, woman with young son in front of family shrine. The prints, from left to right, top to bottom, depict St. Martin of Tours, the Omnipresence of God, St. Raymond Nonnatus, Our Lady of Perpetual Help, St. Anthony of Padua, unknown, the Holy Family. San Antonio, Texas, March 1939 (LC-USF34-032623-D)

not see religious gestures, but we do see the character of women and children linked to their beliefs. In a photograph from Robstown, Texas, Lee sat two children on a bed. Above them are the family's shrine and a framed photograph (fig. 2.12). Lee again composes his picture as a balanced arrangement of the little girls, the sacred characters, and the ancestors. As with the girl from Crystal City, our eyes move between the children, their kin, and their religion. In other pictures Lee eliminates people entirely and concentrates exclusively on the family altar (fig. 2.13). This photograph looks as if it was taken in a store that sold kites and baked goods, although the caption reports that it is a "Mexican home." Christmas ornaments surround a framed print of Our Lady of Guadalupe. Adjoining it is a print of San Ramón. The plain white altar cloth with its rhythmic tatting accentuates the visual complexity by contrasting with the array of the prints, ornaments, figurines, vases, and flowers. While the shrines look exotic and foreign, they also demonstrate the artistry and resourcefulness of the poor.

Russell Lee also photographed Mexican graves in cemeteries in Raymondville and Sinton, Texas.[26] As with some of the shrine pictures, the graves are devoid of people. The pictures do not show Mexican burial practices but, like the altars, illustrate the creativity of people who have almost no material goods. In the same spirit in which they made home altars, Mexican women have decorated the dirt graves of their loved ones. There, on wooden crosses, families placed wreaths of paper flowers. They assembled colorful and interesting pieces of broken pottery, decorative figurines, and even toy chairs on top of the earthen mounds (fig. 2.14). The shrines and graves were places where Mexicans represented the fluidity of all aspects of life. Families did not separate their dead relatives from either supernatural characters or the colorful, everyday articles of domestic life. Sacred and profane was scrambled together.

We can only speculate about why Lee chose to photograph domestic shrines and graves and not other aspects of Mexican culture in Texas. Although Lee took more pictures than any of the other FSA/OWI photographers, he rarely described his work in either captions or in letters to Stryker. Russell Lee's early years, however, may have shaped his sensitivity toward place and the objects displayed in a place. Born in 1903 in Ottawa, Illinois, eighty miles south of Chicago, Lee was five years old when his parents divorced and his father ceased contact with the family. The boy lived with his wealthy grandparents and his mother, but in 1913 she was struck by a car and killed. Russell Lee moved from relative to relative, from legal guardian to legal guardian. Eventually he was sent to Culver Military Academy, where he was a popular student and involved in many campus organizations. Regulations at Culver required cadets to attend Sunday chapel and teachers to be "active Christian men." During his senior year, Lee was president of the Young Men's Christian Association. The YMCA integrated sports and religion, sponsoring a game room with bowling alleys and billiard tables while also promoting Protestant principles. Most of the cadets were members of the YMCA, so membership did not mean that Lee was particularly religious, but it would have been impossible to avoid the rhetoric of Protestant character building at Culver.[27]

After graduating in 1921, Lee enrolled in Lehigh University, studied chemical engineering, met and married a painter, and commenced living the life of a bohemian. The couple spent time in Europe in 1933, traveling as far as the Soviet Union. It was within the circle of artists that Lee developed an interest both in social change and in the camera. Lee joined Stryker's

2.12   Russell Lee, two children sitting on bed under portrait and shrine containing, from left, El Niño de Atocha, St. Helena, St. Isidore the farmer, St. Florian (?), St. Raymond Nonnatus, Sacred Heart of Jesus (statue), Good Shepherd, Immaculate Heart of Mary, Sacred Heart of Jesus (print). Robstown, Texas, February 1939 (LC-USF34-032236-D)

2.13   Russell Lee, shrine to Our Lady of Guadalupe with print of St. Raymond Nonnatus.
San Antonio, Texas, March 1939 (LC-USF34-032678-D)

2.14   Russell Lee, Mexican grave. Raymondville, Texas, March 1939 (LC-USF34-032220-D)

team in 1936, and by the time he was photographing in Texas he had divorced and remarried. Jack Hurley, who interviewed Lee and considered him a friend, theorized that his early years of displacement may have heightened his awareness of the importance of home and family. Hurley observed: "Russell Lee could look with great love and perhaps even envy at the photographs on the mantelpiece or at the cherished old radio — at whatever said to him, 'This is a home; somebody lives here; this is someone's place.'"[28] Lee's fascination with the details of interior spaces, including his interest in religious objects, may have been sparked by envy for a settled domesticity that for many people includes religion. Lee's difficult childhood and peripatetic youth may have heightened his appreciation of (perhaps even romanticization of) home and the symbols of family life. Likewise, while he was familiar with the contours of public Protestantism that supported male camaraderie, the domestic quality of Catholic life in the Southwest must have intrigued him. Lee may have been drawn to home shrines because of the way that they melded artistic creativity, domestic sentiment, and Catholic devotionalism — cultural traits absent from his own religious upbringing.

Faith and the "Common Man"

The fragments of religion found in the early FSA photographs were shaped by the personal and political needs of the photographers to present the poor as dignified and worthy of governmental aid. Shaped by the democratic spirit of the thirties and their own humanistic orientation, they upheld the importance of the "common man." Following in the tradition of reform photography, the staff sought to represent the poor as victims caught in the snares of a world that was not of their making. Breaking with the reform tradition of photographing urban poverty, the FSA project sought to expose economic problems outside of the city. For the New Dealers, rural America was not a romantic paradise of independent farmers but a place where decades of environmental and human exploitation threatened the survival of what many considered to be the "soul" of the nation.

By showing the poor embracing religion, the photographers provided visual evidence that, in spite of their economic problems, rural people had a discernible culture. The ubiquitous appearance of Christian images in the homes of the poor made it possible to illustrate how the poor participated in activities that were not work and were not leisure. The photographers used religious practices to convey the notion that poverty was not reducing people to a point where they might be persuaded by godless communism or socialism; rather, they could be sustained by their enduring faith. Religious images served to enliven pictures of Depression poverty and make them visually more interesting. Like commercial advertisements, they introduced texture and contrast into the photographs. Prints and statues, hymn singing, and Jesus trucks also demonstrated that the poor were connected to beliefs and rituals shared by the "nonpoor."

Russell Lee did not photograph the churches that borderland Mexicans may have attended, just as Dorothea Lange did not linger around Pentecostal meeting houses to observe what migrants were doing inside. Only parts of the lives of religious people attracted them. Institutionalized, communal religion that gave over certain privileges to religious authorities held little interest. Russell Lee would not have been surprised to find out that the Catholic bishop of San Antonio—fearing, along with city officials, that communist agitators were behind the protests—supported the factory owners against the pecan shellers.[29] Mexicans living in Texas may have felt the same way as Lee and so structured their devotions around the home. The intensely interior nature of the photographs of rural poverty, however, does not encourage us to think any differently. The early FSA photographs never bring viewers into communal religious spaces or provide visual narratives of public behaviors.

Instead, they focus on the creative spirit of individual believers. Domestic religion, frequently left out of histories of American religion that focus on institutional and theological change, is emphasized in these government photographs of the poor. Stryker and his photographers upheld the importance of the "authentic" spirituality of the "common man" and presented it as detached from larger national or worldwide religious organizations. Local and ordinary religion, rather than being rooted in the communal practices of churchgoers, was expressed in the individual practices of migrants, elderly men, women, and children. Because the mission of the Farm Security Administration was to concern itself with the rural poor, the photographers made visible what was invisible to many Americans. We can use the file to construct an alternative Christianity of the thirties that privileges the practices of the poor rather than of the middle class.

Up until 1939 photographers included religious images in their pictures in order to evoke certain feelings rather than tell stories. Lange and Lee, as well as the other early photographers, did not try to build those photographs into photoessays. Initially, simply collecting individual photographs was sufficient to present the compelling problem of rural poverty. Exploring religion per se was not their concern. If making pictures to motivate reform had been the only interest of Stryker and the photographers, then the file of religious images would have been minimal. Other goals — to make art, to show America's diverse cultures, to reflect communal solidarity — later lured the photographers into a fuller conversation with religious people and their expressions of faith.

3
Churches Without People

n 1935 Walker Evans was adrift in New York City. At thirty-one, he had no job, no college degree, and no doting family. He had already begun, however, to construct himself as an artist. Ten years earlier, frustrated with his midwestern family, East Coast schooling, and boring New York job, he had left for Paris to pursue an impulse to write. There he hung out at Shakespeare and Company, watching from afar the literary stars of the 1920s. After returning to New York in 1927, he decided not to write but to take up photography as his artistic medium. Three of Evans's photographs were published as illustrations in a book of poems by Hart Crane, but few took notice. In 1932 Evans traveled to Tahiti as the official cruise photographer for a party of rich New Yorkers. The next year he accepted a commission to provide the illustrations for *The Crime of Cuba*. Rather than photographing the country's political unrest, however, he took pictures of everyday Cuban life and drank with

3.1 (facing page)   Walker Evans, Negro church. South Carolina, March 1936 (LC-USF342-008055)

Ernest Hemingway. With those expeditions over, Evans returned to New York to face the economic turmoil of the Depression. While working clerical jobs, he showed his photographs to Bernice Abbott and Alfred Stieglitz and cavorted with writers and artists. He was, according to one art critic, a man "who lived on air and dressed as a dandy."[1]

When some of Evans's friends pulled strings to get him an appointment in 1935 as a government photographer, he gladly accepted the steady job. His duty as "information specialist" for the Resettlement Administration (to become the FSA in 1937) dovetailed with his own growing interest in vernacular architecture and city street life. Walker Evans's photographic style was not the abstract realism of Man Ray or the picturesque palette of Stieglitz. Following in the tradition of the nineteenth-century French photographer Eugène Atget, Evans found art in the "real" of the commonplace. While Stryker and Evans could agree on the importance of recording the art of everyday life, Evans did not believe that the point of his photographs was to document poverty in order to motivate social change. Evans would not tolerate the possibility that his photographs might be used as government propaganda for the New Deal. In thinking about his relationship to the newly formed Division of Information, Evans wrote that he would "never make photographic statements for the government or do photographic chores for gov or anyone in gov, no matter how powerful." In exchange for a set of prints, with their analysis and classification, Evans demanded a car, photographic supplies, and assistants in Washington. He would be a "one-man performance" who would keep his photographic negatives because of his "craftsman's concern" over the quality of the prints.[2] Evans saw himself as an artist who controlled his own art.

Walker Evans (1903–1975) did not last long as a government photographer. He did obtain the use of photographic equipment, as did all the photographers, but he had to buy his own car. He also rarely captioned his prints and never analyzed them. Stryker, not Evans, controlled the photographs. The negatives remained in Washington, where Stryker printed, destroyed, and distributed them as he saw fit. Evans did shoot pictures using his bulky 8×10-view camera, but never enough to suit Stryker's appetite for images. Stryker sent Evans shooting scripts and told him where to travel. Evans, however, spent months out of communication and never hesitated to take up other commissions — photographing African masks for the Metropolitan Museum of Modern Art, for example, or working with the writer James Agee. Early budget cuts that put constraints on the Historical Section forced Stryker to cut one photographer, and he decided that Evans was the most expendable. Evans's contract with the FSA officially ended in March 1937.[3] Perhaps the most famous FSA photographer worked sporadically in the government for less than two years.

Walker Evans's brief but creative stint as a government employee underscores the predictable tensions between artists and bureaucrats. It also is the best illustration of the insistence of photographers on their own ideas about why they were taking pictures, and of how those reasons were ever changing. While Evans apparently shared little of the reforming spirit of the Historical Section, even the socially conscious photographers were not "pure" documentarians. The artistic sensibilities of Dorothea Lange also annoyed Stryker, and she was fired and rehired several times between 1935 and 1942. Many of the photographers who worked for the Farm Security Administration had formal artistic training. Stryker remembered that "most of our people were interested in art. Had some art training, had desires to be artists."[4] In art schools they had learned not only how to paint but the importance of creative independence. Even those who had no artistic training could easily imagine themselves as artists as they wandered across the country, freed from time cards and prying bosses. It was not merely that artists became photographers but that all of the photographers had artistic visions. Anyone who has taken a photograph knows that while recording a particular scene or person is important, it is also pleasing to construct a picture that meets one's aesthetic standards. We want to make pictures that "look good," even at the expense of distorting what we are recording. Within every "sociologist with a camera" there was an artist trying to make well-composed, beautiful pictures.

Stryker explained to an interviewer in 1963 that his photographers were "reporting things that they felt and saw based upon experience; based upon a good deal of investigation." His photographers were not propagandists; they were objectively showing Americans living in poverty. He himself judged photographs in terms of content, "what they have to say about this little group of people, this particular village, this particular dust area."[5] Stryker understood that in order to understand rural life the nation would need to see more than pictures of soil erosion and substandard housing. When photographers like Walker Evans sought to portray more than "this little group of people," however, they asserted a different set of goals from Stryker's. In this chapter and the next, I examine a set of pictures that demonstrate the artistic orientations of the FSA/OWI photographers. These photographs do not merely represent "this little group of people," but rather they attempt to capture the essence of beauty as understood through the canons of modern art. Although Walker Evans was unique in his articulated preference for art photography, all of the photographers made pictures that privileged form over content.

The desire to make modern art, the need to document American cultural life, and the urge to comment on religion were all satisfied when FSA photographers made pictures of churches without people. In order to exercise their artistic inclinations while keeping within the boundaries set by Stryker, photographers turned religious practices into art. As we have seen, Stryker wanted pictures of specific people experiencing difficult circumstances. People standing in front of their pious pictures helped individualize the face of the poor. Other photographs, however, are devoid of people. In these pictures, photographers were satisfied to show religious buildings when they were not being used. Or they waited for churchgoers, with their distracting clothing and expressions, to move away from their church so that the purity of the building's line and form could be exposed. By eliminating people, the photographers could make religion hold still so that a timeless, eternal moment of artistic perfection could be rendered. Some of the photographs in the file explore religious practices as if religion could exist without people — as if religion would be better off if people did not exist.

We have seen that Stryker and his photographers were not involved in religious communities as adults. In this chapter I speculate about what the photographers might have felt was the "truly religious" within religious America. Working from a set of pictures of empty churches, I try to understand what the photographers themselves felt to be "spiritual." Obviously, these conclusions have to be tentative, but I think that the photographs help us understand what secular people of this period saw as meaningful in the religion of others. Rather than always picturing religion as something local and rooted in social interactions among people (as in most of their photographs), "empty church" photographs explore a generalized "spirituality." The fondness of both artists and scholars for pictures of churches without people illustrates the desire — some might say nostalgia — for a pure sacredness that is not profaned by the pettiness of people.[6] This "material spirituality" is represented in vernacular forms, which are then linked to the cosmic, universal, and transcendent. It is this sense of a material spirituality, embedded in form, that defines what the photographers perceived as "good" or "authentic" in form and thus, by extension, in religion. And, as I shall argue in the next chapter, this material spirituality allowed them to connect on an aesthetic level with those people who built and filled the "empty" churches. While a Christian might argue that God and the sacred exist apart from people and from history, a modernist artist would say that beauty transcends and precedes individual personalities. For a Christian, human sin mars God's created perfection. For a modernist artist, capitalism, commercialism, conservativism, and even religious conformity act to sully the mystery of true art. For both groups, at times God or the Transcendent breaks through history and appears in the material world.

God's Mask in the Mediation of the Sun

The formal beauty of churches and synagogues lured the FSA photographers to experiment with composition. Rural churches in particular stood out boldly on the American landscape as examples of distinctive American vernacular architecture. With their strong lines, balanced proportions, and simple iconography, country churches seemed open to the artistic visions of the photographer. The buildings did not make strong visual statements about social respectability or specific denominational commitments. Instead, many rural wooden churches reflected modernist ideals of restraint, functionality, and efficiency. Such churches visually seemed to be beyond the vicissitudes of everyday life that too often marked religious people as pretentious and reactionary. If the photographer wanted to capture forms that suggested timelessness and transcendence, what better way than to photograph something that purportedly spoke to the timeless and transcendent?

In 1936 Walker Evans was given an opportunity to photograph the transcendent in rural churches when his close friend James Agee received a commission from *Fortune* magazine to do an article on southern sharecroppers. Agee persuaded Evans to make a set of photographs for his essay, so between July 16 and September 15 Evans was furloughed from his FSA work. Stryker granted the furlough after securing Evans's agreement that his photographs would eventually become the property of the Farm Security Administration. Agee and Evans picked two families from Hale County, Alabama, as subjects. Agee's article, however, was unacceptable to the *Fortune* editors and eventually was lost. Five years later, in 1941, Agee and Evans published *Let Us Now Praise Famous Men,* a lyrical description of rural life illustrated with Evans's photographs. The book received mixed reviews and sold barely six hundred copies. While Americans in the 1930s wanted stories of the poor, eagerly buying Erskine Caldwell and Margaret Bourke-White's *You Have Seen Their Faces,* by 1941 war was on their minds. Americans had tired of stories and pictures of misery. Agee's wordy prose and Evans's unsentimental photographs were not the stuff of popular publishing.

Walker Evans's photographs were never meant to be a visual depiction of Agee's writing. They were placed at the beginning of the book, were not captioned, and bore no direct relationship to Agee's text. Evans was not making sociological illustrations, but, as always, he neglected to tell Stryker what he *was* doing. James Agee, however, wrote about the process of accompanying Evans while he took photographs. In a short chapter entitled "Near a Church," Agee described an encounter with a rural church. "It was a good enough church from the moment the curve opened and we saw it," Agee wrote, "that I slowed a little and we kept our eyes on it." What caught their eyes was the way that sunlight played on the church's features and transformed it into something that was more than merely a building that held a Protestant congregation. As they approached the church, "the light so held it that it shocked us with its goodness straight through the body, so that at the same instant we said, *Jesus.* I put on the brakes and backed the car slowly, watching the light on the building." [7]

Walker Evans did not include a picture of a church in the 1941 edition of *Let Us Now Praise Famous Men* or in the expanded version of photographs included in the 1960 reissue. Evans did, however, take at least twenty-two shots of churches while he was in the South (see fig. 3.1). Many of those photographs resemble Agee's description. As a good artist unconcerned with rooting an image in history, Evans was indifferent to where he took a particular picture and so did not provide complete captions for his photographs. For a photograph to be artistic, it needed to either rise above time and place or penetrate below. What was important was that photographs demonstrate a recognizable aesthetic. Although he may have only dreamed in 1936 that his photographs would grace the walls of the Museum of Modern Art, that is where several of his church photographs were first seen. In 1938 Evans was the first photographer to have his photographs exhibited at MOMA, albeit in the underground galleries at Rockefeller Center, since the West 53rd Street building was under construction. There the photographs were arranged in a continuous horizontal line with only a few words as captions. When a book was made of the MOMA exhibition, the captions were segregated entirely from the photographs. In spite of the presence of government photographs in the media, only a few critics knew that more than half of the exhibited photographs belonged to the Farm Security Administration file.

Walker Evans's photographs of southern churches are studies in light and form. Like Monet, who would paint the Rouen cathedral or a haystack at different times of the day, Evans studied the effect of light on mass. It was the July light on the church that "even more powerfully strove in through the eyes its paralyzing classicism." Agee and Evans focused on the dominance of geometrical forms in the churches. They followed a trend established in the late nineteenth century by such painters as Cézanne, who believed that the artist must detect in nature the "sphere, the cone, and the cylinder." In the early twentieth century, Corbusier asserted that architecture (by which he meant good architecture) is the "masterly, correct and magnificent play of masses brought together in light." He insisted that our "eyes are made to see forms in light; light and shade reveal these forms." Within the two-dimensional space of the photograph, this meant that Evans would accentuate squares, circles, triangles, and rectangles. Shooting at the right moment and permitting the proper amount of light into the camera produced crisp, sharp, clear lines that defined fundamental shapes. For Agee light enabled the church to become such a powerful statement of basic form that it obliterated any reference to everyday religion, to doctrine, or even to the divine itself. "God's mask and wooden skull and home stood empty," he concluded, "in the meditation of the sun." [8]

Other FSA photographers also presented churches as exercises in abstract minimalist

58

art. In 1939 Lange was in California's Salinas Valley taking pictures of migrant farm laborers and itinerant life. That April she took two photographs of a Pentecostal church that showed the same strong vertical and horizontal lines as Evans's southern churches (fig. 3.2). Lange never photographed the congregation and even refrained from calling the building a church. "Migrants from the Southwest," she commented in her brief caption, "bring their institutions with them."[9] Like Evans, Lange preferred to photograph outside under natural light, using a large-format camera. Her photographs of the Pentecostal church, like Evans's of southern churches, place the church fully and firmly in the center of the photograph. There is little around the photograph that might give the reader a clue about the congregation or distract the viewer from looking at the building's form. Each vertical wooden batten and each horizontal door panel is clearly delineated. Lange places the apex of the roof at the uppermost edge of the photograph. She then establishes a vertical axis from the top of the roof, through the electric light, and downward along the left side of the door. The axis is reinforced by the defining edge of the door along its length. The door also breaks the rhythmic symmetry of the vertical batten. Since the door sits to the right of the axial line and is much larger than the batten, it forces the viewer's eye down to the lower half of the photograph. It not only acts as a balance to the lettering and angle of the roof but also serves as its own statement of repeated lines and shapes.

While it certainly is conceivable that Lange could have composed an equally formal photograph of a migrant picking peas in a field, the nature of vernacular church architecture made it easier to stress form over content. Regulated by a theology that rejected religious images, circumscribed by the carpentry skill of its builder, and limited by the economic standing of its congregation, the Pentecostal church shared an unintended affinity with modernist aesthetic styles. However, it is not just that the church was a simple and minimal piece of architecture; it was imagined and portrayed as simple and minimal. Like Picasso and Georges Braque, who owned African carvings but knew nothing of their ritual functions, Lange was not interested in what motivated these California Pentecostals to build a simple church. Like Picasso, Lange saw only a formal vitality that could be captured in art. Lange's photograph reflects the quintessential principle of modernism: portraying a single, flat, pictorial plane.

Unlike Picasso, Lange did not have the freedom to distort the geometrical forms of her subject into something far removed from the original model. Lange was confined, both by her own preference for straightforward portraiture and by Stryker's documentary goals, to present the church in a direct, unemotional manner. In doing that, she had to capture the large letters that spelled out exactly what the building was. Unlike in a Cubist collage where lettering could be introduced and then scrambled so that the words could not be read, Lange's inclusion of the church's name introduced content into the photograph. In spite of efforts to cause form to override content, the voice of the congregation could still be heard. This is not any old barn; it is the "Pentecostal Church of God Inc."

Given the number of pictures they took, the photographers had many opportunities to explore the artistic possibilities of the camera. Stryker, however, made sure that the artist within

3.2 (facing page)   Dorothea Lange, Pentecostal Church of God. Greenfield, California, April 1939 (LC-USF34-019465-D)

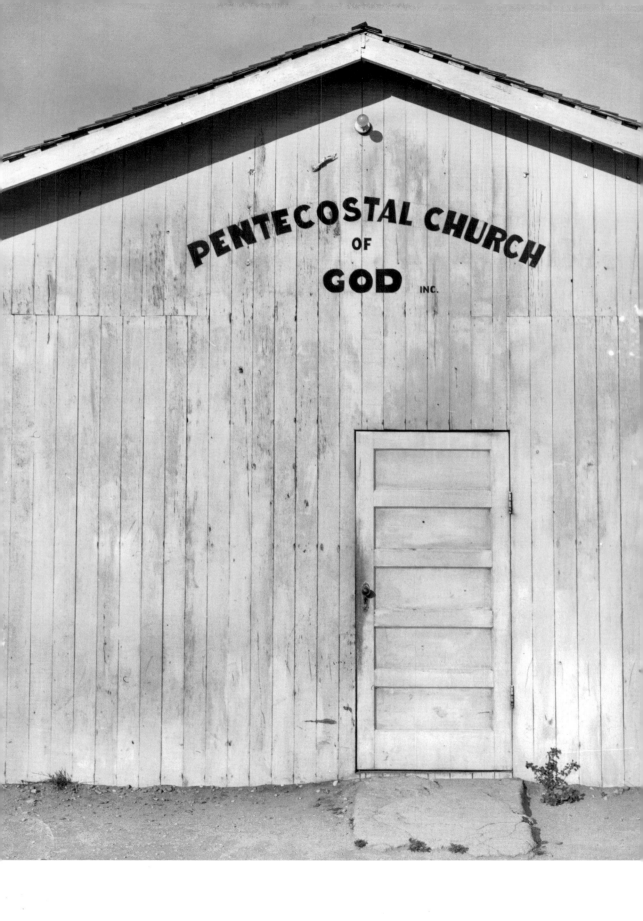

the sociologist did not threaten the production of "genuine" pictures. From Stryker's perspective, if the composition of a photograph became more important than its content, then people could no longer trust the authenticity of the pictorial report. The artistic vision of the photographer would cloud the pure sight of what was "really" out there. When asked whether there were "artistic effects that must be achieved," Stryker denied any concern for form: "The word composition was never talked about. Never mentioned," he insisted. "That was a tabu word. We didn't talk about composition. I don't like the word. I think it's been loaded with all sorts of very spurious things." Indeed, even when Stryker recalled the artistic training of the photographers, he prefaced his thought by remarking, "It's very strange, that most of our people had artistic training."[10] For Stryker, who rarely took photographs himself and who saw photography as a tool for education, not art, the formal qualities of the picture were irrelevant.

Stryker's suspicion of composition, his fear that his photographers could be carried away by their desire to privilege form over content, was not unjustified. Dorothea Lange erased an intruding thumb from the negative of *Migrant Mother* because the child's digit distracted from what she saw as the artistry of the photograph (see fig. 1.2). The print of *Migrant Mother* that hangs in the Museum of Modern Art as a documentary masterpiece has been retouched.[11] The manipulation of the negative was Lange's Pyrrhic victory over Stryker in the battle of who would control the FSA prints. Lange had wanted to make sure that her photographs were being printed properly and that flaws in composition not detract from the beauty of an image. Stryker denied photographers such control in production lest they fail to realize that they were employees of the government and that their artistic sensibilities should never interfere with the educational and historical mission of the section. Consequently, he kept close eye over the negatives, had prints processed and distributed by his staff in Washington, and sent the photographers materials to develop their sociological — not artistic — eyes.

In spite of his efforts, in 1936, a month before Lange asked for control over the *Migrant Mother* negative, a great deal of trouble arose when Arthur Rothstein exercised his artistic eye. While photographing drought conditions near South Dakota, the young New Yorker saw the skull of a dead "steer" sitting in a barren and parched stretch of land. At first, he took a long shot, with the skull taking up only a small part of the picture, in order to emphasize the total landscape. Perhaps Rothstein was thinking about Stryker's concern for contextual documentation of submarginal soil and human land mismanagement. Rothstein could have moved on then, but instead he continued to compose a series of close-up pictures of the skull, moving it around to see how the light created various shadow effects. Those photographs stressed more dramatically the barrenness of the soil and the prominence of death. Rothstein sent the pictures to Stryker, who not only liked them but urged him to make more. Eventually one of the close-ups was published in the Fargo *Evening Forum* as evidence of the drought in North Dakota and linked to a visit of President Roosevelt and his secretary of agriculture, Rexford Tugwell. Critics of the New Deal, however, pointed out that the pictures were taken in South, not North, Dakota, in the badlands, where rain rarely fell, and that other pictures showed that the skull had been moved around. The picture, they insisted, was a fake. While Stryker's response was to turn the criticism into a joke, he knew that he could not risk any more bad publicity linked to publishing "fake" photographs of the Dust Bowl — even if they were beautifully composed. Twenty-two-year-old New Yorkers were going to have to learn something about dried dirt, and they were going to learn to curb their artistic spirits; or at the very least to direct them toward topics less directly related to the Depression.[12]

Photographs of empty churches were less controversial subjects to transform into artistic compositions. By the early 1940s the artistic vision of Walker Evans and Dorothea Lange was so admired by the other FSA photographers that John Vachon wrote Stryker, "There are 4 Walker Evans type R.R. stations in town." Vachon told the historian Jack Hurley that he "went around looking for Walker Evans' pictures."[13] John Vachon had no formal artistic training but had worked since 1936 in Stryker's Washington office filing photographs. Handling hundreds of FSA photographs formed Vachon's modernist aesthetic long before he picked up a camera.

In 1941 Vachon photographed an Episcopal church that closely resembled the southern churches of Evans and the Pentecostal church of Lange (fig. 3.3). Vachon took three photographs of the church, each at a different angle. One of the photographs clearly duplicates Evans's preference for shooting buildings straight on, placing the trees in the background, and including nothing in the foreground. Only the name, Immanuel Episcopal Church, breaks the linear effect of the wooden battens. Unlike Lange's California photograph of the Pentecostal church, the letters can barely be read. Although the pointed arches, open door, and careful paint job tells us that this is not a barn, we have to look closely to see the name of the congregation. The church is angular and blockish, shot in such a way that shadows accentuate the already strong lines of the building. Here is another case in which the play of the sun on mass transforms a rural Episcopalian church into an example of modern, minimal architecture. The church looks as if it is floating off the ground and shows no signs of being rooted in time or space. The composition exemplifies the eternal nature of pure form. Vachon had photographed the "decisive moment" when formal beauty triumphs over social completeness.[14]

While there are many pictures of church exteriors in the file, there are fewer photographs of empty church interiors. Traveling around the countryside, the photographers must have stumbled upon many Protestant churches with their doors locked. To locate the pastor or to return on a Sunday morning would have required time and planning. It would have been far easier to snap a few pictures and move on. In Agee's account of his and Evans's chance encounter with a rural church, the pair actually considered breaking into the church. "While we were wondering whether to force a window," Agee recalled, "a young negro couple came past up the road." After a chat with the couple, Agee admitted that they felt "ashamed and insecure in our wish to break into and possess their church, and after a minute or two I decided to go after them and speak to them, and ask them if they knew where we might find a minister or some other person who might let us in, if it would be all right."[15] The narrative goes on to focus on the couple and Agee's guilt over being a white man in the South. The photographic record, however, reveals that they actually got inside the church, or one much like it.

In the file is a photograph by Walker Evans that matches Agee's description of the interior of the church. "And within," Agee writes as if he and Evans were peeping through the window, "the rigid benches, box organ, bright stops, hung charts, wrecked hymnals, the platform, pine lectern doilied, pressed-glass pitcher, suspended lamp, four funeral chairs, the little stove with long swan throat aluminum in the hard sober shade, a button in sun, a flur of lint, a torn card of Jesus among children."[16] This description matches a photograph of Evans's

3.3   John Vachon, Episcopal church by the roadside. King William County, Virginia, March 1941
(LC-USF34-062663-D)

3.4   Walker Evans, church interior. Alabama, July 1936 (LC-USF342-008285-A)

captioned simply, "Church Interior, Alabama, 1936" (fig. 3.4). The date on the hung chart of the "secretary's report" reads "Sunday July 5 1936," which was during the period when Agee and Evans were in Hale County. Evans was not above moving furniture in order to make his photographs conform to minimalist notions of design, so he might have moved the funeral chairs and pressed-glass pitcher. But the lecture podium still is doilied, and "wrecked hymnals" and bits of lint litter the floor. On the other hand, Agee might have combined several rural church interiors that he and Evans had visited. In June 1937 Dorothea Lange also took an interior shot of an empty "Negro church in Mississippi." The photograph contains the requisite four chairs, stove, and a suspended lamp near the lectern.[17]

The two photographs share an empty and desolate feeling. They present the objects that the congregations use, but not the congregation. A calm stillness pervades the photographs that certainly would be absent from a rural Baptist or Methodist church filled with people. Evans and Lange represent a world where the people once were but are no longer. The scattered hymnals and handmade lectern doily show traces of life but not a full religious life. Lange and Evans placed the religious spirit in the quiet of an empty space rather than in the fullness of preaching, singing, and socializing. The power of the religious, they seem to be saying, is not embedded in the interactions between people and their God. The power of religion is within the form of the space, the arrangement of chairs, the light pouring in the window, the symmetry of the furniture. "Real" religion does not need people. Magic is found within absence and silence.

Religion in Decay

It is impossible to fix the meaning of any visual or literary representation and next to impossible to ferret out the religious intention of photographers as taciturn as Lange and Evans. We do know that Evans was critical of bourgeois society, and it is not unreasonable to suspect that mainstream Christianity may have been included in that appraisal. Evans may have preferred his churches empty — both inside and outside — because he trusted the material world to be more authentically religious than the human world. Lincoln Kirstein, one of Evans's most avid promoters, wrote in 1938 that the photographer's work expressed a "purely protestant attitude: meager, stripped, cold, and, on occasions, humorous. It is also the naked, difficult, solitary attitude of a member revolting from his own class, who knows best what in it must be uncovered, cauterized and why." Evans himself rejected the soft-focus, picturesque photographs of Edward Steichen as full of "parvenu elegance, slick technique," and "the superficiality of America's latter days." While Steichen's photographs were technically impressive, they were "off-track" in their "spiritual non-existence."[18] For the young Evans, the genteel world — of which religion was a part — was corrupt.

In 1934 Evans wrote a friend about his future photographic plans: "I know it is time for picture books. An American city is the best, Pittsburgh better than Washington. I know more about such a place." He then proceeded to describe exactly what he had in mind to photograph:

> People, all classes, surrounded by bunches of the new down-and-out.
> Automobiles and the automobile landscape.
> Architecture. American urban taste, commerce, small scale, large scale, the city street
>   atmosphere, the street smell, the hateful stuff, women's clubs, fake culture, bad
>   education, religion in decay.
> The movies.
> Evidence of what the people of the city read, eat, see for amusement, do for relaxation
>   and not get it.
> Sex.
> Advertising.
> A lot else, you see what I mean.

Here we learn that modern life is not all power, efficiency, and movement. There is also the "hateful stuff," the corruption that needs to be pictured. It is here that we find religion listed — among the women's clubs, fake culture, and bad education. Walker Evans, who was raised in a family where social respectability was preached, even as his father lived next door with his lover, had developed a nose for hypocrisy early in his life.[19] Christianity, like the other institutions of modern America, sheltered the pompous, destroyed the free spirit, and promoted the trivial.

Yet some of Evans's most powerful photographs are of religious spaces. Why did Evans place religion alongside "bad education" and "fake culture" but present southern churches as timeless examples of artistic excellence? Evans, I think, saw the spiritual and the transcendent within the material world. In exploring the forms of religious spaces, Historical Section photographers, like other avant-garde artists of the 1930s and 1940s, felt that they were capturing the transcendental nature of reality. Rather than being profoundly secular and uninterested in the realm of the spirit, many avant-garde artists and architects were preoccupied with questions of ultimate meaning and the spiritual dimensions of life. These artists were not interested in participating in the everyday expressions of faith of Christian and Jewish congregations. They wanted to experience religion with a capital R—a spirituality that they thought was deeper than what people in America were capable of articulating. Although intensely engaged with "modern" America, they shared with thinkers like Carl Jung the belief that "modern man" had lost his soul.[20] That soul, however, could be recovered, and the transcendent known, through art. Walker Evans, in particular, felt that he was capturing something magical in his photographs that permitted him access to a higher plane of reality.

As with many of the pre–World War II avant-garde, Evans was searching for the authentic and the original. In 1971, when asked by an interviewer what "makes a good photograph," Evans replied directly: "Detachment, lack of sentimentality, originality." For him, originality was not to be found in the exceptional or beautiful. Evans "took the thing that, as junk, no longer speaks to us in its original voice, and gave it a new voice in a larger context of dissident values." By focusing on a commonplace object or a vernacular church, Evans restored its individuality by making visual what he saw as the magic embedded in the object. "I think what I am doing is valid and worth doing, and I use the word transcendent," he explained. "That's very pretentious, but if I'm satisfied that something transcendent shows in a photograph I've done, that's it. It's there, I've done it. . . . It's as though there's a wonderful secret in a certain place and I can capture it. Only I can do it at this moment, only this moment and only me. . . . It's there and it's a mystery."[21] The spirit, or the transcendent, did not come through a revealed religion mediated by Christ and his institutional church but was embedded in the natural and constructed universe. The supernatural revealed itself not through relationships with individuals or communities but rather through the visible world of forms. For many modern artists, the search for the eternal meant rooting one's transcendent vision in materiality.

We can see Evans's dualistic attitude about religion—bad religion in decay and good religion in place—in one of his most famous photographs, labeled "Graveyard, Houses, and Steel Mill." In November 1935 Stryker sent Evans south, asking him first to stop in western Pennsylvania to photograph the housing and home life of working-class people. It was here that Evans first was able to photograph modern society in decay. It also is the first time that Evans represented an empty religious space. After being promoted to senior information specialist, Evans was permitted to order a Zeiss triple convertible lens to fit his Deardorff large-format camera. The lens had three different focal lengths, including an unusually long one that allowed Evans to telescope distances. The lens permitted him to collapse a complex scene into a sturdy graphic structure.[22] Evans had gotten a new gadget for his camera, and the photos he took of Pittsburgh and Bethlehem showed that he was eager to use it.

Of the photographs Evans shot, critics have cited one as his most "famous industrial landscape photo."[23] In it Evans collapsed three environments: a cemetery, a series of row houses, and a steel mill (fig. 3.5). While the content of the photograph accomplished Stryker's request to document working-class life, we can interpret the composition in other ways. The new lens enabled Evans to shorten the depth of field so that the cemetery, houses, and smokestacks look like they exist side by side. He places them in three coterminous, horizontal lines—each

3.5   Walker Evans, cemetery, houses, and steel mill. Bethlehem, Pennsylvania, November 1935
(LC-USF342-001167-A)

blending into the other. While the horizontal lines are strong, the vertical upsweeps of the cross, edges of the houses and windows, telephone poles, and smokestacks are also prominent. The contrasting lines make for a visually complex environment. At the same time, there are no people strolling in the cemetery or lounging on the stoops of the houses. The smokestacks reach up to the edge of the photograph, so no billowing fumes are included. In spite of the photograph's noisy visual character, the scene is deadly quiet.

In 1938 the poet Archibald MacLeish noticed the striking character of the photograph and included it in his illustrated poem "Land of the Free." In the poem, a meditation on the doubt raised by the dislocations of the Depression, MacLeish muses:

> Now that the land's behind us we get wondering
> We wonder if the liberty was land and
> the Land's gone: the liberty's back of us . . .
> We can't say
> We don't know

Toward the end of the poem, MacLeish includes in sequence two FSA photographs of graveyards. Marion Post took the first one, of an icy New England scene complete with church and grave markers. "We tell our past by the gravestones and the apple trees," MacLeish reflects about America in the dead of winter. The next photograph is by Evans and is accompanied by these lines:

> We wonder whether the great American dream
> Was the singing of locusts out of the grass to the west and the
> West is behind us now:
> The west wind's away from us

MacLeish uses words to fix the meaning of the photograph. In both stanzas, MacLeish employs a picture of a graveyard to symbolize the death of the American dream.

MacLeish's poetic reflection, as well as later interpretations of Evans's photographs, all present a twentieth-century secular version of a religious space.[24] Walker Evans was in Bethlehem, and so we should not be surprised that when he saw an opportunity to comment on Christianity, he took it. For the secular artist and writer, a cemetery is a nonreligious place, a place for dead bodies, and a reminder that all things must end. Considering that Evans prominently positioned the cross within the photograph, I suspect that he wanted to acknowledge the religious nature of the space and then to associate Christianity with death and a decaying social order. From his perspective, Christianity, as an institutional religion associated with the middle and working classes, was no longer alive. The city, and the people who lived in the city, were struggling for their lives and could no longer rely on religious support. "Bethlehem" — the birthplace of Christianity — had become the place where the death of humanity takes place. Like fake culture and bad education, Christianity was empty and hollow. Like the duplicated smokestacks and windows that all look the same, the crosses and grave markers had no originality or character. Mass production had taken over working-class culture, and middle-class neighborhoods had become desolate, haunted spaces.

Walker Evans and his interpreters spoke only for their own notions of death and religion. I suspect that the residents of Bethlehem in 1935 did not put crosses on graves to symbolize the end of life. In spite of the desperation caused by the Depression, Christians continued to put crosses on graves in order to represent eternal life, not death. Crosses on graves often were empty, the absent body symbolizing Christ's triumph in the Resurrection and the promise of heaven for the righteous. Bethlehem might have been a place of pollution and exploitive labor, but it also recalled the place where the Savior, the giver of eternal life, was born. Evans took another picture in the graveyard, a close-up of the grave of Antonio Castellucci and his wife Maria Fanella.[25] The grave has their portrait carved in stone underneath a cross covered with a wreath of flowers. It is unlikely that this Italian couple or those who commissioned the memorial would have assumed that death brought about the end of life. This famous photograph tells us more about Evans's attitude toward religion than it does about the faith of the people of Bethlehem.

Evans's Bethlehem photograph does not merely serve as a social commentary on the futility of Christianity. If we focus on its style rather than its content, the Bethlehem photograph recalls the photography of Paul Strand.[26] Evans was influenced by the compositional style of Strand, who created photographs reminiscent of Cubist collage painting. More than Evans's photographs of southern churches, the graveyard photograph evokes Cubism. Light — the important quality in abstract minimalism — is almost absent from Evans's industrial photograph. Instead, Evans creates a morass of discontinuous geometry and spaces. The photograph contains broken areas of high and low contrast and repetitious forms. While the content is clear — factory, cemetery, houses — the collapsing of the space makes for an unusual assemblage.

By calling on the techniques of Cubist collage, Evans visually concludes that the religion of explicit meanings and stable values is truly decaying. What must replace it is a spirituality; a sense of the transcendent that produces a new reality that obeys new laws. This is a Cubist world of shifting relationships that includes the onlooker.[27] The essential, the foundational, is not to be found in a set of religious beliefs but rather in the acceptance of the disorder and complexity of modern times. Irony and ambiguity are the only fixed values. While we might think that we know what a factory, graveyard, or row house signifies, when the photographer places them in a tight, overly close relationship, they all become alien. The total picture, while not unfamiliar to the viewer, is still jarring and difficult to interpret. Unlike MacLeish's use of Evans's photograph to indicate the mood of Americans in the 1930s, Evans seems to be saying that the questioning and insecurity of the nation is not a temporary dislocation. What this photograph of a Bethlehem cemetery shares with his later southern churches is the beauty of its emptiness. It is within the negation of the obvious — an empty church, a space that unites work, home, and religion — that transcendent meaning can be found. What is remarkable is not that Walker Evans perceived piety as in decay but rather that he sought to transform piety into transcendence.

Modern Primitive Religion

Transforming one type of religious representation into another was not unique to Walker Evans. The representation of piety so that it becomes more authentically spiritual — and thus more meaningful to the artist — can also be seen in the photographs of John Collier, Jr. (1913–1992). Like many of the Historical Section photographers, Collier had a complicated biography that combined unusual education, foreign travel, and artistic training. Born in Sparkhill, New York, Collier moved with his family in 1920 to Los Angeles when his father became a director of adult education for the state of California. Shortly after their arrival, John Jr. was hit by an automobile, which fractured his skull and damaged the left hemisphere of his brain. Severely dyslexic, the boy had problems with spelling and mathematics, as well as with processing auditory information.[28] John Collier, Sr., who had progressive ideas about education, thought that training in the arts might help his son cultivate an alternative way of understanding the world. So in 1925 Collier's parents apprenticed the twelve-year-old boy to the painter Maynard Dixon. At that time Dixon was married to Dorothea Lange and was working as an artist in San Francisco.

When John Collier, Jr., entered the lives of Dixon and Lange, the couple had been married only five years. Dorothea Lange was struggling to be a professional photographer while raising the couple's two sons and a stepdaughter. Maynard Dixon, twenty years older than Lange, was chafing against his domestic life and spending months away from the family. Eventually John left the family, and at the age of sixteen he apprenticed with a professor of anatomy at Johns Hopkins University in Baltimore. According to his father, his son was "interested in a career in art, and he knew that, like Leonardo da Vinci, he must have a thorough knowledge of human anatomy." Collier's apprenticeship lasted less than a year. He then joined the crew of a sailing ship journeying around the Horn of Africa to Europe.[29] When he returned to the United States in 1930, he trained as an artist and photographer in San Francisco and Taos, New Mexico. At the suggestion of Dorothea Lange, John Collier was hired by Stryker in 1941 when he was twenty-six. Like the other photographers, John Collier had cultivated an eye for the unusual, for the culturally rich. He might make propaganda to serve the needs of the country during a period of war, but it would be creative and thoughtful propaganda.

During his years in California, Collier and his family spent time in New Mexico, living among Native American, Spanish, and Anglo communities as well as colonies of artists and writers.[30] By the early 1900s, artists had discovered the beauty of the Southwest and had settled in the small villages around Santa Fe. In 1918 Mable Dodge Luhan moved to Taos, where her home became a salon for artists making their pilgrimages to paint red hills and colonial Spanish churches. In 1929, at the height of her painting career, Georgia O'Keeffe, the wife of photographer Alfred Stieglitz, had settled in what has been called the "Greenwich Village of New Mexico."[31] Among her New Mexico paintings were those of churches in Ranchos de Taos (1929, 1930) and Hernandez (1931, 1937). John Collier might have known of those paintings and similar ones by his mentor Maynard Dixon, as in 1935 he opened his own art studio in Taos.[32] Like many artists — Paul Strand, for instance, who photographed churches when he lived in New Mexico between 1930 and 1932 — Collier used the New Mexican landscape and churches to serve as a source for his art. In spite of Collier's enthusiasm for Stryker's documentary goals, and his later commitment to using photography as an anthropological tool, there is no question that Collier was following a well-established trend in modern art when he photographed New Mexican churches.

In the winter of 1942–1943, Collier photographed Catholic parish life in several northern New Mexican towns. The town of Peñasco was the site of the area's main church, while Trampas was a tiny mountain village where a colonial Spanish chapel was located. The Peñasco church, San Antonio de Padua, was built sometime between 1911 and 1916 in a gothic revival style typical of Catholic churches across the United States. Its interior decorations were also unexceptional; the pastor could have ordered them from a New York church supply catalogue. Parishioners drove to Mass in cars. There was nothing quaintly "New Mexican" about the Peñasco church. Collier took only two photographs of the church that most of Father Cassidy's parishioners attended.[33]

What caught Collier's attention was the remote mission chapel in Trampas, where only a few villagers came for Mass. Built as early as 1760 by Spanish settlers, the Trampas chapel is one of the oldest churches in New Mexico. Collier never bothered to record its name, the church of San José de Gracias de las Trampas. In 1932 the Society for the Preservation of New Mexico Mission Churches renovated San José, giving it new roof timbers, bases for the towers, and a balustrade and beam for the facade balcony. Consequently, when Collier visited the church in 1943, it had already experienced the hand of historic preservationists. Unlike many mission churches that were crumbling, its physical decline had been halted. It looked old but not too old. Collier took many pictures of the church and later returned to shoot color photographs of the interior. The Trampas church preserves a type of Catholicism that by the

3.6   John Collier, cemetery and the back of the church of San José de Gracias de las Trampas.
Trampas, New Mexico, January 1943 (LC-USW3-013692-C)

1940s was disappearing from larger towns. Most New Mexican Catholics no longer knelt every Sunday on bare wooden floors, stood in sex-segregated areas, and endured winter cold relieved only by the heat of one stove. The larger Peñasco church was more comfortable and modern—something its parishioners appreciated—but far less picturesque than the adobe structure, retablos, and handmade wooden statues of San José de Gracias de las Trampas.[34]

John Collier took two exterior photographs of the Trampas chapel that reflect the same fascination for abstract form, light, and simplicity that we have seen in the photographs by Evans, Lange, and Vachon. As with the Georgia O'Keeffe paintings of the Ranchos church in Taos, Collier shot one of the photographs from the back (fig. 3.6). From that angle the church appears made up of a series of squares and rectangles defined by lines lit by the New Mexican sun. By using a wide-angle lens and selecting the proper focal length, Collier accentuated its form. Holding the camera low and pointing it up to the church created a picture of expanse and massiveness. As with the southern rural churches, the Trampas building assumes a monumental character that may not have been evident to someone looking at the church itself rather than at its photograph. Walker Evans, Dorothea Lange, and John Vachon achieved this same effect when they photographed small, rural churches. The camera transformed a simple structure into a bold piece of modern architecture.

John Collier also shared with other photographers the desire to reduce the design of the church to its simplest forms. In a close-up he took of the front of San José de Gracias de las

Trampas, he carefully composed a balanced picture of rhythmic lines, basic shapes, and duplicating shadows (fig. 3.7). This particular shot was one of several that he took before and after Mass. In the others people linger around the church entrance, but in this one the composition emphasizes repeated right angles. Only the slight curve of the bell, with its balancing shadow, breaks the series of straight lines. The photographer used high contrasts to emphasize the abstract, minimal character of the church and create a study in cadence and order. While the bell and the outline of a cross on the door remind us that this is a building used by religious people, the photograph conveys no information about the congregation.

Collier's vision of the Trampas chapel as modern architecture reflected Corbusier's love of the straight line. In 1924 the French architect wrote, "Man walks in a straight line because

3.7   John Collier, entrance to San José de Gracias de las Trampas. Trampas, New Mexico, January 1943 (LC-USW3-013707-C)

he has a goal and knows where he is going; he has made his mind to reach some particular place and he goes straight to it." Corbusier praised the rational human behavior that produced the line, and he ridiculed disjointed forms. Such forms were, in effect, asinine. "The pack-donkey meanders along, meditates a little in his scatter-brained and distracted fashion," Corbusier wrote. "He zigzags in order to avoid the larger stones, or to ease the climb, or to gain a little shade; he takes the line of least resistance. But man governs his feelings by his reason; he keeps his instincts in check, subordinates them to the aim he has in view. He rules the brute creation by his intelligence."[35] The regulating line, for Corbusier and those designers who subscribed to his vision, kept people from wandering around like beasts of burden. Pure geometry provided order, and order permitted security and happiness. In the back roads of Catholic New Mexico, Collier saw spaces that could be photographed to illustrate the power of the straight line.

In 1991 the art critic Steven Yates saw the spirit of New Mexican culture not in Collier's photographs of everyday life in Father Cassidy's parish but in Collier's exercises in modern art. Yates recognized universal characteristics more easily in empty churches than in the religious people who frequented the buildings. "The church and cemetery are a metaphor for a deeply rooted sense of history and culture," he wrote. Collier's photograph "crystallizes the cycle of life in the community. The universal character of culture is manifest in primary forms that are timeless." For Yates, "the photograph is bold in viewpoint, and its positive and negative patterns of light characterize the strength of the values of the community."[36] Yates interprets Collier's photograph as an effort to express universal rather than regional characteristics.

Yet it evidently did not strike Yates as odd that "history and culture" were represented in a photograph where people were absent; that a decaying graveyard symbolized the "cycle of life in the community." Yates, like Collier, looks past the individuality of the Trampas church and congregation and into the "depth" of the culture. He uses the Trampas church, with its similarity to other famous colonial New Mexican churches, as a metonym. The church represents a whole culture. By offering the church as an example of modernist art, Collier and later critics were able to point to it as a sign of the "universal" spirit of "Culture." Between their births and deaths people are trapped in the fashions and fads of their times. The geometric forms of their handicraft, however, reveal the foundational order of matter. Likewise, if religion were merely the collection of human activities, it could be thought of only in sociological, history-bound terms. When people were eliminated from their creations so that the pure form of a religious space could be seen, then, the truly universal character of religion could be "crystallized." Just as Corbusier defined the truly human as a man walking in a straight line, so did other artists and art critics see the truly spiritual as embedded in the form of certain New Mexican churches.

Collier's original intent in going to New Mexico was to photograph Native American culture. By the early 1940s Native Americans—both as producers of art and as a type of art themselves—had become mainstays of the American modern art scene. The New York avant-garde had discovered (or rather created) Indian "art" in the early twentieth century. By 1941 the Museum of Modern Art's major exhibition, "Indian Art of the United States," had convinced the cultural elite that objects produced by Native Americans were intrinsically fine works of American art worthy of modern consideration.[37] Freed from European influence, native artists could provide the country with its own indigenous art. As we shall see, Collier certainly wanted to provide Stryker with evidence of multicultural patriotism in time of war, but he also wanted to represent Native Americans as art themselves.

For American modernist artists, Native Americans had become the equivalent of Africans for European artists. Like "primitive" Africans, many artists and writers thought Native Americans to be vanishing and rare exotica that were more spiritual and authentic than Western men and women. Africans and Native Americans supposedly had a more elemental connection with the natural order of things, so their simple, agrarian lifestyle more directly expressed humanity. The primitive—from the European folk to the exotic Middle Easterner to the Indian—was seen as living in a world that was organic, whole, sensual, and spiritual. Intellectuals felt that they had lost their soul to progress, a feeling that had haunted the Western mind since the Industrial Revolution. The primitive apparently had not, so could provide a healing remedy for the anxieties that threatened the stability of modern culture as well as strengthening the modern psyche. Unlike the modern who was plagued by individuality, separateness, fragmentation, and dismemberment, the primitive experienced an enviable mind-body unity.

Collier was unable to photograph Native Americans in New Mexico, but he was able to photograph another "primitive" American people—Spanish-speaking Catholics. Like Gauguin, who painted Catholic Brittany before traveling to Tahiti to paint "real" primitives, Collier found in Catholic New Mexico the simple, rural life that fascinated artists. After complaining to Stryker that it was hard to get around without a car, he wrote: "Well, as a 'cure all' for the situation I have turned my back on civilization and have gone to live with a Spanish family in the very ancient and isolated town of Trampas." In another letter to Stryker he referred to the residents of Peñasco as "primitive people." Collier saw Spanish New Mexicans as having, like Native Americans, a mystical culture closely wedded to the land. He told Stryker that he planned to "shoot this town [Trampas] in color particularly the old church which was about as fine [a] primitive religious art as I've ever seen." Photographing the church must have been a welcome relief from what was occupying much of Collier's time outside of the village: doing what he called "sheep stories" to illustrate farming practices.[38]

The photographs that Collier took inside the San José church deemphasize the congregation and focus on the folkloric quality of the interior decorations (fig. 3.8). Rather than shoot from the front of the church, he chose to photograph the congregation from the back. Wrapped up in their winter coats and hats, the women form an undifferentiated mass huddling around a painting of Our Lady of Mount Carmel and the poor souls in purgatory. Collier photographed the congregation gathered in prayer, existing in a time and space separate from our modern world. Prayer is placed in an eighteenth-century chapel because Collier could not see the connection of devotion to the pragmatic world of the everyday. Catholic piety in New Mexico is presented as ancient and mysterious.

Collier took several photographs of the side altars of the Trampas chapel focusing on their statuary (fig. 3.9). Hand-carved and painted, dressed in robes, and draped in gauze, the statues reflect the tight relationship between the sorrowful and crucified Christ and those who care for the objects by clothing and decorating them. The emaciated wooden bodies streaming with blood and bent in agony have a raw quality that evokes the primitive other. As if to contrast with, and thus emphasize, the beauty and ageless character of the statues, Collier commented in his caption, "A Coca-Cola bottle is used as a candle holder." While those who lit candles at the altar probably did not notice the incongruity, Collier may have found the juxtaposition

3.8 John Collier, congregation kneeling in the church of San José de Gracias de las Trampas. Trampas, New Mexico, January 1943 (LC-USW3-014618-E)

humorous, tasteless, or even irreverent. At the very least, he noted the introduction of modern consumer culture into an ancient spirituality.

Collier represented the draped crucifixes, sorrowful Madonnas, and armored angels of the Trampas chapel not as religious images but as art. He domesticated, ordered, and appropriated the supernaturalism of Catholic devotionalism by representing it as primitive folk art — much in the same way that Gauguin represented Brittany processionals or Picasso African ceremonial masks. By setting Catholicism in a timeless, primitive past, Collier was not ridiculing the faith of New Mexicans. I suspect that he was actually trying to make it more religious. For Collier, like Evans, what was authentic about religion was not Sunday church-going but the intense, mystical spirituality that they perceived in primitive design. It was in the beauty of decay, of the rustic, of the raw and unrefined, that real transcendence could be found.

3.9 (facing page) John Collier, crucifix in San José de Gracias de las Trampas. Trampas, New Mexico, January 1943 (LC-USW3-017872-C)

Critics of bourgeois culture felt that the West had lost its true connection with the elemental, foundational source of being. By stressing basic forms and primitive sentiments, modernist artists transcended the ephemeral and discovered the immutable and eternal, the authentic, in the material world. That authenticity supposedly connected "the folk" to modernist art aesthetics, since for both groups authenticity was expressed via simplicity, balance, rhythm, and abstraction. The artist became the conduit to the "real" that could then heal the modern soul. Consequently, for men and women like John Collier, Trampas was a spiritual place not because its people were practicing Catholics. The art and space of the church of San José was spiritual almost in spite of its congregation. I suspect that Collier did not see Catholic spirituality as entirely irrelevant in modern society, but his photographs reveal his discomfort with where piety fit into contemporary New Mexican life.

That a fascination with the "exotic Other" accompanies the colonial agenda of subjugation and domination has been well documented by many scholars.[39] Non-Western people not surprisingly resent Occidental culture's vampirelike pursuit of the Other in order to fill their own spiritual emptiness; an emptiness that was the price paid for progress. Just as modern artists emptied their work of content in order to fill it with form, John Collier emptied the Trampas chapel of people in order to fill it with primitive art. Once the chapel was transformed from being a building for people into being a museum for primitive art, it could become spiritual and thus hold importance for Collier. As with many modern intellectuals and artists, Collier stamped his own brand of spirituality over the religion of other people.

The Emptiest Building on the Fairgrounds

The Historical Section photographers were not alone in their attempt to construct a spirituality that was embedded in the physical world yet freed from any cultural or theological context. In 1939 New York City hosted the grand spectacle of the World's Fair. The thrust of the fair was to present the world, then currently mired in fascism and war, as a place of technological progress and social harmony. The future, the designers predicted, would be a time not of barbarism and horror but of material comfort, consumerism, and international peace. Religion would not be left out of the future in spite of the fair's emphasis on science, rationality, and materialism. While originally three separate buildings were to be constructed for Protestants, Catholics, and Jews, what was dedicated that spring was a Temple of Religion. As fairgoers entered the temple grounds, they passed by administrative offices where representatives of the "three great Faiths" provided "personal counseling," "information about city churches," and "hospitality." Then visitors walked through a garden, cooled by fountains, that the official guidebook called a "landscaped retreat."[40]

Finally, fairgoers moved into the temple itself, a 1,200-seat auditorium with an upper facade rising to sixty-six feet. The simple architectural design included blank white walls with no religious symbols and over the front door only the words "For those who worship God and prize religious freedom." The guidebook instructed visitors that "neither the building nor the ground is consecrated, nor are formal religious services held here." That newspaper accounts praised the blue stained glass, the forty-two-stop organ, and Miss Emma Otero's rendition of "Ave Maria" did not apparently bother Rabbi David De Sola Pool. At the temple's dedication he observed, "Here in the Temple of Religion, men and women of differing creeds, but of one religious spirit, shall meet in full, free, frank fellowship of the spirit, renouncing racialism, learning to love the Lord our God with all our soul and all our mind, and learning to love our neighbor as ourselves." Clergyman after clergyman took to the podium to renounce the demonic forces that "are filling men's hearts with hate and rending the body of humanity asunder" and to promote "a national and personal spirituality that recognizes the universal Fatherhood of God and the brotherhood of man." Religion was formed of "simple concepts" — charity, justice and tolerance — shared by all faiths and necessary for democracy.[41]

The promotion of an American civil religion during a time of impending global war should not surprise us. Nor is it unusual that when imagining the future, Americans in 1939 could see only an all-embracing, peaceful "religion." Not everyone, however, was excited about the message intended by the designers of the Temple of Religion. Father Edward Lodge Curran, president of the International Catholic Truth Society of Brooklyn, did not join the chorus of admirers. Speaking at a congress of the National Laywomen's Retreat Movement, he called the temple "the emptiest and the most unattractive" building on the fairgrounds. "How anybody can erect a building and call it a Temple of Religion without a single symbol of God on the walls is beyond comprehension," he observed. "There is an organ, but an organ does not make a building religious. Nowhere in the construction of the building are to be found two bits of wood put together to represent the Cross of Christ." While *Time* magazine called the Temple of Religion "one of the milk-mildest exhibits in the New York World's Fair," it had no patience with Father Curran ("florid, bald, horn-voiced, hammer-handed"), who "horridly shattered" the temple's "careful neutrality."[42]

Father Curran probably also criticized the ecumenical theology voiced by the temple's proponents but what was reported was his disgust with the emptiness of the building. While the other exhibits were filled to the brim with technological and consumer wonders, the Temple of Religion was stripped down to the bare essentials. Fairgoers had to negotiate administrative offices housing ministers, priests, and rabbis, come through a purifying natural space, and then finally arrive at the proverbial "white box" of contemporary design. The organ and the blue stained glass could not be read as Catholic or Protestant but rather had to be evocative of the general spirit that pervaded all religion. The *New York Times* explained that the spiritual was rooted not in "daily manifestations" but in "eternities."[43] In order to represent visually the transcendent, universal spirit, modernist notions of art were called upon. The progressive future presented at the fair looked surprisingly similar to the primitive past.

To be modern in the late 1930s and early 1940s meant to seek authenticity and purity of spirit. People haunted by absence sought places of presence within modern art and primitive culture. Artists might have used common objects or spaces in their designs, but they had to transform them into forms that spoke to larger concerns and wider visions. Symbols or images that called viewers back into the nitty-gritty of daily life had to be erased in order for a transcendent divinity to appear. This was at the heart of modernism. To introduce a cross, "two bits of wood," either to a rural southern church or to a futuristic temple, would be to introduce Christ, Christianity, Christians, and the burden of history. An empty church, at best freed of people or at least freed of sectarian representations, could better illustrate the universal spirituality that modern man and woman were seeking.

4.1   Jack Delano, men outside church before service. Heard County, Georgia, April 1941
(LC-USF34-043925-D)

4
Another South

Yesterday we went hunting for churches," wrote Irene Delano to Roy
Stryker, "and came upon one small Negro church where we got shots of all
the deacons — the preacher — and the whole 'meeting.' " Accompanying her
husband Jack on his photographic tour of the South in the spring of 1941, Irene
was captivated by rural religion. "One fellow sang in a booming voice — 'Trying
to make one hundred, 99½ won't do,' " she reported, "until all the hills around
rocked in the rhythm! It's amazing how they can sing so beautifully without the aid of any
sort of musical instrument!"[1] Irene and Jack Delano took at least nineteen photographs of this
African-American congregation in Heard County, Georgia. The series began with a picture
of four women, one carrying a child, walking down a dusty road toward the church. Other
photographs show the gathered men dressed in suits and hats, chatting with one another. In
one picture Delano creates an elegant composition by filming the men underneath a massive

tree bounded by a car and the church. The wooden planks of the siding, the shingles on the roof, the curve of the tree's leaves, the uniformity of the men, and the outlines of the car form a textured, balanced scene (fig. 4.1).

Jack Delano probably remained outside for a while photographing people exchanging greetings and catching up on news. Eventually he took a group picture of the deacons and minister, lined up against the side of the church. Moving inside, he filmed the "fellow with a booming voice," prayers and preaching, and the attentive congregation (fig. 4.2; see also fig. 8.3). Three photographs are of the church's minister.[2] Delano explains in his captions that this man lived in an old converted schoolhouse with his wife and two grandchildren, while his children had moved out of Heard County. Delano posed the couple underneath framed portrait photographs taken of them twenty years earlier (fig. 4.3).

While the photographs Delano took were carefully composed to show the beauty of the church and the dignity of the congregation, Delano provides no real details about these people. The captions do not name the church or the deacons. The congregation's leader is referred to as the "Negro preacher." Delano showed little interest in learning about the church and its members; his was not an anthropological study. As we have seen, the Historical Section produced pictures that said as much about modernist canons of art as they did reformist convictions of the New Dealers. The photographs lead us to suspect that what attracted Irene and Jack to the church was the physical beauty they saw in the building and the congregation. Delano photographed the church and its people as if they were figures in an art composition.

Jack and Irene Delano were nonobservant Jews who had little in common with the members of the "Negro church" they photographed. The couple had met in Philadelphia, where Jack Delano (né Jacob Ovcharov) had come as a child with his family from the Ukraine. While Jack's family had struggled to put him through the Pennsylvania Academy of the Fine Arts, Irene's father—an ophthalmologist from Toronto—supplied her with a generous monthly allowance to live the life of a bohemian art student. The car the couple drove through the South was his wedding gift. Jack had made the obligatory artistic pilgrimage to Europe, supported liberal causes, and photographed for the WPA before joining Stryker's team of photographers in 1940. The Delanos, as with the other FSA photographers of southern religions—Marion Post, Ben Shahn, Russell Lee, Walker Evans, John Vachon, Carl Mydans, Dorothea Lange— were artist outsiders who knew the South only through the materials Stryker insisted they read and the images promoted in mass culture and American literature.[3]

The Historical Section photographers took more pictures of religious expression in the South than in any other region of the country. They also provided a more diverse picture of American religious life, filming whites and blacks, Protestants and Catholics, men and women, church services and architecture. This interest in southern religion has many causes. The photographers were in the South for extended periods of time, and southerners were active churchgoers. Consequently, it would have been difficult to avoid photographing southern religion. The "Negro vogue" of the twenties engaged some white artists and intellectuals. Stryker's photographers may have entered African-American churches in order to satisfy their

4.2 (facing page)   Jack Delano, man singing during the collection at church service.
Heard County, Georgia, April 1941 (LC-USF34-043964-D)

curiosity about black culture. On a more ideological level, the photographers had sympathy for the economic plight of rural people, and picturing religion was one way to demonstrate the dignity of the poor. The photographers may have been doing what they did throughout the country, picturing religion when it fit their reformist agenda.

But the pictures the photographers took in the South must be read differently from other pictures of religion in the file. An overwhelmingly negative representation of southern Protestantism dominated the popular culture and literature of the time. Any curiosity or humanistic agenda that the photographers had about southern life would have been tempered by the crushingly critical image of evangelical Christianity in American culture. The Historical Section photographers did not make compelling pictures of southern faith because they came to the region with respect for the complexities of evangelical piety—white or black. I want to suggest just the opposite: in the 1930s and early 1940s cultural representations of southern Protestantism consumed by northerners were exceedingly unsympathetic to local beliefs and worship styles. In many ways, the South had become the symbol for what was wrong with religion throughout the country. The photographers broke with this portrayal of Southern religion not merely because they were expected to picture faith as uplifting. They pictured southern faith communities positively because the visual dimension of southern religion enchanted them. They saw aspects of the South that social critics had missed.

With their stress on the Word of God, evangelicals are noted for their fiery preaching, sentimental singing, and disdain for distracting worldly pleasures. But photographers can use only their eyes, not their ears. Photographers can only "see" religion. They cannot convey in pictures the content of sermons, the rhythms of hymns, the debates over theology, or the struggles with moral dilemmas. A photograph shows the dance that the preacher does when he preaches, not the story he tells. A photograph displays the beauty of the place where the faithful assemble, not the history of why the church was built. In the same way, photographs are not good at eavesdropping on conversations of racial hatred or personal pettiness that come from the lips of religious people. When we look at the FSA/OWI photographs, we see a religious world with its sound turned off.

Photography can present Christianity only as part of a physical world of texture, movement, form, and materiality. The southern religion that Jack and Irene Delano portrayed was different from that of popular novels and newspaper accounts because they were willing to be drawn into the physical beauty and liturgical drama of southern piety. They became engaged with southern Christianity precisely because they were limited in the ways that they could apprehend religious expression. The limits of the camera forced them to explore an overlooked dimension of religion and thus provide a basis for an alternative story of southern Christianity. By privileging sight over hearing, they had to shift their focus to the visual dimension of religion and away from the ethical and theological dimensions. Their artistic orientation provides us a fresh perspective on southern religion. Ironically, what engaged the photographers was the visual beauty of southern faith expressed in ways that we typically think of as being "Catholic"—the elegance of holy places, the intensity of orderly communal worship, the conflation of the sacred and the profane, and the great diversity of popular devotion.

4.3 (facing page)   Jack Delano, preacher and his wife sitting underneath their photographic portraits taken twenty years earlier. Heard County, Georgia, April 1941 (LC-USF34-043918-D)

In this chapter I also address a common idea among cultural critics who write that when photographers stress the beauty of their subjects, they are doing a disservice both to the viewer of the photograph and to those pictured.[4] I want to challenge the notion that the camera's ability to transform an often ugly and boring reality into something beautiful dramatizes the weakness of photography to convey the truth. Rather than criticize photographers for discovering beauty in the poor in order to make poverty less threatening and the poor more manageable, I present a more hopeful outlook: By stressing the visual beauty of congregational life, the photographers opened up interpretive stories that help us understand why people are religious. By allowing themselves to be caught up in the visual beauty of faith, the photographers discovered new and surprising aspects of southern religious experience. Rather than criticize the FSA photographers for romanticizing evangelical Protestantism, we can use the photographs as a means of entering into a religious world not bound up in biblicism and moralism.

Why Scarlett O'Hara Was Catholic

The writer Willa Cather summarized the situation perfectly when she quipped: "The world broke in two in 1922 or thereabouts."[5] Cather was referring to the end of Victorian culture after the First World War and the beginning of a new, modern world populated by the writers and thinkers of her generation. Most of her friends believed that sophisticated men and women were challenging the customs of society and the truisms of their parents. Obviously, this break was not as simple and clean as Cather would lead us to think. Historians have rejected the simple dualism between the "Lost Generation" of the twenties and the supposed "Found Generation" of the Victorians, preferring to name thinkers of the early twentieth century a "Nervous Generation."[6] Nor were members of Cather's generation unique in thinking themselves different from all others. Still, much of the writing in the twenties and thirties was geared to first convincing Americans that there *was* a divide and then to defining who was on each side of the fracture. To help sharpen this divide intellectuals, writers, and cultural critics of the period used religion to accentuate the difference between the two worlds that they felt made up America.

The American South has always evoked a powerful imaginative response from the pens of northern writers and thinkers. Long before the Civil War there was an imagined divide between those living in the North and the South. Following the war, travel and memoir literature reinforced this division. During the period between the world wars, southern *religion* became a critical player in the imaginative world of northerners. Northern cultural modernists configured their progressive beliefs as the polar opposite of southern evangelical Protestantism in order to draw a clear line between two American "worlds." Representations of southern religion were key in the creation of a "modern" world unconcerned with the dictates of community, the superstitions of belief, and the morality of uninhibited fun. The South certainly had its internal critics, many of whom sounded the same notes as northerners, but the construction of a caricature of southern piety was more deeply embedded in the culture of the North. While the pious of the Midwest were also cast on the wrong side of the divide—Sinclair Lewis's *Elmer Gantry* (1927) being a classic example—the South historically served as the place of national "otherness."

Swirling around the FSA photographers in the cultural winds of the twenties and thirties were two events that were used as evidence for the "two worlds" theory. These events—the Scopes trial and Prohibition—form the foundation on which writers could build an image of the backwardness of southern Protestantism. Once this backward world was clearly laid out, the progressiveness of northern modernism would be easier to depict. This was the world in which many intellectuals, including Stryker and his photographic team, imagined that they were living. The FSA photographers, however, produced pictures of religion that implicitly rejected the two-world theory. They presented aspects of religion that secular intellectuals could desire. Like Margaret Mitchell in *Gone with the Wind,* the photographers unintentionally circumnavigated the "problem" of southern Protestantism.

Let me first set out the various ways that southern religion became configured as the opposite of progressive America. Critical to the construction of the modern world is the acceptance of science as a more accurate category of analysis than theology, custom, community, or family. Between 1921 and 1929, twenty-seven states introduced antievolution measures into their state legislatures that challenged the place of science in setting the standards of truth in the public schools. The trial of John T. Scopes in 1925 for teaching evolution brought both newspaper reporters and radio announcers from around the world to Dayton, Tennessee. There they observed on hot summer afternoons that science, technology, critical thinking, and reasoned cultural expressions were not native to southern life. It did not make any difference that religious arguments over the meaning of the biblical text of Genesis had plagued Protestants in the North since the 1870s, or that William Jennings Bryan was born in Illinois and supported Progressive Era reforms, or that the South was experiencing unprecedented social and economic change during the 1920s. To reveal the diversity of southern Protestantism and the prevalence of evangelical beliefs across the nation would have complicated the construction of two conflicting worlds.

The Scopes trial cemented the image of an antimodern southern religion in the minds of the media and many progressive Northerners. It was white Protestant church support of pro-Prohibition presidential candidate Herbert Hoover, however, that convinced the more politically minded of the regressive character of southern Christianity. The South had been a Democratic stronghold since Reconstruction. In the minds of voting southerners, Republicans were associated with northern industrialization and the overturning of the racial social order. Unlike in the North, temperance in the South had become firmly rooted in the upper and middle classes. By the election of 1928 white Methodist and Baptist organizations had widespread grassroots support in preventing Alfred E. Smith—a drinker and a Catholic—from becoming president. Never before had the South's two powerful religious denominations come together to focus their attentions to such an extent on a partisan political campaign.[7] In spite of local grumbling about clergy telling people how to vote, Protestants overcame their theological and institutional disputes and worked to defeat the *Democratic* candidate. While the New Yorker Al Smith's urban ways conflicted with rural traditions, it was his rejection of evangelical religious norms on drinking that sank his candidacy in the South. The Republican Herbert Hoover carried Tennessee, Oklahoma, Kentucky, West Virginia, Virginia, North Carolina, and Texas. With Prohibition and then Smith's defeat, Methodists and Baptists in the South secured their position in the minds of many northerners. They became the new Puritans, who denied individual pleasures and scorned the modern commercial culture increasingly connected with drinking.

While antievolution and antidrinking debates fueled progressive distaste for southern evangelicalism, popular literary and film representations questioned the very morality of southern religion. In 1941, when Jack and Irene Delano were touring the South, *Tobacco Road* had just been turned into a movie directed by John Ford. A hit Broadway play that had run for more then seven years, *Tobacco Road* was based on a novel written in 1932 by Erskine Caldwell. During the thirties, Caldwell made a name for himself by depicting the South in all its degenerate glory. The son of a Presbyterian minister, Caldwell expressed distaste for religion by combining his father's scorn for the piety of the uneducated with his own preference for the secular world. One of the main characters of *Tobacco Road* is a forty-year-old itinerant preacher named Bessie, who "used to be a two-bit slut." Sister Bessie "was always happy when she could pray for a sinner and save him from the devil." When Bessie is not praying for sinners, she is trying to seduce sixteen-year-old "Dude"—a task made difficult because she has no nose. Bessie succeeds in her ambition, marries herself to Dude—"I marry us man and wife. So be it. That's all, God. Amen."—and promises to train him as a preacher.[8] The couple, through carelessness, kill two people with their car. A dark comedy with a rich, earthy dialogue, *Tobacco Road* preceded the controversial *God's Little Acre*, and the two books sold tens of millions of copies. Sister Bessie in *Tobacco Road* helped launched Caldwell's literary career.

Caldwell's later novel *Journeyman* (1935) was met with less critical acclaim, but it too represents evangelical Protestantism as devoid of morality, linked to lust, and designed to maintain a servile southern society. Semon Dye, the preacher in *Journeyman,* has sex with the wives of both black and white men, cheats at cards, and drinks moonshine with his buddies. In spite of his cruel and violent behavior toward the family that offers him hospitality, the community gives itself over to Dye's revival preaching. As the novel ends, the faithful participate in a religious orgy. In both *Journeyman* and *Tobacco Road* an uneducated, duplicitous, and oversexed clergy—both women and men—easily tricks communities made up of simpletons and buffoons. Revivals become the outlets for the repressed sexual energy of people, who can escape from the harshness of southern society only through spiritual excess linked to sexual abandonment. Caldwell was unrelenting in his portrayal of religious people as hypocritical, fatalistic, apathetic, and unaware of larger ethical issues.[9] It should not be surprising that such country bumpkins would support Prohibition and laws against the teaching of evolution.

Caldwell's portrayal of southern piety moved out of the realm of literature in 1937 when he published *You Have Seen Their Faces* with photographer Margaret Bourke-White. By the mid-thirties, Bourke-White was the highest-paid photographer in the nation; her work had appeared in *Fortune* and *Life* magazines. Known primarily for her commercial photographs that transformed the machinery of modern society into pieces of monumental art, Bourke-White had only recently become interested in Depression-era suffering. After traveling through the Dust Bowl in 1935, she learned of the misery with which many Americans were trying to cope. This may have motivated her to respond positively to Caldwell's invitation to help him publicize the effects of the sharecropping system on the South. Caldwell and Bourke-White toured the South in the summer of 1936 and the spring of 1937, producing texts and photographs that represented poor farmers, deteriorating land, uneducated children, and disease-ridden families. Margaret Marshall, writing in the *Nation,* captured the spirit of *You Have Seen Their Faces* when she concluded that the South was the "neglected step-child of the North which has now become so sick from its old infections of prejudice and poverty that it is a menace to the health of the nation."[10]

Not surprisingly, Caldwell and Bourke-White cast religion as a virus that contributed to the sickness of the South. In a black church, a preacher exhorts his congregation with a wide-open mouth. In a white church, women twirl with emotional abandon. In his text Caldwell wrote, "When a minister does not have to appeal to basic reasoning, he can excite men and women as no one else can. . . . He can excite the ignorant who live primitive lives to give vent to their feelings by rolling on the floor, shouting, and dancing in the aisles. . . . The more primitive the ritual, the more exciting the prospect to primitive people." For Erskine and Bourke-White, evangelical Protestantism robbed people of their basic intelligence and replaced it with an all-consuming religious passion that "has its closest counterpart in alcoholic drunkenness." The church in the South was a "burlesque of religion" because it supported without question an unjust social and economic system.[11] Rather than fighting for the welfare of its people, the church offered a sanctified form of intoxication.

Of all the popular discussions of deteriorating southern life, John Steinbeck's *Grapes of Wrath* has joined the canon of American literature as the prime example of Depression-era reformist writing. Published in 1939, *The Grapes of Wrath* also includes a preacher as a lead character in the novel and employs religious symbolism to structure the narrative. The novel won the Pulitzer Prize, and John Ford made it into a movie in 1940. Like Caldwell, Steinbeck intended his work to present the destruction of southern rural life, specifically that in Oklahoma. Steinbeck's portrayal, however, is more nuanced and sympathetic than Caldwell's. In 1936, when Steinbeck was writing stories for the *San Francisco News* about the "harvest gypsies," he met Tom Collins, a Virginian who was managing FSA migrant labor camps in Kern County, California. Steinbeck and Collins became friends and traveled together. Collins helped Steinbeck understand both California's labor problems and "Okie" culture. Steinbeck dedicated the second part of *The Grapes of Wrath* to this manager of the Arvin Camp. (Recall that Dorothea Lange photographed women singing hymns at a meeting at the Arvin Camp in 1938.) Steinbeck's novel captures the language of the southern migrants, their spirit, and their utter social and economic dislocation.[12]

In spite of his writing skill and cultural sensitivity, Steinbeck still cannot remove himself entirely from the "problem" of southern religion. Jim Casy, one of Steinbeck's protagonists in *The Grapes of Wrath,* is a "Burning Busher" preacher who used to "howl out the name of Jesus to glory." By the time he meets up with Tom Joad, however, the spirit has left both him and the people. One of the reasons that the preacher Casy is despondent is that after he would get his people "jumpin' an' talkin' an' passed out" and then baptized, "I'd take one of them girls out in the grass, an' I'd lay with her. Done it ever' time." Not proud of his activities, the preacher would pray, but "Come the nex' time, them an' me was full of the sperit, I'd do it again. I figgered there just wasn't no hope for me, an' I was damned ol' hypocrite." What separates Jim Casy from Sister Bessie or Semon Dye, is his self-recognition, as well as his remorse: "But I didn't mean to be." Steinbeck allows Casy to think about sexuality and eventually his place in the larger world, but he never allows him to return to evangelical Christianity. The preacher becomes a "listener," who trades baptizing in water for working in the field. In the new world of California, far from the South, Casy hopes he will be able to fully participate in the life of the people. "Gonna lay in the grass, open an' honest with anybody that'll have me," he tells Tom. "Gonna cuss an' swear an' hear the poetry of folks talkin'. All that's holy, all that's what I didn' understand. All them things is the good things." Casy embraces a religion of humanism that Steinbeck sharply contrasts to a handful of other Dust Bowl migrants whose piety renders them frightening, judgmental, petty, and puritanical.[13]

Given the ubiquity of this negative portrayal of southern religion in the thirties, it is not surprising that W. J. Cash, in his classic *Mind of the South* (1941), could patronizingly write, "What our Southerner required, on the other hand, was a faith as simple and emotional as himself. A faith to draw men together in hordes, to terrify them, and at last bring them shouting into the fold of Grace. A faith, not of liturgy and prayer book, but of primitive frenzy and blood sacrifice — often of fits and jerks and barks."[14] The South was constructed as a place of fatalism and sentimentality in religion. Sexual promiscuity as well as sexual prudery diverted the attentions of men and women from their social and economic oppression. Whatever the "truth" of such claims might be, the image that made it into books, movies, and photographs was that of a destructive white evangelical culture.

Portrayals of southern evangelicalism in the thirties developed stereotypes once primarily associated with African Americans. Racist literature insisted that blacks were overly emotional, overly sexualized, simple-minded people who would produce religion of hysterical abandon. While racism still ordered the social and economic relations in the North as well as the South, by the thirties the struggles of African Americans were gaining some recognition among liberals. Newspapers reported the horrors of lynching and the injustice of the Scottsboro trials. Exposés like *You Have Seen Their Faces* showed the debilitating effects of the sharecropping system. Fashionable whites listened to jazz and read the literature of what we now call the Harlem Renaissance. *The Green Pastures,* a 1930 Broadway musical and 1936 movie, was a respectful and hugely popular depiction of life in a black heaven. White audiences admired the acting and dignity of Richard Harrison, who played God. In 1939, on Easter Sunday, the opera star Marian Anderson sang to seventy-five thousand people on the steps of the Lincoln Memorial. Anderson had been the first African American to sing at the White House, and Secretary of the Interior Harold Ickes had offered her the public venue when the Daughters of the American Revolution barred her from Constitution Hall. Eleanor Roosevelt had conveyed particular concern about race relations to her husband. This is not to say that racial stereotypes and discrimination were ending but rather that overt racism was becoming less acceptable among moderates in the North. For progressives, it was more acceptable to criticize *white* southerners than black ones.

White southern Protestantism was so thoroughly trivialized during the twenties and thirties that when the Atlanta reporter Margaret Mitchell decided to write a Civil War novel about a South filled with honor, character, strength, and beauty, she made her heroine a Catholic. Scarlett O'Hara, the feisty protagonist of *Gone with the Wind,* is the daughter of Gerald O'Hara, who had been forced to leave Ireland after killing the rent agent of an English absentee landlord. He married Ellen Robillard from Savannah, the daughter of a wealthy and well-established French family. Glimpses in the novel of family prayer and concern about Scarlett's mother's rosary mark the clan as pious but not evangelical. By making the O'Hara family Catholic, Mitchell was able to avoid the sticky problem of how to deal with Protestantism in a book about nineteenth-century southerners. There are no revival meetings or unscrupulous ministers in *Gone with the Wind*. The novel presents a romantic and heroic South without the Gospel.

Bookstores could not keep *Gone with the Wind* on their shelves when Macmillan published it in 1936. It quickly was declared the fastest-selling book in history, and its one-millionth copy was sold a mere eight months after publication. Mitchell, who had written the book over a ten-year period, was awarded the Pulitzer Prize in 1937. Producer David O. Selznick finished the film in 1939. The day of the movie premier the governor of Georgia proclaimed a state holiday, and the mayor of Atlanta ordered three days of celebrations. Part of the reason *Gone with the Wind* was so successful, both in the South and in the North, was that it presented honor and virtue without being caught in the snares of piety. Without the nagging problems of biblical literalism or Prohibition or orgiastic revivals, both southerners and northerners could imagine a South of refined passion. Without religion this southern place fell into neither of Cather's worlds and so could be appropriated by all Americans.

The Beauty of Place

The FSA photographers came to the South with a myriad of mental images that ranged from the extreme poverty of Bourke-White photographs to the glorious costumes of *Gone with the Wind*. The culture of the time told them that the world of the South was not their world. Theirs was a world of the city, of artists and intellectuals, of the privileged and the middle classes, of the unchurched and the secular. And yet the photographers took hundreds of photographs of southern religion that stressed not the stereotypical behaviors of books and movies but the complexity of rural faith.

The FSA photographers spent much of their days on the road. Each had an itinerary, a car, and money for gas. Sometimes accompanied by a FSA field agent or a spouse, the photographer wandered through the countryside trying to find the required tobacco field, sorghum making mill, or successful FSA client. While there are many photographs of southern vernacular architecture—gas stations, schools, stores, and houses—it is churches that consistently captured the attention of the photographers. Every FSA photographer who traveled in the South took pictures of the exteriors of churches.[15] Their photographs underline the importance of place in the religious imagination of southerners. Churches were not merely buildings; they were carefully built and lovingly maintained physical expressions of commitment.

Walker Evans, who had little sympathy for Stryker's reformist agenda, took at least twenty-five photographs of churches in 1936 during his stay in the South. Many of these pictures were taken with a bulky large-format camera that required time and concentration to set up. Every other photographer who toured the South composed an "Evans church" picture: a tightly cropped, centered, frontal photograph of a rural wooden church (fig. 4.4 and see fig. 3.1). Traveling on a back road, the photographer came upon the church, took the picture, and drove on. The photographer was not looking for the church, it just appeared.

4.4   Walker Evans, church [no place or date] (LC-USF342-008262-A)

These "Evans churches" were small, isolated, and picturesque buildings that made for elegant compositions. They were not the brick buildings of colonial Anglicans or the stately edifices of town Methodists and Baptists. The "Evans church" was a wooden-frame church based on a simple, symmetrical rectangle form. The design stressed its solid and balanced character. With their simple cornices and almost no eaves, the churches were made to look even more blocky by eliminating extraneous landscape details from the picture. Atop the rectangle was a gable roof, typically with a short steeple or cupola placed either in the center or on the side. Siding of long wooden planks stressed the building's horizontal lines. Many of the churches had wooden shingles nailed in overlapping fashion that created a variety of patterns. They served to break the horizontal rhythm of the siding and added a contrasting, ornamental detail. Frequently, the churches had two front doors so that men and women could enter separately and sit apart from each other. Air space between the stone foundation and the building allowed for ventilation. Narrow windows were relegated to the side and were often shuttered to prevent the breaking of expensive glass or to keep debris from blowing in. There are never any people standing near the church. With no people, plants, or windows to soften or break their lines, the "Evans churches" are artful compositions that explore the centrality of space in southern religion.

The pictures of church exteriors frequently capture the playful spirit of rural carpenters and congregations. These photographs indicate that congregations enjoyed ornamentation and artistic flair in their churches. Modernist simplicity and restraint was not the only rural aesthetic. Even Walker Evans, who preferred his photographs to have an unsentimental portrait quality, could not pass up taking a picture of a church from Sprout, Alabama (fig. 4.5). With a pair of matching two-storied towers with pyramidal roofs, it looked like a miniature Notre Dame. In 1940 Marion Post photographed two remarkable examples of carpenter Gothic designs from Rodney, Mississippi. Although she did not name the churches, one was Sacred Heart Catholic Church, built in 1869 (fig. 4.6). Local carpenters duplicated in wood what would have been done in stone and masonry in other areas.[16] They built a lovely copy of a Tudor-style English parish church, complete with wooden label hoods over the tops of mitered arched windows. The other photograph, of Rodney's Baptist church, showed a dome cupola, lancet windows, and clapboard siding (fig. 4.7). While the shooting angles of the photographs change, the style of representation remains constant.

While many church exteriors were probably photographed because of their striking simplicity, these churches indicate that even rural people wanted to have fashionable churches. Additions of a porch and bracing poles were made not merely for functional reasons but also to introduce to the church a Greek Revival flair, like that seen in plantation architecture (see fig. 8.10). The photographs illustrate the care that carpenters took to make small design additions, even in modest churches. Southern congregations thought about the spaces in which they worshiped. They permitted those who built the churches to add decorative shingles or lancet windows. The photographers saw the beauty and creativity in these churches and exploited their designs by making the churches dominate the picture frame. As we saw in the previous chapter, these "churches without people" gave the photographers a way to express their artistic and spiritual sentiments as well as those of the congregations.

4.6   Marion Post [Wolcott], Sacred Heart Catholic Church. Rodney, Mississippi, August 1940
(LC-USF34-054738-D)

The photographers did include people in their pictures of southern churches, but members served as elements in an artistic composition rather than as religious actors. On July 5, 1939, Dorothea Lange was in Person County, North Carolina. In her general caption to a series of photographs she took at Wheeley's Church, she mentioned that she "accidentally" had learned that "everybody in the community was gathering at the church" to have lunch and do their yearly church cleaning.[17] Although she missed dinner and most of the cleaning, Lange photographed the women of the congregation at the end of the day sitting in front of their church (fig. 4.8). According to Lange, cleaning the church consisted of sweeping, dusting, and washing the windows. The women told her, "We think we ought to keep [it] as nice as we do our homes." Lange photographed the women sitting on the steps of the church with their brooms and buckets, and she made a series of portraits of a woman called Queen. Queen, Lange explained in her caption, wore her own homemade sunbonnet, apron, and gloves to clean.

The women told Lange that their church was Primitive Baptist and more than a hundred years old. What Lange could not show in her photographs, and what the women did not volunteer, was that Wheeley's church had been a Primitive Baptist Church only since 1832. The original Baptist congregation had actually been founded in 1755.[18] Wheeley's Primitive Baptist Church was one of the many varieties of Baptist churches that southerners could attend.

4.5 (facing page)   Walker Evans, church with double tower. Sprout, Alabama [no date]
(LC-USF342-008260-A)

4.7   Marion Post [Wolcott], Baptist church. Rodney, Mississippi,
August 1940 (LC-USF34-054747-D)

During the first third of the nineteenth century, some Baptists in England and America sought to temper the Calvinist spirit of their theology that taught that God predestined human beings to either heaven or hell. Reformers wanted to begin Sunday schools, missionary societies, religious newspapers, and temperance groups to encourage converts and help members develop a godly life. These Baptists hoped that by organizing congregations into associations or larger "conventions," they would strengthen their presence in the region. They also wanted to introduce instrumental music into church services and pay their ministers so as to ensure good, reliable preaching. When the members of Wheeley's Meeting House passed a resolution in 1832 condemning such innovations in Baptist life, part of the congregation left to begin their own church. Those remaining at Wheeley's added the modifier *primitive* to their church's name. They rejected all moves to centralize Baptist authority in the form of boards, societies, or conventions. They argued that all missionary work, even teaching in local Sunday schools, was contrary to Scripture. God in his sovereign power, they believed, did not need any human means to bring his elect to repentance. Parishioners at Wheeley wanted their ministers to come from the people and to speak in a way that the average person would understand, so they did not pay or educate their preachers.

Lange reported that the members of Wheeley's church met once a month, every second Sunday, for preaching. Such infrequent services were not unusual in the South, as many congregations—both black and white—could not manage to meet every week.[19] Lange returned to the church on July 9. Carefully reading what Lange wrote about her encounter with the church members provides a glimpse into what it must have been like trying to photograph religious southerners. Lange's comments help us understand the negotiations that went on in order to photograph church people. Unlike an inert mitered window or domed cupola, people have their own preferences about how and when they would be photographed.

In order to photograph the church cleaning, Lange had to talk, she wrote, to "a succession of people." The women wanted to have their picture taken because they were "very proud

4.8   Dorothea Lange, women of the congregation of Wheeley's Church on annual clean-up day.
Gordonton, North Carolina, July 1939 (LC-USF34-020017-C)

of their church, spacious well-shaded church yard, well kept (though very simple) cemetery." They had just cleaned about five acres of grounds, and they wanted a print showing how they "keep everything so tidy." On the other hand, there also was a clear hierarchy at Wheeley's church, and something as innovative and out of the ordinary as taking pictures required discussion. Lange had to ask "the others," "older members," and "the head deacon" for permission to photograph. Only later did she receive permission to photograph the women, and "because of hesitation of church members" did not photograph inside of the church.

When she returned four days after her first visit, she talked to Deacon Hugh Moore and the pastor, Mr. Adams. Mr. Adams "was afraid of undue criticism and cautioned us to 'remember what Paul said — that some things were expedient and some things were lawful' — and that that was how it was now." St. Paul, in the verses alluded to by the pastor, twice declares: "All things are lawful unto me, but all things are not expedient: all things are lawful for me, but I will not be brought under the power of any" (1 Cor 6:12 and 10:23). Not quite understanding what he meant, Lange concluded, "With circumlocution [Mr. Adams] gave us to understand that he saw no reason why the pictures should not be taken but that some of the members might object. We agreed not to ask the congregation to pose, not to go inside the church. They gave their approval." Lange then went in for the service, remarking that the congregation began by singing "Amazing Grace." The sermon focused on how members should allow the Holy Ghost into their lives, and it "worked up to a climax through increasing use of rhythmical phrasing and periodical increases in volume." At the end of her report, Lange seemed surprised to note that "there was no shouting and no audible 'Amens' from the audience during the meeting." After the service, she took a series of photographs of the congregation exiting the church, the men going out of the left door and the women the right, corresponding to where they sat in the church.

In general, southern Christians of any race or denomination did not find photography problematic in itself. Rural people could have their pictures taken either by itinerant photographers or in village studios. Family photographs were rare and valued heirlooms that were framed and held with regard. Lange reported that the members of Wheeley's church were "much interested in the photographing" and joked with each other about posing. Since photojournalism was in its infancy, there was no sense that pictures might exploit people. The picture magazines of *Look* and *Life* had only just begun publishing. There was no history among rural southerners of the "poverty photos" that would be a staple of magazine exposés in later years. To the contrary, rural people often used the colorful advertisements in magazines and newspapers to decorate their homes. In 1939 photography and photographers did not carry negative associations.

On the other hand, FSA photographers, with their northern accents and their associations with the federal government, were strangers. Dorothea Lange was not doing portrait photography. She may have explained her larger purpose, but the connection between the Depression and taking pictures of a church service probably did not make much sense to rural congregations. People would have been curious but skeptical; they would not know what to expect. So it would not be surprising that the women, though not averse to having their pictures taken, wanted reassurance that their desires were acceptable to their community.

Dorothea Lange also may have had mixed feelings about the interaction. She wanted pictures, but she also did not want to do surveillance photography. Since its invention, photography had been used by the state to record the bodies of prisoners and slaves and to catalogue as specimens people socially distinct from the photographer. Lange's recollections indicate that she was willing to do a certain amount of talking her way into the congregation but not so much as to force her needs on the group. She took time to find the church leaders. Primitive Baptist "moderators" or "elders" do not wear clerical collars or live in a parsonage next door to the church. They were bivocational preachers who had other jobs. The church leaders themselves would not know exactly how to reply to a request for photographs. While they could have called on a long tradition of Calvinist rejection of the image, their theological knowledge would have been very limited. Mr. Adams relied on a biblical text to conclude that Lange could photograph. On the other hand, he also decided that some of the members might object to having their pictures taken, so he limited where Lange might photograph. Although he cited the Bible as his legitimizing source, Mr. Adams was more concerned with neighbors' feelings than with any fear of profaning a religious space.

Lange did not try to persuade Mr. Adams to reconsider his decision, nor did she find another church service to photograph. She did not find another service, I want to suggest, because she did not really want to photograph inside a church. Lange rarely did interior photography because the flash equipment was bulky and the pictures often were ruined by heavy shadows caused by the bouncing light. She preferred natural light and close to midrange shots. Lange probably knew that Baptist services were mostly about preaching and singing, activities that would be difficult to photograph. Lange, unlike most of the other photographers, felt awkward with people and may not have been comfortable trying to put the suspicious church members at ease. Going to another church could be tricky because southern services did not necessarily begin and end at a particular time, and could continue for hours. Given the time it would take to get inside the church and take the pictures, the resulting images would not be interesting enough to compensate for her trouble. Exterior pictures of churches and their congregations, however, satisfied Stryker's desire for illustrations of people coming to and from church. It was certainly easier to remain outside of a church.

The Liturgical South

The FSA photographers may not have taken pictures of church services for a variety of reasons, but they did photograph many other southern rituals. Photographers preferred rituals that occurred outside, involved the whole community, and were visually compelling, like the yearly church cleaning rite. Out-of-door services eliminated the need for distracting flashes. For northerners used to worship occurring inside a church or synagogue, such rituals seemed more public and accessible. The photographers did not seek out wild revivals, snake handling, or what W. B. Cash called "the pleasures of orgiastic religion."[20] Their photographs of rituals worked against seeing southern religion as the primitive passion of the poor. Stryker wanted pictures of ordinary, everyday life, so the photographers made pictures of rituals that looked "common" by their standards. The resulting pictures demonstrate that the photographers exchanged the drama of the explosiveness of revivals for the controlled but intensely powerful rituals that punctuated southern life. These rituals stressed the communal elements of southern Christianity and thus contrast with the familiar emphasis placed on individual conversion and personal salvation. The photographs also downplay the importance of the church leader in the community by surrounding him (often dwarfing him) with his congregation. Just as the rituals are under control, so is the minister.

In August 1940 Marion Post was in eastern Kentucky. "I've done country fairs and horse shows," she wrote to Stryker, "[a] church supper, [an] American Legion fish fry . . . fences, highways, a few landscapes, and chased around trying to find a good big all day (with dinner served on the grounds) farm auction."[21] She complained to Stryker (in the third person) that "chiggers nearly ate out her belly button, among other delicate spots on her anatomy" during an evening spent sitting on old wooden benches "and climbing around in dry grass and weeds at the church picnic supper." Post jokingly commented, "It's the church that will do you dirt every time." While Post never told Stryker the name of the offending church, her photographs indicate she was at the picnic supper of St. Thomas's Catholic Church. In spite of the chiggers, Post took many pictures of the Catholic parishioners preparing their picnic meal: all-you-can-eat fried chicken with all the fixings for fifty cents.[22] Post might have been filming summer outings because a drought had ruined much of the harvest and "the country [was] not luscious and juicy any more." During the summer months, southerners—both Catholics and Protestants—moved their religion out-of-doors, where it became more easily accessible to strangers.

Like many of the photographers Stryker hired, Marion Post (1910–1990) had no positive experience of how religion structured community life. Born in Montclair, New Jersey, Post was the daughter of the local physician and homeopath. Marion and her sister Helen attended church with their parents. All was not right in the family, however. When Post was in her early teens, her parents began a bitter divorce, and Marion was sent to a "regimented" private school where she "marched to church every Sunday." Post rebelled and was sent to the Edgewood School in Greenwich, Connecticut, where she and her sister "thrived in a progressive atmosphere which fostered open inquiry, flexibility, and individuality."[23] Post's mother, Nan, moved to Greenwich Village in New York. There she worked with Margaret Sanger, helping to set up health and birth control clinics. On the weekends and in the summer, mother and daughter enjoyed the life in "Mongrel Manhattan," where they hung out with musicians, artists, writers, and the theatrical crowd. In 1932 Marion Post left for Europe, eventually studying dance, psychology, and photography. After returning to the United States, she continued her interests in photography while teaching at a progressive high school. Post studied at the New York Film and Photo League School, at the time the only noncommercial photography school in the United States. There she worked with Paul Strand and Ralph Steiner, men committed to transforming photography from a picturesque pseudoart to a source for analysis of the social world of Americans. In 1935 Post joined the staff of the *Philadelphia Evening Bulletin* but found that as a woman she was asked to cover stories about the latest fashions for the ladies' pages. Frustrated, she complained to her former teachers, and in 1938 Ralph Steiner took her portfolio to Washington. He showed it to Roy Stryker, and Stryker offered Marion Post a job.

Two years later, Post was in the South taking pictures of what must have seemed an exotic religious world. "I'm going to get a creek baptizing here tomorrow," Post reported. "I hope

4.9   Marion Post [Wolcott], congregation leaving the Primitive Baptist church.
Morehead, Kentucky, August 1940 (LC-USF33-031004-M3)

there will be no objections. Tried to get permission to take pix inside the church (Baptist) of the annual 'footwashing' service, but was unsuccessful." The church that Post photographed is still sitting on a hill about a mile from downtown Morehead, Kentucky. The same sign is on the building that was there in 1940, proclaiming that the church was built in 1927 and the congregation "constituted" in 1869 at Poplar Grove (fig. 4.9). According to Elijah Tackett, whose father, Abel, administered the baptism, there were several Primitive Baptist meeting houses in Morehead. Before the war, people would travel from church to church so that no one would be inconvenienced for too long.[24] The members might have met at the Poplar Grove Church that Sunday because they could easily walk to Triplett Creek for the baptism. Marion Post does not explain the reasons the community gave for not letting her photograph the foot washing. If she had gone, she would have seen the men and women separate and divide into pairs. Then they would wash each other's feet in a tin bowl, wiping them with a white towel worn around the waist. Following the foot washing, the community would go outside for a midday meal.[25]

Marion Post began her photographic series with the members leaving the church. Shooting with a 35 mm camera, she took several shots of the group walking down a footpath, through the bushes, and across boards placed in the creek.[26] Her pictures show parents carrying little ones in their arms and women gingerly walking on the planks in their high heels, using their pocketbooks to balance themselves. Several people open umbrellas as shade against the August sun. Standing on a bridge across from the gathering congregation, Marion Post changed cameras, and with her press camera took four photographs of the actual baptism. These pictures show Abel Tackett, another elder, and two candidates entering the water until they are about waist deep. The elders stand on each side of two candidates, raise their hands in prayer, and then submerge the couple face up into the water (fig. 4.10).

Marion Post had documented the importance of baptism in southern evangelical culture. Baptism in the South, either inside or outside of a church, was a rite more important than the Lord's Supper.[27] Her photographs stress the communal nature of the rite of passage as she follows the community to the creek. The members of the church are dressed as anyone might be in 1940, so they do not set themselves apart from society. At the creek, she photographs the whole congregation standing together. There is not one minister and one candidate, but two elders and two candidates. They do not baptize the couple as individuals, one at a time, but dunk them both together as a couple. By moving away from the congregation and standing slightly above them, Post is able to show the candidates as separate from the congregation but soon to join them as full church members. Marion Post does not photograph the baptism as

4.10   Marion Post [Wolcott], river baptism. Morehead, Kentucky, August 1940 (LC-USF34-055314-D)

4.11   Marion Post [Wolcott], court day church supper on the courthouse lawn.
Campton, Kentucky, September [?] 1940 (LC-USF33-031086-M3)

an individual experience moderated by clergymen. Instead she presents it as an orderly rite for which the elders emerge from the congregation. She does this, I propose, not because she understood the theology of the Primitive Baptists but because she had to look very carefully at the congregation in order to compose her pictures. Since she could not see the individual conversion experience, she could only take pictures of the group's recognition of the validity of the individual experience. She photographed what she saw, rather than what she thought, about the beliefs of these southern Protestants.

Traveling to Campton, the county seat of Wolf County, Post continued her portrayal of life in Kentucky. There she photographed the bustling "court day." Courts functioned as places of entertainment for small-town southerners when once a month a judge would arrive in town to conduct trials. Post photographed the farmers and their families who came to Campton to watch the trials, shop, gossip, and trade mules and horses. She also photographed what her captions call a "church dinner" and "community people listening to [an] itinerant preacher" on the courthouse lawn. According to contemporary residents of Campton, in 1940 there were no restaurants to feed the influx of people who came for court day.[28] So the women's missionary association of the local Methodist church offered a midday meal (fig. 4.11). Bertie Center, who was active in the church during the forties and who lives near the courthouse, explained that the women borrowed the benches and tables from the courtroom. They made the food at home and brought it to the courthouse yard, where they sold it to help fund the women's religious and social causes. Since at that time the Methodists did not have a full-time minister, the women might have invited a visiting preacher to address the assembled crowd. In the South courthouse lawns, because of their size and central location, served as places of preaching

4.12   Marion Post [Wolcott], itinerant preacher's car. Campton, Kentucky, September [?] 1940 (LC-USF33-031067-M3)

open to all Protestant groups. Marion Post photographed both the preacher and his car with its out-of-state license plates, "JESUS SAVES" visor, and warning to "REPENT" (fig. 4.12).

As with the photographs she took of the creek baptism, Post emphasized the communal nature of Campton's court day. She composed photographs that are loosely framed to give the rituals emotional distance. Post arranged the actors in her photograph such that the community surrounds the preacher, watching him dance but looking only partially involved. The photographs are straightforward descriptions that do not seek to accentuate the power of the preacher over the assembled townspeople (fig. 4.13). In her photographs, and in others taken by Ben Shahn and Russell Lee, revivalists do not evoke ecstatic religious reveries.[29] Ministers may move with dramatic gesticulation, but their listeners have more ordinary responses to their words and gestures. The photographs indicate that enthusiastic preaching was common not only in churches and at summer revival meetings but on courthouse lawns and in the streets. While the spirit at times certainly could overcome both white and black southerners, it was also common for them to be only mildly attentive to the preacher's exhortations. Post's photographs stress the routine, ritualized nature of southern preaching where the actions of the sermon giver and the sermon receiver were culturally scripted.

Russell Lee's photographs of Catholics celebrating All Saints' Day also privilege communal behaviors over individual spontaneity, group participation over clerical control. In 1938 Lee photographed the graveside rituals of white and black Catholics in New Roads, Louisiana. Like Marion Post, he photographed the rites from middistance so that the white priest who blesses the black families does not dominate the scene. Even though one caption mentions that the congregation first "assembled at the church for preliminary ceremonies and then marched en mass to the cemetery," Lee did not photograph the church or the service.[30] Most of the pictures show families kneeling in prayer at the graves, painting fencing that surrounds family plots, or whitewashing crosses (fig. 4.14). Their actions are deliberate and planned. While no rubrics in a prayer book outline what families should be doing, their actions are dictated by agreed-upon custom. Lee took only three pictures at the white section of the cemetery, and those photographs eliminated any clerical presence. Both white and black Catholics in New Roads are pictured commemorating the dead in the same manner. The size of the graves differs, but the ritual is the same (fig. 4.15).

The photographers present southern Christianity as intensely local and integrated into the fabric of community life. The pictures are composed as if the photographers were charmed by the public intimacy of small-town life that permitted Methodist women to use the benches from the courthouse and African-American men to kneel in cemeteries. Rather than depicting the sexualized frenzy of revival meetings, the photographers sought out church picnics. There, priests dressed in summer white shirts and preachers with rolled-up sleeves moved easily among their congregations. While religion still provided entertainment and sociability for southerners, church life was tightly integrated into the daily rhythms of rural life—black,

4.13   Marion Post [Wolcott], preaching in courtyard on court day. Campton, Kentucky, September [?] 1940 (LC-USF33-031088-M3)

4.14   Russell Lee, African-American family praying at graves of their relatives on All Saints' Day.
New Roads, Louisiana, November 1938 (LC-USF33-011875-M1)

4.15   Russell Lee, woman decorating a family vault on All Saints' Day. New Roads,
Louisiana, November 1938 (LC-USF33-011901-M3)

white, Protestant, Catholic. Creek baptisms and repairing graves on All Saints' Day were predictable, serious rituals that assured the community of the continuity of life and faith. Religious expression certainly could be spontaneous and unpredictable, but the southern photographs reflect what brought people together into community rather than illustrating their individual relationships with the sacred.

At this point, I must reiterate that photography can present only a partial perspective on religion. That the FSA/OWI photographers took pictures of typical southern rituals does not mean that the "primitive" dramas critics described did not exist. Nor should we be seduced into thinking that representations of communal harmony was the full story. The Primitive Baptists of Poplar Grove may have returned from their communal ritual at Triplett Creek and convened a church court to condemn a member's cardplaying activities. The black Catholics of New Roads may have tuned in to Father Coughlin's anti-Semitic radio broadcasts from Royal Oak, Michigan. The photographs help us remember that religion is about yearly church cleanings and the importance of sacred places, but they are not comprehensive. Photographs, like all cultural representations, are limited in their scope. While the stress on the democratic nature of southern Christianity serves as an antidote to the stereotypical pairing of manipulative clergy with mindless congregants, it cannot present a total picture of the complicated and often contradictory lives of religious people.

The Diversity of Devotion

In early October 1938 Russell Lee was on his way to the National Rice Festival at Crowley, Louisiana. While driving between Lafayette and Scott, he saw a couple pushing a wagon. Lee stopped his car, grabbed his 35 mm camera, and took five pictures of the pair of traveling evangelists. Three of the photographs show the couple pushing their wagon. The other two pictures are portraits of the evangelists, who look unconcerned about the photographer's intrusion on their journey. The man wears a tie and hat, and the woman has a cross around her neck (fig. 4.16). She leans against their three-wheeled wagon that has the painted warning:

REPENT YE

SHALL ALL PERISH

JESUS IS COMING SOON

Lee's caption explains that the "couple have spent twenty-five years on the road preaching the gospel, sharpening knives to meet expenses."[31]

In an era when millions of Americans were forced from their homes because of the economic disruption of the Depression, Lee must have thought the couple's voluntary migrancy both charming and bemusing. The evangelists were following a long tradition of itinerant preaching that began with Jesus and his disciples and came to the American South with the Baptists and Methodists in the eighteenth century. That they were pushing a vehicle instead of driving it, and that they — like gypsies and tinkers — sharpened knives for a living sets the couple apart from ordinary preachers. Like their predecessors who turned away from settled family life with its worldly distractions, this couple indulged in a type of spiritual virtuosity. By focusing on the democratic and local character of religion, the photographers explored the

4.16   Russell Lee, traveling evangelists standing in front of their wagon. Scott, Louisiana,
October 1938 (LC-USF33-011702-M5)

innovative and diverse nature of southern Christianity. Working within the idioms of evangelical culture, southerners were exceptionally creative in how and when they expressed their faith. The photographers, always on the lookout for the clever picture, were attracted by the improvisational. Devotion in the South was not limited to churches and revival tents. It spilled out onto the streets.

As more and more Americans bought cars, roadways and vehicles became a new type of literary text. Signs in the South were a folk art that used color and design to convey messages to the traveling public. The hand-painted posters and carefully drawn billboards that dotted rural America captivated all of the photographers. Southerners joked that ministers needed to know how to paint a sermon as well as preach one. Religious people also used signs to present information and exhortations. Like commercial advertisements, religious signs and billboards had to catch the attention of the busy motorist. Sign painters altered the size and style of their letters. They broke horizontal lines with words printed in curves or laid out vertically. Signs combined image and word; they were the meeting point between the visual and the verbal. Signs had drawings of eyes ("EVERY EYE SHALL SEE HIM") or mantel clocks ("WATCH! FOR YE KNOW NOT WHAT HOUR YOUR LORD DOTH COME").

Signs changed with the holiday seasons ("UNTO YOU A SON IS GIVEN HIS NAME IS WONDERFUL, THE MIGHTY GOD") and current events ("WAR BRINGS DEATH O AMERICA! PREPARE FOR ETERNITY 'PREPARE TO MEET GOD'"). And as with both commercial and evangelical culture, the message was blunt and uncompromising: "GOD WILL JUDGE YOUR THOUGHTS," one sign read. "'THE THOUGHT OF FOOLISHNESS IS SIN.' WHAT WILT THY JUDGMENT BE?" (fig. 4.17). "GOD IS NOT MOCKED," warned another; "A LIFE OF SIN REAPS EVERLASTING PUNISH-

MENT." Signs addressed individuals: "HARK! THE VOICE OF JESUS CALLS *you*," and gave them specific admonitions: "WHOSOEVER WILL BE A FRIEND OF THE WORLD IS THE ENEMY OF GOD. HEAR GOD'S WORD."[32] Neither evangelical nor commercial culture expected people to think carefully about making decisions because the correct choice was obvious. Evangelical culture, however, was so ubiquitous in the South that its terrifying messages could easily be ignored.

While the rural southerner may not have noticed such signs or thought them unusual, sign painters were successful in capturing the attention of the visiting photographers. Although they never referred to evangelical signs in their letters to Stryker, the number of examples of religious advertisements in the file is significant. Signs thus made it possible to take a picture of a belief. The mixing of religion with society and culture in the South grabbed the attention of the FSA/OWI photographers. Southerners did not keep religion inside of churches. Enthusiastic statements of belief could appear out of nowhere, between the pine trees and the telephone poles. Religion visually marked the southern landscape in ways that it did not in the urban Northeast. Or at least the photographers never noticed the ways that religion marked their home territory. But of course signs on southern back roads did not appear randomly. Even though the photographer might have felt that he or she was in the middle of nowhere, rural people knew the roads that were well traveled. Why waste a good sign where no one could see it?

Religious people do not assume that religion takes place only in churches. God can reach people in their cars or while they work. A well-placed sign might be just what is needed to begin

4.17   Marion Post [Wolcott], religious sign between Columbus and Augusta, Georgia, December 1940 (LC-USF34-056454-D)

4.18   Jack Delano, storehouse along the road between Greensboro and Siloam. Siloam, Georgia,
October 1941 (LC-USF34-046166-D)

the conversion process. On a cotton storehouse that sat alongside the road between Greensboro and Siloam, Georgia, someone had painted, "LORD JESUS IS COMING AGAIN," and hung
an arrow off the portico pointing to the admonition. On one side, in carefully designed script,
was the observation: "YOU ARE GOING TO HEAVEN OR HELL FOR ALL ETERNITY" (fig. 4.18).
Throughout rural America, including Greene County, Georgia, advertisers painted signs on
barns and storehouses. Most likely the sign painter wanted his or her sign noticed but did
not expect it to be funny or unusual. Religious messages could be painted on whatever was
available.

Jack Delano probably was amused at the conflation of the South's cotton culture with its
evangelical culture. The juxtaposition of the two images made for a good picture because it
was both visually dynamic and illustrative of the public dimension of southern faith. Such a
picture could generate humor because those outside of evangelical culture would not be used
to seeing such a serious message mixed with a commercial building. The FSA/OWI photographers often took pictures of contrasts; perhaps the most well-known of these is Dorothea
Lange's 1937 photograph of two men walking with their suitcases next to a billboard that read,
"NEXT TIME TRY THE TRAIN, RELAX."[33] Delano most likely expected the sacred and the supernatural to be separated from the profane and the natural. That he made a photograph of the
building indicates that both its design and its message was notable.

The difference in perspective between the religious believers *in* Greene County and the
secular observers *of* Greene County becomes clear when we look at the ways that Delano's

photographs were used. In the spring of 1941 Jack and Irene had been photographing in Greene County to create a set of illustrations for Arthur Raper's book on life in the share-cropping South. Raper was a sociologist who produced some of the first intra-regional critical scholarship. His book, *The Tragedy of Lynching* (1930), was published by the Commission on Interracial Cooperation. Will Alexander, the director of the Farm Security Administration, had been one of the chief architects of this bi-racial organization. Raper was quite familiar with the goals of the FSA and knew that their photographs could enrich his writings. The Delanos visited both African-American and white Protestant church services to make pictures for what would become *Tenants of the Almighty* (1943).

The storehouse did not make it into the published book, even though it is a striking example of the public and visual nature of evangelical Protestantism. The pictures chosen for the book confine the religious of Greene County to their churches and reflect assumptions about the purity of religion. Raper would write that there were more churches than any other kind of institution in Greene County, "about 30 churches for Whites, 50 for Negroes." While he does mention that revival meetings are popular "during the slack-work season of mid-summer, when watermelons and fried chicken are in their prime," none of the illustrations of *Tenants of the Almighty* uncouple faith from a church building.[34] Black and white Protestants are pictured singing hymns in their separate churches. White congregants greet each other outside of their white clapboard church. Delano and Raper included a picture of the interior of Bethesda Baptist Church, one of the oldest churches in Greene County. The photograph was taken from behind the pulpit, from the perspective of a minister preaching to his congregation. On the pulpit lies the Bible (fig. 4.19).

Even though Delano photographed evidence of the diversity and innovation of devotion in Greene County, he and Raper published a perspective on religion that fit predictable notions of what religion was. By picturing faith inside of the church, they placed religion under the control of ministers and larger denominational bodies. Those photographs are less intriguing because they are conventional representations of what we assume goes on in Protestant churches. By assuming that religion takes place only in church, *Tenants of the Almighty* presents black and white Protestantism without its innovative, less predictable aspects. As with *You Have Seen Their Faces* the photographs appearing with a text are highly edited selections that are chosen to support the point of the book. Even before Raper's editing, Delano knew that the Greene County photographs had their limits. "The pictures so far are predominately *factual*," he wrote Stryker, "and very little *human*. I'm sure Arthur realizes it but feels that these factual things must be gotten first."[35] The larger file of photographs, which correspond more closely to the reality the photographers witnessed, is more diverse. Confined by the medium of print, the published version of southern religion returns us to the world of the word, as contained in the bible or sung from the pews. This is a world not easily accessed through photographs and thus the pictures in *Tenants of the Almighty* do not have the same power as other photographs in the file.

Unbroken World

The FSA photographers were not particularly disposed to like religion. The literary and cultural expressions of their day told them that they were modern men and women who were not

PLATE 68

Revival meetings are held in mid-summer when fried chicken and water-melons are at their best. Most churches have women's missionary societies; only the largest ones have young people's organizations.

4.19   Two images used as plate 68 in Arthur F. Raper, *Tenants of the Almighty* (New York: Macmillan, 1943): top, Jack Delano, services at a Methodist church. White Plains, Georgia, October 1941 (LC-USF34-046206-D); bottom, Jack Delano, Bethesda Baptist Church. Union Point, Georgia, May 1941 (LC-USF34-044304-D)

confined by genteel religious conventions or supernatural beliefs. They wanted to live, and in fact did live, in a world where organized religion held little sway. And yet, they did not project their desire to be separate from the traditional world of faith on to the religions of the South. Rather than distance themselves from what they saw by making patronizing or stereotypical pictures, they engaged southern Christianity on its own terms. The photographers, I believe, were successful in representing what it was about religion that made people religious. They were able to do this because the camera forced them to recognize the compellingly visual elements of the southern religion of the thirties and early forties. The diversity and richness of the pictures they produced leads me to conclude that southern Christianity spoke to the photographers not as a moral system but as a sensual experience. Although evangelical Protestantism stresses the importance of the words in the Bible and their plain-folk heritage scorned the image, what the secular photographers saw was a faith that was built, danced, painted, and designed. The photographs present a southern landscape that demonstrated the creativity of religious people as they construct a physical and sensual religion. It would be the intensity of the visual dimension of southern religion that would turn the photographers away from stereotypes and toward a different understanding of faith. While they certainly still harbored religious stereotypes and critical attitudes, their art moved them to see another South as well.

The photographers did not create a visual southern religion. Southerners made a sensual religion and the visual dimension was one of many dimensions. This dimension, however, has been overlooked by many scholars as well as participants in southern congregational life. One of the reasons a people crushed by poverty and plagued by racial division could find deep solace and strength in congregational life is because it brought beauty into their world. It is the appeal to the senses that Jack and Irene Delano shared with the "Negro church" in Heard County, Georgia. In spite of the ideas that circulated about southern religion, the photographers were seduced into seeing the South in a way that connected them to the participants. They did not share their belief systems and they did not even pretend to participate in their rituals, but the photographers did enjoy the visual and auditory delights of southern faith. Those delights were strong enough, coupled with Stryker's and their own populist predilections, to pull secular people into religion—if only for a moment.

Certainly what they saw for that moment was defined by all of the ideological limitations described in earlier chapters. The camera can never record the totality of religious expression, just as the pen cannot. However, this limit can also be a freeing experience that opens the photographer to aspects of faith ignored by writers, anthropologists, theologians, and participants. Visual representations are not merely nostalgic representations of ideas contained in the photographer's head. Especially with documentary photography, pictures are the combination of the worlds of the photographers and the worlds of the subjects. At the same time, the pictures that he or she produces *can* be so powerful that they urge the viewer to forget other, more destructive elements of congregational life. By silencing certain voices in religion the photographers enabled other voices to be heard. While we can enjoy the positive results that happen when the photographers are seduced by beauty, we the viewers must never be totally seduced ourselves. We must always assume that all cultural expressions are inadequate to the complexities of faith, while remembering that faith will always express itself in form and thus create visual expressions.

5
Christian Charity

've had two dark rainy days on which it was impossible to work outside so, I did a pretty complete story on the City Mission, community chest financed and operated by a Baptist minister who is quite a little stinker." John Vachon was photographing in Iowa, and in April 1940 he was in Dubuque. "It really breaks my heart to hear this little Baptist say, 'all right men, upstairs to bed' after the hymns had been sung," he wrote to Stryker. "They go up, fumigate their clothes, take showers, and go to bed about 8:30." The only Catholic to work for the Historical Section, and probably the only photographer who went to church every Sunday as a child, Vachon did not take the evangelical tone of the charity very seriously. "The first night I sat through the services and raised my hand on the third call that yes I wanted to be saved. I never realized before what a lousy situation it is to have 'charity' operate this way." The "lousy situation," however, was interesting enough to prompt Vachon

5.1 (facing page) Paul Vanderbilt, nun collecting money outside of Macy's department store. New York, summer 1939 (?) (LC-USW3-056230-E)

to return one more day. "I am going back once more to get shots of children coming to get pails of the stew that's left over," he explained to his boss.[1] A few days later, Stryker dashed off a letter in support of his young clerk. "The City Mission story sounds good. I hope your pictures portray the real character of the Baptist minister. I know the type. Will save my comments about them until you get back."[2]

A year earlier, in April 1939, Dorothea Lange had also left the fields to photograph in the city. She had taken a break from traveling through the migrant labor camps in California to return to San Francisco, where she had her photographic studio. During her time in the city, she photographed the activities of a group of Christians who had dedicated their lives to evangelizing the poor and meeting their physical needs. Her pictures of members and officers of the Salvation Army were sent to Washington without comment by Lange. We do not know why she photographed a street revival and Sunday service. We can only speculate from the pictures about what she might have thought about the Salvation Army.

These two photo-essays of John Vachon and Dorothea Lange are unusual in the file. In spite of the efforts of many local congregations and larger religious organizations to address growing poverty during the Depression, government photographers gave little attention to their activities. The New Deal was not intended to fund religious organizations, and there was no reason to photograph the distribution of privately generated funds. Liberal reformers like Stryker and his photographers were interested in the innovative and massive changes going on in the federal government, not the struggles of churches to attend to the material needs of their parishioners. Religion, understood by the photographers as a set of ritual practices, sacred spaces, and mythic stories, had a place in American culture. Specific religious visions of social justice articulated through the practice of Christian charity did not. Especially in the early years of the project, when the photographers were building a file of images of American poverty and governmental reform, religious communities were ignored. New Deal programs were understood by their proponents as replacing a hodgepodge of private and religious charities that were not only unable to cope with the Depression but were out of step with modern notions of reform and social justice. The FSA photographers had no motivation to provide evidence of successful Christian charity.

In those few instances when the photographers did take pictures of Christian charity coping with poverty, the ideology of the New Deal limited the depth of their portrayal. When religious charities were pictured, they were represented as totally disconnected from the reforming spirit of the era. John Vachon represented Dubuque's Rescue Mission as old-fashioned, patronizing, and inefficient. Like Paul Vanderbilt's single picture of a nun begging outside of Macy's department store, Christian charities were shown as isolated endeavors clothed in unproductive restrictions that limited their usefulness (see fig. 5.1). Vachon did not like what he saw in Dubuque, and he used his camera to harshly judge the practices of religious people. Dorothea Lange ignored the impressive social welfare system of the Salvation Army and concentrated on its explicitly evangelistic rituals. Lange cleverly avoided condemning evangelical forms of social reform and charity by constructing respectful representations of prayer and preaching detached from any real concern for the physical lives of the poor.

Roy Stryker and the FSA photographers felt that they were promoting the dignity and worth of "the common man." Typically, this meant focusing on those not in power rather than those who had power. The FSA photographs do not sharply criticize the social and economic forces that led to the woes of the Depression. In these two instances, however, photographers resented what they saw as the manipulation of powerless people. I have argued that the limits placed on the photographers, both by the medium in which they worked and by the worth of the "common man," worked to provide a more nuanced and diverse picture of southern religiosity. As artists, the photographers shared with the people they photographed a feeling for the beauty and intensity of communal piety. But sensitivity to the visual beauty of faith could not sustain the photographers through all of their encounters with America's pious. Religious people often behave in ways that are strange and problematic to those outside of their communities. Even if the ministers and preachers had explained and interpreted their behaviors and denied that they were manipulating the powerless, the photographers still probably would not have approved of such religious activities. They shared with the supporters of the New Deal a commitment to the state as the dispenser of social justice. The City Mission photographs of John Vachon and the Salvation Army photographs of Dorothea Lange are examples of how pictures can close down—rather than open up—communication between outsiders and insiders.

John Vachon's City Mission

Roy Stryker hired John Vachon as a clerk, not a photographer. Vachon had come to Washington in 1935 to begin graduate study in English literature at Catholic University. An adventurous twenty-one-year-old, he had just graduated from another Catholic school, the College of St. Thomas in St. Paul, Minnesota. Vachon's academic career came to a halt after one semester at Catholic University when he was dismissed for violating the school rules against drinking. Rather than return home, he decided to stay in Washington and used the support of Minnesota's congressional delegation to help him find a job. Unlike other young men who had come to Washington to work in the New Deal, planning to exploit their prestigious law education or graduate studies in economics, Vachon hoped for a job at the Library of Congress. That position never materialized, but Roy Stryker interviewed him for a temporary position with the Historical Section, and in May 1936 he joined the section as an "assistant messenger."[3]

Vachon's job was to write captions on the backs of mounted photographs and run errands for the staff. Looking at photographs all day inspired Vachon to take up the camera, and eventually Stryker permitted him to contribute pictures to the file. In 1941 Vachon officially became classified as a photographer, but in 1940 he was still a twenty-six-year-old clerk who was only photographing on temporary assignment for Stryker. That spring he was in the Midwest photographing farms and agricultural communities. Wandering throughout the countryside, Vachon used a 35 mm camera to take pictures of whatever struck his fancy—spring planting, tractors and horse teams, boys playing marbles, grass growing in the cracks of sidewalks, the inside of his car. The photographs taken by Vachon reflect his enthusiasm for the Historical Section's mission, but they are not of the same caliber as those taken by the more experienced photographers. We need to keep in mind that the art of all of the photographers evolved while they worked for Stryker; none entered government service as a senior, sophisticated reform photographer. Vachon's photographs, more than Dorothea Lange's, reflect an unfiltered response to what the photographer was seeing. Although Vachon eventually became a more skilled photographer, at this point he did not have the technical abilities to create more complicated compositions. His statements about the "lousy situation" revealed emotions that can be detected in his pictures and that a more seasoned photographer may have toned down.

While Vachon was still pursuing the stated goal of the Historical Section by taking pictures of the challenges of life in rural America, his Iowa photographs also reflect an important change that was occurring in Stryker's project. By 1940 the photographers were also taking more pictures in towns and cities. Stryker probably told Vachon to follow his rural "subjects" into town and try to photograph the impact that the Depression was having on agricultural cities like Dubuque, Iowa, where the City Mission was located. As a railroad and shipping center on the Mississippi River, Dubuque was a popular destination for transient workers. Vachon's pictures range from illustrating architectural details of Victorian buildings to showing people foraging for food in the city dump. Vachon thought his photographs to be "all inconsequential"; writing to his wife, Penny, that he was taking pictures of the "same old crap. Must make myself stop taking pix of signs, billboards, arrangements of unimportant building, etc." He told her he had missed the chance to photograph romantic newlyweds because he was "self conscious, afraid to take good pix."[4] A few days of bad weather in Dubuque forced Vachon to move inside and switch cameras.

Using a more complicated press camera, Vachon shot a series of photographs of the activities of Dubuque's City Mission, a religious charity that lodged and fed twenty-five transient men. Vachon had found something more "consequential," and several days later he wrote both his wife and Stryker of his visit. The letters are practically identical in their sentiments about the City Mission, with Vachon concluding in his note home, "Really, it's a crime that Community Chest money is spent on a thing like that."[5] Vachon chose to photograph the City Mission on his own, but his attitude toward what he was seeing reflected common assumptions among progressive reformers about the role of religion in social welfare. Vachon, who as Stryker's clerk had looked at literally thousands of pictures of poor people and governmental relief efforts, was not at all impressed with what he saw at the City Mission of Dubuque.

John Vachon's photo-essay of the City Mission begins with photographs of a line of men waiting in the alley outside the mission (fig. 5.2). His captions explain that the men are waiting for an evening meal served at five o'clock. There is no clear beginning or end to the line of men. Vachon's caption explains that only the first twenty-five will be fed, and we are led to assume that the others will be turned away hungry. A line of unemployed white men—waiting for relief checks, waiting for news of jobs, waiting for soup—was a common image used to represent Depression-era misfortunes. John Vachon, however, modified this familiar picture by including in the center of the photograph a sign with a curt warning: "PLEASE HELP US KEEP THIS YARD CLEAN." Placing the sign in a prominent position gives us a clue about what Vachon hopes we will think about men having to wait in this particular line. We already are saddened by the sight of healthy men unemployed and reduced to taking charity. With the sign Vachon is telling us that not only must they wait for dinner; there is a disembodied voice telling them what to do, pushing them around. Vachon wants us to see that someone else is adding an extra expectation onto the already humiliated men. They must submit to a certain standard of cleanliness. And cleanliness, as we all know, is next to godliness.

5.2   John Vachon, line of men waiting in the alley outside of City Mission.
Dubuque, Iowa, April 1940 (LC-USF34-060517-D)

Vachon's photograph of the building's exterior shows a sign displaying the times for meals and the name of its director, William Masters. Vachon filmed the men saying grace and eating their meal. At 7:30 P.M. a "gospel meeting" was held, and there are several pictures of both the leaders of the service and the men. Sitting in high-backed wooden chairs, the men bow their heads, pray, sing, and listen to a sermon by a visiting preacher. Then we see the "transient men" waiting in line to have their clothes fumigated before taking showers. Vachon even enters the dormitory room, where he photographed the men dressed in their nightclothes, lying in their beds, ready for the lights to be turned off. Vachon returned the next day and filmed in the kitchen, where neighborhood children brought buckets to collect the leftovers from dinner. Dressed in his apron, the "Baptist minister" ladles out soup to the boys and girls.[6]

In his pictures, Vachon does not try to preserve the illusion that the events took place without the camera being noticed (fig. 5.3). In these photographs, the transient men stare back grimly at the photographer, recognizing his presence, and in some respects ours. During the gospel meeting, Vachon might have stood at the back of the room, photographing the preacher and the pianist, but not the faces of the men. This would have been a safer place for a newly minted photographer. Instead, he positions himself in the front and directs his camera at the men in the pews. In one of the pictures, a man looks up at the distracting flash of the photographer. He gazes directly, even confrontingly, at Vachon. The men are aware of what is happening to them. They are standing in line to be fumigated; they are about to sleep in dormitory beds. Vachon has made pictures that acknowledge our voyeurism. The men look

5.3   John Vachon, prayer service following dinner at City Mission. Dubuque, Iowa, April 1940
(LC-USF34-060485-D)

at us. We feel embarrassed, as if we have caught them doing something that they should not be doing. In effect we have. The men are not behaving as adult males should behave. Vachon sets up the photograph so that we feel the humiliation of having to accept this type of charity. The men are represented as if they are captives.

The City Mission photo-essay—one of the few series of photographs that show religious groups addressing poverty and unemployment—casts Christian charity in the model of pre–World War I social reform rather than the state-welfare model of the New Deal. Rather than employ professional social workers trained at universities, for example, a Baptist minister heads the City Mission. This minister is never named in the captions; he represents, in Stryker's words, "a type." Instead of hiring staff that would be familiar with sociological methods and developmental psychology, the minister has invited a guest preacher and a pianist to play hymns for the men. Rather than exploring the source of male unemployment through economic studies, the minister sets up a rigid schedule. The schedule is designed to control the behavior not of the captains of industry but of the victims of capitalism. As with Victorian charities, the City Mission is pictured as being preoccupied with the individual behavior of men, not with the collective actions of the country. Unlike the New Deal, which was centrally organized, nationally run, and geared toward the well-being of millions of Americans, the City Mission meets the basic needs of only twenty-five men. A local center of charity, it passes out food and institutional housing. From Vachon's perspective, no larger economic or social system is being restructured by their efforts. No movement toward social justice or creating long-term entitlements for citizens is being created by the "little stinker."

Vachon took several photographs from various directions of the men attending the "evening service." He wanted us to see both religious activities and the social services of the City Mission. Although he never mentions whether or not the men are expected to attend the prayer meeting before they can be fed, the assumption is that soup and salvation go together. Vachon intends us to see the negative results of the inappropriate mixing of prayer and reform. Those men who are not staring at Vachon are bowing their heads in quiet reverence. They appear to be submitting to the religious intentions of the minister. The regimentation of the City Mission and the passive attitudes of many of the men create an image of a helpless people being forced-fed religion in order to receive a bowl of soup and a good night's sleep.

Vachon emphasized in his photographs the passivity and humiliation of the transient men and the poor children. His disapproval of the City Mission appears in the decidedly infantalized and feminized picture of charity he produces. The photographs stress how the City Mission transforms adult men into children by forcing them to act as if they are in an institutionalized home. There is a kitchen, dining room, and bedroom, but instead of seeing it filled with a mother and her children, we see ministers and poor men. As in an orphanage the men sit at long tables, each man with a bare bowl in front of him and a tin cup at its side (fig. 5.4). A severe and elderly man leads the prayer before the meal. Like children, the men

5.4   John Vachon, prayer before dinner at City Mission. Dubuque, Iowa, April 1940
(LC-USF34-060518-D)

will be in bed before nine. Vachon's only portrait of William Masters shows him in the kitchen surrounded by huge pots and pans that sit on a monumental stove. Wearing an apron, he is a man doing woman's work (fig. 5.5). In another photograph Masters pours soup from a kettle into the waiting bucket of a poor boy. Children have been waiting patiently to be fed, and Vachon photographs a pair of boys with their mouths slightly ajar and their eyes wide with curiosity (fig. 5.6). The City Mission, like a Victorian orphanage, is a place where "normal" family relations are inverted. Vachon's photographs represent the City Mission as a type of unnatural and institutionalized home.

We do not know whether John Vachon's Catholic upbringing, in addition to his feeling for the "common man," made him particularly intolerant of the Christian charity of evangelical city missions. Vachon's attitude toward Catholicism was complicated. In 1938 he wrote in his journal, "I still go to church, but only to avoid the complex. I never pray, or use the sacraments. I am truly out of the church. I have the intervals of fine feeling about being out, but now I am just unmoved. O I guess not, I'd like to dig myself up a religion sometime. I'd even like to be able to use it in the Catholic Church." When he married a non-Catholic, both sets of parents disapproved, but apparently the families quickly made peace with the newlyweds. Indeed, it may have been Vachon's own experiences growing up in an Irish Catholic family and going to Catholic schools that made him particularly sensitive to the ways that faith and power can be institutionalized in ways that demean and destroy the human spirit.[7]

John Vachon never took photographs of any of the many Catholic charities that were active during the Depression and early war years. He did, however, take a second and a third set of pictures in March 1941 of evangelical charity. There must have been something about this form of religious behavior that both repulsed and attracted him. In coastal Virginia flocks of unemployed workers had come to try to get jobs building ships for the prewar military buildup. The influx of people caused severe housing shortages in many areas of the country. Vachon photographed the Salvation Army feeding men in Newport News and the Helping Hand Mission conducting services in Portsmouth. Vachon's captions explain that one destitute family of five had found shelter in one room at the Helping Hand mission. Several photographs of the Helping Hand Mission focus on the pianist who played hymns at the evening services, showing him as profoundly grim. As with the Dubuque photographs, these pictures also focus on interiors.[8]

No Rival to the State

John Vachon presented a different picture of charity when he photographed federally sponsored programs. In May 1938 Vachon went to Irwinville, Georgia, where he photographed the Irwinville Farm Project—a cooperative farm funded through the Federal Emergency Relief Administration (FERA) and the Resettlement Administration. He made no pictures of men waiting in line or being fed. There were no bowed heads or soup pails. There are no images that might be construed as negative portrayals of government charity. In Vachon's Irwinville

5.5 (facing page)   John Vachon, Baptist minister in kitchen of City Mission. Dubuque, Iowa, April 1940 (LC-USF34-060516-D)

5.6   John Vachon, boys waiting in kitchen for soup after the meal. Dubuque, Iowa, April 1940
(LC-USF34-060590-D)

Farms pictures, men are pictured as active partners in their community's improvement. They are shown building cotton gins and dynamiting stumps in fields. Boys are pictured working in cooperative stores and playing baseball after "May Day–Health Day" festivities. Vachon's pictures include children being inoculated for typhoid, and a caption reports that Dr. Herman Dismude treats families at reduced rates. The homes built by the Resettlement Administration are overseen by women who make beds, work in kitchens, and put food into their own electric refrigerators. A pretty girl is even crowned May Queen. Community building is carried out by men and women in ways appropriate to the gender-role expectations of the period. New Deal reforms may have been innovative in form, but they actually served to reiterate traditional sex roles. Federal assistance was designed to enable men to be breadwinners and women to maintain their homes. The photographs of Irwinville are similar to Dorothea Lange's of the FSA camp at Tulare, California (1939), Arthur Rothstein's of Sinton, Texas (1942), or Marion Post Wolcott's tenant purchase homes in Isola, Mississippi (1939).[9] Men are never portrayed as anything less than fully active, adult partners in governmental reform.

When Dorothea Lange ventured onto a cooperative farm not funded by the Farm Security Administration, she carefully avoided mentioning why it was constructed and who paid for it. In June 1937 Lange photographed the cabins, cotton fields, and residents of the Delta Cooperative Farm in Hillhouse, Mississippi. As with other cooperative farms, this one was set up to improve the lives of sharecroppers and tenant farmers by providing decent housing and common ownership of basic industries. Lange took pictures of their cooperative store and poultry units. Her caption describing the new community building mentions a library, a clinic, and meeting rooms. Another explains that the community garden supplies fresh vegetables to twenty-eight families. Lange took a portrait of a boy whose family was evicted from their Arkansas farm and whose father was beaten. What Lange does not mention is that this cooperative was the brainchild of a former Protestant missionary to India, Sherwood Eddy (1871–1963). The Delta Cooperative Farm was organized in March of 1936 in order to help poor sharecroppers who had been evicted from their homes in Arkansas because of their membership in the Southern Tenant Farmers' Union. Half of the families were white, half black. A religious progressive, Eddy intended the cooperative to "exemplify the return of Christianity to its prophetic mission of identification with the disposed." The noted theologian Reinhold Niebuhr was one of five trustees of the project, and reports of its accomplishments appeared in *The Christian Century*. The Delta Cooperative Farm was a private experiment by liberal Protestants in "realistic religion," but Dorothea Lange represented it as no different from any other government-funded cooperative.[10]

From our perspective in the twenty-first century it might be difficult to understand such a rosy picture of government reform. Historical Division photographers, like the other Roosevelt New Dealers, were optimistic that the federal government could make substantial changes in the lives of the poor and unemployed. We might fault them for going not far enough (or too far) in their reforms, but they believed that the economic crisis had provided an excellent opportunity to remedy many of America's social problems. New Deal ideology stressed that only bureaucratic centralism and a caring state patriarchy could cope with the Depression. Private agencies and religious groups had a place in the reform movements of earlier times, but in the twentieth century their efforts were fragmented, limited, and often amateurish.

Let us move away from the photographs for a moment and concentrate on what might have shaped Vachon's attitude toward Christian charity. The development of America's "semi-welfare" state has a complicated and controversial history. One way of understanding that history is to briefly look at the biography of the chief architect of federal relief—Harry Hopkins. In Hopkins's biography we can see a shift from Protestant progressivism to belief in state welfare reform. Like Stryker, Hopkins became committed to a distinct separation of church and state, secularized social work and public welfare, and the establishment of a comprehensive program of old-age, health, and economic insurances. And like Stryker, Hopkins eventually rejected organized religion, pursuing his passion for serving humanity within the federal government. The ideals of the New Deal that shaped the outlook of the FSA/OWI photographers were created by men and women who believed, like Harry Hopkins, that private and religious charities could neither appropriately address the problems of the Depression nor act as a foundation for protecting Americans against future economic and social instability. The New Dealers' response to the reality of the industrial world looked significantly different from the one that William Masters crafted at Dubuque's City Mission.

Harry Lloyd Hopkins began his federal career in 1933 as director of the Federal Emergency Relief Administration, then went on to head the Works Progress Administration from 1935 to 1938. Roosevelt placed a tremendous amount of confidence in Hopkins, who was one of his most influential and powerful advisers. Hopkins developed stomach cancer in 1938, and from 1940 until his death in 1946 he lived as a guest in the White House. From 1938 to

1940 he was Roosevelt's secretary of commerce, and during the Second World War he administered the lend-lease program and sat on the War Production Board. He accompanied Roosevelt to the wartime summit conferences at Tehran (1943) and Yalta (1945). He died in 1946, ten months after Roosevelt's death.

Like Roy Stryker, Hopkins was raised in a rural community where he personally felt the effects of "genteel" poverty. Born in 1890 in Sioux City, Iowa, Hopkins eventually settled with his family in Grinnell. His father was skeptical about religion, but his mother was an enthusiastic Methodist whose grandfather had been a circuit-riding preacher in Canada. Anna Hopkins passed on to her children the ideals of Methodism: "A spirit of voluntarism, a commitment to service to others, and a sense of an interdependent Christian community."[11] She also managed to persuade four of her children to attend Grinnell College, a center of Social Gospel reform. Harry Hopkins entered Grinnell College in 1908 and was exposed to the principles of "applied" Christianity.[12] Grinnell's atmosphere combined progressive thought with evangelical piety. Women had been admitted since 1861, labor unions were supported, and radicals were invited to address the students. At the same time and without any sense of conflict, the Gospel was preached, and drinking and dancing were condemned. From the perspective of Grinnell College, the personal sanctity of the students was necessary in order to create an atmosphere supportive of social change. Piety coupled with economic and cultural reform produced social justice. Change needed to occur both in the community and within the individual. Protestant progressivism instilled a humanitarian spirit in college students and provided a theological rationale for reform.

After graduation in the summer of 1912, Hopkins followed his sister Adah, who had also attended Grinnell, to a Christian settlement house in New York. There they put into practice the ideals of the Social Gospel, as they worked to change the conditions of the urban poor. As with Stryker, religious connections enabled Hopkins to move from a rural community to New York City. Protestant progressivism did not merely establish an ideology and cultivate youthful enthusiasm; it provided a set of national networks to support reform. The workers at "Christodora" (Gift of Christ) settlement house had no pretensions of creating a secular charity organization. Workers were expected to base their lives on biblical principles and to support both the physical and spiritual conversion of the poor. The environment in which Adah and Harry lived and worked inculcated Protestant ideals of work and family to the poor Catholics and Jews who came to its doors.[13]

Like Stryker, however, Hopkins did not stay long at the settlement house, leaving after one year. Hopkins later wrote, "I have fully decided that if this house is on the side of the Lord, I am going to straightaway apply below."[14] His departure from the settlement house probably had to do with his frustration with the limitations of Christodora and the rapidly changing landscape of social welfare. By 1912 social reformers were arguing against the effectiveness of religious volunteers conducting charity or providing social welfare. Secular charity organizations wanted their volunteers to contribute money, not time. In that way casework, program development, and administration could be left to better-trained paid professionals. Comprehensive city departments were being created to impersonally distribute relief, inspect housing and factories, and run employment agencies. New ideas were being promoted, like pensions for older workers and compensation for on-the-job injuries. Changes in state laws made it easier for workers to bring injury claims to court. By the end of 1913, twenty states had authorized the distribution of "mothers' pensions" — small stipends for women who had to support children.[15] The pious character and small-scale nature of a Christian settlement house must have increasingly looked anachronistic and paternalistic to Hopkins.

The "charity wars" of New York City may also have provoked Hopkins to seriously consider what should be the appropriate relationship between private and public forms of welfare.[16] Historically, religious and private charities took care of orphans and children who could not be raised by their families. By the mid-nineteenth century, because of the number of indigent Catholics in New York City, the church had become the major caregiver for poor children in the growing metropolis. Catholics established orphanages, hospitals, industrial schools, institutes for the blind, residences for the "feeble minded," and homes for unwed mothers. Although Catholics staffed these institutions, they were supported by public funds. As early as the 1870s, charity reformers and politicians tried to alter the ways that Catholics conducted charity in New York. Reformers wanted to eliminate the institutionalization of children, restrict the amount of relief given to the poor, professionalize caregiving, and eliminate religious orientations in charity organizations. Politicians wanted to wrest control away from the city's Catholics, keep Catholics from getting state aid for the growing number of parochial schools, and make sure that the graft from charity aid went into the appropriate coffers. Critics accused Catholics of running unsanitary and crowded facilities that worked children long hours without providing proper education or other services. They noted the high death rate for babies placed in Catholic asylums.

From the Catholic point of view, so-called secular reformers were merely Protestants who wanted to place poor Catholic children in Protestant foster homes and thus change their religion. Catholic leaders could document a long history of anti-Catholicism among New York's elite. The supposedly neutral state charities actually were trying to undermine Catholic control over the Catholic poor. Catholic bishops and clergy defended the quality of their institutions and supported the work of the Catholic sisters who took care of many children for little recompense from the city. In 1916 this "simmering battle" exploded into an open war when the New York mayor demanded a full-scale public review of the connections between city government, the State Board of Charities, and the Archdiocese of New York. By then Hopkins was working for the Board of Child Welfare, and he would have seen that the secularization of social welfare would not be either easy or straightforward. As reformers attacked Catholic institutions and Catholics fought back, Hopkins must have seen how fraught with problems were such private-public partnerships. While the Catholic sisters may have been willing to help any child or adult regardless of religious background, the whole issue of personal belief interfered with the just and dignified distribution of charity. For Hopkins, and for other reformers of the early twentieth century, the days of religious groups influencing social welfare were ending.

Hopkins's reevaluation of the role of Christianity in social reform may also have been fueled by the love he felt for a non-Christian. A year after arriving in New York, Hopkins courted and married another Christodora settlement house worker, Ethel Gross. A Hungarian Jew, Gross had left the traditions of her Orthodox family as a part of her movement into American society. Gross introduced Hopkins to the excitement of New York City as well as the possibility that one could be a moral person concerned about the lives of others without being a Christian. Ethel Gross never embraced Protestantism, and Harry Hopkins never became a Jew. They looked for organizations that would support their beliefs without asking them to adhere to a specific theological system. In 1913 the couple was married at the Ethical Culture Society.

Founded in 1876, the New York Society for Ethical Culture promoted the philosophical commitments of Felix Adler. Adler was the son of a rabbi whose family had come to America from Germany in 1857, when Felix was almost six. Felix's father, Samuel, was already a rabbi of some repute for both his command of Jewish history and Scriptures and his work in the Reform movement in European Judaism. Samuel Adler had been called to the rabbinate of Temple Emanu-El of New York City, a rapidly growing center of Reform Judaism. Felix, however, broke further from rabbinical Judaism than had the Reform movement. Adler preached that all religions should be based on intellectual truth rather than on theology. A champion of social reform, Adler stressed the common humanity of all people and the need for righteousness and justice. He started the first kindergarten in America, developed a visiting nurse service, established a "Workingman's school," and lectured on the rights of laborers. Harry Hopkins and Ethel Gross shared with Felix Adler the notion that service to others was the most important way to manifest religion.[17] "Deed then, not creed," Adler preached. "The ethical end is itself the supreme end of life to which every other is subordinate," he reminded Americans in 1931. "The right relations between men and women, between employers and employees, between people and people, are not to be regarded as the means for making mankind happy, but that right relations are supremely worthwhile on their own account, that to act rightly is to do the right for right's sake."[18] Adler, like other turn-of-the-century progressive thinkers, felt that the essence of religion could be expressed without recourse to sectarian doctrines or rituals.

Although Hopkins eventually divorced Ethel Gross, he never rejoined a church. He had discovered that one could be committed to social justice without being involved in a Christian community or having a theological rationale for service. While his mother's Methodist enthusiasm for education enabled a poor boy to go to college, progressive Protestantism fired his humanitarian spirit, and church networks got him out of Iowa, Hopkins became a secular man of the twentieth century. His experience at Christadora and in observing the New York "charity wars" convinced him that private and governmental welfare should be detached from religious communities. In these thoughts he was not alone. By the 1920s, public spending for social welfare in the United States exceeded private spending by a ratio of three to one.[19] The Depression so depleted the coffers of private and religious charities that by January 1933 they were providing only 1 percent of the total wages lost by unemployed men and women.[20] Although Catholics and Social Gospel Protestants could provide some help, only the government had the resources to address the effects of widespread unemployment and economic instability.

Before moving to Washington, Hopkins worked in a series of social service organizations that had no overt religious associations: the Association for Improving the Condition of the Poor (1912–1915), the Board of Child Welfare (1915–1917), the American Red Cross (1917–1922), and the New York Tuberculosis Association (1924–1933). In 1931 he was appointed by New York Governor Franklin Delano Roosevelt to head the state's Temporary Emergency Relief Agency. When Roosevelt became president in 1933, he appointed Hopkins as director of the Federal Emergency Relief Administration. Roosevelt had established FERA to help relieve the suffering of the 15 million unemployed Americans by providing direct cash grants to city and state work relief projects. FERA eventually employed nearly 2.5 million workers, aided millions of farmers, and created a special bureau to deal with transients. By 1935 FERA had spent more than two billion dollars on relief.[21] Hopkins made it clear that religious groups should play no role in the disbursement of FERA monies. One of the FERA guidelines, what would be called "Regulation No. 1," eliminated the fuzzy line that had existed between public and private agencies by stating that only public officials would administer FERA funds.[22] States could no longer use private or religious organizations as avenues to distribute federal monies but would have to create new agencies staffed solely by public employees. Since city and state coffers had already been emptied, Regulation No. 1 effectively eliminated public subsidies to private charities by cutting off any new funding by the federal government. Although some Catholic dioceses were able to circumvent Regulation No. 1, a New Deal attitude toward religion and charity had been established.[23] The "modern" model of charity would be the isolation of the worlds of rituals, doctrines, and the supernatural from the rational world of social workers, policy, and economic reform.

Even after the Works Progress Administration replaced FERA in 1935 and distribution of aid returned to communities and states, religious charities played only a minor role in the New Deal. The federal government's entry into charity dwarfed religious efforts to assist the poor. Soon not only the elite New Dealers but Roosevelt's vast grassroots supporters saw to it—at least for the moment—that only the state had the presence and the money to address the current economic problems. While the government would need influential religious leaders to support New Deal reforms, the spotlight was on the government. Such Catholic activists as Father John Ryan found an open ear in Washington, but only because their vision of social justice dovetailed with that of the government. The New Dealers did not trust religious communities to distribute federal monies or to be creative partners with the state.

Evangelical Social Work

For supporters of the New Deal like John Vachon, it was clear that Christian charity may have been appropriate in the nineteenth century but that the modern industrial world demanded new ways to think about how to cope with economic instability. Not all of those who practiced Christian charity, however, were as optimistic about the ability of the state to eradicate poverty. Roosevelt's new Social Security system certainly would help the elderly, and state unemployment insurances would temper the impact of economic downturns, but for many Christians there was something missing from these policies. Consequently, for various practical and theological reasons, many people continued to run their own faith-based organizations rather than give control over the poor to secular professionals. Not all Americans joined the trend to secularize social work. To cope with poverty, Catholics, Jews, African Americans, and conservative Protestants continued to "take care of their own" and provide an alternative or a supplement to state welfare. Even when it was obvious that only the government had the resources to cope with the massive problems of the Depression, many congregations and religious organizations struggled to maintain their social services. Some groups saw their entire religious calling as focused on the spiritual and physical welfare of the poor.

The Dubuque City Mission photographed by John Vachon and the Salvation Army photographed by Dorothea Lange were two organizations that continued Christian charity during the period of secularizing welfare. Although these groups evolved in different ways during the twentieth century, both began in response to the deteriorating situation of Western industrial cities. Unlike Catholics, who had developed a theory of social justice and charity within a preindustrial European setting, the "rescue mission" movement and the Salvation Army were "modern" in that they took seriously a changing economic and class order. What Vachon and Lange recorded but did not appreciate was the refusal of the City Mission and the Salvation Army to accept the state's isolation of belief, rituals, and supernaturalism from welfare and social reform. Evangelical social workers provided an alternate model of reform from that offered by the New Deal.

The city mission movement was part of a larger movement of Protestants taking seriously the social and economic conditions of the city. While scholars have examined the impact of the liberal response to urban America via the Social Gospel movement, they have taken the efforts of evangelicals less seriously. Evangelical social work included that done within denominations as well as that of new groups like the Salvation Army, Volunteers of America, and the Christian and Missionary Alliance. These Protestants would have agreed with the ministers of the Social Gospel that industrialization caused immense human suffering, but they were less interested in working toward political or economic change. Evangelical social workers took a "hands-on" approach and tried to respond to the pressing needs of the poor. In the first three months of 1900, for example, the Volunteers of America housed 45,400 men in their New York lodge, and in 1913 the Bowery Mission provided 200,000 breakfasts.[24]

As evangelicals, these reformers believed that only a personal relationship with Christ and a commitment to biblical truth—by both social workers and the poor—would enable permanent social change. They drew their inspiration from the words of Jesus in the Gospel of Matthew: "I was hungry and you fed me, thirsty and you gave me a drink; I was a stranger and you received me in your homes, naked and you clothed me; I was sick and you took care for me, in prison and you visited me" (25:35–36). Evangelical social workers set up "rescue missions," and unlike the founders of settlement houses, they fostered the notion that a focused approach to the poor was the most effective. They offered basic food and shelter, accompanied by straightforward preaching. Prominent late-nineteenth-century revivalists like Charles Haddon Spurgeon (d. 1892), Thomas DeWitt Talmage (d. 1902), and Charles N. Crittenton (d. 1909) promoted this alternative to the Social Gospel movement. Evangelical social workers believed that the city would be saved when the gospel was preached and charity given to all who needed it.

Unlike the settlement houses of the turn of the century, rescue missions were often staffed and run by men who themselves had been poor and defined as social misfits. In this way the movement differed from the genteel charity of Victorian churches, the progressive Protestantism of Christian socialists, and the secular spirit of the New Deal. This class difference marked both the style and content of both the rescue mission movement and the Salvation Army. Jeremiah McAuley, for example, the founder of the Water Street Mission in New York City, was serving a fifteen-year term at Sing Sing prison when he was converted to evangelical Protestantism. In 1872 he opened the mission with the intent to provide physical and spiritual help to men like himself. That year on Thanksgiving the mission provided food for 150 men, then had religious services. As men were converted at the New York rescue missions, they went on to establish other missions. Between 1872 and 1892 more than one hundred city missions opened throughout the United States. By 1900 they had formed a loose federation, and by the twenties three thousand rescue missions were operating across the country.[25]

Vachon's photographs reflected this understanding of Christian charity. One Baptist minister in Dubuque dealt with the economic dislocation of the Great Depression just as other evangelical social workers had coped with the little depressions of the nineteenth century. William Masters (d. 1941) preached to them, fed them, and housed them. Joining with a Dubuque businessman, Edward Beach, he opened the doors of the City Mission on February 14, 1932. As "superintendent," Masters used money generated from local businesses to support a city ministry that reached even more men because of the dislocation of the Depression. His involvement, as with earlier generations of evangelical social workers, was intimate. He cooked and distributed food; he preached the Gospel. Essential to Masters's understanding of poverty was the opportunity it provided for people to create a personal relationship with Christ through their acceptance of their weakness and God's greatness. Neither poverty nor charity was detached and impersonal; both stimulated emotion and thus the possibility of conversion.

Masters and Beach probably perceived their charitable activities not as old-fashioned but rather as resourceful in bringing together business and church to help those crushed by the economic turmoil of the Depression. President Herbert Hoover encouraged local communities to take care of their unemployed, and a coalition naturally formed between business leaders, Protestant congregations, and ministers committed to caring for the urban poor. A year after the City Mission was established, Masters and Beach received funds from Dubuque's Community Chest. The Community Chest, forerunner to United Way Services, had been established by Dubuque businessmen in 1928. It initially served as a funding source for groups like the Boy Scouts, the Visiting Nurse Association, and the YMCA. Additional agencies were supported in the thirties, and their names reflected the changing times: the Cooperative Unemployed Exchange (1933), the Milk Fund (1933), and the Council of Social Agencies (1937).[26] We do not know what William Masters was thinking about when he posed for John Vachon (see fig. 5.5), but we might well imagine that he was wondering why in 1940—seven years after Roosevelt had proposed his New Deal and as the country's economy was heating up due to an emerging military buildup—men were still waiting in line for prayers, soup, and bread.

Salvation in San Francisco

In 1939 Dorothea Lange photographed the Salvation Army in San Francisco. Although Salvation Army activities were more expansive and developed than city rescue missions, and Dorothea Lange a more experienced photographer than John Vachon, her photographs share with those of Vachon a negative representation of Christian charity. Vachon dealt with the problem of Christian charity by setting up his pictures to stress the paternalistic nature of the City Mission, thus directly challenging the "goodness" of religious communities. Lange addressed evangelical social work more subtly. By the 1930s the Salvation Army was a respected welfare organization. Many Americans would have been surprised to discover that Salvation Army officers were as evangelical as the Baptist minister in Dubuque. The Great Depression may have presented Salvationists their greatest challenge, but they had not retreated from their commitment to the poor and dispossessed. Rather than showing Salvationists performing activities she felt were better performed by the federal government, Lange simply limited her pictures to their religious services. Lange pictured the Salvation Army doing what New Deal reformers thought Christians should do: preaching the gospel and leaving the business of welfare to the state. Through her visual silence she eliminated the part of religion that made secular people uncomfortable.

We do not know why Dorothea Lange interrupted her study of migrant workers to photograph the Salvation Army in San Francisco. Lange had been a studio photographer in San Francisco; she might have been in the Bay Area for personal reasons. The photographs were taken in April, on Palm Sunday, the Sunday before Easter. Frequently FSA/OWI photographers took pictures of religious activities during the Christmas and Easter seasons. Lange may merely have wanted to show what looked like a revival service — something that visually said "religion." The Salvation Army had a long, historic presence in San Francisco. It was in San Francisco in 1891 that the first "red kettle" was used to collect money to fund Christmas dinners for the poor. Lange might have known about Salvationists' work among the poor because of their presence on San Francisco's streets.

The Salvation Army is a Protestant denomination that came to the United States from Britain in 1880. Its founders believed that earnest experiential religion would eventually convert even the most difficult persons. During its early days in America, the Army built up its membership by converting poor and working-class people to its message of Christ and Christian service. Its members, called soldiers, wore distinctive dress and devoted their lives to bringing the Bible to the most marginal workers of industrial England and America. Some members — both women and men — were promoted to officers and functioned as ministers. One way of getting the poor and working class to listen to the Salvation Army message was through rowdy and spontaneous outdoor preaching. On Thanksgiving Day of 1909 in New York City, a whole regiment of the Salvation Army paraded down the street with a walking whiskey bottle and a "water wagon." Men were encouraged to jump aboard the water wagon, which took them to a trial of "John Barleycorn" and a free Thanksgiving dinner.[27] Until the early twentieth century, the Salvation Army promoted itself as a faith for the enthusiastic Christian concerned with righting the wrongs of industrial society.

The Salvation Army was established in the United States precisely during the period when many reformers argued it was important to give support only to the worthy poor. Many religious groups disagreed with this approach. Like the City Mission movement, the Salvation Army sought to direct its attention toward the most troublesome part of the urban population. Former prisoners, prostitutes, alcoholics, unwed mothers, vagrants — these were the people the movement hoped to reach. The organization built homes for single mothers, day care centers, and inexpensive hotels for men and women. It staffed unemployment agencies and developed salvage operations. In San Francisco, Salvationists provided emergency aid collected from around the world to victims of the 1906 earthquake. Members felt that their intimate knowledge of poverty helped them provide practical and sensitive care. Unlike the men and women who staffed the settlement houses, evangelical social workers did not assume that coming to Christ meant adopting a set of middle-class values. While some evangelical organizations, like the Volunteers of America, eventually became secular charities, the Salvation Army worked to survive as both a religious denomination and a welfare organization.

By 1939, when Lange was taking her pictures, the Salvation Army had changed immensely from its days of street theater. The majority of the members of the denomination were no longer the former drunks and destitute women drawn into the group through street preaching. The very success of the movement had meant that the class status of members was changing. Membership in the thirties was made up of the grown children of the converted, some of whom were second- and third-generation Salvationists. They did not come off the streets but were raised in the tradition. After World War I officers sought more professional training in social work and in music. The denomination was struggling to successfully integrate the middle-class perspectives of some of its members with its history as a working-class religion. While they still preached in the streets, Salvationists were less spontaneous and more ritualistic in their preaching, because most of the people who were listening were already members. When Lange made her pictures, Americans would have remembered that "lassies" had given out doughnuts during the First World War and would have defined the Salvation Army as a charity organization rather than as a group of working-class evangelicals.

Working against this common perception, Lange did not photograph unemployed men receiving shelter or destitute women getting clothing. She pictured the Salvation Army as a religion, not as a social service organization. Her photographs illustrate a typical Sunday service that is spatially and philosophically distinct from the daily charitable work of the Army. The Sunday service of the Salvation Army began in the streets, and Lange took several pictures of soldiers playing music and officers preaching (fig. 5.7). The remaining pictures that Lange took were of the "Corps meeting," during which officers conducted a traditional evangelical service for the soldiers (fig. 5.8). Lange's photographs should be read this way: from the outside (on the streets) to the inside (the Corps meeting house) rather than from the inside out.[28] After the street preaching, which symbolically connected the Salvationists to their more rowdy religious past, the group moved inside to the Corps, their storefront church.

Lange explained in her captions that the public music and preaching were not really noticed and that onlookers were only "mildly attentive." This would be expected since the street preaching was not really meant to grab the attention of nonmembers. The Sunday activities were directed at the families of the Salvation Army, not drifters collected off the street. Lange filmed venerable officers and pious-looking Salvation Army women, none of whom looks very appealing (fig. 5.9). In one photograph Lange uses hackneyed visual conventions to create a sentimental picture of piety. A little girl sings alongside an elderly officer whose glasses slip down his nose while he holds his hymnbook. Old and young sing together while each holds onto an American flag (fig. 5.10). Lange has cast the Salvation Army as a pietis-

5.7   Dorothea Lange, street preaching. San Francisco, April 1939 (LC-USF34-019278-E)

tic, evangelical organization made up of portly men, prissy women, and devoted children. By leaving out middle-aged men and charitable activities she eliminates the avenues that would connect their religious community to public, nonsentimental, modern reform.[29]

Representing Evangelical Charity

Lange's depiction was not any more sophisticated than other popular media representations of the Salvation Army. Because of their easily identifiable visual symbols (military hats, insignia, capes), their simple theological message, and their urban presence, the Salvation Army was portrayed on stage and in the movies. Since women could preach, plots could be constructed with romantic twists and turns. In 1897 a musical comedy, *Belle of New York*, featured a Salvation Army lassie rescuing Bowery boys and rich men from perdition. In 1908 *Salvation Nell* was heralded as a new type of play because of its realistic depiction of the poor. In the early thirties, *Laughing Sinners* (1931) with Clark Gable and *She Done Him Wrong* (1933) with Mae West and Cary Grant put Salvationists on the silver screen. Damon Runyon wrote about virtuous soldiers for Christ in *Guys and Dolls* (1931). His stories of tough life in New York City was eventually made into a Broadway musical in 1950 and a film in 1955. The Salvation Army became entertainment shorthand for urban, evangelical Christianity. In the film *Miracle Woman* (1931), one of Frank Capra's first movies, Barbara Stanwyck played a revivalist preacher modeled after Aimee Semple McPherson. When she finally sees the error of her ways, and turns from flashy stage life to true religion, she joins the Salvation Army. During the first decades of the twentieth century, stage and screen used Salvation Army officers to signal devotion and commitment. When someone donned an Army uniform, he or she sincerely pursued the good and the pure. Even Clark Gable was able to resist the charms of Mae West, as long as he was disguised as a Salvation Army worker.[30]

Lange's photographs continued this outsider depiction, but they empty it of the con-

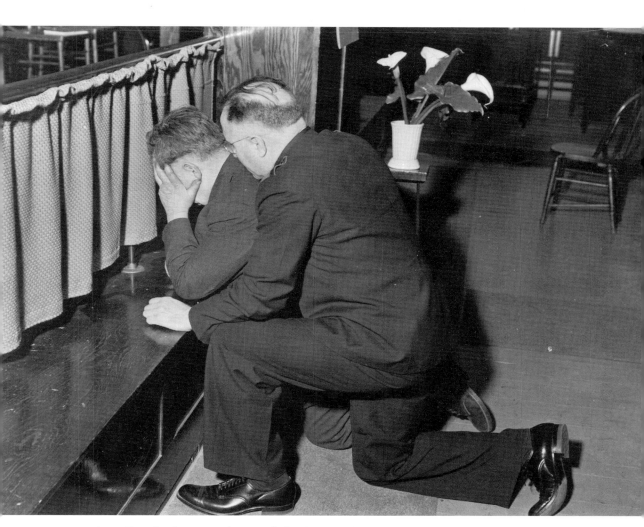

5.8   Dorothea Lange, men in prayer during Corps meeting. San Francisco, April 1939
(LC-USF34-019239-D)

5.9   Dorothea Lange, Salvation Army officers at Corps meeting. San Francisco, April 1939
(LC-USF34-019243-D)

trolled sexuality exploited by the plays and movies. There is no conflation of religious and romantic passion in Lange's representations. For her, this is a religion of elderly men and women surrounded by children, not of pretty girls and handsome men seducing sinners to Christ. Her Salvationists hardly even smile. This portrayal of the Salvation Army has a parallel in John Steinbeck's *Grapes of Wrath*. In his novel Steinbeck works hard to distinguish his ex-preacher Jim Casy from other religious leaders. Casy has decided to listen to the people and to grow from their wisdom. In a conversation with Tom Joad on their way to California, the two discuss the problems with "preachin'." "Preachin' is tellin' folks stuff," concludes Casy. "Preachin's a kinda tone a voice, and preachin's a way a lookin' at things," reflects Tom. Tom then goes on to report a story from his days in prison. The previous Christmas the Salvation Army "come an' done us good. Three solid hours a cornet music, an' we set there. They was bein' nice to us." As it was for the characters in John Vachon's photographs of the City Mission, however, this "niceness" was founded on forced compliance: "But if one of us tried to walk out, we'd a-drawed solitary. That's preachin'. Doin' good to a fella that's down an' can't smack ya in the pus for it." No, Tom Joad agrees with Casy, he was not a preacher. Just in case Casy missed the point, however, Tom reminds him: "But don't you blow no cornets aroun' here."[31]

Steinbeck softens his criticism of the Salvation Army by humor in this part of *The Grapes*

5.10 (facing page)   Dorothea Lange, Salvation Army officer and child. San Francisco, April 1939
(LC-USF34-021993-C)

of Wrath, but by the end of the book the author enthusiastically condemns Christian charity as practiced by the Salvation Army. The Joad family have made it to California, where they have taken refuge in a federally supported migrant camp. A group of women from the "Ladies' Committee of Sanitary Unit Number Four" have come to welcome the Joads and to explain to them the ways of government-supported charity. Like John Vachon's portrayal of the Irwinville Farm Project, the ladies present a very positive picture of New Deal charity. They speak to the family in "dignity and kindness" about how resources are shared and decisions communally agreed upon. They tell the Joads how committee members were elected. The women insist that the groceries given out in the camp store are not "charity," and that when a poor mother resists getting food for her children, she is told that she has "no right to be stiff-necked . . . not with our own people." For Steinbeck and the characters he creates, government support is not the same thing as charity that "makes a burn that don't come out." [32]

Charity is what one receives from religious groups like the Salvation Army. One woman, Annie Littlefield, tells Ma Joad of her experience "las' winter," when someone told her to go to the Salvation Army. "Her eyes grew fierce," Steinbeck writes. " 'We was hungry — they made us crawl for our dinner. They took our dignity. They — I hate 'em!' " The paragraph ends with a condemnation of Christian charity: " 'I hate 'em,' she said. 'I ain't never seen my man beat before, but them — them Salvation Army done it to 'im.' " Steinbeck has Annie explain that what goes on in the camp is not charity because "we don't allow nobody to give nothing to another person. They can give it to the camp, an' the camp can pass it out. We don't have no charity!" In *The Grapes of Wrath* Steinbeck represents Christian charity as the opposite of New Deal social welfare. Government-sponsored camps do not rob people of their dignity and autonomy. The state has provided in the FSA migrant worker camp a place where the poor have agency over their lives. Democracy and symmetrical power arrangements have been established between those who have and those who have not. For "New Deal modernists" like Steinbeck, the future of social reform is the welfare state.

Lange's refusal to photograph the Salvation Army's social services may be taken as an effort to unmask the intentions of private charities that reformers like Steinbeck felt they understood so clearly: the Salvation Army may appear to be like the state by setting up shelters and employment agencies, but in actuality it is a Bible-pounding, hymn-singing, Jesus-preaching church. From the perspective of New Dealers the mingling of piety and social reform was an old-fashioned Victorian hangover that could only hamper the progress of a secular nation. In 1933 liberals and workers had managed to overturn Prohibition, thus disentangling religion from social reform. Their success signaled the end of Protestantism's ability to determine national moral behavior. The churches had marshaled enough support to get the Eighteenth Amendment passed, but they could not persuade Americans to stop drinking. The failure of Prohibition proved to many Americans like Dorothea Lange and John Vachon that mixing piety and social reform could not be sustained in a modern nation. Even charity, if given by religious organizations that did not seek to alter existing economic arrangements, was suspect.

These two photo-essays visually represent the suspicion that New Dealers had about religion's place in reform. Religion made sense to the photographers when it stayed in its own sphere — the sphere of rituals, devotion, and personal faith. New Dealers could accept religion as a part of culture, not as a reformer of culture. Hymn singing was fine, as long as it remained in people's tents and did not come out into the streets and demand change. Ministers could preach, but they could not be shown asserting their authority over their flock in such a way that the flock looked like they could feel their power. Christianity was not represented as a cause of poverty — as it might have been by more radical reformers — but it certainly did not provide a foundation for social change. Religion was acceptable to reformers as long as it was bound by its own inward looking nature. From this perspective, while religious faith may give the poor strength to carry on in a migrant labor camp, it could not provide a foundation for demanding social justice. Since religious communities were not efficient providers of charity, the state can — and should — absorb the social welfare dimension of religious behavior. As long as the Depression and the New Deal preoccupied the government, the FSA photographers had no reason to picture Christian charity in any other way. Much would change, however, when President Roosevelt, in his state of the union address for 1941, called on all Americans to support those fighting against the "new order of tyranny" and thus to secure "four essential human freedoms," among which freedom of religion loomed large.

6.1   John Collier, photograph of Roosevelt with drawings in home of New Mexican.
Taos County, New Mexico, January 1943 (LC-USW3-017273-E)

6
New Mexico's Patriots

n late December 1942 John Collier, Jr., was overjoyed to be back in New Mexico. Although he had been born in New York and raised in California, he had lived for several years in New Mexico. "This is my home Roy," he wrote to Stryker. "I can't stay in the East indefinitely." Collier's letters reveal the excitement of a photographer who has happened onto what he called a "grand story." The FSA was sponsoring a rural low-income medical program in the remote mountain area of northern New Mexico. Seven hundred fifty families with incomes of less than one hundred dollars a month were receiving health insurance. "In the town of Peñasco," Collier wrote, "there is a clinic run by a young nurse who left her husband (sick) to do this job. It is 100% war on the home front and a perfect set up to get a series on the sacrifices and hardships of fighting a war." The nurse not only lived in an adobe house, cooked on an old range, and hauled her own water, but "She is young and attractive enough to lend herself to a grand story." "I am starting at once," Collier concluded.

"First, a record of the town, its people, its problems, and then the clinic and what it brings to these primitive people."[1]

While Collier followed the general plan he had outlined to Stryker, his attention shifted from the nurse to two young priests who also were on the board of directors of the Taos County Cooperative Health Association. According to Collier, Fathers Walter Cassidy and Patrick Smith were "deeply concerned with the particular rural economic problem of these Spanish American villages and are keen on supplying all the help they can on obtaining stories that might be helpful in the post-war period as well as functional in the present program of the O. W. I. [Office of War Information]."[2] The "Portrait of America" pamphlet that was produced out of Collier's photographs celebrated the activities of Catholic clergy. Collier stayed in the area for almost three months, from the end of December 1942 to the middle of March 1943. He shot hundreds of photographs of New Mexican social life and local reform efforts, including more than 130 pictures that showed the activities of the priests.

John Collier's photographs of New Mexico, their captions, his correspondence, and "Portrait of America" exemplify how the changing mission of the Historical Section was altering the place of religion within the FSA/OWI file. Before the United States joined the Allied forces in World War II, photographers used religious activities as evidence of the culture of the poor. Their photographs illustrated the physical beauty of rural church life and stressed elements of American religion often overlooked by writers and even the participants themselves. In other cases, pictures of religious behaviors were used to demonstrate the need for social reform while at the same time marginalizing the charitable activities of faith communities. Before Pearl Harbor, photographers' commitments to the New Deal and their attraction to vernacular forms of art shaped how they understood religious behavior.

After war broke out in Europe in 1939, additional pressures were placed on the photographers that shaped the kinds of pictures they took. Both governmental and private groups asked Stryker to send them images that spoke to a rapidly changing international and domestic climate. Roosevelt directed his personal charisma toward moving Americans out of their isolationist position and into direct involvement in world affairs (see fig. 6.1). Internationalists within the government were convinced that dictatorships in Europe and Asia would eventually affect the stability of the United States. The national economy was still shaky, however, and historians are still divided in their opinions about the successes of Roosevelt's New Deal remedies. By 1940, 14 percent of all Americans were still unemployed. No one would deny, however, that America's military buildup eventually moved the nation to full employment. As a government photographic agency, the Historical Section was poised to provide pictures that showed that the United States had the physical and spiritual resources to fight—and win—a war against fascism.

While Stryker never told his photographers to make propaganda, he did know that the section needed to make more "American background" photographs to satisfy the changing needs of the nation. The photographers could still pursue their reform-oriented stories, but they would also have to provide examples of the economic and social strength of the American people. In September 1940 Roy Stryker wrote a letter to Jack Delano, laying out, in his typical humor, the kind of photographs that the staff now needed to take: "Please watch for 'Autumn' pictures, as calls are beginning to come in for them, and we are short. These should be rather the symbol of Autumn. . . . Emphasize the idea of abundance—the 'horn of plenty' and pour maple syrup over it—you know; mix well with clouds, and put on a sky-blue platter. I know your damned photographer's soul writhes, but to hell with it." Stryker ended his sentiment by joking, "Do you think I give a damn about a photographer's soul with Hitler at our doorstep? You are nothing but camera fodder to me."[3] The Nazis had marched through France that June, and Americans watched as Europe became engulfed in war. Images stressing the American way of life were needed to neutralize fascist propaganda spreading in the United States.

Photographs of religious practices were useful in a variety of ways for this new mission of the Historical Section. The pressures of war required that all elements of American society work in concert. Americans needed to put aside their labor disputes, racial tensions, gender roles, and generational misunderstandings and work for the common good. This notion of a "common good" linked the reforming spirit of the thirties to the patriotic spirit of the forties. In the crucible of propaganda, Christian charity was transformed into community service. Catholic priests were presented as partners—rather than rivals—to the state. Collier's photographs served as examples of why federal assistance *should* support faith-based social reform.

Religious practices were also presented as the social glue that connected people in communities and gave them the spiritual sustenance that enabled them to create a democratic nation. For religious behavior to be useful in propaganda, it needed to reflect the strength of the nation. Collier took photographs that demonstrated how contemporary religious people were rational, predictable, communal, and practical. They were comfortable with modern media, technology, and government. Their religious leaders had the support of the people with whom they worked. Patriotic religion—true religion—supported and reflected democracy. Securing freedom of religion around the world was worth the personal sacrifices of the American people.

But there were limits to what could usefully be depicted. A photograph showing faith spinning out of control and shaping people in odd or unpredictable ways made poor propaganda. Religious voices should not argue against the government but rather should rearticulate national goals. Whatever did not portray the strength of religious communities would be ignored or reworked. Not surprisingly, Collier did not document the struggles between Catholics and Pentecostals that divided the New Mexican villages he photographed. In order to transform New Mexican piety into the pragmatic faith of patriotism, he downplayed Catholic rituals and transformed objects of devotion into folk art. From our vantage point of more than sixty years later, we know that Collier's idyllic pictures of cooperation and mutual respect were not entirely accurate. We do not know to what extent Collier knew this. But the disjunction between the image and the reality is significant because it highlights the strong desire that Americans had during the early forties to assuage or erase the conflicts between and within religious communities.

Religion and the Making of Propaganda

Once war broke out in Europe, in September 1939, America was increasingly called up to provide assistance to what would become her military allies. Government agencies outside of the Farm Security Administration asked Stryker for pictures that showed America's economic strength and the population's determination to oppose fascism. Stryker, along with most intellectuals of the thirties, was reluctant to label such pictures propaganda.[4] Propaganda had become closely associated with the deliberate lies distributed by the various governments engaged in World War I. By the thirties, people assumed that Nazis and communists produced propaganda in order to undermine democratic ideals. Propaganda was not merely the ways the government manipulated cultural symbols and images for its own purposes but was a dangerous weapon that foreign forces directed at the United States. Consequently, even when the Historical Section became a part of the Office of War Information, Stryker did not tell his photographers to make visual propaganda. Rather, he joined a wider cultural effort to defend against fascist propaganda by providing justification for America's participation in the war effort.

A key aspect of preparing America for war in the late thirties and early forties was countering the rise of German nationalism by promoting the values of freedom, democracy, and material abundance. While propaganda during World War I also evoked the American way of life, during the late thirties and forties the government recognized that all immigrant groups had joined in the building of America, and their unique cultures were worthy of acknowledgment. In 1938, for example, the federal Office of Education, in conjunction with CBS radio, acknowledged the contribution of ethnic and racial minorities in its series *Americans All, Immigrants All.* Nationally broadcast over a twenty-six-week period, the popular series sought to expand the narrative of American history beyond the melting pot image of assimilation. The show worked to offer the children of immigrants a sense of inclusion as "Americans." Once the United States entered the war, it was not sufficient merely to recite the contributions of immigrants. The American government came out strongly in support of the importance of difference, specifically ethnic difference, for democracy. Different ethnic groups could maintain their traditions while still being true Americans and supporting national unity. While racial difference was handled cautiously, and segregation was still normative in the military and across much of the country, black intellectuals eagerly promoted American war aims, often for their own purposes. The goal was to craft an image of the United States where people of all races and ethnic groups lived in peace and prosperity. This celebration of diversity was "without precedent in the country's history."[5]

Stryker was well aware of the notion that cultural tolerance was essential to the war effort, and he directed his photographers to make community studies that showed both the diversity and unity of the American people. Photographers were given more time in an area and expected to photograph a wider range of cultural activities. Stryker knew that he could more easily place such photographs if they told human interest stories that engaged the viewer. Magazines like *Look* and *Life* had set a standard for using pictures to carry the main narrative of a story. A single poignant picture, like Lange's *Migrant Mother,* no longer was enough to tell a compelling tale. "The emphasis from now on," Stryker's secretary wrote to Russell Lee in August of 1940, "is going to be on stories and getting sets of pictures into publication."[6] Under the pressure of the war buildup and the changing nature of America's print media, the photographers would need to spend more time thinking about the stories their pictures could tell.

In November 1939, three years before Collier photographed in northern New Mexico, Stryker wrote Russell Lee about an idea he had that would connect his growing interest in community studies with the political needs of the government. Stryker wrote that "we have a suggestion" before the Cultural Relations Division of the State Department to send a set of pictures from the FSA file to Latin American countries that would be distributed to local papers and picture magazines. The Spanish Civil War had ended that April, and Stryker might have thought that the United States could solidify its reputation in Latin American countries by showing the lives of Spanish-speaking U.S. citizens. Or he might have listened to the Office of Education's radio broadcasts on Latin America that had aired for twenty-six weeks in 1938. In any case, the State Department was looking for images of everyday American life to counteract the movie representations of Americans as rich tycoons, glamorous dancers, and violent criminals. Stryker wrote Lee, "There is no reason why we shouldn't be making up sets of materials which will show the people of South America that we do farm in this country, that people wear old clothes, that we too have an interesting cattle industry, what small town America looks like, etc." Aware of the problems entailed in working with the State Department, Stryker concluded, "We have an ample supply of pictures here which can pass the hardest boiled patriotic censor any place in the government."[7] In July 1940 Lee was in New Mexico taking pictures to satisfy the need for images of everyday life in the Spanish-speaking United States.

In order to make these pictures, Lee stayed with a private family in the small town of Peñasco, photographing there and at nearby Chamisal. He wrote to Stryker that he had met the priest, the postmaster, the majordomo, some merchants, and several farmers.[8] The photographs he took range from portraits of the villagers to descriptive illustrations of hog slaughtering and adobe brick making. He also photographed local churches and a religious procession. As with the other FSA photographs, Lee's pictures show that the strength of the United States resides within the lives of average people. Stryker realized that the political climate had changed since the mid-thirties, but he still worked from the conviction that examples of the "common" lives of Americans would make for goodwill and help spread democratic ideals. Lee's photographs would accurately show how New Mexicans worked hard at simple jobs, lived with loving families, and worshiped in Catholic churches—in ways not that different from people in other Spanish-speaking countries.

Russell Lee included only a few pictures of religious practices in his photo-essay of Peñasco and Chamisal because he was following the New Deal model of understanding religion as merely one aspect of society. The stress in Lee's photographs was on ethnic, not religious, difference. By the early forties, however, the federal government had developed a specific rationale for American involvement in international affairs that would alter the place of religion in the preparation of propaganda. Almost a year before America's entrance into the war, religion ceased to be merely one element of culture and became one of four essential freedoms upon which a moral order could be built.

In January 1941, during his state of the union address, Roosevelt discussed the "new order of tyranny" that was eliminating peace and democracy outside of the United States and thus threatening the security of the nation itself. In addition to pledging ships, planes, tanks, and guns to those who sought to maintain a free world, he outlined the foundations of "a healthy and strong democracy." Roosevelt called for personal sacrifice in order to secure "four essential human freedoms." The first was freedom of speech, the second "freedom of every person to worship God in his own way," the third freedom from want, and the fourth freedom from fear. Roosevelt was articulating an ideological basis for eventually engaging in war. Americans would not be fighting for land, for prestige, or even against a common enemy. Americans would be fighting to secure the freedoms on which an international moral order could be built. Religion thus became a cornerstone in the rationale for military buildup and war, as well as a key element in Roosevelt's blueprint for the future world. When the clause on freedom of religion was left out of a draft of the Atlantic Charter, criticism of this omission motivated Harry Hopkins to send Roosevelt a memo insisting that it appear in the upcoming Joint Declaration by the United Nations (the Allies). Roosevelt personally assured the Soviet ambassador, Maxim Litvinov, that he could tell Stalin that religious freedom also meant the right to have no religion at all. Stalin must have been convinced, because the clause was inserted in the final August 1941 draft.[9]

It is important to note that Roosevelt did not phrase this second freedom as the freedom to have one's own individual beliefs or to participate in a diverse set of cultural traditions. Roosevelt developed the sentiment expressed in the Bill of Rights that Congress should not make laws that would prohibit the free exercise of religion. As with the framers of the Constitution, Roosevelt assured Americans that religious practice, not simply belief or diverse ethnic cultures, must be made secure. Roosevelt's Four Freedoms made religious practices fundamental to American liberty. Americans would not be fighting to secure the rights of people to speak languages other than English or eat special foods or structure their households in a particular manner. With the Four Freedoms speech, the toleration of minority difference was imbued with more significance because of its association with religion. In addition, this was not merely a generalized notion of religion. Roosevelt specifically cited "freedom of worship" as what should be guaranteed to produce a moral order. Since worship, unlike belief, involves the senses, it could be visually depicted. During the war years, freedom of worship would be *the* aspect of culture — *the* unquestioned expression of difference.

By the end of 1941 the Japanese had bombed the American naval base at Pearl Harbor, and the country had declared war on Japan and Germany. In 1942 the Treasury Department published and distributed *Our War . . . Our Victory*, which used FSA photographs to convey the reasons Americans were waging war. Freedom to worship was one of those reasons. Across from one photograph was the poem "What We Fight Against":

> We are against tyrants.
> We are against people who push others around.
> We are against hatred of anybody because of his race.
> We are against hatred of anybody because of his religion.
> We are against people who do not believe "that all men are created equal."
> We are against people who wish to rule others by force.
>
> Fascists and Nazis are such people.
> We are at war against the things Fascists and Nazis believe in and do.
> We are at war against Fascism and Nazism.[10]

The text was set across from an illustration of a mealtime prayer that Jack Delano took of the Lemuel Smith family in their Carroll County, Georgia, home (fig. 6.2). Lemuel Smith had received a loan from the Farm Security Administration, and in other pictures Delano showed him feeding his chickens, working in the garden, and sharpening farm implements on a rainy afternoon. Only the image of the Smith family bowing their heads in prayer before eating their midday meal made it into *Our War . . . Our Victory*. Dinner grace, perhaps the most common religious ritual in the country, was threatened by the dictatorship imposed by Nazis and Fascists. The family's four neatly dressed children pray at a table set with a spotless tablecloth, flawless plates, and plenty of food. Indeed, the same photograph was used in another government pamphlet with the caption "America fights so that people—everywhere—will be free from want, the want that causes dictatorships and wars. Men must enjoy economic security."[11] Economic and spiritual security were conflated in the mealtime prayer, and the enemies of democracy endangered both.

Other photographers took similar pictures of families praying at mealtime (fig. 6.3). In 1942 Marjory Collins photographed a prosperous Pennsylvanian family saying grace before carving their turkey at Thanksgiving (fig. 6.4). That same Thanksgiving, Gordon Parks made pictures both of the black residents of a public housing project and of the president of historically black Howard University and his family saying holiday grace (fig. 6.5). It was important to demonstrate that Americans of all classes and races enjoyed the benefits of freedom. These government photographs may have served as models for the most widely distributed poster of the World War II era. In December 1942 Norman Rockwell made four paintings of Roosevelt's Four Freedoms, and two share images common to the FSA/OWI photographs. *Freedom of Worship* is a gray monotone assemblage of people of various ages and sexes praying, and *Freedom from Want* is a Thanksgiving scene of holiday abundance. The Treasury Department sent the original paintings on tour, and the Office of War Information distributed four million posters of the Four Freedoms—captioned "OURS . . . to fight for"—as premiums for war bond purchases. By the end of 1942 the government was hard at work creating an association between freedom, religion, patriotism, and abundance.

Photographing "freedom to worship" within America's communities became a new focus of Stryker's team. Stories about American people had to include accounts of their religious activities. In the summer of 1940, after filming in New Mexico, Russell Lee traveled to Utah, where he photographed rural Mormons farming and going to church. At the same time, Jack Delano was putting together a "day in the life of" story about Boyd Jones, an African-American boy from Greene County, Georgia, that included photos of him attending Sunday School and saying his bedtime prayers. That fall Delano filmed a community of farming Jews in Connecticut. Marjory Collins's photographs of New York (August 1942, 1943) included the city's Italian, Chinese, and Jewish neighborhoods. She did a series in November 1942 on a Mennonite community in Lititz, Pennsylvania (fig. 6.6), and one in April 1943 on a Polish-Catholic church in Buffalo, New York. John Collier's New Mexico photographs were preceded by a series on the Amish in Pennsylvania (March 1942), Portuguese Catholic fishermen in Massachusetts (April 1942), and French-Canadian Catholics in Maine (August 1942). All these photographs follow the general pattern of Collier's pictures of northern New Mexico: ethnic and religious differences flourish under an American system of freedom, democracy, and abundance.[12]

At the same time that the demands on the Historical Section photographers were changing, the Farm Security Administration was coming under closer congressional scrutiny. As the nation shifted its attention from "butter to guns," many New Deal agencies had a diffi-

We are for Freedom of Religion

6.3   Gordon Parks, Mr. Branch saying grace. Washington, D.C., November 1942 (LC-USW3-010684-C)

cult time maintaining their levels of funding. The Farm Security Administration, historically one of the most controversial programs of the New Deal, was increasingly being attacked for its purportedly socialist leanings. In early 1942 the conservative Farm Bureau Federation revealed that the FSA was paying poll taxes for poor southern farmers. The implication was that if the poor farmers could vote, they would vote for progressive legislation. Congressional critics argued that paying poll taxes was just one of the many frivolous ways that the FSA spent taxpayers' money. They condemned the agency for supporting socialized medicine, and a senator from Tennessee even accused an FSA administrator of being a communist. When the debate was over, the FSA's total budget was cut 43 percent below its requested level, and the Historical Section's was 27 percent lower than the year before. The FSA had met congressional challenges before, but Roosevelt's war-oriented government was quickly shifting national attention away from economic and social reform. The established farming community, which never had liked the government messing in their business, came out in full force against "do-gooders, bleeding hearts, and long-hairs who make a career of helping others for a price and according to their own peculiar, screwball ideas."[13] The future of one of the FSA's weakest divisions, a group of photographers, looked bleak.

Stryker knew that the photographic project had a better chance of survival if it could suc-

6.2 (facing page)   Jack Delano, Lemuel Smith and his family saying grace at the afternoon meal as reproduced in *Our War . . . Our Victory*. Carroll County, Georgia, April 1941 (LC-USF34-043863-D)

6.4   Marjory Collins, family saying grace before carving the turkey at Thanksgiving dinner in the home
of Earle Landis. Neffsville, Pennsylvania, November 1942 (LC-USW3-011874-D)

cessfully unite its mission of social reform to the growing focus on patriotism. In February
1942 he sent out a shooting script to the photographers, asking for "pictures of men, women
and children who appear as if they really believed in the U.S. Get people with a little spirit.
Too many in our file now paint the U.S. as an old person's home and that just about everyone
is too old to work and too malnourished to care much what happens." Stryker's hyperbole
indicates that he was not enthusiastic about the shifting identity of the section; he reassured
the photographers in his letter that the "FSA is still interested in the lower income groups
and we want to continue to photograph this group."[14] Stryker also realized that in order to
continue the photographic project, he had to find a more secure home for the section than the
Department of Agriculture. Seven months after the bombing of Pearl Harbor, the Office of
War Information had been created to consolidate government information services. It coordinated the release of war news for domestic use and launched a huge propaganda campaign at
home and abroad. Stryker knew the new agency would need pictures, and so he negotiated
a transfer for the Historical Section. Beginning at the start of the new federal fiscal year in
October 1942, he and his staff were reestablished as the Division of Photography, Bureau of
Publications and Graphics, Domestic Operations Branch of the Office of War Information.

Consequently, when John Collier, Jr., traveled to northern New Mexico during the winter
of 1942, he could call on well-established patriotic ideals to explain to his boss why he was
returning to a region so fully photographed by Russell Lee. Collier wanted to photograph
the Southwest because he loved the landscape and the people, but he also knew that Stryker

was under pressure to produce useful pictures. Like the other photographers, Collier did not turn away from the reformist, cultural, and artistic goals that shaped how they took pictures. Rather he added patriotism to the list of things that Stryker, the OWI, and the photographers valued.

The Great Arsenal of Democracy

At some point in the forties, Collier sent an undated shooting script to Stryker describing a series of photographs on a "New Mexico Winter" that would develop the concept of "What Is America?" "In this remote region," Collier explained, "this pioneer stock has remained unchanged, retaining characteristics that are 'Fundamentally American,' the sinew and steel of our history." His photo-essay was to illustrate how "the many cultures and diverse races which fuse together in this region" are an "arsenal" for the "strength of America." Collier was paraphrasing one of Roosevelt's "fireside chats," in which he told Americans that they must work to produce implements of war in order to help Great Britain fight the Nazis and defend democracy. Our arsenal comprised not only guns and tanks but also the character of the American people. Rural New Mexico could contribute to a "nationality study" of American culture that would demonstrate the "spiritual strength that is dominant in the American spirit." Collier cast the people of New Mexico into the mode of New England patriots: The "accent," he

6.5   Gordon Parks, Dr. Mordica Johnson, president of Howard University, saying grace before Thanksgiving dinner. Washington, D.C., November 1942 (LC-USW3-012027-C)

6.6   Marjory Collins, Mennonite husband and wife at a public sale. Lititz, Pennsylvania,
November 1942 (LC-USW3-011705-E)

explained, "will be on the hardihood that these colonials still deal with [in the] life around them, simple rugged living that won a place for their forefathers in the wilderness." [15] Collier's rationale reminds us of an important theme in the history of photography. Pictures not only could catalogue the various types of people that inhabited a country; they could prove that all of those groups shared a set of common characteristics.

Collier originally intended to photograph the "democratic spirit" not only among Spanish-speaking Catholics but also among Native Americans. In his script, Collier explained to Stryker that he wanted to document "Indian youth" in order to show how development through "the democratic system" (of the native communities) allowed the individual a "place in society that is wholly his own." "What finer story could there be," Collier wondered, "of the Four Freedoms?" Unfortunately for Collier, the Indians were not interested in the Four Freedoms. "Your errant photographer," Collier later confessed to Stryker, "spent three hours speaking in the grand manner to a room full of elderly blanketed Indians on 'their place in the war effort' and how important was a record of their ultra democratic way of life." The Indians were not impressed: "Possibly it was my interpreter, possibly it was my own limitations but after all was said and done I was limited to a coverage wholly inadequate for my story." Stryker must have been relieved that the native elders were not willing to be photographed. "I was opposed most decidedly," he wrote to Collier, "to our getting involved in the Indian problem." Stryker did not want the Bureau of Indian Affairs to feel that the OWI was moving in on its territory. [16] Taking pictures of Indians was too controversial.

Collier should have realized that his attempts to photograph Native Americans in New Mexico would provoke suspicion both from the native communities and from the government. Collier's father, John Collier, Sr., had in 1923 become executive secretary of the newly formed American Indian Defense Association (AIDA), an organization that called for an end to the selling off of native property and the suppression of Native American culture. When in 1933 Roosevelt appointed a former AIDA director, Harold L. Ickes, as his secretary of the interior, Ickes convinced the president to appoint John Collier, Sr., as his commissioner of Indian affairs. Collier remained Commissioner until 1945 and became the architect of what has been called the Indian New Deal; he worked to funnel New Deal funds into Native American projects, support Indian leadership, and restore traditional lands and customs. Through his father, John Collier, Jr., was well aware of the landscape of New Mexico, the cultural significance of minority communities in America, and the ideology of New Deal reforms. The son of the commissioner of Indian affairs should have known that years of exploitative photography of native people, coupled with long-standing government mistreatment, would make the Taos Pueblo Indians skeptical of bureaucrats with cameras.

When Collier shifted his attention to Spanish-speaking Catholics, however, his intuition about the "strength of America" residing in New Mexico paid off. Sometime in the early forties, the Office of War Information selected some of John Collier's photographs to be made into a pamphlet called "Portrait of America." Number 38 in a series, the pamphlet assembled a few of Collier's photographs with their captions into a narrative that boasted, "OLD AND NEW CULTURES BLEND IN SOUTHWESTERN COMMUNITY OF THE U.S." "Portrait of America" is a celebratory story of religious people working together for the common good. It includes pictures of Father Walter Cassidy attending meetings of the Taos County Cooperative Health

Association, visiting with new mothers, saying a memorial mass, leading the Boy Scouts, and playing the organ. The script describes Cassidy's Irish parents and reports that many of the children of the parish "speak the soft, archaic Castilian Spanish, which has been retained by those descendants of the early pioneers from Spain, as well as they speak English. These children are as American as Father Cassidy himself, and the spiritual values of their lives are similar." Over and over again "Portrait of America" repeated the refrain that "many of the people are bi-lingual, speaking Spanish and English with equal ease." The pamphlet reports, "Today with the United States at war, the young men of New Mexico are serving with the armed forces of their country on the battlefronts of the world. At home, the older men, the women, the younger boys and girls are working their farmlands to the utmost to produce vitally important food for the war effort."[17]

"Portrait of America" sought to connect the long history of the residents of New Mexico with a patriotic, Eurocentric colonial heritage. Developing the self-understanding of many New Mexicans that their ancestors came from Spain and not Mexico, the pamphlet stresses the noble history of what Collier called the "pioneer stock." These pioneers had a "church that was built in 1700," and it was the "best preserved colonial mission in the Southwestern US." The hearty colonial spirit that Collier described to Stryker resided not only in New England but could be found in the Southwest. Irish priests and Spanish villagers both reflected the success of European immigration. While only a few of Collier's many New Mexican photographs were used in "Portrait of America," there is no difference in tone or content between the government pamphlet, Collier's correspondence with Stryker, his photographs, or the captions he wrote for his pictures. Collier saw the people of New Mexico through a patriotic lens that transformed these Spanish-speaking Catholics and their Irish-American priests into rugged New England patriots imbued with the American spirit.

John Collier entered into the life of rural New Mexico through his interactions with two parish priests, Walter Cassidy and Pat Smith. Collier met the priests at the Taos County Cooperative Health Association, where they were on the board of directors. According to Collier's correspondence, the FSA had provided $50,000 to the cooperative to set up clinics and provide health insurance. The cooperative ran two medical and dental clinics per week, funded a resident nurse, and organized an ambulance service. The Taos Health Cooperative was one of 787 such medical programs, along with 221 dental programs, that operated in forty-one states. Funded through the FSA, with the cooperation of local physicians and dentists, the cooperative served more than 140,000 client families.[18] It was an innovative and successful program that connected local people, community leaders, medical professions, and government agencies to provide health care to rural areas.

Unlike the Native American elders, the Catholic clergy of the area were enthusiastic about helping Collier photograph their work on FSA projects and the lives of their parishioners. There is no sense in Collier's correspondence or other archival materials that either the priests or the bishop of Santa Fe was skeptical about the FSA cooperatives, the intentions of the photographer, or the impropriety of taking pictures of religious services. Collier, who was having a difficult time getting from village to village without a car, wrote to Stryker, "My transportation problem is nicely solved by the Catholic church who takes me anywhere I need to go — leaves me — and comes for me in the evening. . . . The church is very enthusiastic and wants to help me in every way."[19] Collier was able to take a full range of pictures — of the activities of the village priests, the homes of their parishioners, and the FSA-funded social services. His personal and professional needs, the goals of the OWI, and at least some of the ideals of the clergy clearly dovetailed.

Collier may have been eager to film the social welfare activities of New Mexican priests because he had recently photographed a similar priest in Maine. In August 1942 Collier took pictures of Father D. Wilfred Soucy, who worked with his parishioners on projects funded by the FSA (fig. 6.7). Father Soucy was fluent in French and English, familiar with community customs, and able to communicate with government bureaucrats. The priest had organized crocheters and knitters into cooperatives, founded a credit union, persuaded the government to build roads linking small communities, and used FSA monies to support a creamery co-operative. He even opened a community theater that showed movies. In 1939 Soucy had tried to generate community support for an FSA health cooperative, but lack of physician involvement kept it from being implemented. Soucy was influenced by a Catholic social activist movement in Nova Scotia. He was among the generation of young priests in the thirties who were trying to create new models of economic action and social reform.[20]

John Collier did not invent the reform activities of Catholic priests any more than John Vachon invented the reform activities of the Baptist minister he met in Dubuque, Iowa. In both cases, however, the photographers designed their pictures to convey a particular story about charity in America based on their understanding of religion and reform. In the case of John Vachon's pictures of the City Mission, the New Deal's distrust of religion was the dominant paradigm through which the activities of William Masters were ordered. As we have seen, evangelical Protestants approached social reform in ways distinct from those of either New Dealers or even liberal Protestants. Vachon had no interest in exploring those distinctions or the ways that evangelical ideas about charity might actually improve the strategies of the New Deal toward the poor. By the time Collier was taking his pictures of Christian charity, however, freedom of worship had become one reason why Americans were fighting in Europe and Asia. Collier's patriotic optimism about religion led him to construct a portrait of Christian charity very different from that of John Vachon. Catholics, for generations the outsiders in America, now were represented as demonstrating the appropriate relationship between church and state.

Key to Collier's portrayal of appropriate Christian charity was his understanding of who received charity. Collier discussed and photographed the Spanish Catholics of New Mexico as long-term residents who had the self-confidence to articulate their own needs and then to take advantage of government assistance. All of Collier's photographs of the people of New Mexico stress their self-sufficiency and dignity. No one in Collier's pictures stares blankly at the camera or looks hostile; they are not caught off guard nor seem as if they do not want to be photographed. Instead, many of Collier's photographs are formal portraits for which he has taken time to arrange people next to objects that he felt conveyed something about their lives. Probably influenced by Lewis Hine and Russell Lee, Collier's pictures stress his respect for the people he photographed. In the village of Trampas, for instance, Collier positioned "Grandfather Romero" underneath other photographs and religious prints (fig. 6.8). There is no embarrassment in the subject's eyes. Romero looks directly at the camera as if he is sitting

6.7   John Collier, Jr., Father D. Wilfred Soucy on the steps of the community theater he organized.
Aroostook County, Maine, August 1942 (LC-USF34-083722)

6.8   John Collier, Jr., Grandfather Romero sitting in his room with prints of Jesus and
El Niño de Atocha. Trampas, New Mexico, January 1943 (LC-USW3-017796-E)

in a photographer's studio and has purchased a portrait for his family. This was only one of
several photographs Collier took of the daily life of the Juan Lopez family.

Collier's photographs, their captions, and the pamphlet "Portrait of America" were all
designed to present an optimistic story about New Mexican villagers and one parish priest,
Walter Cassidy. Collier's captions, echoed in "Portrait of America," establish Cassidy's context: "The Catholic priest of the parish of Peñasco was born in Mora county, New Mexico, and
spent his boyhood working cattle and helping his father to operate a flour mill. His mother and
father both came from Donegal county, Ireland, and were early settlers in the Mora region."
Cassidy is not merely another Irish priest—a type—but a man who, like his parishioners,
has a name and a distinct history. He is not an outsider or just another Irish American missionary, but a Spanish-speaking native like the members of his congregation. The presence
of Cassidy moves the New Mexico story away from becoming a narrative of an ethnic group.
With Cassidy as the focus, the stress is placed on the multiethnic Catholics of New Mexico.
Father Cassidy, dressed in his cassock, sits in front of his roll-top desk and looks directly at the

6.9   John Collier, Jr., Father Walter Cassidy at his desk. Taos County, New Mexico,
January 1943 (LC-USW3-017399-C)

camera (fig. 6.9). He places one hand on his papers and books, the other formally at his side. Letters fill the desk's pigeonholes, telling us that this is a busy man. In other photographs the priest is shown relaxing at his fireside or enjoying his hobby of woodcarving.[21]

  Roman Catholic priests and nuns have always played complicated roles in the imagination of Protestant Americans. Nuns and priests were celibate people whose sexuality could not be easily defined — or more worrisomely, controlled. From the Protestant perspective, Catholic clergy promised obedience to their bishops, and the bishops were under the control of a foreign leader, the pope. Like their parishioners, many priests were recent immigrants who spoke English with an accent and ate strange foods. Their churches and religious services were exotic by Protestant standards, with complicated and sensual symbol systems. Protestants wondered how Catholics could support democracy if they allowed themselves to be influenced by authoritarian priests and bishops. Years of anticlerical writing in the United States had made many Americans suspicious about the activities of Catholics and their clergy. Catholic sisters gained the goodwill of some Protestants by nursing Civil War soldiers and staffing elite schools for girls, but for Protestants, priests had no obvious use.

In more recent years, the voice of one Catholic priest had come to symbolize the ability of religion to sow cultural and political division in the country. As early as 1932 Father Charles Coughlin was employing twenty-six secretaries to handle the 200,000 letters he received in response to his national Sunday afternoon radio broadcasts. Coughlin had caught the attention of the American people with a mixture of Catholic piety, political populism, anticommunism, isolationism, and anti-Semitism. By 1936 Father Coughlin could be heard telling his listeners that he would not support either the Republicans or the Democrats, but that Americans should vote for his new third party, the Union Party. Two years later in his magazine *Social Justice,* Coughlin freely plagiarized the anti-Semitic writings of Joseph Goebbels, Nazi minister of propaganda. Goebbels, flattered by the attention and furious at Roosevelt's support of Great Britain, praised Father Coughlin in one of his own radio broadcasts in 1940.[22]

Historians have stressed Coughlin's demagoguery and virulent anti-Semitism while overlooking the devotional content of his radio ministry. Coughlin broadcast from the top floor of the "Crucifixion Tower." His "shrine" in Royal Oak, Michigan, was named after St. Theresa, the "Little Flower," a popular saint of the thirties. From there he sent out blessed medals of the Holy Ghost, explaining that they had "touched the relic of the True Cross."[23] Coughlin was not merely another populist agitator presenting an alternative social plan to the New Deal. He was decidedly *Catholic,* and he never tried to hide or downplay his priestly role.

After the European war broke out, the number of people who listened to Coughlin's broadcasts declined, and by 1942 both his radio show and his newspaper had been silenced. But this particular Catholic priest had played an unquestionable role in disrupting the national consensus. Coughlin's presence called into question the assumption that religion was a private activity unconcerned with politics. Instead, Coughlin's popularity introduced an uncontrollable, pietistic element into the public world of opinion making. Collier's photographs of Father Cassidy and Father Smith must be looked at with Father Coughlin's disruptive voice fading in the background.

If Catholics were to be represented as good Americans essential to the war effort, then their clerical leaders had to shake off any questions about their loyalty and predictability. As with all OWI propaganda, the government had to show that everything connected to the war was under control. Censors sought to erase images of mass death, racial mixing during "off hours," and psychological strain in battle. Catholic priests needed to reflect the responsible voice of religion, not its extremes. Father Cassidy and Father Smith's parish activities thus were represented as the serious business of adult males, in spite of their celibacy and feminine-looking cassocks. These young men—who were not away at war—had to look like they, too,

6.10   John Collier, Jr., Father Walter Cassidy smoking and talking things over with a parishioner.
Taos County, New Mexico, January 1943 (LC-USW3-017401-C)

were sacrificing for their country's benefit. They would not, as Father Coughlin did, be calling their president a "great betrayer and liar."[24] Like the people of northern New Mexico, the
priests had to reflect the American spirit.

To accomplish this, Collier's pictures stress the public, rational, and masculine nature
of clerical social service. Unlike Vachon's Baptist minister, who is never shown outside of his
institutionalized "home," the priests are photographed inside and outside of the houses of
their parishioners, in the community's schools, and in the health cooperative offices. They go
in and out of their own cars as they travel through the backwoods of New Mexico. While John
Vachon photographed the City Mission superintendent wearing an apron in a kitchen, John
Collier photographed Father Cassidy smoking a cigarette (fig. 6.10; see fig. 5.5). Vachon's
Baptist minister pours soup into the pails of hungry children, but Father Cassidy leads his
Boy Scouts on hikes and explores the wilderness (fig. 6.11; see fig. 5.6). Father Cassidy and
Father Smith are active, young, masculine priests who take seriously their role to serve the
community. They make sacrifices like men do, not like women. One gets the message that if
the priests had not been committed to the religious life, they would have made good soldiers.

Collier represents the Catholic priests of Questa and Peñasco as modern men who are
sophisticated in the ways they use the state to benefit their congregation. The photographs
accentuate the progressive nature of the priests' social work, and in this way we see the New
Deal promotion of scientific reform blend into the patriotism of the war years. These clergy-

men are represented not as feeding a passive clientele but as enabling their fellow citizens to lead fully productive lives. The priests are never shown directly giving people food, clothing, or shelter. Instead, Collier's photographs show them meeting with FSA agents to discuss the needs of the community. Father Cassidy is photographed helping a parishioner appraise the worth of a farm and equipment in order to apply for a loan.[25] In another picture, Father Smith and Dr. Onstine of the Taos County Cooperative Health Association are photographed caring for a tubercular patient in her home, accompanied by two family members (fig. 6.12). Representatives of medicine, religion, and government function as a team in order to heal the sick. Vachon's portrait of the Baptist minister shows him rooted in another age, with no sense of modern social work techniques. The priests, on the other hand, have mastered the bureaucratic world around them. Catholic social service, or so the photographs encourage us to think, is fully scientific and supportive of state goals. The priests do not give Christian charity.

As modern men, the priests are characterized as conversant with technology and mass media. John Collier was intrigued by Father Smith's use of loudspeakers mounted on the top of the parish house to broadcast the nightly news in Spanish. Collier took two pictures of the priest, including one in which it looks like Smith has been asked to put his hand strategically on the globe (fig. 6.13). Collier gives no hints that Father Smith might have had additional uses for his loudspeakers. According to Smith's own account, however, the equipment pur-

6.11   John Collier, Jr., Boy Scouts on mountaintop with scoutmaster, Father Walter Cassidy. Peñasco, New Mexico, January 1943 (LC-USW3-017346-C)

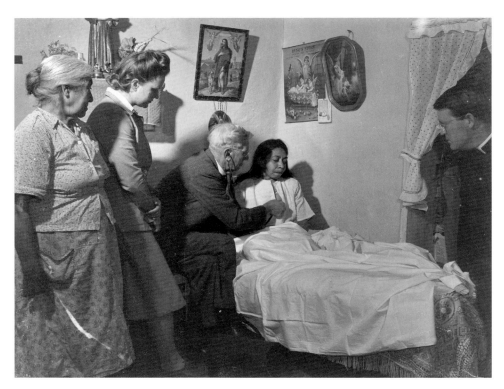

6.12   John Collier, Jr., Father Patrick Smith, Dr. Onstine of the Taos County Cooperative Health
Association, tubercular patient, and family members under prints of St. Roch (Rocco) and two of guardian
angels. Questa, New Mexico, January 1943 (LC-USW3-017918-C)

chased allowed him to drown out the preaching of the "Alleluiahs." Some of the villagers of
Questa were Pentecostal Protestants, and their preacher broadcast sermons on Sunday night.
Father Smith boasted to the bishop of Dallas, "My equipment reaches out for miles in each
direction," and "for that reason it is of great benefit in bombarding the town with Catholic
doctrine." When the Alleluiah preacher began to "rant and rave, I play operatic arias. The
people in his vicinity have assured me that they would rather listen to the music, even opera
(?), so it has been continued."[26] In his letter Father Smith mentions his nightly broadcasts of
the Office of War Information bulletins, but he is much prouder of his efforts to defeat rival
religious groups in the village.

Collier's pictures, however, reveal no cracks in the image of mutual cooperation between
religious leaders, local community people, and the federal government. The photographs are
nostalgic in representing ethnic and religious difference as orderly and contained. While there
were frequent periods of antagonism between Catholics and Protestants, and even between the
parishioners and their priests, such social dysfunctions had to be ignored. Both propaganda
and nostalgia depend on "local color" to be predictable and quaint, not uncontrollable and
divisive. Including a priest's image in governmental propaganda assumed that most Americans understood Catholics as patriotic supporters of the war and not potential foreign "fifth
columnists."

It would have been difficult for Collier to miss Father Smith's "Catholic doctrine" broadcasts in Questa, but it would have been far more important for him to depict the democratic orientation of the priests rather than their community power. Collier's photographs ignore the priests' authority over their congregations and instead show them helping the people achieve their own self-defined educational, social, and financial goals. Typically the young priests were filmed either sitting or standing on the same level as the people. In one case Cassidy sits at a desk and listens intently at a parent-teacher association meeting in the high school (fig. 6.14). Collier sets up the pictures so that a patriotic poster is in the center of the frame. Even when Collier is with his Boy Scouts, he is either nestled among them or raising his hand giving the Boy Scout pledge just as they do (fig. 6.15). In only one picture, in which Collier goes to visit a mother in bed with her newborn baby, does he stand over someone. The mother's obvious joy and excitement about her new baby, however, eliminates any sense that she is intimidated by the visiting priest (fig. 6.16).

Collier's pictures, his captions, and "Portrait of America" all illustrate how American Catholics are—as he wrote to Stryker—"fundamentally American." Catholics do not disrupt

6.13   John Collier, Jr., Father Patrick Smith broadcasting the news in Spanish.
Questa, New Mexico, January 1943 (LC-USW3-018103-E)

6.14   John Collier, Jr., parent-teacher association meeting in the high school.
Peñasco, New Mexico, January 1943 (LC-USW3-014569-C)

communities by trying to gain the upper hand in reform or by promoting a set of values different from that of the government. Catholicism is not an alien or foreign religion because — like the government — it serves the interests of the community. Catholics, even those in remote New Mexican villages, are just like "us." They join the Boy Scouts, have babies, attend PTA meetings, and go to church. American priests, Collier vigorously states through his photographs, are young and modern. They are familiar with local customs and languages, and they use this knowledge to help their congregation improve their everyday lives. Rather than flee from modern forms of charity or technology, the priests embrace new ways of social reform and communication. Religious commitments do not hinder social progress or national goals. They actually strengthen the resolve of people to work for the common good. The photographs insist that Catholics and their clergy are partners with the state in nation building. Collier's photographs are visual examples of constructive American citizenship. No one has to be in bed by nine in order to get a bowl of soup.

Catholic Power

In 1943, the year that Collier finished his photo-essay of the Catholics of New Mexico, Jennifer Jones won an Academy Award for her performance in *The Song of Bernadette*. The young actress beat out Ingrid Bergman, whose performance in *Casablanca* solidified her American movie career. *The Song of Bernadette* is based on a story well known in American Catholic

6.15   John Collier, Jr., Father Walter Cassidy giving out Boy Scout merit badges in church.
Peñasco, New Mexico, January 1943 (LC-USW3-018001-C)

circles about a young woman who has a series of visions of the Virgin Mary in the village of
Lourdes in France. In the film a pious but rather simple-minded Bernadette steadfastly keeps
to her convictions in spite of the challenges of her family, her church, and the officials of the
French state. Bernadette is portrayed as consistently attacked by the powerful authorities, but
she never doubts that she has seen a vision of "a beautiful lady" who causes the appearance of
miraculous healing water. Based on the 1941 novel by Franz Werfel, a German Jew, and produced from the studio of Jewish film magnate David Selznick, *The Song of Bernadette* said as
much about the pressures of World War II as it did about a Catholic miracle story. As Jennifer
Jones concluded, the movie was needed "when the world was in upheaval. I think that's why
the picture went right to people's hearts. It gave them something to believe in; it refreshed their
memories of undying faith."[27] Hollywood filmmakers could have used any religion to show
how "undying faith" could triumph over mighty institutions. But they chose a Catholic story
to tell how the average person, even an absentminded teenager, could develop convictions that
no one could overturn.

A year after Collier took his photographs, another Catholic movie swept the Oscars at
the Academy Awards. In 1944 *Going My Way* won seven Academy Awards, including Best
Picture, Best Actor, and Best Director. The film is a lighthearted tale of a young priest, Father
Chuck O'Malley (played by Bing Crosby), who is sent to rescue the financially failing St.
Dominic's parish, run by an old curmudgeon, Father Fitzgibbon (played by Barry Fitzgerald).
Father O'Malley's American charm is gently contrasted to Father Fitzgibbon's Old World

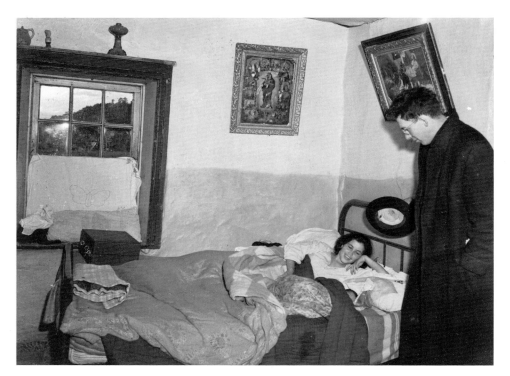

6.16   John Collier, Jr., Father Walter Cassidy visiting a mother and her new baby. Print is of
Our Lady of the Rosary. Taos County, New Mexico, January 1943 (LC-USW3-017371-C)

Irish spirit. Father O'Malley plays baseball, wears sweatshirts, has a former sweetheart, and
can calm wayward boys with his golden voice. More important, however, Father O'Malley
serves his community. "His great gift," the novelist Mary Gordon perceptively writes, "is to
see everyone's need and so provide for it. He is infinitely flexible, infinitely equipped with
resources." [28] Father O'Malley continues this service in the sequel, *Bells of St. Mary's* (1945),
joined by Sister Benedict (Ingrid Bergman). While *Bells of St. Mary's* did not win any of the
three Oscars for which it was nominated, it was a box office hit. At the time, only *Gone with
the Wind* and *You're in the Army Now* had grossed more money for its makers.

Throughout the forties, Catholic stories fascinated filmmakers. The Catholic (often Irish-
or Italian-American) soldier was always included in the multiethnic platoon that was the staple
of war movies. In *The Fighting Sullivans* (1944) Catholic heroism is accentuated as the action
follows the story of five Catholic brothers, all of whom die in a naval battle. Catholic women also
were portrayed as cultural heroines. Ingrid Bergman brought her stage performance of *Joan
of Lorraine* to the movies as *Joan of Arc* (1948). Directed by Victor Fleming, the film—like
The Song of Bernadette—depicts a self-confident young woman ready to die before altering
her convictions. In *Come to the Stable* (1949) Loretta Young and Celeste Holm play Benedic-
tine nuns determined to build a hospital in the countryside. The movie was very popular, and
Young was nominated for an Oscar for her performance. During the forties, Hollywood was
confined by the Production Code and under close scrutiny by the Catholic Legion of De-
cency.[29] Father Daniel Lord participated in writing the Production Code, and Joseph Breen,
a devout Catholic, administered it at the time. Moviemakers had no alternative but to conform

to Catholic standards when films dealt with Catholic subjects. If they used priests and nuns as characters in movies, they had to represent them in ways that met the expectations of both the church and the moviegoing populace.

In the popular imagination, the images that John Collier made of Father Walter Cassidy, Father Patrick Smith, and their New Mexican parishes were not unique. In spite of continued anti-Catholic sentiment among the intellectual elite, during the forties most Americans came to accept Catholics as loyal Americans.[30] War had given a boost to the positive portrayals of religion in the media. In fact, if Collier's OWI photographs and Hollywood movies are an indication of general cultural sentiments, during the forties Catholicism became *the* religion for conveying essential American values. The Catholic saint, like the innocent Bernadette and the heroic Joan, became the symbol of the "little guy" who could withstand the onslaught of unjust institutions and be emboldened by the power of God and of their convictions. Catholics' unwavering assertion of the truth became a symbol of the nation's fight against the foes of democracy rather than a sign of dogmatic supernaturalism. Catholic priests, like Father Cassidy and Father O'Malley, were understood as strong workers for their community in ways that were acceptably male, patriotic, and — most important — effective. Like the Sullivan brothers who died in a burst of flames, priests exchanged a normal life of family and career for a life committed to the greater good. Catholics benefited from the war ethos.

Obviously, the Catholicism of government propaganda and Hollywood movies is a certain type of Catholicism. It is not, for instance, the Catholicism that Russell Lee pictured among Mexicans in Texas. The Catholicism that Lee saw was confined to the home and maintained by women. This Catholicism was intensely visual and overtly supernatural. Likewise, films and propaganda downplayed the religious authority of priests, especially as it was displayed in rituals in which the clergyman was the active performer and the people were passive recipients. While Bing Crosby's Father O'Malley struggles to get his parish out of debt, we never see him saying Mass. A critic from the *Pittsburgh Catholic* newspaper called the film "unCatholic throughout," and part of his concern was that priestly duties were reduced to social work among the poor. Father Cassidy is shown with his Boy Scout troop, but there are no similar pictures of Catholic children learning their catechism. Father Smith broadcasts the news over his loudspeakers, but we hear nothing about his blasting of "Catholic doctrine" over the airwaves. Catholic consultants to Hollywood continually pointed out that "religious indifferentism" — the idea that all religions were good and that there were many routes to heaven — contradicted Catholic teaching.[31] Moviemakers, however, ignored Catholic critics as much as they could and presented Catholics as possessing ecumenical humanism.

John Collier could not fully understand the complicated nature of Catholicism in New Mexico. Catholicism made sense to him when it could be refigured into practical community service or, as we have seen in an earlier chapter, folk art. Collier was, in effect, promoting "religious indifferentism" because his photographs flattened the truth claims of Catholics in New Mexico. Highlighting priestly duties — which would have been highly undemocratic activities in the forties — would have necessitated the separation of the priest from the people. Religious convictions could not be portrayed as detracting from patriotism but rather had to parallel the strength of the state. In the environment of war, Catholics were represented as possessing both the power of unwavering democratic convictions and the creative spirit of "the common man."

7
Farming Jews

e're still in Norwich and getting fed up with the rain," Jack Delano complained to Stryker in November 1940. "The only heartening thing that happened in the last 5 days was yesterday when I spent some time in Colchester, (Conn). The town is an old New England settlement that has at various times been dominantly Yankee, Irish, German, and now Jewish." From August 1940 to February 1941, Jack Delano and his new bride, Irene, traveled throughout the Northeast photographing shipyards, steel mills, aircraft factories, and a submarine base—in addition to the more typical dairy farms, tobacco fields, and potato farmers. As the nation prepared for war, Delano was told to illustrate America's strengths by documenting New England's agricultural resources and its industrial

7.1 (facing page)   Jack Delano, Abraham Lapping in his dairy barn.
Colchester, Connecticut, November 1940 (LC-USF34-042322-D)

167

installations. A few days earlier, Delano had written that he was photographing poultry and dairy farmers in Connecticut, trying to illustrate what he called "the part-time farmer problem." The "problem" was that people who both farmed and worked in light industry were not eligible for assistance from rural relief programs. According to an FSA supplemental file, "the social effects of extending assistance to this 'part-time' farmer group is of the utmost importance," since these farmers were "sound citizens . . . not susceptible to social agitators."[1] If Delano could put a human face on people who moved back and forth between industry and farming, it might bring governmental attention to their economic plight. As a secular Jew himself, what better way to spend a dreary fall day than photographing farming Jews?

When Delano visited Colchester, approximately a quarter of the population of this town in rural Connecticut was Jewish. This number had decreased from its high point (between 1910 and 1925), when more than half of the residents of this village thirty miles from Hartford were Jewish.[2] Jews also had settled in other Connecticut towns, and pictures were taken of Jewish poultry farmers living near Tracy, Ledyard, Windsor Locks, and Newton (fig. 7.2). The Jews who came to Colchester established dairy and poultry farms, started clothing factories, and ran retail businesses. Colchester was also close enough to New York City — only two hours by train — that Jews could maintain social and economic ties with those who remained in the city. Although the number of Jews had been declining, the main businesses and political positions in Colchester remained in Jewish hands.

Jews had come to rural New England because the Baron de Hirsch Fund and later the Jewish Agricultural Society provided them with small loans for farms and to help them in hard times. In 1889 the Baron Maurice de Hirsch (1831–1896), a wealthy German Jew, donated $2.4 million for agricultural resettlement of displaced Russian Jews in the United States. He eventually established the Baron de Hirsch Fund in 1891 to continue his dream of Jews renewing their ancient tradition of tilling the soil. Successful farmers, the Baron believed, would counter the stereotype of the Jew as an unscrupulous petty trader and unproductive business middleman. Baron de Hirsch was certainly the most influential figure in the "back to the soil" movement that promoted the redemptive value of agriculture among Russian Jews. By funding agricultural colonies and vocational schools, Baron de Hirsch sought to enable Jews fleeing persecution in eastern Europe to create productive lives in the New World. "Colchester was a place to come if you wanted to get out of the Lower East Side," remembered one resident in 1986. "If you wanted to get away from the squalor that apparently was associated with the ghettos of Manhattan, this was the place to come." Approximately half of Colchester's Jews had received help from either the Baron de Hirsch Fund or the Jewish Agricultural Society.[3]

Jews were able to purchase farms in Connecticut because by the turn of the century many Yankee farmers had given up on the rock-infested lands of New England. As one Colchester farmer put it, the "fields in Connecticut are good for raising dairy cows that ate grass from around the stones." Small-scale industry had also fallen on hard times. When Jews began arriving in Colchester in the 1890s, its rubber plant had closed, as well as its bank, canning factory, creamery, and even the town newspaper. Land was cheap and available. By 1920 one-

7.2 (facing page)   John Collier, Jr., farmer, perhaps a *schochten* (ritual butcher), holding Torah scroll. Near Windsor Locks, Connecticut, August 1942 (LC-USF34-083882-C)

third of Connecticut farms were owned by immigrants. The first Jewish family bought a farm near New London in 1891 with money saved from working in a New England woolens mill. Jews then began to settle in the vicinity of Oakdale, Montville, Palmerton, Chesterfield, and Salem. In 1931 the director of the Jewish Agricultural Society estimated that there were about one thousand Jewish families farming in Connecticut.[4]

Jack and Irene Delano must have seen the inherent human interest angle of a story about Jewish farmers. For the most part, America's Jews had little to do with farming and were not Farm Security Administration clients. Before World War II, 40 percent of the Jewish population lived in New York City and most of the remainder in a handful of big cities: Chicago, Philadelphia, Boston, and Cleveland. Although Jews settled independently as farmers, and Russian Jewish farming colonies were established in the early 1880s, the 1936 *Census of Religious Bodies* noted that only 3.8 percent of the Jewish population lived in rural communities.[5] In rural Connecticut, however, a community of Jews maintained a synagogue and sent its children to Hebrew school. Colchester's Jews may not have been representative of Jews in America, but their story is significant because it provides an alternative to the urban story of Jewish life during the interwar years.

Jack Delano spent only one day in Colchester, but he took many pictures of life in the town. He had been hired only that May of 1940 and was eager to comply with Stryker's request for pictures that could be easily made into photo-essays. The series, like John Collier's photographs of rural New Mexico, exemplifies the changing orientation of the Historical Section as it responded to the pressures a war in Europe placed on the American government. Documenting poverty—with quick bows to rural culture and art—could no longer be the sole goal of the division. Delano's photographs of Colchester are another example of how religiously committed people, sacred spaces, and ritual practices entered into the FSA/OWI photographic file in the last few years of its existence, when religion became important to government propaganda.[6] These pictures are quite different from those of the Jersey Homesteads, a Jewish community photographed at the beginning of the project in 1935. In 1940 it was not enough merely to show ethnic diversity; the photographs needed to present America as diverse in its religious rituals and institutions.

At first glance, Delano's photographs present the Jews of Colchester as small-town Americans who "pray" and have their own "churches," "ministers," and "Sunday Schools." What we see in the pictures should make sense to a Christian population that experiences religion in its own particular way. The pictures might have made good illustrations for Roosevelt's Freedom of Religion. Although I will point out the gaps in Delano's portrait of Colchester, a second glance at the photographs will show that this is not just one more nostalgic picture of small-town America. The photographs illustrate Jewish distinctiveness. Jews do things differently. The Colchester photographs are important to the issue of identity because they present a picture of Jewish life that is neither that of a fully assimilated Yankee farmer nor that of a New York Jew struggling with the meaning of Jewishness. Archival materials, oral histories, and interviews with surviving members of the community indicate that the interwar years were economically hard but socially satisfying in Colchester. Unlike Jewish photographers of New York, who liked to picture the residents of their city as "jumpy" and their communal solidarity as "a created and always liquid condition, as reversible as a tide," Jack Delano saw a far more stable community in Colchester.[7] His photographs do not merely reflect a hope that Jews could feel comfortable with their ethnic and religious identities in America, nor are they simply propagandistic constructions useful for the government. The Jews of Colchester had, in reality, revitalized this New England village, and they felt comfortable with being both Jewish and American.

Roosevelt, New Jersey

Prior to Jack Delano's series on Colchester in 1940, there had been only one other effort to represent an American Jewish community by Stryker's photographers. This was a series of pictures designed to document federal support of what might be considered an experiment in Jewish socialism. In 1933 Benjamin Brown, a Ukrainian Jew, was awarded $500,000 from the Department of the Interior to bring two hundred Jewish garment workers and their families from New York City to establish cooperative farms and factories in New Jersey. The hope was one frequently expressed in the United States: if the urban poor had a chance to get away from their polluted streets and crowded tenements, then they could successfully be taught new skills and live more healthy and productive lives. Brown began his subsistence homestead project near Hightstown in Monmouth County, fourteen miles east of Trenton. It was called the Jersey Homesteads. Initially, Brown had the support of various Jewish charitable organizations and such prominent Jews as Albert Einstein. The New York families contributed $500 each, and the government built houses and schools and put in streets and utilities. In 1935 the Resettlement Administration (which became the Farm Security Administration in 1937) took over from Brown the administration and funding of the project. The Jersey Homesteads was one of ninety-nine communities created across the nation during the New Deal.[8]

Roy Stryker officially joined the staff of the Resettlement Administration in May 1935, but his contract was only for three months and no one knew whether his picture project would survive. By October, however, Stryker had been given the go-ahead by the administrator of the Resettlement Administration, Rexford Tugwell, and the photographic project commenced. A month later, Stryker sent Carl Mydans to document how the former urbanites were benefiting from government support for their new rural life. Mydans, Arthur Rothstein, and Walker Evans were Stryker's first full-time photographers. After he photographed the Jersey Homesteads in 1935, Mydans took another set of pictures in August 1936, shortly before he left the division. Arthur Rothstein photographed the Jersey Homesteads in May 1938, Russell Lee in November 1936, and Dorothea Lange in June 1936. The file contains hundreds of photographs of every aspect of the construction and programs of the Jewish experiment.

The Jersey Homesteads was a community of light industry and mixed agriculture. The settlers also planned to run a cooperative bakery, cannery, store, laundry, garage, and hospital. Shooting in both 35 mm and large-negative format, the Historical Section made pictures of new buildings, factory workers, and community leaders. They photographed the dairy and poultry farm, as well as the women's wear factory. Russell Lee and Dorothea Lange also traveled back to New York City to photograph the Lower East Side and the Bronx, where many of the applicants for resettlement had lived. Lange's captions express a feeling common among many New Dealers in 1935 that the government needed to support the construction of decent

7.3   Dorothea Lange, member of Jersey Homesteads cooperative asking, "Who says Jews can't farm?"
Hightstown, New Jersey, June 1936 (LC-USF34-009174-E)

housing for American workers and help them create a cooperative lifestyle of industrial and agricultural production. Rexford Tugwell, after a trip to the Soviet Union in 1927, became enthusiastic about the possibilities of collectivized farming and industrial planning. The Jersey Homesteads, along with other cooperative experiments, heralded an end to both the Depression and capitalism's evils. In one of her captions, Lange explained that the man in the picture was "accepted [as an] applicant for resettlement on the Hightstown project. Jewish-American. This man is already employed on the project as carpenter, working on the nearly completed first unit of thirty-five houses. He says, 'Will we succeed? Any people who will go through what we did—any people with such patience—will succeed.'"[9] Perhaps the most telling of Lange's photographs was of a farmer in a field of grass, his muscled arm placed confidently on his hip. She quotes him as saying, "Who says Jews can't farm?" (fig. 7.3).

Although almost everyone who settled in the Jersey Homesteads was Jewish, Judaism did not figure prominently in the photographs. Only Russell Lee showed the religious life of the community, making four pictures of a visiting rabbi teaching Hebrew to a small group of children (fig. 7.4). A permanent synagogue was not built until 1956. It was in no one's interest to photograph Jewish rituals or religious customs. After the government took over the funding and administration, it would have been politically unwise to advertise the fact that all of the settlers were Jews. The settlers themselves also had reasons not to want religion highlighted in the photographs. The New Yorkers who settled in the Jersey Homesteads had socialist leanings and understood their Jewishness primarily in ethnic and cultural terms. Religious commitments, rather than uniting the community, divided it. Those few who felt inclined to celebrate the holidays or pray together on the Sabbath gathered in homes.

The government succeeded in moving workers in the needle trade out of the city slums and sweatshops, but the transplants could not make the experiment work. Like most of the Jewish agricultural colonies founded a generation earlier, the Jersey Homesteads project proved not to be profitable. The cooperative factory was a failure and ceased operations in 1939. In July 1940 the government foreclosed its mortgage on the farmland. Only the food store remained a cooperative enterprise by the time Jack Delano was photographing farming Jews in Connecticut. The government was never able to recoup its investment, but the community changed and survived. Among its residents were two members of Stryker's staff. In 1936, after Ben Shahn and his wife, Bernarda, painted a mural of the history of the settlement for its elementary school, they decided to rent one of the worker's houses. They settled permanently in what later became Roosevelt, New Jersey. Eventually, they motivated the photo editor Edwin Rosskam and his wife, Louise, to join the colony of working-class Jews.

The photographs of the Jersey Homesteads have all of the hallmarks of the prewar New Deal attitude toward religion. By focusing on the cooperative work of the residents, the photog-

7.4   Russell Lee, visiting rabbi teaching Jewish children at Jersey Homesteads cooperative. Hightstown, New Jersey, November 1936 (LC-USF33-011049-M4)

raphers emphasized that what motivated the idealism and spirit of the Jersey Homesteads was not Judaism but socialism. The series presents as carpenters and farmers "Jewish-Americans," an ethnic identity just like that of "Italian-Americans" and "German-Americans." Rituals, theology, sacred history, religious laws — these were not important community markers as far as the photographers were concerned. Religion was superfluous in the process of remaking worker communities. The photographers could easily drop any reference to religious practices because the people they were photographing did not emphasize the significance of Jewish ritual in their lives. The residents of Jersey Homesteads were very much like the Jews who worked for Stryker. Carl Mydans, Arthur Rothstein, Ben Shahn, and Edwin Rosskam were secular Jews who as young men dreamed of having communal security not shackled by the evils of capitalism nor by the confines of ritual practices.

Who Says Jews Can't Farm?

There is no written evidence that Jack or Irene Delano saw or knew about the photographs of the New Jersey Homesteads, but there is no question that they would have found the idea of such a cooperative experiment exciting. Like the earlier photographers (with the exception of Walker Evans), Delano believed that showing Americans pictures of Americans would make for a better country. In 1939 Delano was a former art student who had been doing freelance photography. Hired by the WPA Federal Arts project to photograph folk art, he persuaded the agency to let him photograph Pennsylvania miners. He sent Stryker his pictures of unemployed coal miners with the hopes of getting his foot in the FSA door. "Sorry. No openings available," Stryker wrote back. "Do not give up hope. Read the following books." Delano kept persisting, and when Arthur Rothstein resigned to join *Look* magazine, Stryker hired him. Delano's philosophy of photography — later articulated in his autobiography — matched Stryker's. "To do justice to the subject has always been my main concern," Delano wrote, "Light, color, texture, and so on are, to me, important only as they contribute to the honest portrayal of what is in front of the camera, not as ends in themselves." In 1938 Delano had seen Walker Evans's photographic exhibit of Alabama sharecroppers at the Museum of Modern Art. Although he was "stunned by the simplicity, sureness, power, and grace of the images," he was also disappointed. The photographs were "too cool, precise, and emotionally aloof." Evans had produced "technically perfect, interesting specimens of humanity rather than human beings of flesh and blood and joys and sorrows." Delano and Stryker shared a common fascination: "My favorite subjects happen to be people," Delano explained simply, "and the world they have created."[10]

Delano's background was not radically different from that of many of the Jews he photographed in Colchester, except that he ended up in photography and they on a farm. Like them he was an eastern European Jew whose family had immigrated to a large American city. Born Jacob Ovcharov in 1914, he lived with his family in the Ukrainian town of Voroshilovka, a settlement the Nazis were to destroy during World War II. The village was typical of communities in the Pale of Settlement. "It had no electricity, no running water, no telephone," recalled Delano. "Its most characteristic feature was a long, dusty main street that ran to the marketplace, where we children could buy a pickled apple for a kopek. Merchants and tradesmen made up most of the population, and on market days the town would be filled with peasants coming from the countryside bringing in their produce."[11] Delano's parents were not typical shtetl Jews, however. His mother, Sonia, was a dentist who had graduated from St. Vladimir's University in Kiev. His father, Vladimir, taught Russian and mathematics in the village school and felt himself to be a part of the local intelligentsia. These were upper-class, educated Jews. As a child, Delano could remember only amicable relations between Christians and Jews, but his parents worried about the possibility of pogroms and what would happen to Russia after the Revolution. In 1923 the family moved to the United States, eventually settling in Philadelphia.

Like many immigrant Jews, the Ovcharov family was not particularly observant in their new homeland. Delano remembers receiving Christmas presents (one roller skate for each brother) and attending a summer camp run by Catholic charities. His autobiography never mentions celebrating Jewish holidays or having a Bar Mitzvah. Shortly before joining the FSA, Jacob Ovcharov officially changed his name, "with my parents' blessings," to Jack Delano. On the other hand, his parents belonged to the Workmen's Circle, a socialist Jewish fraternal organization that Delano credits with heightening his awareness of social injustice. In spite of the family's shaky financial situation, Delano and his brother studied art and violin; Delano's brother went on to become a concert violinist. In 1935, while studying at the Pennsylvania Academy of Fine Arts, Delano went on the Grand Tour to Europe and returned with a new love for contemporary art. "Cubism, abstract expressionism, surrealism," he recalled, "had changed my attitude toward the [art] academy. I began to rebel at what seemed to me the stodginess and old fashioned concepts that prevailed in all the classes."[12] As an eastern European Jew, Delano must have found elements of the Colchester community to be familiar, and yet in his correspondence with Stryker and in his memoirs he positions himself as an outsider. The Jews of Colchester were observant Jews and farmers, people with whom the Americanized Delano had little experience.

Even though these Jews did not resemble the Jews that Delano's family associated with in Philadelphia, he easily recognized a good picture story. By 1940 the FSA project had reached its fifth birthday, and the file was overflowing with pictures of farmland, farmers, and the problems of rural life. Delano had been employed with the agency only a few months, but he already was seeing how difficult it was to photograph "problems." After a while all problems looked the same. "I've found it necessary to consider carefully how to deal with similar problems in different localities without treating them in the same way," he wrote to Stryker. "Outwardly," Delano confessed, "they are often quite similar. A farm family in New York might look very much like a dairy farmer family in Connecticut."[13] For a young man raised in Philadelphia who enjoyed an urban bohemian lifestyle, a cow was a cow was a cow. How could someone who had almost no experience of rural life visually represent its problems in such a way as to capture the unique character of the local? What could he possibly photograph that would shed new light on the problems the FSA was trying to resolve while also provoking visual and cultural interest? How could a twenty-six-year-old barely out of art school make pictures that could compare with those of Dorothea Lange, Walker Evans, and Russell Lee?

The Colchester Jews proved an excellent photo opportunity for Delano because they provided a unique angle on the generalized problem of the part-time New England farmer.

They were simultaneously representative of, and not representative of, rural Connecticut. As farmers who also worked in factories, they struggled with the land and their animals while also facing the tedium of industrial life. They suffered the economic woes of the Depression but were not as downtrodden as southern sharecroppers, who had become a visual cliché by the forties. Most important, these Jews had a synagogue, a Hebrew school, and a rabbi—all of which could be photographed to illustrate the diversity of religious life in America. As John Collier found in New Mexico, religions had distinctly material sides that lent themselves to photography.

Perhaps in order to emphasize the religious angle and free himself from making still one more picture of a field and farmer on a rainy day, Delano downplayed the agricultural activities of the Colchester residents. Only one photograph shows a Jew on his farm with his animals (see fig. 7.1). Delano's caption explains that Abraham Lapping and his wife run a small poultry and dairy farm and take in tourists during the summer. From other sources we know that Lapping and his wife, Anna, were both born in Latvia. As with many of Colchester's farmers, they had first settled in New York, where Anna worked in a millinery factory. Abraham, however, could not adapt to city life and "spent his days reading, studying [the Torah], and yearning for his own piece of land." In 1918 the Lappings moved to Colchester and purchased their farm. Many years later, Delano still remembered his meeting with Abraham Lapping, "a tall, white-haired, long-bearded Jewish farmer wearing a skullcap and looking for all the world like a biblical prophet, tilling his field behind a horse-drawn plough." [14]

Delano, however, did not photograph Lapping tilling the field or, more realistically, attending his chickens. By 1940 poultry farming was the major cash producing agricultural activity for Colchester Jews. Poultry farming, in Connecticut and more prominently in New Jersey, provided rural Jews a sustainable income. Unlike other forms of farming, raising chickens demanded only small plots of land with little start-up capital. Both the slaughtered chickens and their eggs could be sold, so income could be realized almost immediately. Droughts and storms were not as problematic as with dirt farming, and the physical labor not as back-breaking. Not knowing much about rural life, and certainly nothing about Jewish farming, Delano did not understand the significance of the chicken. Delano, who confessed that he had "trouble with chickens," thought raising poultry was akin to establishing a "factory for the manufacture of potential chicken pies." [15] Milking cows must have seemed the quintessential farming activity for a "biblical prophet," so he pictured Lapping standing in front of his cows carrying two pails of fresh milk. Jews who farmed with cows possessed a charming, romantic quality that linked them to the Jeffersonian spirit of the yeoman farmer, in contrast with the industrial nature of chicken factories.

In a photograph more characteristic of his Colchester series, Delano positioned Abraham and Anna under the watchful eyes of their ancestors, reading a Yiddish newspaper (fig. 7.5). Rather than show them struggling with rocky soil and unruly chickens, he photographed the Lappings in their comfortable farm home enjoying their leisure time. Given Delano's own family background, reading newspapers probably seemed like a good Jewish activity to com-

7.5 (facing page)   Jack Delano, Abraham Lapping and his wife, Anna, reading Yiddish newspaper. Colchester, Connecticut, November 1940 (LC-USF34-042320-D)

7.6   Jack Delano, junk dealer Jacob Kalmanowitz outside a store. Colchester, Connecticut,
November 1940 (LC-USF33-020697-M1)

plement milking cows. Delano also focused on the many Jewish-owned businesses in the town center. In his general caption to the series, he mentioned the existence of a Jewish general store, saddle maker, feed store, lumberyard, coat and dress factories, shoemaker, tavern, restaurants, and professional offices. One of his more compelling portraits of the town center is tersely captioned "Outside a Jewish store." When I showed a copy of the picture to seniors in Colchester, they quickly recognized Jacob Kalmanowitz, town junk dealer, resting on a bench (fig. 7.6). The photograph captures the feel of a small town, avoids the problem of the unglamorous nature of poultry farming, but still has an air of Depression dreariness.[16]

Delano may have been looking for evidence of the small-town character of Colchester because Roy Stryker had been encouraging his photographers to create photo-essays of American communities. Russell Lee had photographed Pie Town, New Mexico, in June 1940. His photographs of a community sing and a square dance stressed the vibrancy of the small town. When the photographs were displayed at the town fair a year later, one citizen wrote, "The pix you sent are certainly appreciated by the community." In San Francisco the prominent photographer Ansel Adams was directing "A Pageant of Photography," and he wanted a series of photographs on "The American Small Town." Adams had not always been a supporter of the FSA photographic project. His comment to Stryker—"What you've got are not photographers but a bunch of sociologists with cameras"—privileged his own artistic orientation over the FSA's documentary goals. In April 1940, however, he needed pictures for the Golden Gate International Exhibition. Edwin Rosskam, who was organizing the file for the Historical Section, sent Adams a selection of prints. Rosskam also chose the images from the FSA file to illustrate Sherwood Anderson's *Home Town*. Colchester provided an unusual and original angle on life in small-town America. Here was a Jewish small town that had a Jewish mayor, justice of the peace, and president of the school board. On Saturdays the town was as quiet as a Sunday in any New England village, and on Jewish holidays the public schools closed. Just as Jewish poultry farmers lent specificity to the generalized problem of part-time farmers, Jewish Colchester gave a twist to small-town life.[17]

Delano captured the small-town feel of Colchester in the picture he captioned "Having a beer in 'Art's Sportsman's Tavern'" (fig. 7.7). "Art" was Arthur Zupnick, who had moved to Colchester in 1931 when he was twenty-one. His father was a kosher butcher from Russia, and his mother was Hungarian, but Zupnick had been born in New York City. After marrying in 1933, he and his wife ran the tavern from 1935 until 1955. They offered a ten-cent glass of beer and a place for idle chat. "I used to do a fairly good business," Zupnick told an interviewer in 1986. "The farmers used to be there in the winter because they didn't have anything to do

7.7   Jack Delano, men chatting in Art's Sportsman's Tavern. Colchester, Connecticut, November 1940 (LC-USF34-042315-D)

after milking."[18] Both Zupnick and his wife remembered Delano's visit. They also knew that one of Delano's tavern pictures was published during the war in the military newspaper *Stars and Stripes,* and another was displayed in 1942 at the Museum of Modern Art as a part of the "Road to Victory" exhibition. The photographs of Sportsman's Tavern celebrated male camaraderie and the reintegration of drinking into American culture after the end of Prohibition. Jewish men—like men all across the nation—drank beer, talked sports, and listened to the radio. Like John Collier's picture of a PTA meeting in New Mexico, the flag gives the scene a patriotic air. On the other hand, the giant beer bottles and the rifle save it from being sentimental. With a touch of humor, Delano shows that the American Way of Life includes the freedom to enjoy one's leisure time.

Colchester, however, was not merely a small town made up of farmers. As with the Jersey Homesteads, this New England farming community needed the income from industrial activities. Jews worked at the Levine and Levine factory making tweed coats. During the 1930s and 1940s Colchester also had dress and leather factories. David Adler, who was born in 1913 in New York City, remembered that garments were made seven or eight months out of the year; the rest of the time workers were laid off. Adler's wife, Ruth, who was born the same year in Colchester, recalled that in the 1930s she worked a fifty-four-hour week in a dress factory and earned twenty cents per hour. The work was tedious, and frequently after the factory work was over, the farm chores began. Delano captured the intensity of the factory work in his photographs but expressed none of the exhaustion and boredom that accompanied industrial life.[19]

Had Delano been satisfied with the usual pictures of people at work and leisure, he would have duplicated what most of the FSA photographers saw in American towns, including the Jersey Homesteads. Colchester's citizens, however, were practicing Orthodox Jews who by 1940 had established religious organizations that were successful in meeting the spiritual and social needs of the community. Unlike Jews in New York, who either slowly slipped in and out of religious practice or defiantly cultivated a secular perspective on their Jewishness, the Jews of Colchester had a different attitude toward Judaism. Rather than finding religious life confining, old-fashioned, and un-American, they actively engaged with their spiritual traditions. A small community that held the upper hand in town life, Colchester's Jewish families kept control over religious expressions and the pace of acculturation. In November 1940 the community was stable and the religious rhythms of Judaism seemed natural and comfortable.

When Jews began arriving in Colchester at the end of the nineteenth century, their first concern was not to build a place for worship. Although communal worship is important, Jews can conduct their religious rituals at home or in rented spaces. So there was no pressing reason to spend the time and money building a synagogue. Of more immediate concern was the proper burial of the dead. In 1893, fifteen men established the Love of Brotherhood (Ahavath Achim) Cemetery Association in order to purchase land for a cemetery, which they did a year later. By 1898 the Love of Brotherhood Cemetery Association had evolved into Congregation Ahavath Achim, holding regular services in the home of Hirsch Cohen and High Holidays celebrations in the Grange Hall. Farmers who could not walk to town organized minyanim (the minimum ten men for prayer) at neighbors' homes. As the community grew, a larger building was needed, so in 1902 Hyman Mintz donated a house on Windham Avenue for use as a

7.8   Jack Delano, men entering synagogue for afternoon prayer. Colchester, Connecticut,
November 1940 (LC-USF33-020701-M2)

synagogue, calling it Pische Tshuvah (Beginning of repentance). The Jews of Colchester were
delaying synagogue construction until the community had the resources to purchase land and
construct a building. It was only when an even larger building was needed that disputes in
the community began over where to place the new synagogue and what to call it. When a new
synagogue was finally built in 1913 as a compromise between contending families, it carried the
combination name of Ahavath Achim Upische Tshuvah (Love of brotherhood and beginning
of repentance).

Delano's photographs of Colchester's synagogue present it as a simple house of prayer
(fig. 7.8). The community had built a one-level wooden structure in a Gothic Revival style.
Decorative ironwork fencing also gave the synagogue a Victorian flavor that enabled it to blend
into the New England ecclesiastical landscape. The synagogue's architecture harmonized with
the modest nature of the community and provided a place of prayer for those people living
close to the town center. The design of the building did not make a statement about Jewish
political power or serve as a challenging piece of art. It did not try to provide a place for Jews
to learn about "Jewish civilization" or to engage in activities other than prayer. Unlike Reform

Jews, who sought to broaden the role of the synagogue, Orthodox Jews used the building more selectively. Delano underlined the unpretentious character of the synagogue by downplaying its architectural features and focusing only on its function as a place of worship.

After the new synagogue was built, some families continued to hold services in their homes. Bernice Abrams, whose family ran a dairy and chicken farm on 150 acres of land, recalled that her uncle gave her family a Torah, and "our Jewish neighbors worshipped in our house on all the holidays." She explained to an interviewer, "We had engaged a rabbi, Rabbi Solomon, a very Orthodox man, who would stay at our house. I can still see them dancing on Shemini Atzeres and Simchas Torah and Purim and all the gay holidays. My mother would do all the cooking. . . . Those who couldn't walk home would sleep at our house."[20] The rhythms of Jewish life were rooted in the yearly celebrations in which the whole community participated. The synagogue was a convenient place for assembling, but it was not a powerful institutional force within the community. The Colchester Jews continued to use their homes as ritual centers, and the synagogue was first and foremost a building.

Unlike their cousins in New York, who may have acculturated too well to America's secularized culture, the Jews of Colchester were maintaining their traditions. They were first generation Americans who were still conversant with the rituals and rhythms of Judaism. Even at midday some men took time out from their farming or businesses to attend to their obligations as pious Jews. Wives still sat separate from their husbands in the women's gallery at the synagogue. Delano took considerable trouble to photograph a group of Colchester men assembled for afternoon *(mincha)* prayer in the synagogue. Since he was in town only for the day, Delano had to find out quickly who could give him permission to photograph and then counter the concerns of the community leaders. "I've never seen such buck-passing in all my life!" he wrote to Stryker. "The main objection seemed to be that only a few people attended the weekday service and the rabbi feared that it wouldn't make a good impression in a photograph. Now, if I could come on Saturday, there would be a whole crowd there—but of course they wouldn't permit me to take any pictures on the *Sabbath!!*"[21] Since photography was rabbinically defined as work, it would not be permitted in the synagogue on the day of rest. Delano persevered and photographed afternoon prayers from several places in the building, including the women's gallery. He recorded the men entering the shul, conducting the service, and visiting afterward (figs. 7.9, 7.10). The pictures show that Colchester's synagogue followed the traditional style of *bimah* placement. Seating positions in the front of the synagogue were considered a great honor for men and were purchased by the town's influential families.[22] The women sat upstairs in their own space.

Unlike other FSA photographers, who did not seem to mind being restricted to photographing church exteriors, Delano did not give in to the "buck-passing" of the community leaders. Both he and the Colchester congregation wanted to demonstrate that the community had an active religious life, that members were not merely poultry farmers and factory workers. Delano's photographs stress the importance of the synagogue as a place for people to worship. The synagogue is presented not as a form of folk art but as a building for communal religious practices.

Since Jewish public worship in Colchester was sex-segregated, the synagogue photographs were unusable as examples of an "American" worship style that reflected the "univer-

7.9   Jack Delano, men during afternoon prayer photographed from women's gallery.
Colchester, Connecticut, November 1940 (LC-USF34-042243-D)

7.10   Jack Delano, men talking in the synagogue after afternoon prayer. Colchester, Connecticut,
November 1940 (LC-USF34-042338-D)

sal" spirit of prayer. By 1940 the "family pew" perspective of Christians had been universalized in visual culture to the point that representing prayer as being conducted only by men would have seemed somehow "unnatural." Prayer and worship, in order to be useful for the government, had to involve all the members of American society — children and adults, men and women. By photographing afternoon prayer in the synagogue, Delano presented the town's ritual life as dominated by men. It would have been next to impossible for Delano to go to any other New England town and find men praying without women present. Even in a Catholic church, which might sponsor men's sodalities or even special times for men to attend confession apart from women, the chances of finding pews without women sitting in them would be slim. Delano's pictures depart in a significant way from representations of communal prayer taken in Christian contexts. Leisure, however, was still acceptably sex-segregated in the 1940s. A picture of Jewish men chatting in a bar could be used in the Museum of Modern Art's 1942 exhibition "The Road to Victory" because women in the forties were not expected to be whiling away a rainy afternoon drinking beer. Sex-segregated leisure activities could still be read as "American" and not "Jewish." Viewers might wonder why two of the men were wearing hats indoors, but even those do not mark the picture as "Jewish." Orthodox worship, however, still looked too exotic to be universalized.

The Jews of Colchester continued the traditional separation of men from women in worship and the gathering of men for daily prayer at the synagogue. But as if to make a statement that in the future women and girls would play a more visible role in American Judaism, Delano composed a careful portrait of a girl copying her lesson (fig. 7.11). Delano used children to represent the lively continuation of the religious community in a way similar to Collier's representation of New Mexican Boy Scouts. Delano's photographs are captioned "Hebrew school" and show children intently studying. Colchester's seniors recalled that both boys and girls were expected to assemble in the afternoons to study Hebrew and learn Jewish history and rituals. Their Hebrew school was a variation of the traditional Talmud Torah school that passed on the language and meaning of the Scriptures to the next generation.

In Colchester, however, children attended Hebrew school as a supplement to their public school education and a sign of their Jewish commitments. Boys and girls studied both Hebrew and Yiddish. Delano probably posed the girl but may not have known she was practicing writing a Yiddish poem. Primarily designed for elementary school children, Colchester's Hebrew school tried to transmit a complex body of knowledge in a limited amount of time. Ruth Adler, who went to Hebrew school in the 1920s, recalled that she spent a little more than an hour, five times a week, learning to "read Hebrew and study the Bible." While she might not have been serious about her studies, she did attend classes. Colchester differed from urban New York City, where a 1929 study revealed that almost 80 percent of its Jewish children received no formal religious training whatsoever and had never learned the Hebrew alphabet.[23] In Colchester, Jewish education was a part of community life.

Delano's photographs of the Hebrew school show rows of boys and girls with their books

7.11   Jack Delano, girl studying Yiddish text in Hebrew school. Colchester, Connecticut, November 1940 (LC-USF34-042454-D)

opened wide on their desks. Their eyes are fixed on the texts before them, and they obviously have been told not to pay attention to the classroom visitor (fig. 7.12). In a picture that is compositionally similar to the one taken of Abraham and Anna Lapping, Delano arranges his shot to show two boys studying under the watchful portrait of a learned rabbi. Delano used the sentimental convention of combining the old with the new, the wise with the youthful, in order to emphasize the continuity of tradition. In other photographs, boys practice their Hebrew letters on the blackboard. By showing the diligence of the students as they study Hebrew, Delano acknowledged the scriptural traditions of Judaism. Like Catholic altar boys learning Latin, Jewish boys also studied the language of their faith. At the same time Hebrew was a secular language that was being promoted as the language of Palestine. Only an insider would notice that some of the children were actually reading Yiddish texts, which use Hebrew letters.[24]

Photographing children illustrated the positive future of the Jewish community in America, a theme that would sit well both with Colchester's Jews and with the political aims of the FSA Historical Division. Delano's photographs of Colchester were taken at the same time that Jewish communities throughout Europe were being destroyed. From the beginning of Hitler's rise to power, Jewish publications had documented the systematic attack on Jews. Even *Life* magazine in April 1938 ran a picture story on "the Jews" that showed contemporary persecutions in Germany, Austria, Poland, and Rumania. From various sources American Jews learned of the removal of Jews from professional and commercial life, the revocation of their civil rights, and the confiscation of their property. By 1940 American Jews knew of forced emigration, slave labor, mass arrests, and executions. That year *The American Jewish Yearbook* reported that the Nazis had established a Jewish "reservation" in the area of Lublin, Poland.[25] Images of children in Colchester busily studying Hebrew demonstrated the desire and ability of American Jews to socialize the next generation. Delano probably was aware of the propagandistic possibilities of photographs of healthy, happy, Jewish children studying literature. No religious community would be able to flourish unless the world was made safe for democracy.

For Jews, however, America was not the only hope for Jewish survival. As the situation in Europe became more and more threatening, American Jews came to believe that Palestine could provide both a refuge and a Jewish cultural center. During the thirties, Zionism acted as a central focus in American synagogue life, educational curricula, and popular sentiment. Young people were especially open to the idealism of the Zionist message, which combined a socialist spirit with a program for economic justice. Among Jewish educators Zionism served as a tool for Jewish renewal.[26] Colchester's educators participated in this trend, and Delano photographed two boys "studying a map of Palestine" (fig. 7.13). Zionist commitments, however, did not require Jews to relocate to Palestine. Zionism was a social and cultural ideology that solidified Jewish identity but did not detract from American patriotism.

In 1922 Henrietta Szold visited Colchester and helped set up a Hadassah chapter for women to support Palestine. That same year a small community center, which was to house the Hebrew school, was built and named Zion Hall. Bernie Goldberg remembers that his father,

7.12 (facing page)   Jack Delano, boys studying texts in Hebrew school. Colchester, Connecticut, November 1940 (LC-USF34-042457-D)

7.13   Jack Delano, boy pointing at a map of Palestine in Hebrew school. Colchester, Connecticut,
November 1940 (LC-USF34-042567-D)

7.14   Jack Delano, Rabbi Golinsky teaching in Hebrew school. Colchester, Connecticut, November 1940 (LC-USF34-042575-D)

the mayor and *shochet* (a slaughterer who prepared kosher meat), was active in Zionist causes. "You know," he told an interviewer, "my father was not only a Zionist and a Jew and a Eretz Israelnik and all those things, but he was an American."[27] For Jews in Colchester as elsewhere, Zionism and American patriotism were not mutually exclusive.

It is among the photographs of the Hebrew school that we see a glimpse of Colchester's rabbi (fig. 7.14). Delano's photographs of the rabbi illustrate his limited role in the community. According to Delano's captions, the rabbi was the instructor of the Hebrew school, but there is no mention of his name or any of his other duties. When I showed the rabbi's picture to older members of the community, his name did not immediately come to them. They knew the names of the prominent men and even the name of the junk dealer, but the rabbi . . . they were unsure. Synagogue records do not list the names of past rabbis. Eventually the seniors decided that the rabbi's name might be Galinsky. In an interview conducted in 1986, Edward Scott mentioned that the first rabbi the community hired who lived in the town came in the 1930s. His name was Golinsky.[28] Delano's photograph of Rabbi Golinsky presents him sitting at the front of his classroom of students, looking downward at the books and papers lying across his desk. This rabbi is not represented as either a community leader, judge of legal disputes, or ritual expert. Rabbi Golinsky is portrayed as one trained in the language and meaning of Jewish texts. This, of course, would be held in high esteem—at least symbolically—by the community. But given that Colchester's Hebrew school was an afternoon extracurricular activity primarily set up to prepare boys for their Bar Mitzvah, placing the rabbi in that environment limited his prestige. Delano did not photograph him studying Torah or preparing his weekly sermon. While the rabbi may have been much more active in the community than we see in the photographs, he apparently did not resist Delano's desire to portray him as a teacher of young Jews.

If we compare the photograph of Rabbi Golinsky with that of another Colchester resident, we can see more clearly where the power in the community resided. While education was certainly valued in Colchester, there is no question that Leon Broder's portrait shows him to be more influential than the rabbi (fig. 7.15). Leon Broder (né Brodsky) came to Colchester in 1906 as a young man and eventually established a large feed and supply store that sold grain, lumber, and farm goods to the area's farmers. Broder was a member of a triumvirate of synagogue leaders, along with the owners of Colchester's factories, Ike Cohen and Harry Levine.[29] He is among the men at afternoon prayer. In 1940 his son Morris was the chairman of the school board. Leon Broder, whom Delano called "one of the leading Jewish citizens," is pictured as friendly but busy. Delano photographed him looking directly at the camera, as if he is chatting with a prospective customer. Pencil in hand, Broder commands the center of the photograph with his face. Unlike Golinsky, who gazes downward at his books, Broder looks outward. Broder sits alone in his own office surrounded by his business memos, calendars, and papers while Golinsky sits in Zion Hall surrounded by children. Considering that Delano only spent one day in Colchester, he had no trouble finding the most powerful man in town.

Laymen led the Jewish community of Colchester. As with all Jewish congregations, the rabbi was hired and fired by the synagogue board. In the case of Colchester the rabbi was not in a position to divert power from influential lay leaders. For much of Colchester's history, rabbis and cantors were retained on temporary contracts to conduct holiday rituals or tutor children. Unlike the townspeople, rabbis came and went, so they had no long-term connection to the community or its problems. If the congregation had economic problems, its members could fire the rabbi and go back to conducting services themselves or hiring part-time rabbis. Not until after the war did conflicts between families and changing notions of Jewish life become serious enough to cause a division in the synagogue. In the 1950s dissension among residents in Colchester required the mediating force of a rabbi. But in November 1940 community authority rested in the hands of a small number of families.

Jack Delano's photographs of Colchester reveal a community that had not yet experienced the social and religious divisions typical of larger, urban communities of Jews. During the thirties many rabbis in New York felt that the Jewish community was undergoing a "spiritual depression" in addition to an economic depression. Eastern European Jews, who had brought Orthodox traditions to America, were having a difficult time passing on their language and religious habits to their children. In order to capture the interest of the Americanized children of the immigrants, Reform rabbis began to create multipurpose Jewish community centers that went beyond the ritual and teaching activities of the traditional synagogue. The "shul

7.15 (facing page)   Jack Delano, Leon Broder in his office. Colchester, Connecticut, November 1940 (LC-USF34-042580-D)

with a pool" sought to provide a social and cultural focus for Jewish life.[30] Jewish synagogue-centers attempted to provide social alternatives that would give their members alternates to the home, the street, or the movie house.

As Orthodox worship became more formalized, cantors were hired and rabbis became more numerous. Over the years, the rabbinate had professionalized, and rabbis took on more and more pastoral and administrative responsibilities. This institution building that had been enthusiastically undertaken in the prosperous 1920s came to a halt with the crash of the stock market. Families who felt the pressures of unemployment let their membership fees lapse, and synagogue income declined. The "modern" rabbi was left with the burden of sustaining or re-creating some kind of Jewish community during a period of economic depression. Consequently, it is not surprising that many rabbis in New York and other cities were concerned about the future vitality of American Judaism.[31]

From the perspective of Colchester, however, the picture was not so gloomy. These Jews were successfully maintaining their religious traditions while constructing themselves as efficient businessmen, productive farmers, and industrious (if underpaid) factory workers. Disputes did not divide the community. There were no alternative Jewish organizations to compete with village traditions. Acculturation occurred, but at a pace with which the people could cope. The synagogue and community center were firmly under the control of laymen who knew the limits of the community's finances and understood its social and religious needs. Even though the Jewish share of the population had declined to 25 percent, Colchester was a decidedly Jewish town. Unlike the Jews of New York, who struggled with identity and economic issues, the Colchester Jews benefited from their historical dominance and enjoyed cultural and religious stability.

This is not to say that the residents were unaware of the ritual, psychological, and social disputes that shaped Jewish life in cities like New York. Since Delano photographed in November, he missed filming Colchester's third major "industry"—tourism. Situated only two hours by train from New York City, Colchester was known as the "Connecticut Catskills." During the twenties and thirties Jewish families from New York took up residence for the summer in the farms and boarding houses of Colchester. Delano's caption for his photograph of Abraham and Anna Lapping mentions that they took in summer boarders. Farmers moved their children out of their rooms and rented every available space to paying guests. Enterprising Colchester residents built hotels and boarding houses to accommodate the Jews from the city. While the increased population provided hardships to those who had to share kitchens and bedrooms, the tourists enthusiastically bought the farmers' fresh produce, eggs, and dairy products, bringing cash into the community. Even during the difficult days of the Depression, Colchester residents remember the interactions between themselves and the visitors. Bernie Goldberg reported that his parents first met during the summer when his mother, who was working in New York, came to vacation at his father's family's farm.[32] One reason that Colchester was able to flourish—financially and socially—in rural Connecticut was this constant interaction with the urban Jews of New York. Unlike those in other rural communities, Colchester residents were not isolated from the ideas, conflicts, and culture of city Jews. Colchester Jews most likely enjoyed the stimulation of their New York summer visitors, but they were different from their big city relatives.

7.16   Jack Delano, Armistice Day parade. Colchester, Connecticut, November 1940
(LC-USF33-020714-M5)

Jews as Jews

Jack Delano arrived in Colchester as its citizens were celebrating Armistice Day, the end of
World War I. They had assembled on the town green and, carrying American flags and beat-
ing on drums, paraded down Main Street (fig. 7.16). One who saw only these photographs
of the town might have concluded that this was merely one more New England village demonstrating its Yankee patriotism. And to a certain extent this was true. Colchester's residents
understood themselves to be part of small-town America, where industrious citizens worked
in factories and farms. Like other Americans, their men socialized in local taverns and their
children dutifully studied their books. Businessmen looked serious but could take time out
for prayer and reflection. Times could be difficult, but with hard work and a little luck one
could succeed.

This perspective on Colchester could go only so far. In the context of violent anti-Semitism
in Europe and the war buildup in the United States, it became unthinkable to represent the
Jews of Colchester as assimilated Yankees. In 1935 it fit the agenda of the government to present
the settlers of the Jersey Homesteads as only ethnically Jewish. This representation harmonized with the self-perception of the Jews who staffed the factories and plowed in the fields. It
also was in keeping with the sensibilities of the Jewish photographers who took the pictures.
What was important during a period of economic experimentation was to document the will-
ingness of Americans to trade life in the sweatshop and slum for a cooperative community in
the country. By 1940, however, portraying Jews in photographs to look exactly like other rural
Connecticut farmers would have tacitly conceded the disappearance of Jewish life in America.

7.17   Jack Delano, synagogue that serves fifteen Jewish families. Near Newton, Connecticut,
September 1940 (LC-USF34-041885-D)

Emphasizing acculturation and assimilation would be an American version of Hitler's wish to make the Jews "disappear"—more benign, certainly, but devastating in its own way. Neither Delano nor Stryker would have been satisfied with that depiction. Portraying economic innovation was no longer the overriding point of the photographic project. The Colchester Jews had to be Jews and not Yankees because it was imperative that America be presented as a place where religious minorities not only survived but flourished.

Key to emphasizing the pluralism of democratic America was acknowledging both the universality of faith and the variance in religious practices. Delano represented Colchester Jews as having a religion that would make sense to the Christian majority in 1940. Jews worship in a particular space, they pray, and they socialize their children into their traditions. The photographs take structures common to Christian practice and present them as universal characteristics of religion. Delano did not, however, ignore the substantial differences that separated the Judaism of Colchester's citizens from the Christianity of other Americans. He photographed inside of the synagogue, illustrating that Jewish ritual space looked different, even if the synagogue's exterior was designed to look like a Gothic church. Men, not women, were conducting a midday prayer, and there were no clergy in sight. In nearby Newton, he photographed a small synagogue with a large Star of David (fig. 7.17). While there are many FSA/OWI photographs of ministers and priests, only Rabbi Golinsky's portrait stresses the intellectual duties of a religious leader. Christian women were frequently photographed leading Sunday school but never at a desk surrounded by books and papers. Delano made pictures that, on one hand, supported a universal, humanistic understanding of the common elements of religion and, on the other, illustrated the unique characters of Orthodox Judaism as practiced by Connecticut's farmers and businessmen.

Unlike Collier, who seemed uncomfortable with the devotional lives of Catholic parishioners and preferred to photograph the social activism of their priests or the beauty of their Colonial churches, Delano moved easily between synagogue and factory, home and Hebrew school. While this might be due to his own childhood in a Jewish village, it also may be because of the stability of the community. Colchester was a Jewish community that happened to hire a rabbi named Golinsky, and Delano did not try to see religious life through his eyes. If anything, Delano used the eyes of Leon Broder to evaluate Jewish life in the village. While Rabbi Golinsky—like the rabbis in New York—may have had a negative opinion about the education and observance of the children he taught and the parents he interacted with, the congregation evidently thought that they were "good Jews."

Delano's photographs, the history of the community, and memories of some of its residents all indicate that in Colchester a spiritual depression did not occur in the thirties. In spite of a declining population, the period before America's entry into the war may actually have been the apex of Jewish life in Colchester. By the late thirties, the war in Europe caused an expansion of agricultural production and thus an increase in farm income. Sons were not yet being called away to fight, and daughters were still being courted by city Jews who came for summer holidays. The religious disputes that motivated the proliferation of synagogues in both urban and rural settlements did not occur in Colchester.[33] From the twenties through the forties, Jewish life was under the control of its long-term residents, who moderated its change and strove for communal unity. They shared a set of religious values and exerted control over the institutional aspects of their faith. Cultural change and institutional expansion did happen, but on a reasonable scale and at a pace that the community could manage. Delano's photographs, although certainly shaped by his own need to provide a positive picture of minority culture in America, actually do reflect a community without major cultural and religious divisions. Only in the fifties did Colchester experience the divisions that plagued many urban Jewish communities in the twenties and thirties.

... out of our deepest need
we have built the Negro Church

8
The Negro Church

F or weeks the churches on the South Side were gearing up to celebrate the Resurrection of Christ. Bethel African Methodist Episcopal Church had presented
its eleventh annual Palm Sunday "musicale," featuring their hundred-voice
choir singing Sir John Stainer's "Crucifixion." Opera singer Marian Anderson
had performed at Chicago's Auditorium Theater for the benefit of the Good
Shepherd Community Center. The children were busy preparing for the Bud
Billiken Easter music festival sponsored by the city's African-American newspaper, the *Defender*. Many churches had held fund-raising fashion shows of spring finery, and everyone was
trying to gather the appropriate clothing for the special day. Advertisements in the *Defender*
announced that Count Basie would be coming to town, and indeed, the Easter Sunday dance
drew record numbers to the Savoy ballroom. As it turned out, April 13, 1941, was a scorcher,
with the temperature setting an all-time Easter record high of 82.2 degrees.[1]

8.1 (facing page)   *Negroes and the War,* np (LC-USF34-044013-D)

For many Americans, Easter Sunday is one of the few days of the year that they go to church. Even those who are not religious know that Easter is a special day for Christians. Such was the case with Russell Lee and Edwin Rosskam, who were in Chicago for two weeks taking pictures of African Americans living on Chicago's South Side. They must have felt the excitement in the community as they moved from church to church photographing religious life on Easter day. The pair began the day at a Church of God in Christ congregation, where they took pictures before the worship service.[2] They then moved down the street to catch Elder Lucy Smith preaching at All Nations Pentecostal Church. By the time they got to St. Edmund's Episcopal Church, the mass was over and the choir had begun the recessional. The photographers' last stop was Pilgrim Baptist, where they arrived in time only to take pictures of worshipers leaving the church. Since most Protestants have their services at eleven o'clock on Sunday morning, Lee and Rosskam had to dash between churches to catch this glimpse of ritual life in Chicago's "Black Belt." One can only hope that they enjoyed a good Easter lunch after the demanding morning was over.

Edwin Rosskam, Russell Lee, and Lee's wife, Jean, had come to Chicago on specific assignment. They were to take pictures of African-American life in the urban North to supplement the file's portrait of rural life in the South. The impetus behind the trip came from a project that Rosskam was coordinating with the black novelist Richard Wright. The pair had agreed to create a book that would tell the story of African Americans as they were transformed from slaves to sharecroppers to urban proletarians. Wright explained shortly after the publication of *12 Million Black Voices: A Folk History of the Negro in the United States* that the book combined words and images to document that "the development of Negro life in America parallels the development of people everywhere."[3] For Wright, and indeed for anyone who sought to comment on "that which is qualitative and abiding in Negro experience," black Christian practices required attention.[4] Of the eighty-seven photographs chosen for the book, almost one in ten was an illustration of religion.[5] There is no evidence that Wright accompanied Rosskam and Lee on their photographic expeditions, but for Lee and Rosskam, what better day to experience black Christianity in Chicago than by photographing church life on Easter Sunday morning?

12 Million Black Voices was widely read when it was published that autumn. Its text clearly acknowledged the Farm Security Administration, and Richard Wright specifically thanked Roy Stryker for his "never-failing interest, courtesy, and co-operation" (149). Credits at the end of the book listed the individual FSA photographers responsible for the illustrations. In spite of this, the photographs have been consistently misattributed or ignored by reviewers and scholars. Richard Wright's prominence as an African-American writer has drawn attention to the text of *12 Million Black Voices,* but there has been almost no analysis of how his narrative of black life relates to the book's illustrations.[6] Wright's discussion of African-American religion, however, demonstrates that there can be a complex relationship between text and image. Although there are only eight illustrations of religious practices, a close analysis of the way that *12 Million Black Voices* represents black Christianity provides insight into how modernist writers and photographers represented the "Negro church." The Chicago photographs — more than other pictures of religious behavior in the file — were defined by a clearly articulated ideology that shaped which congregations would be photographed, what would be photographed, and which pictures would make it into print. *12 Million Black Voices* offers a unique opportunity to see how the FSA photographs of religion were used.

The visual and literary complexity of religion in *12 Million Black Voices* reflects Wright's own ambiguous relationship with the religion that was echoed in the writings of many post–World War I black intellectuals. As a child, Richard Wright felt the harsh and restrictive character of his family's Seventh-day Adventist faith. Like many artists and writers, his early experience of religious abuse led him to reject the church community. Wright's desire to free himself from the restrictive world of his Seventh-day Adventist family parallels the experience of other black modernists who criticized African-American Christianity. In the last two chapters of *The Negro's God* (1938), Benjamin Mays, then the dean of the School of Religion of Howard University, summarized their discontent: Uneducated preachers distracted their congregations from altering their social situation and offered them heavenly promises instead. Church life may have given people the strength to endure, but it did not show them how to rid themselves of what they had to endure. White people supported the black church because they knew that it kept social revolution at bay. While older intellectuals like W. E. B. Dubois and Carter Woodson may have held out some hope that the churches could direct their attention toward Christian social activism, a younger generation of poets and writers rejected both Church and God. If God existed at all, he must be a sadistic God of white people. "A man was lynched last night," wrote the poet Countee Cullen. "God, if He was, kept to His skies / And left us to our enemies." Echoed the novelist Nella Larsen: "God must laugh at the great joke He had played on them!" Langston Hughes brashly summarized these sentiments in 1932 in "Good-bye Christ":

> Listen, Christ
> You did all right in your day I reckon
> But that day's gone now
>
> .   .   .   .
>
> Make way for a new guy with no religion at all.
> A real guy named
> Marx Communist Lenin Peasant Stalin
> Worker ME —
> I said, ME.[7]

Given the sentiments of his generation of writers, Richard Wright could have sharply criticized religion in *12 Million Black Voices*.

But Richard Wright could not simply turn away from his religious roots. Nor could he have left Christianity out of a "folk history." Wright knew on an intimate level the power of religion to control the individual while simultaneously transporting the believer into a supernatural world rich with images. The vivid images contained in the Adventist plan of salvation stimulated the imagination of the young writer and introduced him into a creative, imaginary world. The religious language of Seventh-day Adventists, initially articulated by the prophet Ellen G. White and then elaborated on by generations of Adventist elders, was one not of dispassionate theology but of storytelling. Wright was well aware of the intense power of religion to excite the senses, not merely to control them. Comfort may have been what some members found in their church, but what must have engaged Wright was the mythological dimension of belief. For a poor child whose family could not afford books or music or travels, it was through the church that fantasy could be explored. The price of that exploration was high. After a long struggle, Wright rejected the church, but he understood the allure that kept the pews filled.

Consequently, what Wright does in *12 Million Black Voices* is to use the FSA photographs to stress the beauty and dignity of black "folk" Christianity while simultaneously telling a story of religious decline. By fixing black Christianity in a southern rural past and by ignoring its creative adaptations to city life, Richard Wright constructs a false sense of the impending end of religion. Edwin Rosskam, Russell Lee, and Richard Wright promoted a kind of "Negro church" that resonated with both black and white readers but simplified the dynamic character of African-American religion between the wars. Text and image work together to subtly control and define religious practices and to eventually eliminate Christianity from an imagined future world of racial equality.

In the spring of 1942, a year after Edwin Rosskam and Russell Lee had finished their project, Stryker sent another FSA photographer to Chicago. Jack Delano also made pictures of black life on the South Side, including black church life. The Japanese had bombed Pearl Harbor the previous December, and the federal government was launching a propaganda campaign to persuade the American people to support the war effort. Delano's photographs were among those used to create an illustrated pamphlet to be distributed by the Office of War Information. *Negroes and the War* was the first major piece of government propaganda directed specifically at securing the commitments of African Americans to a patriotic cause (see fig. 8.1). Edwin Rosskam also helped with its production. Although it was highly criticized after its publication by the black elite, *Negroes and the War* was a sought-after publication. While the OWI judged it as a failure in stimulating black support of the war, the pamphlet accomplished the more important task of distributing representations of black life — including church life — to people who possessed few visual images of themselves.

The illustrations in *Negroes and the War* provide a less predictable and more intriguing picture of Christian practices than *12 Million Black Voices.* In the next chapter, I explore the complete file of photographs taken both for Richard Wright and for the OWI project. When those pictures are supplemented with written texts and interviews, a fuller representation emerges of the religious practices of city congregations. The FSA/OWI photographs provide a perspective on what some people — African Americans at the very least — found exciting in city religion. The modernist fantasy of the "Negro church" that Richard Wright and Edwin Rosskam present in *12 Million Black Voices* must be understood as only one response to the vibrant religious world of African Americans during the thirties and forties.

The Worlds of the Observers

Edwin Rosskam and Russell Lee were good friends and had similar personal histories. Both were well-traveled artists who expressed their progressive social concerns through photography. And, like Lee, Rosskam has left us with only the bare bones of his early biography.

Rosskam's ancestors probably came to America with other German Jews during the mid-nineteenth century. His father was born in 1865 in Elmira, New York. Although his family had established a successful candy-making company in Philadelphia, for some reason Rosskam's parents returned to Germany. Perhaps business or personal matters drew the couple back to Munich, where Edwin was born in 1903. When World War I broke out, these American citizens became noncombatant prisoners of war and were not permitted to leave. Although Rosskam remembered that they were treated with no unpleasantness, his father died during this period. At sixteen, Rosskam returned to Philadelphia, where he mastered English and finished high school in a short six months. After a year at Haverford College—an institution with Quaker roots—Rosskam "got out of there" and trained as a painter at the Pennsylvania Academy of Fine Arts.[8]

Rosskam returned to Europe in the twenties to paint and experience the flourishing of avant-garde art and society. Although he had a one-man show of his work in Paris, Rosskam decided, "I was not a painter." His friendship with Man Ray made him think about photography as an appropriate art form. After his new bride "walked off with his best friend," Rosskam went to the Musée d'Homme, telling administrators that he was going to Tahiti and offering his services as photographer and translator.[9] After a brief stay in the West Indies, Rosskam ended up in the South Pacific, as had Walker Evans. For more than three years he photographed and wrote a novel (never published) about leper colonies. By the time he returned to the United States, the Depression was in full force, and Rosskam had to string together a series of writing and photography jobs to make ends meet. Like Russell Lee, he met and married a woman who shared his photographic interests and supported his professional projects.

Louise Rosenbaum was trained as a biologist but developed skills in the darkroom and behind the camera. She came from a Hungarian Jewish family, and her father was a prominent banker in Philadelphia until the stock market crashed. Morris Rosenbaum wanted his children to be "American Jews" and was an active supporter of the Reform movement in Philadelphia. The youngest of eight children, Louise remembered going to Jewish Sunday School and being confirmed. Like Rosskam, however, she did not integrate Judaism into her own life or her family's. "'I'm not going to belong to this Synagogue when I grow up,'" she told the rabbi friend of her father's. "'Nope, I don't believe in it.' . . . And I never did go back until my father died."[10] Louise and Edwin eventually moved to New York City, where they lived in Greenwich Village. There they met other Jews who shared their artistic and political views. Among those friends was the photographer Sol Libsohn, one of the founders of the Photo League. Libsohn helped Rosskam make the transition from art photographer to documentary photographer.

Louise Rosskam recalled that her husband had been "very religious" in Germany, but when he came to America, he "wanted to forget the whole thing if he could." She explained, "We had lived a very free life of artists, writers, painters" and said, "We never really thought about being Jewish, although we didn't say we weren't or anything like that."[11] When the family lived in Puerto Rico after the war, the Rosskam children got presents at Hanukkah as well as from the Three Kings and Santa Claus. In the fifties, Edwin Rosskam moved his family to Roosevelt, New Jersey, the former Jewish cooperative of Jersey Homesteads. Although a synagogue was built "after so many years of getting along in the old construction shack," Rosskam did not join it.[12] Like many Jews who had come from the Lower East Side to Roosevelt, Rosskam had only limited connections to Jewish religious practices.

In 1939 Rosskam was finishing a picture book about San Francisco and putting together another on the nation's capital for Alliance Book Corporation when he met Roy Stryker in Washington and learned about the Historical Section. Stryker eventually hired him as a "visual information specialist" who would organize the file and prepare exhibitions. Not thrilled about working as a well-paid clerk, Rosskam remembered that he and Stryker had an "understanding" that he would stay only a year. In August 1940 he left the Historical Section to become the managing editor of Alliance, a firm founded by a family friend and fellow German Jewish immigrant. By November the company was faltering, so Rosskam again worked with Stryker as a freelance editor.

Rosskam continued to produce books for Alliance Book Corporation.[13] He persuaded Sherwood Anderson, who had painted a barbed portrait of small-town life in *Winesburg, Ohio,* to produce a gentler version for "Faces of America." *Home Town* was published in 1940, and Rosskam selected FSA photographs to accompany the text. According to Louise Rosskam, Edwin then decided to produce a series on minority groups in America, beginning with Native Americans. Rosskam was finishing *As Long as the Grass Shall Grow* when he contacted Viking Press to gauge the publisher's interest in a short book by Richard Wright that would be illustrated with FSA photographs.

"I had no knowledge that I would get hold of Richard Wright," Rosskam told an interviewer in 1965. Wright, it turned out, had been mulling the possibility of writing a series of historical novels about the black experience. He later recalled, "I told him I had already been thinking of the idea and that made the whole thing come easily." Rosskam must have been ecstatic about a positive response from such a rising star on the American cultural scene. Richard Wright's first novel, *Native Son,* was a best seller and the first book by an African American to be marketed as a Book-of-the-Month Club selection. Published in March 1940, it sold a quarter of a million copies in its first month. By April it was number one on the best-seller list, ahead of John Steinbeck's *Grapes of Wrath.* Wright was swiftly moving from being an unknown writer, living off paychecks from the Federal Writers' Project and a fellowship from the Guggenheim Foundation, to being a literary spokesperson for the African-American experience. Rosskam and Wright's collaboration enabled an influential African-American writer to look at "thousands of pictures" in the FSA file, leading Wright to conclude, "It is one of the most remarkable collections of photographs in existence."[14]

While Stryker had supported Rosskam's productions of commercial books, he was uneasy about the *12 Million Black Voices* project. "You know, of course," Stryker's secretary wrote Jack Delano, "that we are doing a coverage of the negro in Chicago for the book Ed is doing with Richard Wright. This of course is off the record information, and not to be talked about."[15] Stryker's plea for silence was due to several reasons. Perhaps foremost was the problem of how a government agency should interact with a commercial press. Rosskam was stretching the truth when he asserted in *12 Million Black Voices* that "none of the photographs here reproduced was made for this book" but rather that they "were taken by Farm Security photographers as they roamed the country during a five-year period on their regular assignments" (149). Stryker had sent Russell Lee, who was a full-time employee of the Historical Section and skilled at interior photography, along with Rosskam to Chicago. Rosskam was not working for the Historical Division at the time, but he worked as both a consultant and as a full-time employee on and off until Stryker left in 1943. The Farm Security Administration had already been facing criticism and budget cuts from Congress. Could Stryker explain how photographs of Chicago's South Side were relevant to the agency's mission? Accommodating Rosskam's picture needs could be risky.

The topic of the book was also controversial. Since the outbreak of war in Europe and Asia, the photographers were taking pictures that reflected the strength of America. While pictures of urban poverty were in keeping with the earlier reformist agenda of the division, such photos also vividly illustrated the failure of American democracy and capitalism. How could such images stimulate wartime patriotism? In addition, Richard Wright was a controversial character. His association with communists as well as his biting social criticism alienated conservatives. In 1938, during an investigation of the Federal Writers' Project, Congressman Martin Dies condemned Wright's autobiographical sketch "The Ethics of Living Jim Crow," published in a WPA anthology of writing. *Native Son* had been banned from libraries in Birmingham, Alabama. If southern congressmen felt that supporting black tenant farmers with small loans would lead to socialism, what would they think of government photographers making pictures for a member of the Communist Party?[16] Conservative criticism of Wright eventually evolved into government harassment. In 1943, after the publication of *12 Million Black Voices,* the FBI interviewed Wright's neighbors and associates to determine whether the sentiments in the book constituted sedition. While that specific inquiry came to nothing, the FBI continued to investigate Wright until his death in 1960 in Paris. Stryker had good reasons for keeping this particular project "off the record."

It speaks to the enduring reformist vision of Stryker that he was willing to risk the future of his division in order to provide Richard Wright with pictures of urban poverty. Stryker must have realized that FSA photographs in a book written by Richard Wright and marketed by Viking Press would be seen by millions, who would grasp that racism and economic serfdom was the fate of far more than southern black sharecroppers. At the very moment when Lee and Rosskam were traveling to Chicago, African Americans across the country were gearing up for a major march to Washington to protest continued segregation in employment. Only when President Roosevelt signed Executive Order 8802 in June 1941, prohibiting discrimination in the government-funded defense industries, was the march called off. Stryker's acceptance of Rosskam's project was a part of a larger movement by African Americans and some New Dealers to bring to the attention of the public what was to be dubbed the "American Dilemma" of race relations.[17]

Published in late October 1941, *12 Million Black Voices* sold well and received positive reviews. The *New Yorker* called it a "moving and powerful work." George Streator, writing for the liberal Catholic journal *Commonweal,* concluded, "We have a good book to hand to our policy formers." The Book-of-the-Month Club, exemplar of middlebrow taste in the forties, advertised it to subscribers. At the same time, communists offered it as a bonus for subscribing to the Party newspaper, *New Masses.* While some reviewers rankled at the absence of the middle class from Wright's story of Negro life, they praised his rich and earnest text as well as the emotional impact of the photographs. African-American newspapers around the country noted the one-sided portrait but upheld the representation of poverty as accurate.[18]

Richard Wright's involvement in the project gave FSA photographers an unprecedented entrance into black urban culture, which was one reason the book was successful. His support enabled Lee and Rosskam to travel freely throughout the South Side, efficiently photographing key black institutions and activities. Richard Wright had come to Chicago in 1927 and, like most black migrants, had scraped by with menial and often humiliating jobs. Wright was also a writer who associated with whites and politically aware blacks. In 1935 the Federal Writers' Project (FWP) hired him as a supervisor. The FWP was collecting information about American communities by hiring the unemployed to collect statistics, conduct interviews, do "participant observation," and write up their research as essays and short stories. Volumes of typed manuscript pages describing life in the Black Belt, including religious life, were produced by Chicago's FWP. In 1938, for example, FWP workers surveyed 327 churches on the South Side, describing their buildings and clergy. Investigators returned to many of the churches and filed hundreds of reports on black religious behavior.[19]

Typically the results of the FWP surveys that Wright and others produced ended up in rather conventional tour books on the various states. The Chicago African-American social scientists Horace Cayton (1912–1970) and St. Clair Drake (1911–1990), however, were hired by the WPA to conduct further research. While Cayton focused on administering the staff, Drake organized fieldwork. A Julius Rosenwald Fund grant helped the pair finish the project, and in 1945 *Black Metropolis: A Study of Negro Life in a Northern City* was published. Richard Wright was a close friend of Horace Cayton's, and he introduced the book with "keen pride," calling it a "landmark of research and scientific achievement."[20]

Black Metropolis saw African-American life on the South Side through the theoretical lens of the Chicago School. Richard Wright and Edwin Rosskam adopted the same sociological theory to inform how religion was represented in *12 Million Black Voices.* Under the influence of the sociologist Robert E. Park and the anthropologist W. Lloyd Warner, the Chicago School stressed the importance of intensive fieldwork. By conducting personal interviews, reviewing historical sources, and analyzing statistics, social scientists sought to construct accurate and responsible descriptions of specific communities.[21] The scholars of the Chicago School saw themselves as having an approach distinct from that of the more theoretically orientated European sociologists or from those Progressive Era reformers who conducted research in order to provoke change. The social scientists of the Chicago School understood their work as scientific and objective, geared toward pragmatic reporting rather than social improvement. During the school's influential period between 1915 and 1930, its sociologists wrote monographs on organized crime, delinquent boys, hobos, and even taxi-dance girls. When Park came to the university in 1913, the first course he taught was entitled "The Negro in America." Park had studied and researched in the South and worked for nine years as Booker T. Washington's secretary. He was keenly interested in black culture in the city.

Shaped by the theoretical orientation of the Chicago School, *Black Metropolis* concentrated on where African Americans lived, how they conducted their businesses, what their families looked like, and who worked at what jobs. Material life was of primary interest, but religion was hard to ignore. "The church and religion have been displaced from the center of the average man's life," Drake and Cayton observed in *Black Metropolis.* But "Bronzeville" (as they called the South Side) "is tinctured with religion." Secularization had not yet reached the ghetto. For Chicago School scholars, the only way of assessing the "real importance of the church" was by "relating it to the economic and social status of the various groups in Bronzeville." Class was the strongest predictor of religious behavior, and church life reflected class divisions in direct and obvious ways. "The tiny churches in deserted and dilapidated stores, with illiterately scrawled announcements on their painted windows," the authors explained, "are marked off sharply from the fine edifices on the boulevards with stained-glass windows and electric bulletin boards."[22]

Drake and Cayton understood church life as an outgrowth of a static, tripartite social structure that was defined as either lower, middle, or upper class. According to this sociological theory, African Americans (as well as other urban dwellers) went to churches with people of their same educational and economic levels. The authors included statistical tables to show how churches were distributed by "desirability of neighborhood" into "best areas," "mixed areas," and "worse areas."[23] Their worship styles and beliefs reflected their unique culture (defined by class) as well as their place in the pecking order of the South Side. Religious communities did not challenge existing social structures but rather reflected and reinforced them.

In his role as photo editor, Edwin Rosskam even further reduced the tripartite class division of religion in *Black Metropolis.* Rosskam wrote in his "supplementary reference file" on the "Negro church" that there were "hundreds" of churches on Chicago's South Side. In spite of that observation, he lumped all of Bronzeville's congregations into one of two categories. The first category was made up of lower-class congregations, including the "majority of churchgoers" who attended "storefront" churches: recent migrants from the South who "have brought their religion with them as they tried to bring their gardens." These "humble churches" retained the "ecstatic character and native poetry of the revivalist prayer meeting" and were located in "former grocery, drug or notion stores vacated by their original tenants when the white population relinquished the neighborhood." "Fundamentalist sects" of "Hardshell Baptist, Pentecostal, Seventh Day Adventist, Holiness and the like" were "transported intact from the Southern land." On Sundays one could hear "fervent crescendos issuing from three or four places within the same block."[24]

Rosskam probably did not consider his description disparaging or patronizing, because many modernists believed true genius resided in the "native poetry" of the "humble." As with Lee's fascination with shrines in the homes of Mexicans living in Texas, Rosskam probably admired the "primitive" creativity of storefront religion. John Collier, Jr., expressed similar sentiments about Catholics in New Mexico. Walker Evans and Dorothea Lange never revealed to Stryker their thoughts on the subject, but their attraction to vernacular southern architecture indicates that they shared the same affection for "plain folk." The FSA photographers and the Chicago School of social scientists were drawn to communities they felt were disappearing under the impact of modern civilization. Rosskam's observation that specific denominations were "transplanted intact" from the South also reflected the notion that these vanishing communities had core beliefs and norms around which all members naturally and organically cohered. Since Chicago School sociologists agreed that economic structures determined culture, it was assumed that when African Americans moved north into an urban world, traditional values would hold the communities together for only so long.

Rosskam's second category of congregations folded together the middle-class and upper-class congregations described in *Black Metropolis.* His account explained that most of those congregations own "imposing buildings and [employ] preachers who are men of the world." Having a large "physical plant" would be "an almost certain index to the comparative wealth of the congregation." This type of church was made up of high school graduates with some money ("no matter how little"), who want a more "literate approach to their faith." Their services are "much more decorous and formal and less inspirational than in the old shops and stores." The documentation notes that "Pilgrim Baptist Church" and "an Episcopal Church" have "given up all [their] specifically Negro character." Such churches "are all exact duplicates of a fashionable white church." Rosskam concluded his statement on the "Negro church" by explaining that Christian communities still revolve around "the preacher" whose "distinction and influence rises in inverse ratio to the social and income scale of his parishioners."[25]

Richard Wright reduced even further this portrayal of Christian practices on the South Side. Unlike Rosskam and Lee, whose experience with black Christianity was limited, Richard Wright knew the power of religion on a very intimate level. It was this very familiarity with religion that kept him from taking seriously its role in South Side life. Raised in a strict Seventh-day Adventist home in the South, Wright depicted childhood memories that stressed the brutality and narrow-mindedness of Christian people. Beaten by his grandmother and aunt, Wright remembered in his memoir, *Black Boy,* "the half dozen or more daily family prayers that Granny insisted upon; her fiat that the day began at sunrise and that night commenced at sundown; the long, rambling Bible readings; the individual invocations muttered at each meal; and her declaration that Saturday was the Lord's Sabbath and that no one who lived in her house could work upon that day." Scornful of all worldly distractions from faith, Granny destroyed a radio Wright built and forbade moviegoing. Seventh-day Adventist beliefs meant that Wright could not supplement the family income by working on Saturday or satisfy his hunger by eating pork. All-night prayer meetings left him "squirming on a bench, longing to grow up so I could run away . . . wondering when it would be safe for me to stretch out on the bench and go to sleep." Wright had no romantic appreciation of the "Negro character" or "native poetry" of Granny's church. "There were more violent quarrels in our deeply religious home," he wrote in *Black Boy,* "than in the home of a gangster, a burglar, or a prostitute."[26]

Even when Wright's mother broke free from the constraints of her own mother's faith and went to a Methodist church (where "we don't holler and moan"), her son found nothing but oppression, boredom, and hypocrisy. The Methodist church was a pretentious copy of white religion filled with "prim, brown, puritanical girls who taught in the public schools; black college students who tried to conceal their plantation origins . . . snobbery, clannishness, gossip, intrigue, petty class rivalry, and conspicuous displays of cheap clothing" (151). Although Wright's writings reveal that he was profoundly shaped by the religious worlds of his family, he never participated in any church after he left the South. He married two Jewish women, both of whom were members of the Communist Party, as he was. Like other intellectuals and artists of the thirties, he had experienced religion and turned away from it: "Whenever I found religion in my life," he concluded, "I found strife, the attempt of one individual or group to rule another in the name of God. The naked will to power seemed always to walk in the wake of a hymn" (136).

Off to Church

Wright did not directly explore the "naked will to power" of religion in *12 Million Black Voices*. Writing primarily to a white audience, he knew that his readers expected to see black piety. At the same time, he must have realized that if he articulated a Marxist critique of religion as the drug of the ignorant, he would only be playing into racist hands. Richard Wright instead chose to reiterate common notions about the function of faith in the black community while simultaneously undermining the possibility that Christianity could survive in an urban world. Using the FSA photographs, Wright bowed to the significance of religion in black life but then quietly denied religion the power he knew well it had. Rather than trying to draw the reader into the complicated world of the faithful, Rosskam picked photographs that simplified the religious practices of South Side residents. Rather than trying to understand how or why Christianity could be so powerfully destructive, Wright warned readers to escape from the controlling grasp of belief.

Wright begins his story of religion in the first pages of *12 Million Black Voices*. In Africa "we had our own civilization" that included systems of "law, religion, medicine, science, and education" (13). Religion, while not described, is listed along with other rational pursuits. It was Western slavery and Christianity that "blasted our lives," killing the orderly world of African society. "Our gods were dead," Wright laments, "and answered us no more" (15). Even though radical Christians like the Quakers and a few Puritans called for the "humanitarian belief in the rights of man," the order of the universe was defined by those who had a "love of gold and God" (18). Christianity legitimized slavery, established a deadening paternalism, encouraged casual cruelty, and promoted despotism.

Following a long description of southern misery, the reader arrives at the middle of *12 Million Black Voices* and the first illustration of a black religious practice (fig. 8.2). The transition from white economic exploitation to black religious agency is eased by a brief discussion of education; then Wright abruptly announces, "Sunday is always a glad day" (67).[27] Above this text, Rosskam places an illustration of five adults and two children. Although the two boys are barefoot, one wears a sailor suit and the other a double-vested jacket. One woman carries a stylish purse, and the man standing next to her wears two-tone shoes. Their clothing stands out from earlier illustrations of overall-wearing sharecroppers. Under the picture, Wright relates in painful detail the Sunday ritual of getting ready for church. He explains how girls had "red ribbon[s]" tied on their heads rubbed with "hog fat." We can perhaps imagine that girls liked their fancy hair wraps, but could boys possibly look forward to wearing stocking caps "stretched taut upon their skulls" to straighten their hair? Is the mood somber in the photograph because everyone is wearing "clean clothes ironed stiff with starch made from flour"? Or could it be because "*we* rub the hog fat upon *their* faces to take that dull, ashy look away from skins made dry and rough from the weather of the fields" (emphasis mine). Wright finishes by stating: "And we are off to church."

Nothing in either the text or the photograph makes me think that going "off to church"

Sunday is always a glad day. We call all our children to us and comb the hair of the boys and plait the hair of the girls; then we rub their heads with hog fat to make their hair shine. We wrap the girls' hair in white strings and put a red ribbon upon their heads; we make the boys wear stocking caps, that is, we make them pull upon their heads the tops of our stockings, cut and stretched taut upon their skulls to keep their hair in place. Then we rub the hog fat upon their faces to take that dull, ashy look away from skins made dry and rough from the weather of the fields. In clean clothes ironed stiff with starch made from flour, we hitch up the mule to the wagon, pile in our Bibles and baskets of food—hog meat and greens—and we are off to church.

would be a pleasure. Wright's discussion of Christianity begins with memories of what it was like to go to church as a child. In beginning his discussion of religion by making the reader feel uncomfortable, he tells us that churchgoing has several faces. While Sunday might be a glad day, it also demands the proper appearance of adults and asserts control over the bodies of children. Wright reinforces the notion that Christianity is the one southern institution that offers an alternative to work, but he also tells us that churchgoing has its own pressures. Wright knew from his own childhood that ritual shapes and regulates bodily movements. For Wright that control was oppressive, especially for boys. Church for him was not about spirituality; it was about social conformity and control. Wright introduces the power of religion to discipline and to encode negative memories of religion on the body.

The illustration used in this section on churchgoing supports Wright's perspective on the rituals of religious comportment. Perhaps he and Rosskam were playing a joke on readers when the pair decided to illustrate the "glad day" of Sunday with a photograph of Jack Delano's originally captioned "Family who had just come back from a funeral." When Rosskam credited this illustration at the back of *12 Million Black Voices,* he incorrectly cited it as: "Rural Negroes dressed to go to church" (150). The illustration does show a family looking strained, but the original caption reveals that it is not because hair has been pulled and collars have been starched. FSA photographs and captions are manipulated elsewhere in *12 Million Black Voices.* In another illustration, Rosskam erased the tongue of a little girl who was sticking it out at the white men who had come to photograph her in her home (110). Since playful children distracted from the seriousness of their poverty, and rebellious behavior among blacks was threatening, the offending appendage was eliminated from the illustration.[28] As with the altered caption, preserving the "authenticity" of the photograph was of less importance than intensifying the message. That message moved back and forth between the text and the image.

After having "dressed" for church, Wright brings his readers visually and textually into a place of worship. He and Rosskam chose five photographs to illustrate southern religious practices, three that Jack Delano took at a "Negro church" in Heard County, Georgia, and two that Russell Lee took at All Nations Pentecostal Church in Chicago (figs. 8.3–8.7). Since Wright saw little difference between rural and urban Christianity, we should not be surprised that Rosskam felt free to include Lee's pictures of Chicago to illustrate Wright's reflections on southern religion. Wright and Rosskam had no interest in defining denominational differences or in pointing out the changes that were occurring in black Protestant worship. The photographs chosen were tightly framed, stressing the piety of people, not the space of their church. We are given no contextual clues about the traditions of those particular churches. In one illustration, Rosskam cropped the photograph to eliminate a woman playing a tambourine (fig. 8.5). An extraneous element like a tambourine might have raised questions about the presence of such a flashy instrument in a "country" church.[29] The illustrations are presented as examples of pure religious experience, untouched by local differences, divisive theologies, or modern sensibilities.

All five of the illustrations in this section reflect the practices of the "lower-class church"

8.2 (facing page)   Richard Wright, photo direction by Edwin Rosskam, *12 Million Black Voices: A Folk History of the Negro in the United States* (1941; rpt. New York: Thunder's Mouth, 1995), 67 (LC-USF34-025348-D)

The preacher tells of days long ago and of a people whose sufferings were like ours. He preaches of the Hebrew children and the fiery furnace, of Daniel, of Moses, of Solomon, and of Christ. What we have not dared feel in the presence of the Lords of the Land, we now feel in church. Our hearts and bodies, reciprocally acting upon each other, swing out into the meaning of the story the preacher is unfolding. Our eyes become absorbed in a vision. . . .

. . . a place eternal filled with happiness where dwell God and His many hosts of angels singing His praises and glorifying His name and in the midst of this oneness of being there arises one whose soul is athirst to feel things for himself and break away from the holy band of joy and he organizes revolt in Heaven and preaches rebellion and aspires to take the place of God to rule Eternity and God condemns him from Heaven and decrees that he shall be banished and this Rebel this Satan this Lucifer persuades one-third of all the many hosts of angels in Heaven to follow him

69

8.4   Wright and Rosskam, *12 Million Black Voices,* 69 (LC-USF34-043933-D)

8.3 (facing page)   Wright and Rosskam, *12 Million Black Voices,* 68 (LC-USF34-043965-D)

*and build a new Heaven and down he comes with his angels whose hearts
are black with pride and whose souls are hot with vengeance against God
who decides to make Man and He makes Man in His own image and He
forms him of clay and He breathes the breath of life into him but He warns
him against the Rebel the Satan the Lucifer who had been banished from
Heaven for his pride and envy and Man lives in a garden of peace where
there is no Time no Sorrow and no Death and while Man lives in this*

8.5   Wright and Rosskam, *12 Million Black Voices,* 70 (LC-USF34-038779-D)

*happiness there comes to him the Rebel the Satan the Lucifer and he tempts
Man and drags him down the same black path of rebellion and sin and
God seeing this decrees that Man shall live in the Law and not Love and
must endure Toil and Pain and Death and must dig for his bread in the
stony earth but while Man suffers God's compassion is moved and God
Himself assumes the form of Man's corrupt and weak flesh and comes
down and lives and suffers and dies upon a cross to show Man the way back*

71

8.6   Wright and Rosskam, *12 Million Black Voices*, 71 (reverse printing of LC-USF34-043854-D)

up the broad highway to peace and thus Man begins to live for a time under a new dispensation of Love and not Law and the Rebel the Satan the Lucifer still works rebellion seducing persuading falsifying and God through His prophets says that He will come for a second time bringing not peace but a sword to rout the powers of darkness and build a new Jerusalem and God through His prophets says that the final fight the last battle the Armageddon will be resumed and will endure until the end of Time and of Death. . . .

as defined in *Black Metropolis* and depicted in Rosskam's supplementary note on the "Negro church." Cayton and Drake explain that the services of the "faithful few" of the lower-class church "are highly charged with emotion. They involve group singing, individual prayers, and 'testifying.'"[30] The illustrations show exactly this—singing, attentive listening, meditative prayer, and ecstatic praise. While the illustrations are not disrespectful, they do echo Rosskam's belief that "humble churches" retain the "ecstatic character and native poetry of the revivalist prayer meeting." The five illustrations are arranged in a linear order and culminate as readers might imagine a black church would—with a woman's arms spread out and her mouth wide open (fig. 8.7). To heighten its effect, Rosskam had Lee's original photograph tightly cropped. The illustrations are intense and dramatic; there is a spirited enthusiasm, but it is balanced by other images of attentive listening and meditative contemplation (figs. 8.4, 8.6). Rosskam and Wright picked images that reinforced what most readers—black or white—assumed happened on most Sundays in southern black churches.

The text that accompanies the illustrations, however, has none of the clarity and simplicity of the visual message. Wright's words do not summarize rural religious practices or give examples of their continuation in the city. He does not develop the compensatory function of faith in a racist society. Rather, the text around the illustrations is an imaginative, prophetic reverie of the author's. After a brief introduction, Wright observes, "Our eyes become absorbed in a vision" (68). He then changes both the print font and the tone of his writing (fig. 8.4). While scholars have argued that Wright is preaching a sermon to his readers, what we read in italicized type is not a sermon text.[31] With the font change, Wright signals a move away from straightforward historical and sociological descriptions or even evangelical preaching. Under the photographs of prayer and worship, Wright uses a visionary language to creatively present his plan of salvation. Wright returns to childhood memories and uses the visions of the Seventh-day Adventist prophet Ellen G. White as a model to articulate what he sees as the struggle of the individual against religious authority.

Starting when she was seventeen, Ellen White had visions. They began in 1844 and reassured Ellen that, although William Miller's prediction of the end of the world had not materialized, the Adventist message was true. Ellen White became an Adventist preacher and writer. In March 1858, after a funeral service at Lovett's Grove near Bowling Green, Ohio, Ellen White fell into a trance that lasted more than two hours. The vision she had that day was one of two thousand revelations that she experienced during her lifetime. Her visions formed the basis of her writings and thus serve as a source for Seventh-day Adventist theology. As a child, Wright must have heard them recounted in many sermons and read about them in Granny's pious literature. The power of apocalyptic imagery would not have been new to the writer.

White's "Lovett's Grove vision" depicted the "great controversy" between Christ and Satan—the great war in heaven before the creation of the earth. In her vision, White saw that Lucifer was a "high and exalted angel" whose "high and broad" forehead revealed a "powerful intellect." Lucifer's "form was perfect; his bearing noble and majestic. A special light beamed in his countenance and shone around him brighter and more beautiful than around the other

8.7 (facing page)   Wright and Rosskam, *12 Million Black Voices*, 72 (LC-USF34-038745-D)

angels." Lucifer, however, became jealous and envious of Christ, who was preeminent "over all the angelic host." He "turned from the loyal and true angels, denouncing them as slaves." Lucifer promised those angels who would rebel with him "a new and better government than they then had, in which all would be freedom." Then Lucifer appeared with his followers before God and demanded that he "should be equal with God and should be taken into conference with the Father and understand His purposes." The "angels needed no law but should be left free to follow their own will," which Lucifer claimed "would ever guide them right." Law was a "restriction of their liberty," and Lucifer sought to abolish law. "The condition of the angels," Lucifer believed, "needed improvement." Such rebellion could not be tolerated, so there was a "war in heaven." Lucifer, along with his sympathizers, was "expelled from heaven." Heavenly order was reestablished, but Lucifer continued his evil rebellion by tormenting God's creation, humankind, until he was finally vanquished at the end of time.[32] In other visions, Ellen White saw the end of time, when a renewed earth was prepared for the righteous saints to live on in peace for all eternity.

Richard Wright retells the Lovett's Grove vision in *12 Million Black Voices* and inverts Ellen White's salvation narrative. He makes Lucifer into a heroic figure and denies the Righteous their final victory over evil (fig. 8.4). Wright, like White, begins his vision in heaven before time, when "there arises one whose soul is athirst to feel things for himself and break away from the holy band of joy" (69). The rebellious soul, named "Rebel the Satan the Lucifer" (70), is "hot with vengeance against God." Lucifer asserts the primacy of independence and freedom over the servile conformity of God's angels (fig. 8.5). He is, in effect, the first Enlightenment individual. This Rebel builds a "new heaven" along with his angels, "whose hearts are black with pride" (70). Wright's black angels are a play on Ellen White's "slaves." These black-hearted angels revolt against their masters, and Wright uses them to symbolize all oppressed people who seek to create and experience freedom on a new earth. According to Wright's vision, God responds to this challenge by making "Man in His own image." The Rebel tempts Man "and drags him down the same black path of rebellion" (71). Then come the Fall, the Incarnation, and the Second Coming, but in Wright's vision there is no happy ending (fig. 8.6).

Ellen White's cosmic narrative, like other Christian stories of the End Times, finally comes to a close with the establishment of a New Heaven and a New Earth. Cayton and Drake in *Black Metropolis* relate that lower-class Christians knew that after a cosmic drama at the end of time they would be among the "righteous dead" living on a new earth free of suffering.[33] "Sin and sinners are no more," Ellen White writes on the last page of *The Great Controversy*. "The entire universe is clean. . . . From the minutest atom to the greatest world, all things, animate and inanimate, in their unshadowed beauty and perfect joy, declare that God is love." [34] Richard Wright, however, sees no such positive resolution to the cosmic battle in his vision: "The final fight the last battle of Armageddon will be resumed," he reveals, "and will endure until the end of Time and of Death" (72). For Wright, there is no godly time after historic time. Nothing exists beyond the battle (fig. 8.7). For modern men, reality is always in process; it never becomes fixed and eternal. The world is never completely remade; a utopian society can never be definitively established. More important, in Wright's vision religion never triumphs. Everlasting struggle and annihilation are better than an eternity in the New Jerusalem living with the righteous. Richard Wright does not want to return to an earth cleansed of all sinners and populated with the likes of his Seventh-day Adventist grandmother.

After his powerful retelling of the plan of salvation, Wright changes voice and returns to a predictable description of, and justification for, the religious practices of lower-class blacks. He turns from his own vision of eternal strife and restates the opposite — yet socially acceptable — notion that religion brings peace and humanity to the oppressed. "It is the courage and faith in simple living that enable us to maintain this reservoir of human feeling," Wright suggests. "Our enchanted vision" is what "drains the gall out of our years" (73). This "enchanted vision," which is at odds with Wright's own childhood memories and his membership in the Communist Party, cannot be maintained for long. Soon after Wright acknowledges that religion has helped African Americans endure racism and economic exploitation, he predicts that it cannot form the foundation for societal change. "We know," he reminds us, "that if we could but get our feet planted firmly upon this earth, we could laugh and live and build" (73). Like other black and white critics of the southern piety, Wright sees the church as uncritically supporting otherworldly preoccupations that ensure the continual servitude of the uneducated.

Wright ends this section on southern Christianity by presenting readers with a modernist understanding of religion: religious practices are not childlike activities as racists would have one think, but rather are the profound ways by which poor people maintain their humanity. But such religious communities cannot provide the impetus for eliminating racial and economic oppression and remaking the earth. For Wright and other modernists, change can occur only with "feet planted firmly upon this earth." Although never stated directly, the implication is that once oppression is over and freedom secured, there is no longer a need for the "enchanting vision" that "purges the pain from our memory of the past" (73). Since Wright sees Christianity as intimately linked to the dynamics of oppression, the black church can do nothing but provide emotional sustenance for weary people.

When Wright moves his "folk history" north, he continues to acknowledge and then subvert religion. Playing with the popular interpretation of the Great Migration as a salvation event, Wright begins his chapter on black life in the city with a shout: "LORD IN HEAVEN! Good God Almighty! Great Day in the Morning! It's here! Our time has come! We are leaving!" (92). Just as the Israelites escaped from Egypt to the Promised Land, so do black southerners move north into cities of freedom.[35] Rosskam visually stresses this millennial hope by placing an illustration of spirit-filled women over Wright's text. Caught in rapture, the women wave their hands in praise (fig. 8.8). There is, of course, no Promised Land. He titles his chapter "Death on the City Pavements," and it chronicles the disappointment and despair of urban blacks. "We went innocently," Wright reports, "longing and hoping for a life that the Lords of the Land would not let us live" (98). Even the earth rejects the newcomers: "Here in the North cold forces hit you and push you. It is a world of *things*" (100).

To illustrate Christian practices in the urban world, Rosskam and Wright picked two photographs of storefront churches. In one, two women intently read their religious books during a service while a clergyman stands behind them in his pulpit (fig. 8.9). Under the photograph in bold print is a phrase that Wright has used earlier in the text: "We, who needed the

LORD IN HEAVEN! Good God Almighty! Great Day in the Morning! It's here! Our time has come! We are leaving! We are angry no more; we are leaving! We are bitter no more; we are leaving! We are leaving our homes, pulling up stakes to move on. We look up at the high southern sky and remember all the sunshine and the rain and we feel a sense of loss, but we are leaving. We look out at the wide green fields which our eyes saw when we first came into the world and we feel full of regret, but we are leaving. We scan the kind black faces we have looked upon since we first saw the light of day, and, though pain is in our hearts, we are leaving. We take one last furtive look over our shoulders to the Big House—high upon a hill beyond the railroad tracks—where the Lord of the Land lives, and we feel glad, for we are leaving. . . .

ritual and guidance of institutions" (95). The use of the past tense is significant, as this phrase is included in a string of descriptions of black life in the South, not in the North. In the South, where blacks were "landless upon the land" struggling to maintain families with "personalities blasted," they needed the guidance of the church. "We were such a folk as this," Wright observes, "when we moved into a world that was destined to test all we were, that threw us into the scales of competition to weigh our mettle" (93).

As with the "glad-day" churchgoing photographs of Delano, the illustrations do not fully support the text. Russell Lee's church interior does not convey the impression that southern rituals and institutions of guidance have any relevance or influence in the urban North. Neither of the two women appears interested in meeting the "test" of urban living, as they look downward, busily studying their books. Even the preacher looks as if he is not speaking to anyone; the women have their backs to him. Although Wright and Rosskam picked a picture that illustrates the intensity of religious study, the orientation of the churchgoer is not outward. The illustration is characteristically ambivalent: we see literacy, but it is misdirected. Wright provides no sense that religion might have to change in order to meet the challenges of a new environment. Nor did he or the photographers seem interested in any of the social welfare activities of South Side churches. In spite of this visual evidence of otherworldliness, Wright repeats his earlier observation, "It is only when we are within the walls of our churches that we are wholly ourselves . . . that we maintain a quiet and constant communion with all that is deepest in us" (131). It is unclear how "quiet and constant communion" relates to a northern world "of things."

Richard Wright did not "maintain a quiet and constant communion" with what was deepest in himself in a church. While the northern city did not eliminate racism and economic discrimination, it did offer more alternatives where African Americans could experience a "hint of a full life lived without fear" (126). In the city there were places of music and dance where the emotional strain of living in a racist society could be imaginatively expressed and partially expelled. It is significant that Wright presents a description of these secular expressions of creativity and spirit in the city before his paean to the church. In the section on the South, such pursuits were discussed after churchgoing (73). Even more persuasively, when discussing northern life, he and Rosskam included three illustrations of dancing in which young men and women look like they are having fun. The disciplined body at church may have looked "quiet and constant," but it did not look as modern and appealing as the body caught up in the rhythm of jazz. The dancers' uninhibited movements, their smiles, and their stylish clothes sharply contrast with the calm of the church service, the simple dresses of the women, and the formal attire of the clergyman.

In a place where Wright could have illustrated the continuity between dancing in church and dancing at the Savoy, he chose to separate the sacred from the profane. For Wright it is in secular pursuits like music and dance—rather than in the church—that "we are wholly ourselves." The city offers liberating cultural activities as communal alternatives to religion. If music and dance could free the spirit, could they replace churchgoing? For Wright, who hated the endless church services of his family and their constant bickering, the emotions generated

8.8 (facing page)   Wright and Rosskam, *12 Million Black Voices,* 92 (LC-USF34-038774-D)

We, who needed the ritual and
guidance of institutions

from beliefs and rituals were either debilitating or mind-numbing. Why not encourage young people to dance and relegate the disciplined, moral life of black congregations to preachers and older women?

The final illustration of church life "on the city pavements" reiterates Wright's perspective on the future of religion in the city (fig. 8.10). Under a picture of a church exterior, Wright explains: "So they keep thousands of Little Bethels and Pilgrims and Calvarys and White Rocks and Good Hopes and Mount Olives going with their nickels and dimes. Nurtured in the close and intimate folk culture of the South, where each person knew the others . . ." (134). Storefront Christianity, the black religion of the Promised Land of the North, is a church with closed doors and young people standing on its doorsteps waiting for something to happen. A man and child quickly walk by.[36] The sign tells outsiders this is a "Church of God" but no one can see what is happening inside. The reader is no longer included in the hidden community: Wright now tells us that "they" keep the Little Bethels, and "they" group themselves about a "lonely young black preacher," and "they" perform religious rituals on "fervid levels" (135).

It is not mere coincidence that Wright includes in his final discussion of Christianity a reference to "elderly black women" who "cultivate tiny vegetable gardens in the narrow squares of ground in front of their hovels" (135). In spite of his earlier comparison of churchgoing to experiencing the "murmur of the human heart," congregational life will not survive the modernization process (131). Richard Wright puts his Granny, who prohibited him from reading and smashed the radio he painstakingly built, finally in her place. "More than even that of the American Indian," Wright concludes the paragraph, "the consciousness of vast sections of our black women lies beyond the boundaries of the modern world, though they live and work in that world daily" (135). Wright populates the premodern world with black women. Granny and the American Indians, the photograph could be interpreted as saying, remain inside the church, waiting to die or to vanish. We, the young men and women of the future, stand outside the church waiting for something better to come along.

Wright ends *12 Million Black Voices* with a chapter entitled "Men in the Making." For Wright, the future is not a fixed utopia waiting to be achieved but rather a continual process of change. Like Walker Evans, who found strength in seeing the world as a Cubist painting, always changing and re-creating itself, Wright saw the world to be "in the making." Rosskam set the "Men in the Making" chapter title over a photograph that Arthur Rothstein took in 1938 of a black steelworker from Pittsburgh (141). Although his clothes are sweaty and his hat tattered, the man conveys an outward-looking strength that is absent from Lee's photograph of the churchwomen or the waiting children. The world-in-the-making is adult, male, youthful (but not childish), and work-oriented. There is no mention of religion in this last chapter. There are no inverted visions or paeans to churchly succor. Wright does not make even a feeble attempt to move African Americans toward the Social Gospel of liberal Protestantism as he did in his earlier short story "Fire and Cloud." Humanity "in the making" is represented as a black version of the fully secular, epic worker of Depression-era art and literature.[37] "As our consciousness changes, as we come of age," Wright reflects, "as we shed our folk swaddling-clothes, so run our lives in a hundred directions" (143). The modernist division between old

8.9 (facing page) Wright and Rosskam, *12 Million Black Voices*, 95 (LC-USF34-038802-D)

So they keep thousands of Little Bethels and Pilgrims and Calvarys an White Rocks and Good Hopes and Mount Olives going with their nickel and dimes. Nurtured in the close and intimate folk culture of the South where each person knew the others, where the basic emotions of life wer

and new, with religion siding with the old, has been repeated yet again. Wright's worker of the imaginary future has banished from his mind the illusion of trying to grow vegetable gardens in front of hovels.

To understand how the church was shed along with the "swaddling-clothes" of premodern consciousness, we must return to Wright's penultimate chapter, "Death on the City Pavement." Here Wright explains why teenagers are loitering on the church steps: "We lean upon our God and scold our children and try to drag them to church with us," Wright tells us, "but just as we once, years ago, left the plantation to roam the South, so now they leave us for the city pavements. But deep down in us we are glad that our children feel the world hard enough to yearn to wrestle with it . . . for our instincts tell us that those brave ones who struggle against death are the ones who bring new life into the world" (136). Like Wright, who rejected the religion of his mother and grandmother and came to Chicago to live among communists, scholars, and artists, "we" should struggle against the stranglehold of religion even if it means death. The city does turn out to be the Promised Land, even if it means that the land is no longer a place of ministers and churches.

It is in these last reflections on religion that Wright finally confesses what he really believed all along. Independence, even if it means death or demonization — as it did for Lucifer before time began — must be embraced. The church cannot be a place where "we are wholly ourselves" because it brutally enslaves the individual to the community. It is in the city, not in a romanticized rural world of wooden churches and prayerful deacons, that freedom can be anticipated. Christianity will not be a partner in the process of making a socially and economically egalitarian world because it looks too much beyond this world. Using a selection of FSA photographs of religion, Wright presents in *12 Million Black Voices* an imaginative story of the end of religion.

Negroes and the War

The publication of *12 Million Black Voices* came barely a month before the bombing of Pearl Harbor. Perceiving that their society and culture were under attack, Americans and the government shifted attention away from social problems. The messages of *12 Million Black Voices,* along with that of James Agee and Walker Evans's *Let Us Now Praise Famous Men,* also published in 1941, were soon drowned out by war concerns. The FSA file of photographs, however, continued to be used as a source of representations of African-American life. During the forties, the Office of War Information distributed 2.5 million copies of a pamphlet filled with FSA photographs of black life. *Negroes and the War* cost $85,000 to produce and was widely distributed throughout the country. Unlike *12 Million Black Voices,* this piece of propaganda was directed exclusively at one segment of the population. Chandler Owen, the black journalist who wrote the text, believed that African Americans would respond positively to a message that characterized the war against Hitler as a war against slavery.[38] One hundred forty-one illustrations of black life and culture were included in the seventy-two-page pamphlet. Ted Poston, a black editor who headed the OWI's Negro Press section, chose the photographs

8.10 (facing page)   Wright and Rosskam, *12 Million Black Voices,* 134 (LC-USF34-038810-D)

from the FSA file in consultation with Edwin Rosskam. Rosskam was working as a visual information specialist for the OWI after it took over the Historical Section. Poston also worked with Alfred Palmer, an OWI photographer who was familiar with Stryker's trove of images.

After the publication of *Negroes and the War*, the OWI conducted a series of surveys to see whether African Americans had gotten the message about the war. They had not. Readers of the pamphlet could not see that Hitler was a particular enemy of Negroes. From their perspective, Hitler's hatred of the Jews was only slightly more destructive than white attitudes toward blacks in the United States. African-American activists did not respond to the pamphlet's message either. From their point of view, *Negroes and the War* failed to address American racism and lacked any sense that progress could be made in the area of social justice. Southern congressmen also hated the pamphlet. "All over this country we are having race riots, even in the North," Congressman James Allen of Louisiana lectured his fellow representatives, "and the type of propaganda the OWI has been sending out certainly does not hold that situation down." Conservatives not only rejected the pamphlet's implication that the races were equal, they succeeded in forbidding the OWI from issuing any more pamphlets of any type. Despite the criticism, the black public could not get enough of *Negroes and the War*. The OWI observed it was "going like hot cakes."[39]

One reason for the popularity of *Negroes and the War* was that it provided African Americans with pictures of themselves. *Negroes and the War* was in demand not because of its patriotic sentiments but because it presented visual evidence of black values and accomplishments. In a society that had succeeded in erasing most black images from the public sphere except those that promoted racist stereotypes, pictures of everyday life in African-American communities were rare. *Negroes and the War* was filled with illustrations of ordinary people doing everyday things, seemingly without the pressures of racism and poverty. These were the very representations that many critics — black and white — felt were missing from *12 Million Black Voices*. In addition, *Negroes and the War* was a visual "who's who." It had illustrations of almost every black notable — from Marian Anderson to Jesse Owens to E. Franklin Frazier. Unlike the illustrations in *12 Million Black Voices*, which continued the tradition of reformist photography, *Negroes and the War* showed blacks as full American citizens — who could be housewives or opera stars.

Poston was able to include such photographs in a piece of propaganda because during the early forties Stryker directed his photographers to make pictures of middle-class black life. A year after Russell Lee and Edwin Rosskam were in Chicago, Jack Delano photographed South Side life. The primary goal of Delano's visit was to show Chicago as a powerful railroad transportation center. But, perhaps in preparation for *Negroes and the War*, he also took pictures of successful African Americans. Delano photographed the technological sophistication of black medical personnel working at a segregated South Side hospital. He photographed jazz musicians playing both in nightclubs and at home with their children. Delano went to the recently opened government-financed Ida B. Wells housing project on the South Side. His photographs do not show destitute families thankful for decent housing but rather tenants who seem fully accustomed to organizing "town meetings." Residents are shown taking first-aid classes, publishing a community newspaper, providing art classes for their children, and attending Sunday afternoon forums.[40] While life on Chicago's South Side had not changed in a year, the need for a certain kind of pictures had.

Other FSA photographers also made pictures of black life unencumbered by debilitating poverty. That March and again in July, Marjory Collins photographed teachers, technical schools, dance classes, and patriotic activities among African Americans in Washington, D.C. Before leaving for New Mexico, John Collier, Jr., took pictures of a black employee at the Library of Congress whose husband was an intern at Howard University. Gordon Parks also filmed middle-class life in the nation's capital. After the Historical Section was moved to the OWI in October 1942, part-time photographers like Howard Liberman, Alfred Palmer, and Terry Pat continued to produce black images. These photographs are not as well known as the rural pictures of black sharecroppers, but because the government wanted evidence that African Americans also enjoyed the Four Freedoms, this slice of city life exists.[41]

Given that Americans were now fighting to preserve the Four Freedoms, it is not surprising that religion was included in this portrait of black life. What is surprising is *which* pictures of religion were used. Gone is the sense that southern evangelicalism defines the "Negro church." A photograph that Russell Lee took at St. Edmund's Episcopal Church was made into an illustration. During Jack Delano's visit in 1942 he photographed at two Catholic churches that were made up exclusively of African Americans, and one from this series was printed. Gordon Parks contributed a curious picture of a "storefront" minister preaching next to a statue of the Virgin Mary. Of the five illustrations of religious life in *Negroes and the War,* only the first two reflect the "Negro church" of *12 Million Black Voices.*

Unlike Richard Wright, who stressed the similarity between church life South and North, *Negroes and the War* makes a clear delineation between rural and urban worship. The first two illustrations, both from photographs taken in the South, introduce the section with large headlines telling readers that "From the humblest beginnings . . . out of our deepest need we have built the Negro Church" (ellipsis in original). Rather than showing a family supposedly dressed for church, photographs in *Negroes and the War* dramatically command our attention with the church itself. Using a photograph taken by Walker Evans, who delighted in picturing churches without people, the building is a testament to durability and elegance. Solid and relentlessly symmetrical, it conveys the stability of rural belief (fig. 8.11). Inside this church, as the next illustration lets us imagine, we see no women. It is only men who have their heads bowed and their hands covering their eyes in prayerful concentration. Even the shadow created by the camera's flash serves to heighten the male presence in church (fig. 8.1).

These two illustrations of a rural church present southern piety as calm and focused. There is no ecstatic praise or even heartfelt song. Bodies are fully under the control of their owners. The primitive, emotional, "Negro character" that Rosskam and Wright were both drawn to and repelled by is absent. Likewise, the men seem fully comfortable assuming their prayerful postures. There is a feeling of power in these two photographs, but it is not the "naked will to power" that oppressed Wright in his Seventh-day Adventist family. *Negroes and the War* has erased the dark side of giving oneself over to God and his community of the saints. Surrounded by pages and pages of successful black men and women, religion no longer is burdened by representing the only place of agency in the African-American community.

Churches are merely one more place where African Americans have displayed their energy and creativity.

Turning the page, readers are moved into an urban world (figs. 8.12, 8.13). Unlike in *12 Million Black Voices,* where urban faith is only a vanishing version of rural piety, government propaganda accentuates the discontinuity between rural and urban Christianity. While a rural congregation might own nothing more than a wooden chair, pulpit, and some benches,

8.11   *Negroes and the War* (LC-USF342-008054-D)

AN EPISCOPALIAN CHURCH IN CHICAGO

OUR NATION IS AT WAR. This war will decide whether the Christian Church as an institution will survive. This war will decide whether Negro Americans will have the right to continue their march to freedom or will sink into slavery.

There can be no question as to where anyone of us stands in this grave world crisis. The democracy which the United Nations fight to preserve has its deep fountain in the principles of Jesus Christ. Our Nation is builded on Christian principles. WE STAND BEHIND OUR NATION AND OUR PEOPLE FOR VICTORY OVER HITLER AND SLAVERY.

Because we know the great stake involved in this war, we have lost no time in throwing the full weight of the Negro church behind the task of mobilizing the Negro people for victory. That is why we declared to the President of the United States on February 17, 1942:

"WE PLEDGE EVERY SPIRITUAL AND MATERIAL RESOURCE AT OUR COMMAND IN SUPPORT OF OUR COUNTRY IN THE IDEALS OF FREEDOM AND DEMOCRACY . . ."*

*From an address by the Rev. W. H. Jernagin, president of the Fraternal Council of Negro Churches of America

8.12   *Negroes and the War* (LC-USF33-013013-M2)

city congregations are awash in Christian material culture. Churches are built of bricks, and they have clocks, statues, crucifixes, and electric lights. Men dress in suits, and servers put on laced cottas. Choir members wear mortarboards and starched collars. African Americans in the city participate in rituals that are not spontaneous expressions of religious enthusiasm but carefully choreographed symbolic statements of faith. In the city, African Americans can choose from black evangelical traditions or high-church liturgies. Whites do not hold a monopoly over certain styles of worship, just as they have not succeeded in restricting all African Americans from being writers or chemistry students.

GOD IS LOVE

SAINT MARTIN'S

SUNRISE

STORE FRONT CHURCH IN WASHINGTON, D.

YOUTHFUL WORSHIPERS IN A CATHOLIC CHURC

The illustrations in *Negroes and the War* are not only crowded with objects, they are packed with people. City churches are as communal and congested as Chicago's pavements. Men have not left religion to their women and children. They preach from the pulpit and sit attentively near the minister. A teenage boy swings a censer, younger boys carry a cross and candles, and male elders watch knowingly. Unlike in *12 Million Black Voices*, where teenagers and children stand aimlessly outside of the church's closed doors, in *Negroes and the War* they cram the pews. Since children are the future of the church as well as of the nation, they are represented as active and intent participants in religious practices. It is only women who are pictured somewhat at a distance from the centers of faith. We have to look carefully at the illustrations to see the nuns watching their charges or the women's choir sitting behind the church elders. Women do not dominate these churches. Just as they are not the primary actors in war, they are not the key players in religion.

Negroes and the War, designed to appeal to African Americans, presents a perspective on city congregations that is not shared by Richard Wright. The illustrations in *12 Million Black Voices*, while respectfully avoiding negative stereotypes of black religious behaviors, never challenge what "the" Negro church "is." They continue to present African Americans as pious and simple evangelicals. Instead, it was a piece of government propaganda that insisted that African Americans participated in a range of religious practices.

8.13 (facing page)   *Negroes and the War* (LC-USF34-013384-C)

9
City Congregations

eft Chicago this morning after a hell of a grueling job," Russell Lee complained to
Stryker. "I'm afraid I was tired when I started the job and by the end was not really
much good and inclined to make errors. Then, too, Chicago is a very depressing place
when taking pictures in the negro neighborhoods."[1] Lee and Rosskam did make a
series of errors in Chicago that shaped how the photographs were later "read." They
assumed that African-American religions were best understood through the lens
of the Chicago School of sociology and that the "Negro church" had a set of unifying characteristics. Later, when the Office of War Information produced a piece of patriotic propaganda to emphasize the strength of the black community, a different set of "errors" were made.
Negroes and the War may be justly criticized as portraying African Americans as religiously
"successful" only when their men engage in the rituals of white Christians. In the case of

9.1 (facing page)   Russell Lee, Elder Lucy Smith. Chicago, April 1941 (LC-USF34-038803-D)

both publications, the "errors" stem from the desire to use African-American religious practices to support a larger purpose — to explain where the "Negro church" fit into the story of either black oppression or black success.

To dismiss the illustrations in *12 Million Black Voices* and *Negroes and the War* as mere visual representations of the ideologies of their makers, however, is to overlook their cultural importance. In this chapter I return to the full FSA/OWI file of photographs that served as the source for those publications. When that visual record is supplemented with written records, a fuller representation of the "Negro church" emerges. African Americans experienced in city congregations in Chicago and Washington, D.C., a complex and intense religious life. The photographs of Russell Lee, Edwin Rosskam, Jack Delano, and Gordon Parks provide us an entrance into that world. While the photographers may have intended for their images to illustrate the class structure of "Bronzeville" or the success of African Americans in joining traditionally white churches, we can also use the pictures to tease out what churchgoing was like for men, women, and children in the early forties.

Church of God in Christ

One of the "errors" that Russell Lee, Edwin Rosskam, and Richard Wright made in Chicago was to assume that one "Negro Church" was the same as any other "Negro church." Consequently, nine photographs of a Church of God in Christ congregation on the South Side were miscaptioned as pictures of a "storefront Baptist" church. Downplaying the significance of religious difference, the photographers followed the lead of the Chicago School and overemphasized class while underestimating denominational history, theology, and ritual. Unfortunately, later historians working with the Chicago photographs never questioned the accuracy of Lee's and Rosskam's notations.[2] Their scholarship continued the flattening of regional and religious difference presented in *12 Million Black Voices*. In order to move away from generic descriptions of the "Negro church" and toward a more accurate representation of African-American life, we must understand that Baptist churches are not interchangeable with Church of God in Christ congregations.

If scholars had observed the visual evidence as well as the written, they would have immediately questioned the accuracy of Lee's caption. Both Lee's original photographs and the illustrations published in *12 Million Black Voices* indicate that what was photographed was not a Baptist church (see fig. 8.10). The sign on the building reads "CHURCH OF GOD IN CHRIST" and lists the name of the pastor as Elder W. A. Hicks. Numbering above the door gives a hint at the church's street address (07). "Church of God in Christ" is the name not of an individual church but of a denomination. A list of South Side churches compiled in 1938 by a worker for the Federal Writers' Project includes a Church of God in Christ congregation pastored by W. A. Hicks located at 3307 State Street. Members of Church of God in Christ congregations still living on the South Side recognized Elder Hicks's picture and remember that he "always dressed well."[3]

We can connect the exterior photographs with the interior ones by looking at the banner hanging behind the minister that reads: "STATE S.S. BANNER/ELDER/W. M. ROBERTS/STATE

OVERSEER" (see fig. 8.9). The Greek word *epískopos,* translated by some Christian communities as *bishop,* is rendered as *overseer* by members of the Church of God in Christ. W.[illiam] M. Roberts was an important figure in Chicago's Church of God in Christ community. In 1907 in Memphis, Tennessee, he joined with Charles H. Mason and a handful of other men to establish the denomination. Eventually he moved to Indiana and then to Chicago. In 1938 FWP investigators filed twenty-six reports that described W. M. Roberts's church located at 4021 State Street. Overseer Roberts would have supervised churches in his district, including Elder Hicks's congregation located seven blocks away.[4]

Traditionally in the South, African Americans joined either Baptist or Methodist churches, and a few Catholics lived in Louisiana and Maryland. By the turn of the century, however, Pentecostal, Holiness, and Spiritualist movements had come to provide significant competition to mainstream Protestantism, both black and white. Robert and Helen Lynd noted in 1937 that the "smaller and more primitive sects" were growing at a fast clip, and they quoted one white minister as saying that "my church has grown from 40 to 200 during the past four or five years as it is one of only two churches of our denomination [locally] and draws working people from all over the city."[5] While outsiders may have considered all these "sects" as merely fundamentalist "storefront" congregations unmarked by denominational differences, this was not the case.

The Church of God in Christ, established by Charles Mason in the late nineteenth century, was one of the "primitive sects" that flourished in the black neighborhoods of America's cities. By 1938 there were at least thirteen congregations in Chicago.[6] Like many Baptist congregations, the Church of God in Christ (then and now) stresses the fervor of spiritual life. Preachers teach the infallibility of Scripture and the need for regeneration. Like Baptists, they emphasize repentance and justification by faith. A person's sins are forgiven through the atoning death of Christ. Unlike Baptists, however, they believe in entire sanctification, which comes after one has accepted Christ as Savior. Sanctification enables believers to live a holy life apart from the sinning world. Church of God in Christ members (known as Saints) feel that their community has restored the excitement of early Christianity. In black neighborhoods in Chicago, Saints separated themselves from other Christians by their dress and behavior. They spent most of Sunday in church. During services Saints experienced the gifts of the Holy Spirit by speaking in tongues or by healing. Their ritual practices included full-immersion baptism, as well as monthly Holy Communion and foot washing services.

Since most Protestant congregations on the South Side scheduled worship services to begin at eleven o'clock, the photographers had to arrive either before or after the main service of some of the churches in order to visit several religious communities on that one Easter morning. Lee and Rosskam's first stop on that special morning was the Sunday School of Elder Hicks's Church of God in Christ. According to the announcement of services shown in Lee's photograph, Elder Hicks's congregation held Sunday school at nine o'clock in the morning (see fig. 8.10), so they were probably just finishing when the pair arrived. The historian Nicholas Natanson speculates that Lee and Rosskam made the series of photographs in order to balance the "holy rolling" of black fundamentalism with glimpses of "contemplative activity." Such images would help defuse racist myths about inherent black emotionalism and primitive spirituality. According to Natanson, here were "Baptists" celebrating Easter like a "seminar [rather] than a holiday service."[7] The congregation, however, was not a Baptist congregation, and they were not "celebrating" Easter.

Sunday school in the Church of God in Christ precedes the main worship service. At nine o'clock in the morning all in attendance assemble into small groups to sing hymns, study the day's lesson, and recite memorized Bible verses. Men and women form separate discussion groups, and children are divided by age. These small-group discussions typically go on for several hours and could be very animated. Around eleven o'clock the congregation reassembles and summarizes the main topics of the day's lesson. Lee photographed the group when they were intensely focused on reading the Bible and examining the Sunday lesson. His close-up of a woman marking pages in her Bible summarizes the involvement of the community with the Scriptures and conveys the importance of education and literacy for many South Side residents (fig. 9.2).

A photograph can catch only one moment out of many. At other points during the two-hour Sunday school the mood would have been different. Church members interacted in multifaceted ways with the Scriptures. In 1938 the FWP investigator Edward Rembert observed Sunday school classes at William Roberts's church. While this was a different church from Elder Hicks's church just up State Street, the congregational attitude toward Sunday school was probably the same. "When the classes reassembled and formed one body to review the lesson," Rembert reported, "everybody again wanted to be the teacher, everybody wanted to be heard, each individual thought he was right and the other fellow was wrong."[8] Different interpretations of biblical texts made Sunday school sessions lively. Rembert voiced concern that the congregation could not reach a consensus on the meaning of a "simple verse." When a biblical text is taken seriously, religious people can become quite committed and enthusiastic about their interpretation of it. Fundamentalists in particular debate what God intended in "His" revealed Scripture, what the linguistic origin of a specific word is, and how the meaning of a passage relates to one's own life. Believing in the literal truth of the Scriptures does not mean that everyone in a church will agree on a single interpretation. Rembert may have thought he knew the meaning of a "simple verse," but he also had only one interpretation. Those outside of the church community often have a difficult time understanding what all the fuss is about.

Since Lee and Rosskam left the church just before the main worship service began, they failed to see what happened after "the seminar." In order to understand what is in photographs, we must also consider what is left out. Essential to all Church of God in Christ worship is the ecstatic expression of spirit-filled devotion that includes shouting, dancing, hand waving, speaking in tongues, and other spontaneous manifestations. On any one Sunday morning Saints move between "holy rolling" and "contemplative" activity. Lee and Rosskam, however, did not photograph the ecstatic aspect of Sunday worship. Edward Rembert reported that after Sunday school a "testimonial service" occurred that included singing, reading a scriptural lesson, and chanting. "With hands raised, faces long and solemn, with what seemed like the burden of the world on their shoulders," he reported, "these people followed their leader in 'yes Lord,' until sufficient spiritual enthusiasm was worked up to inflame the audience."[9] After an hour of testimonials, the preaching began.

9.2   Russell Lee, worshiper searching the Scriptures during Sunday school at Church of God in Christ.
Chicago, April 1941 (LC-USF34-038828-D)

9.3   Russell Lee, the Rev. W. A. Hicks. Chicago, April 1941 (LC-USF34-038829-D)

Rembert's description of Hicks delivering a sermon contrasts sharply with the portrait taken by Lee (fig. 9.3). While Lee's photograph supports the idea that this man could run a "contemplative seminar," Rembert's description firmly places the minister in the evangelical tradition of vibrant preaching. "Elder Hicks clapped his hands together with clock-like regularity," Rembert reported, "as he sang and whipped up the spirit. His hand clapping sounded like pistol shots, or like the striking of two planks together. In the course of whipping up the spirit these people, led by Elder Hicks' singing, actually danced. . . . They goose-stepped, fox trotted, eagle-rocked, snake hipped, and carried on so many types of primitive contortions it was impossible to follow all of them. . . . Elder Hicks, in the pulpit, was doing a backward tanglefoot dance that defies description, and at least thirty-five persons were out on the floor dancing." Eventually Elder Hicks grabbed one of the chairs on the rostrum, dragged it in front of the pulpit, and lifted it up demonstrating how "Jesus restored the man who was sick of the palsy." After his sermon, the congregation "broke into wild demonstrations." "Amid this clamor," Rembert reported, "the services came to a close. The collection was taken and church dismissed."[10]

Edward Rembert attended Church of God in Christ congregations many times, but he never ceased to be amazed by their holy dance. Russell Lee's photograph of a calm, intellectual congregation is misleading. A fuller portrayal of the congregation would have shown a community that could, and did, experience the Spirit of God in a variety of ways. While it might be considered meritorious to record and publish the intellectual rituals of a black congregation, it would have been more accurate to illustrate how this community mastered the various spiritual moods of study, praise, and prayer. For members of the Church of God in Christ, there was no carefully laid-out hierarchy between religious expressions. The Saints were expected to attend Sunday school as well as all the other services and meetings. Members experienced intellectual and enthusiastic rituals.

Lee's interior photographs of Hicks's church remind us that a faith community that builds its life around the Bible and the gifts of the Holy Spirit may also create a visible worship environment. While the biblical text is certainly central in Church of God in Christ congregations, this particular congregation also used images to draw themselves out of the everyday and focus their minds and feelings on the life, passion, and resurrection of Christ. If we look at the pictures that Lee took, we can see that Elder Hicks and his congregation were not anti-iconic Protestants. A large painting of Christ crucified hangs behind the pulpit (fig. 9.3). Blood drips from the wounds, and Jesus' head is bowed in agony. In addition to the painting, an Easter cross is displayed with a crepe paper shroud, and three simple wooden crosses adorn the sanctuary. A print of Leonardo da Vinci's *Last Supper* is hung to the right of the pulpit, and a close-up of the head of the young Jesus from Heinrich Hofmann's *Christ and the Rich Young Ruler* is placed on the far left wall above the piano (fig. 9.4). A print of the Sacred Heart of Jesus hangs on the right wall across from the Hofmann print (fig. 9.5). Care has been taken to transform these mass-produced prints into something special by having them framed and placed in prominent places. Elder Hicks also wears a gold Gothic-style cross.

Since the turn of the nineteenth century, Protestant denominational publishing houses and commercial companies have made and sold religious prints and biblical sayings, some of which are put in churches. The print of the young Jesus displayed in Elder Hicks's church was sold both by Perry Prints and by the Gospel Trumpet Company. By the 1930s Gospel Trumpet sold stationery with religious sayings, lamps bearing the face of Jesus, Christian wall mottoes, Sunday school games, and puzzles that illustrated Bible stories. In the South, traveling Bible salesmen peddled such religious goods, and during the Depression itinerant salesmen became popular in the North as well. Men who could not find permanent work could sell door-to-door on commission. Church groups also sold prints and calendars to raise money.[11] African Americans, like all Protestants, used material culture to dramatize and secure their evangelical message.

9.4   Russell Lee, interior of the Church of God in Christ with Hoffman print at left.
Chicago, April 1941 (LC-USF34-038812-D)

Perhaps more unexpected in a Church of God in Christ congregation were the images of the Passion, images more closely associated with Catholics and Episcopalians. Visual evidence from elsewhere in black religious culture suggests that such images occurred in the interwar years. In June 1941, for instance, Jack Delano photographed inside the home of a black woman whose former residence in Caroline County, Virginia, had been destroyed to make room for army maneuver grounds. She was now living in a prefabricated house that the FSA had built her. In her living room was a large framed picture of the wounded head of Christ. That fall, Delano was in Woodville, Georgia. There he took an interior picture of a "Negro church." Tacked on the wall of the church a pennant reads "Baptist World Alliance." In this apparently Baptist church, a large crucifix hangs down over the chair where the minister sits. In the same year Spencer Williams wrote, directed, acted in, and financed a film he called *The Blood of Jesus.* The "race film" was produced by an African American for an African-American audience.[12] *The Blood of Jesus,* like other Spencer Williams movies, had an all-black cast. It also contained many bleeding Christ images. Women wear crucifixes when they go to the river for baptism, and the main protagonist prays in front of a print of the Sacred Heart in her bedroom. In the dramatic climax to the movie, blood drips from the wounds of a crucified Christ onto the forehead of a virtuous woman.

These African Americans were giving visual life to long-standing themes in Protestant theology and spirituality that stressed the importance of the atoning sacrifice of Christ (Rom

3:25) and the "blood of Jesus" (Heb 10:19). Embodied, sensual depictions of salvation have appeared in American Protestant piety since the Puritan days. Blood imagery in particular became popular in evangelical hymns. Hymn writers from Isaac Watts and William Cowper to Fanny Cosby and Phoebe Palmer described gruesome visions of fountains "fill'd with blood" and warned Christians to "Trust only in the precious blood / That cleanseth white as snow."[13] Revival hymnists of the early twentieth century also employed graphic language to stimulate conversions. A 1904 hymn by Nellie Edwards observed,

> My sins are all covered by the blood
> Mine iniquities so vast
> Have been blotted out at last
> My sins are all covered by the blood.

Verbal and visual depictions of the "precious blood" of Jesus intimately reminded the Saved of the costs of their salvation and put their own suffering into a divine context. Although gospel music was becoming popular in Chicago after Thomas Dorsey's appointment in 1932 as music director of Pilgrim Baptist Church, older images in hymnody shaped the imaginative world of black as well as white evangelical Protestants.

Catholic religious goods companies may have produced the prints and crucifixes used

9.5   Russell Lee, interior of the Church of God in Christ with Sacred Heart print at right.
Chicago, April 1941 (LC-USF34-038813-D)

by African Americans. Catholics and their churches were everywhere in Chicago, so African-American congregations had easy access to Catholic material culture. In addition, in the early twentieth century Catholics had increased missionary activity in the South. Religious orders like the Josephites (St. Joseph's Society of the Sacred Heart) directed their attention to African Americans. In the twenties and thirties, other rural missionaries traveled the South in motor homes that doubled as catechetical centers. Crucifixes and prints of the Sacred Heart may have originally been designed as devotional aids for potential rural black converts. The objects may have traveled north with their owners who then used them in other settings.

The space of Elder Hicks's church was not a purified, orderly universe where everyday objects were kept from tainting (or at least distracting from) the biblical narrative contained in holy pictures. The interior photographs show that these African Americans put coat hangers on the wall behind the pulpit and left a hat in front of one of the wood crosses. A moneybox, a collection basket, and a clock sit on the table. Books, and probably music, are scattered on top of a piano. Both the table and piano top are covered with decorative cloths. Just as their services are filled with debate, music, and dance, the congregation's visual space is packed with evocative images. There is no clear-cut division between sacred and profane, cross and coat hanger. Protestant African Americans used images in ways similar to Catholics in Texas and New Mexico. The photographs help us see that the church, like the home, was a place of mixing rather than separating. Both of these Protestant and Catholic communities engaged the religious imagination by creating a complicated visual environment that blended the supernatural and the natural.

Chicago's Church of God in Christ congregations, photographed by Russell Lee and documented by FWP workers, employed an aesthetic of excess. There is nothing plain, pure, simple, or straightforward about either their religious practices or their visual environment. Ritual was explored in its fullness — from quiet reading to ecstatic praise. Objects and images were layered and repeated with apparently little concern about what they might convey about class or taste. There is no sense that a print of a painting by a Renaissance master would be inappropriate because it symbolizes upper-class fashions. The fact that hangers are in full view of the congregation (lower-class) does not keep Pastor Hicks from wearing a Roman collar and pectoral cross (upper-class). The congregation sought to experience the life, and perhaps more poignantly the death, of Christ. For them, the more varied the ways that the Christ event could be experienced, the better.

All Nations Pentecostal Church

After Sunday school was over, Lee and Rosskam dashed to another Pentecostal church. Of all the churches that he and Rosskam visited on Easter, this was the only one where they stayed for most of the worship service. Lee took twenty-three photographs of Lucy Smith's All Nations Pentecostal Church, which was less than a mile away from Hicks's Church of God in Christ. At least twenty FWP field reports were filed on Smith's congregation. St. Clair Drake and Horace Cayton in *Black Metropolis* include only two churches on their map of "The World of the Lower Class" — Cobb's Church (a spiritualist church) and Lucy Smith's church. Elder Smith had little in common with the "lonely young black preacher" that Richard Wright imag-

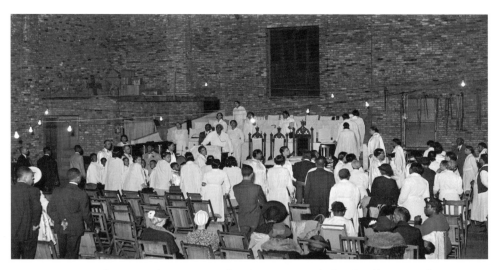

9.6   Russell Lee, opening prayers at All Nations Pentecostal Church. Chicago, April 1941
(LC-USF34-038804-D)

ined ministering to women on the South Side.[14] By the early 1940s, Lucy Smith was one of the
most important black ministers in Chicago (see fig. 9.1). Her radio program had been on the
air since 1933, and a multiracial group of believers and nonbelievers listened to her broadcasts
and attended her prayer services. An even larger and more diverse audience listened to the All
Nations choir singing gospel music over the airwaves. Smith's healing capabilities were known
citywide, and the wall behind and to the right of the pulpit held the braces and crutches of
those who no longer needed them (fig. 9.6). A 1936 FWP report, perhaps edited by Richard
Wright, noted that Smith had "an ardent following" of about three thousand. In 1940 Cassel Gross speculated that All Nations had the largest regular attendance and membership of
any Sanctified church in the city. When Smith died in 1952, more than sixty thousand people
viewed her body, and her funeral was one of the largest in Chicago history.[15]

Lucy Maddox Smith was born in 1875 in Oglethorpe County, Georgia. She married in
1892 and eventually had nine children. In 1910 she traveled northward with thousands of other
southern blacks and arrived in Chicago. After attending several Baptist churches, she joined a
white Pentecostal assembly in 1914. Lucy Smith did not simply transplant her southern practices to Chicago. Like many residents of the South Side, and twentieth-century Christians in
general, she visited and considered various congregations, beliefs, practices, and even racial
settings to see which fit her spiritual needs. Then, when she heard God call her to be a healer,
she established her own church. Intending that both white and black would worship together,
she called her church All Nations Pentecostal Church.

As in other Pentecostal and Sanctified churches, active members of All Nations separated
themselves from others in the black community. The Saints of All Nations, Alvin Cannon reported in 1938, "are a society all of their own, but they are not recognized by the so-called
respectable society." A member reflected, "You are in a sort of hypnotic state from the time
you enter the church until the time you leave the service. The services have a certain liveliness

and zip. You feel a sense of independence. You say to yourself: 'Here is something which I can depend on.' There is a close, very close bond and union between the members."[16] Shunning things of the world, the Saints rejected movies, makeup, smoking, and playing policy (betting on numbers). They sought to stand apart from the things of the world that they perceived to be sinful. Like the members of the Church of God in Christ, the rhythms of their lives were closely entwined with their church. And like the membership of most black congregations, the majority were women.

That the Saints spent long hours in church did not mean they were antimodern. Elder Smith chose those elements of modern society that supported her religious orientation and condemned those she felt distracted from it. Just as members of the Church of God in Christ did not distinguish between Catholic and Protestant holy pictures, Lucy Smith's followers had a pragmatic approach to life. Members of All Nations embraced contemporary forms of music; Lee's photographs showed their church's drum set. The choir read music and sang gospel hymns from songbooks, unlike their rural cousins who preferred unaccompanied music sung by rote. One of Lucy Smith's daughters recorded gospel music with a quartet. While they believed along with other Pentecostals in the literal existence of angels, demons, and the devil, they also produced a radio show using modern technology. All Nations assumed that the current economic unrest and foreign wars of the thirties and forties were signals of the imminent Second Coming, but Lucy Smith also was able to include in her sermons the details of the Italian Fascist invasion of Ethiopia.[17] She knew what was going on in the world. Just as Elder Hicks's congregation rejected the hierarchical dichotomy between book rituals and spirit-filled rituals, so did Elder Smith's congregation intermingle the modern world of radio with the supernatural world of demons and Armageddon.

If Lucy Smith had followed the class-based prescriptions detailed in *Black Metropolis* and *12 Million Black Voices,* she would have set up a church in a storefront, where her followers would have felt comfortable with her spirit-filled services. Smith did start small, but she eventually built a grand brick church at 518 Oakwood Boulevard. Unlike many African-American churches that were hand-me-downs from Protestant and Jewish congregations, All Nations was designed explicitly for Elder Smith by the architects Newhouse and Burnham. This large "physical plant" should have contained an upper class or at least upwardly mobile membership. Lucy Smith's congregation, however, could not afford to maintain her dream church. FWP reports from 1940 mention that the interior of the church was still not finished and that the building lacked proper heating. Lee's photographs show electric wires and bare lightbulbs dangling only a few feet above the choir members' heads (see fig. 9.6). What social scientists could see from the outside did not always mirror what was in the inside. Lucy Smith was a skilled organizer whose congregation bragged about her healing powers, but her big church did not reflect the economic status of her flock. Only a very few people on Chicago's South Side were economically prosperous, while many endured financial sacrifices to support the church they attended.

Lucy Smith herself illustrates the problem of making simple associations between class and religion. Smith was a popular healer, counselor, and marriage therapist, but her daughter insisted that she was not a wealthy woman. On the other hand, Cassel Gross reported in July of 1940, "While she says, 'I'm not a salary preacher,' it is evident that her congregation has

9.7   Russell Lee, Brother Holly. Chicago, April 1941
(LC-USF34-038772-D)

taken exceptionally good care of her. She now owns considerable real estate, including several apartment buildings, [and] a fine chauffeured limousine, generally a new eight-cylinder Packard. This, her congregation evidently approves for she has asked for separate collections, a 'free-will' offering for a new dress or other necessary luxuries." Lucy Smith had an imposing presence in black Chicago, and Russell Lee succeeded in capturing her impressive mien (see fig. 9.1). In this photograph, unlike her illustration in *12 Million Black Voices,* Elder Smith is very much of this earth. Cassell Gross noted that she did not "become emotionally excited to the degree that some of her members do" but was "rather phlegmatic." The body of Lucy Smith, like the size of her church, fascinated government reporters. They all commented on her massive weight and dark skin, and some even described her feet.[18]

Russell Lee photographed several members of All Nations, although he did not give their names in his captions. FWP reports provide enough biographical information on one of the male Saints to support my contention that there was an unstable relationship between religion and class on the South Side. "Brother Holly" came to the United States from Haiti in order to study agriculture at Tuskegee Institute (fig. 9.7). Like Lucy Smith, he arrived in Chicago in 1910. Lee photographed Holly, a former Episcopalian, on Easter dressed in a natty suit with his hands folded and face uplifted. He is pictured as a dignified male member of the congregation. Holly's education, demeanor, dress, former religion, and place of birth all might move us to think he should belong to a middle- or upper-class church instead of Lucy Smith's "lower class" church. Brother Holly probably would have been the first to say that Lee's portrayal of his serious religious spirit and dignified appearance should not be taken as a fixed identity. "I used to play the piano in the Episcopal church merely for form," Robert Lucas recalled Brother Holly saying. "'But now,' and—he smiled—'maybe you've noticed, I play from the heart.'"[19] Brother Holly could express his heart with both quiet reserve and enthusiasm. His participation in a church dominated by women did not mean that he had to uphold masculine rationality to balance their female emotionalism. Just as Lucy Smith was a cagey organizer and an enthusiastic preacher, Brother Holly could become spirit filled.

St. Edmund's Episcopal Church

When Brother Holly arrived in Chicago, he decided to join a Pentecostal church and leave Episcopal formalism behind. Other African Americans, however, decided to exchange the spontaneity of Pentecostal and Baptist worship for the liturgical precision of the Episcopalians. Not everyone who came to the city continued southern evangelical forms of piety. Edwin Rosskam wanted evidence of the church life of the black upper class, so he and Russell Lee photographed one such Episcopal congregation. Jack Delano wanted evidence of black accomplishment for *Negroes and the War,* so he photographed the same congregation again.[20] While a nuanced examination of class and religion can be informative, more impressive is the growth of Episcopal and Catholic communities of African Americans in the thirties and forties. African Americans did not merely use Catholic material culture; some joined high-church liturgical communities.

The story of St. Edmund's Episcopal Church provides an excellent entry into the growth of nonevangelical Christianity in the cities. Founded as a mission church for whites in 1905, St. Edmund's did not initially flourish. Its establishment came precisely at the time when whites who could afford to were leaving city neighborhoods. Those city neighborhoods then became the places where new African-American migrants found housing. In 1928 the Episcopal bishop Charles Palmerton Anderson decided not to sell the church, although most of its white parishioners had moved. Instead, he assigned an African-American deacon, Samuel J. Martin, to the church. Bishop Anderson gave Martin the charge to "secure your congregation at St. Edmund's."[21] St. Edmund's thus became one of two Episcopal churches in Chicago made up exclusively of African Americans.

Bishop Anderson was following a pattern familiar in Roman Catholic, if not Protestant, circles. For Protestants and Jews, when membership declined buildings were sold and congregations disbanded. The black members of Chicago's Pilgrim Baptist church, for example, had bought the synagogue of the oldest Jewish congregation in the city, Kehilath Anshe Ma'ariv. The synagogue was designed in 1890 by the famous architecture firm of Dankmar Adler and Louis Sullivan. The change from synagogue to church signaled the transformation of the South Side from white to black. In the thirties and forties, however, Roman Catholic bishops did not permit the movement of parishes to accommodate white flight out of changing neighborhoods. City parishes either struggled for survival or they became exclusively African-American congregations. Such was the case with St. Edmund's, as it was with two Catholic churches photographed by Jack Delano. White Episcopalians had moved out of the South Side, and Deacon Martin was given their church and told by his bishop to fill it with new members. This was to be a tremendous task.[22]

By all accounts a remarkable individual, Samuel Martin met his bishop's expectations. Martin was ordained a priest a year after he arrived at St. Edmund's, and he served as pastor there until 1970. Father Martin not only had to maintain the physical plant of a church built by white people during far more financially flush times, he had to convert low-church southern migrants to high-church Episcopal ways. In 1928 St. Edmund's had 150 black communicants, but ten years later it could boast 800 members. By the mid-thirties the church was respected throughout Chicago for the beauty of its liturgy. When the revered actor Richard B. Harrison ("De Lawd" from *Green Pastures*) died in 1935, seven thousand fans and dignitaries attended his memorial service at the Episcopal cathedral of St. John the Divine in New York City. The body was then sent to Chicago, Harrison's home, where Father Martin oversaw its presentation at St. Edmund's before its burial in Lincoln Cemetery.[23]

Father Martin is remembered for his exacting sense of ritual correctness. On the Easter that Rosskam and Lee took their photographs, there were so many people at the service that latecomers had to sit on folding chairs at the back of the church. At the end of Mass, Father Martin expected them to remove their temporary chairs at the beginning of the last hymn and exit the church so that the congregation could leave gracefully. This was why Lee and Rosskam could photograph churchgoers waiting outside of the church. As the congregation was finishing the last hymn, the servers, choir, and priest recessed through the front door, walked a short distance around to a side door, and reentered the church (figs. 9.8, 9.9; see fig. 8.12). The recessional lasted only a few minutes and was a common ritual that occurred on all feast days. Once back inside, Father Martin said a final prayer and dismissed the congregation. He then removed his clerical robes and walked to the door of the church, where he greeted the people. This was no "Easter parade" of Negro society, as Rosskam and other historians have implied, but a highly choreographed ritual that celebrated the Resurrection of Christ.[24]

The biography of Samuel Martin, like that of Lucy Smith and Brother Holly, also warns us not to assume that "high-class" churches were run by "high-class" people. Class and religion during this period were slippery identity markers for African Americans. Born in 1905 in Huntsville, Alabama, Samuel Martin was the son of a Baptist minister who preached in Alabama for thirty years. His mother was a teacher and an educational administrator. When Samuel was fourteen, Dorrence Martin died and her family was broken up. Whatever precarious economic stability the family enjoyed was lost. Samuel was reared by a Roman Catholic aunt in Alabama who passed her love of liturgy on to her young charge. Like so many others, Martin joined the Great Migration north and came to Chicago. In the process, he left the Roman Catholic Church and joined the Episcopal Church. Samuel Martin eventually received a Master of Sacred Theology degree and a certificate in excellence in Hebrew from Seabury-Western Theological Seminary in Evanston, Illinois.[25]

Samuel Martin was well aware of the fragile nature of black achievement. Racism prevented African Americans from enjoying a fixed class status — even among the most talented

9.8   Edwin Rosskam, Father Samuel J. Martin and two altar boys in the recessional after Easter Mass. Chicago, April 1941 (LC-USF33-005156-M4)

tenth. The liturgical formality of St. Edmund's and the prominence of some of its parishioners did not mean that the church could concentrate its energies on purely spiritual matters. During the Depression, Father Martin, like Elder Smith, organized soup kitchens and clothing distribution points. Martin accompanied church members and nonmembers to their court hearings and at times posted bail bonds. And, like Elder Smith, he was concerned with renovating and expanding the physical plant of his church. By 1945 the congregation had increased to the point that they needed a larger building, so they sold their original church and bought another. In 1948 they began a parochial school. St. Edmund's church is still active in its neighborhood, where 60 percent of the residents now live below the poverty line.[26]

St. Edmund's Episcopal Church did not merely survive on the South Side during the thirties and forties, it flourished. One of the reasons it did was that men and women, boys and girls, all found a place within the congregation. During the 1930s, for every four Christian men who went to church, there were five women. For African-American congregations the ratio of churchgoers was nearly three women to every man.[27] While there may have been a more balanced gender ratio at St. Edmund's, the all-male portrait in *Negroes and the War* is misleading (see fig. 8.12). Women were active at St. Edmund's, and they too had their place in the recessional (see fig. 9.9).

Children also had various reactions to churchgoing. For every boy like Richard Wright who hated getting dressed up to go to church, there were two girls who liked it. For every boy who thought his body was being disciplined by uncomfortable shoes, there were two girls who took pride in wearing their Sunday best. For every boy who could not wait to get out on the city pavements, there were two girls who felt secure and safe sitting in the pews. And for every boy who chafed against having his hair prepared for churchgoing, there were others who looked like they enjoyed lounging around in their robes.[28] Since many of those girls grew up to have sole control over their children (as we have seen so starkly in the memoirs of Richard Wright) they insisted that their children go to church with them. Women did not let children wander on the "city pavements," as Wright imagined, but found places for them in church.

Women who attended St. Edmund's in the thirties and forties recall that children did not merely sit bored in the pews. They were involved in almost every aspect of church life. When young people came back to the "home church" for holidays like Easter, they were integrated into the liturgy. This is what made the holiday recessionals look like parades, crowded with boys holding candles and choirs singing (see fig. 9.9). As with many Roman Catholic churches, St. Edmund's had a children's Mass at 9:30 on Sundays, and the five o'clock Easter Sunrise Mass was sung by the children's choir. Seniors at St. Edmund's explained that children were highly trained and disciplined and — at least according to their grandmothers — took pride in their liturgical knowledge and considered it an honor to participate in the Mass. The photographs by Lee, Rosskam, and Delano provide an alternative perspective from Wright's on how children experience the rote learning of prayers and ritual gestures. Rather than simply oppress the body's "natural" spontaneity, memorized movements and texts also allowed children to participate in an ordered, adult ritual world. Children, like their parents, could feel spiritually secure within the predictable and manageable routines of their church.

The FSA/OWI photographs of South Side churches and the corresponding FWP reports indicate that other children, not only Episcopalians, were involved in the practice of their

9.9   Russell Lee, women of the choir recessing after Easter Mass. Chicago, April 1941
(LC-USF33-013014-M5)

religion. Russell Lee took several pictures of children from All Nations Pentecostal Church putting on their choir robes and singing enthusiastically on Easter.[29] In 1938 the government investigator Alvin Cannon observed this about children and teens at Elder Roberts's Church of God in Christ church: "One was constantly impressed by the fact that for the most part the congregation was composed of young people. The young people it seemed were a vital part of the service. They played the musical instruments, ushered, sang in the choir and not a few of them testified and danced. The balcony seemed to be the rendezvous for most of the very young folk." Cannon did not want to speculate as to what extent the young people were actually interested in the services, but he did comment, "They were there and in large numbers, whether they were compelled to come or not."[30] In African-American communities, Episcopalian or Pentecostal, children were expected to go to church, and young people were counted on to participate in services. Lee's photographs of the Church of God in Christ Sunday School show children nestled among the adults (see figs. 9.4, 9.5). A child's refusal to go to church was a strong statement of the inability of the community and the family to socialize the next generation into proper communal and spiritual behavior. Children were the physical symbols of the future of the community. Their innocence and enthusiasm were seen as models for the devotional behavior of adults.

During the 1930s Protestant churches in general paid increased attention to children. Churches started vacation Bible schools and organized "release time" for children to leave school for short periods to attend religious education classes. Following the conflicts over the Scopes trial, conservative leaders lobbied for laws that mandated that the Bible be read in school and pushed school boards to grant high school credit for Bible study. In spite of declining membership among mainstream white denominations between 1926 and 1936 (Methodists were down 14 percent, Presbyterians down 5 percent, Episcopalians down 6 percent), congregations increased their religious education staffs.[31] While the propaganda potential of a picture of a child—a giggly one or a hungry one—is high, it is also important to recognize how critical real children were to churches in black neighborhoods.

St. Elizabeth's and Corpus Christi Catholic Churches

As we have seen, white Episcopalians built St. Edmund's church, then abandoned it when they no longer wanted to live on the South Side. Rather than sell the church, their bishop decided to see whether the new southern migrants might join the congregation. This reluctance to abandon property in the city was shared by the Roman Catholic leader of Chicago, George William Cardinal Mundelein. Far more than the Episcopal bishop, Mundelein had experience dealing with changing urban neighborhoods. Chicago was home to many immigrant Catholics, and since the turn of the century, "national parishes" had been established to address their spiritual and corporeal needs. By 1915 there were at least 202 well-defined national parishes for sixteen ethnic groups in the Archdiocese of Chicago. St. Joseph's (founded in 1900) was for Lithuanians, St. John the Baptist (1909) was one of nine Slovak parishes, St. Florian (1905) was one of many Polish parishes. In the first part of the century, only St. Monica's was for African Americans. While changes in canon law in 1918 mandated that the territorial parish be the Catholic norm, national parishes continued in Chicago. Poles in particular were not interested in giving up their Polish-language parochial schools and voluntary societies to accommodate either Rome or American bishops.

Consequently, when Irish Americans moved away from the parishes of St. Elizabeth's and Corpus Christi, Cardinal Mundelein declared them "colored" parishes. Mundelein wanted to fill empty churches with converts. In 1924 St. Elizabeth's was merged with the existing African-American congregation, St. Monica's. St. Elizabeth's was then "given over" to the Society of the Divine Word priests and the Sisters of the Blessed Sacrament, religious orders that ministered to African Americans (see fig. 8.13). Corpus Christi parish underwent a similar process. By 1928 there were only one hundred white families left and twenty-one children registered for school. After a failed attempt in 1932 to make Corpus Christi into an urban retreat house, Mundelein reopened the church as an exclusively "colored" parish. He gave control of the parish to Franciscan priests and brought in Franciscan nuns to run the school. A shrewd administrator, Mundelein had no qualms about handing over faltering parishes to religious orders and expecting them to make Catholic converts from Baptists, Pentecostals, and Spiritualists. Religious orders specialized in caring for certain types of people—for fellow Italians, for Native Americans, for "fallen" women—and the money to fund this care was generated from outside the diocese. A critical difference, however, was that African-American Catholics were not permitted to worship elsewhere in Chicago, and whites were not permitted to belong to those congregations. St. Elizabeth's and Corpus Christi were not merely national parishes; they were segregated parishes.

Mundelein's strategy was successful. The interwar and war years were times of growth for black Catholics in Chicago and other urban centers. In 1935 the Franciscans at Corpus Christi already had 2,100 "souls in your care," and by the end of 1943 the number had risen to 2,500. St. Elizabeth's parish reported at the end of 1943 having between three hundred and four hundred families and caring for 2,000 souls. During 1942, the year of Delano's visit, 128 adult African Americans had been baptized and joined Corpus Christi church, and 158 new Catholics had joined St. Elizabeth's. The number of converts was high throughout the thirties and early forties. In 1938 the priests of Corpus Christi reported baptizing 322 adults. Both parishes had the standard array of Catholic societies and sodalities, with the addition of the Knights and Ladies of St. Peter Claver, a guild exclusively for African Americans.[32]

Catholic schools facilitated the increase of black conversions in Chicago and other urban centers. Parochial school children introduced their parents, guardians, and friends to Catholicism. Since 1884 Catholics had been required to send their children to their own schools. Parochial education was a critical Catholic institution, and parishes often built a school before the church. African Americans took advantage of the schools located in "colored" parishes. In 1923, when St. Elizabeth's congregation was still biracial but its schools segregated, Mercy Sisters taught 168 white children, and Blessed Sacrament Sisters taught 281 black children. Three years later, after the declaration that St. Elizabeth's parish would serve colored Catholics only, the number of black children enrolled in its parochial school increased to 505 (fig. 9.10). By 1943 the Sisters of the Blessed Sacrament were teaching 908 elementary students at St. Elizabeth's. The parish also ran the only Catholic high school in Chicago that accepted African-American students.

In the fall of 1933 the Sisters of St. Francis of Dubuque, Iowa, had reopened Corpus

9.10   Jack Delano, altar boys before Mass at St. Elizabeth's Roman Catholic Church.
Chicago, March 1942 (LC-USW3-000155-D)

Christi's parish school as an all-black school and had to turn away applicants because of lack of
space (fig. 9.11). By the end of that school year, they were teaching 381 black pupils. The sisters
estimated that one-third of those students were non-Catholics and commented that although
all public schools in Chicago accepted black pupils, "in cases of over-crowding or other non-
accommodation, the colored children are the first to be dismissed." By the early forties the
Franciscan sisters were teaching 800 children a year at Corpus Christi. The Franciscan sisters were committed to their schools, one of them writing, "We have found that the colored
child is not inferior to the white in regard to secular knowledge." They boasted that on the
archdiocesan examinations black children "compare very favorably with [white children] and
in some instances are superior." They even were experimenting with a curriculum "in which
Negro heroes and Negro leaders figure prominently," so that the "Black race" could "admire
and emulate their own rather than the Caucasian race." [33]

During the thirties and forties, all parochial school children—Catholic or not—went to
Mass, and their families were expected to learn what they could about Catholicism. Given
the number of African-American children who went to these schools, it would not be unreasonable to imagine that their mothers and fathers might have become interested in Catholicism because of the practices of their children. While we do not have statistics on the gender
makeup of the churches, parish reports indicate that women especially were motivated to convert to Catholicism (fig. 9.12). Consistently throughout those decades almost twice as many

African-American women as men became Catholics. Of the 267 converts who joined Corpus Christi in 1935, 177 were women. Of the 158 adult baptisms done at St. Elizabeth's in 1943, 99 were women. Many African Americans converted, apparently not put off by the formality of Catholic liturgy, the rote memorization of the catechism and prayers, the long history that had little to do with Africa, or the racism of Cardinal Mundelein and his fellow Catholics. The Catholic parish offered to the residents of the South Side an education for their children and a disciplined spiritual life that was rich with symbol and ritual.

Delano's photographs show that Catholic churches were also worship environments of "aesthetic excess." Not only did parishes continue when whites left the South Side, the departing parishioners were not permitted to take with them the statues, altar linens, and stained glass. White Catholics were required, in effect, to leave their "class markers" behind in the city. Consequently, Delano's photographs show African Americans worshiping in beautiful sacred spaces that have no relationship to the economic status of their congregations. Corpus Christi parishioners worshiped under high arched ceilings and watched priests pray at altars made of imported Italian marble (fig. 9.13). St. Elizabeth's priests and altar boys wore elaborately stitched robes, and parishioners lit candles in front of popular saints (see figs. 9.10, 9.12). When a fire destroyed St. Elizabeth's church in 1930, the members added paintings of St. Peter Claver and the Ugandan martyrs to their new sanctuary.

As with All Nations Pentecostal Church, the upkeep of these churches put a financial

9.11   Jack Delano, choirgirls with Franciscan sister at Corpus Christi Roman Catholic Church. Chicago, March 1942 (LC-USW3-000148-D)

9.12   Jack Delano, women attending Sunday Mass at St. Elizabeth's Roman Catholic Church.
Chicago, March 1942 (LC-USW3-000156-D)

strain on their congregations, especially during the Depression years. Creating a visually dense, theologically correct, and symbolically layered environment was expensive, even with white "hand-me downs." When the cost of maintaining an appropriate worship space was added to the cost of supporting a school and social services, the burden was high. To pay for this, Catholic orders of nuns and priests were eternally raising money (at home and across the nation) to fund their efforts on behalf of "colored" Catholics. African Americans supported their parishes as best they could for many of the same reasons that early generations of immigrant Italians and Irish did: parish schools and social services compensated for political, cultural, and economic systems that showed little concern for the lives of the poor. Sensual and dramatic churches fulfilled the desire to create a magnificent worship space appropriate to house Christ's physical presence on earth in the Eucharist. Parish organizations attempted to compensate for the world of woe of city Catholics, and churches provided a glimpse of the future glory waiting for the redeemed in heaven.

While immigrants and migrants shared a common commitment to Catholic parish life, they did not share equal access to Catholic leadership positions. Italians and Poles sent their own priests to Chicago, but the clergy at black parishes were white. Between 1854 (when the first African-American priest was ordained) and 1934, only fourteen black men had received

9.13 (facing page)   Jack Delano, view from choir loft of pulpit and altar of Corpus Christi Roman
Catholic Church. Chicago, March 1942 (LC-USW3-000144-D)

9.14   Jack Delano, Father Vincent Smith distributing Holy Communion at St. Elizabeth's Roman Catholic Church. Chicago, March 1942 (LC-USW3-000139-D)

Holy Orders in the United States. African Americans were worthy enough to become Catholics but not considered worthy enough to enroll in the vast American seminary system that trained priests. The one aspect of Jack Delano's photographs of Catholic life on the South Side that was not typical of African-American parishes was the image of Father Vincent Smith, one of a handful of African-American priests in the country (fig. 9.14).

On the Sunday that Delano visited St. Elizabeth's Church, he photographed in the basement, where Mass was being said by "Father Smith." In the forties there were so many African Americans attending St. Elizabeth's that Mass was said simultaneously in the upper and lower sanctuaries. In his captions Delano mistakenly (but perhaps hopefully) identified the priest saying Mass in the basement as the "Negro pastor" of St. Elizabeth's. The captions never mention Smith's first name, nor have other historians who have reproduced the photos.[34] Like Lucy Smith and Samuel Martin, Vincent Smith was a remarkable individual whose name needs to be attached to the photographs and whose biography challenges us to rethink stereotypes about the "Negro church."

Vincent Smith was born in 1894 in Lebanon, Kentucky, the twelfth of thirteen children. His parents were Catholics; his father was a Creole from Louisiana. As a boy, Smith was employed as the chauffeur and valet for the Catholic bishop of Covington, Kentucky. When the United States was brought into World War I, Smith joined the army and fought in France. After his discharge from the military in 1919, he decided that he had a calling to the priesthood. In 1921 he started high school at a recently established segregated seminary of the Divine Word

Fathers in Mississippi. There, the nearly twenty-seven-year-old black man who had fought in the trenches of Europe studied with fourteen younger black men. Although the Divine Word Fathers had worked in the South with African Americans since the late nineteenth century, it was unclear whether Pope Benedict XV would actually permit the ordination of the black men as order priests. There also was controversy over whether Divine Word Fathers would integrate the black priests into their white order or make them form their own segregated province.

In 1934, thirteen years after he began his studies, Vincent Smith was finally ordained. He was one of four African-American men who would be accepted as full members of the Divine Word Fathers. At the age of forty, Father Smith accepted his first assignment as a black parish priest in Lafayette, Louisiana, where he stayed until 1938. His religious order soon recognized his exceptional oratorical skills and booked Father Smith into a nationwide preaching circuit. He conducted missions throughout the country until he came to St. Elizabeth's in the fall of 1940. Shortly after Delano photographed him, Father Smith was transferred to St. Peter Claver Church in Asbury Park, New Jersey. In 1948 Father Smith left the Divine Word missionaries to become a contemplative Trappist. In 1952, a year after taking his final vows with that community and being appointed novice master at the new Genesee Monastery in upstate New York, Vincent Smith died.[35]

At first glance, Jack Delano's photographs of Father Smith merely show a black priest saying Mass. We can say little else about the photograph if we confine ourselves to the visual evidence. The photograph can be used, however, to open a wider world of black Catholic practice within a white Catholic world. The photograph provides a starting point for exploring an undervalued aspect of black religious life. That exploration leads us to speculate about the importance of formal liturgy and rich symbolism to urban African Americans. It also reminds us that children play many roles in religious life. Photographic portraits can direct us toward remarkable lives when biographical information helps us understand who is in the picture. The very "realness" of the photograph lends a texture to stories that tend not to be told because they complicate the established narrative of the "Negro church."

Verbycke Spiritual Church, Washington, D.C.

To conclude this chapter, let us consider another series of overlooked photographs of African-American congregational life. As with the other FSA/OWI photographs of black religious practices, these also stress an eclectic, innovative, and intense urban Christianity. One of the illustrations in *Negroes and the War* was of a "store front church in Washington, D.C." It was taken by Gordon Parks, the only African American to work under Roy Stryker. Parks (1912–) eventually became one of America's premier photographers. Immensely talented, Parks worked for *Life* magazine, directed movies, published poetry, and wrote music—including a ballet commemorating the life of Martin Luther King, Jr. His several memoirs include descriptions of his youthful days working with Stryker and his team of photographers. Parks's fame, and the availability of his own reflections on his life, make him unique among the FSA/OWI photographers. More than for any of the others, Gordon Parks's days working for Stryker were only the beginning of a long, diverse, and successful artistic life. Consequently, instead of presenting his government photographs as the height of his photographic career, Parks has described his days in Washington as his introduction into the guild of concerned photographers. Not surprisingly, he places himself at the center of the story.

The story, however, is knottier than Parks has portrayed. In Parks's narrative, he came to Washington as an innocent. Although he attended a segregated elementary school, his experiences in Kansas, Minnesota, and Chicago had not prepared him for the racism he encountered in the nation's capital. At thirty, Parks was now a Rosenwald Fellowship scholar who had chosen to use his $2,000 stipend to train with the most famous documentary photographers in the country. Parks remembers Stryker telling him to go out—without his camera—and experience Washington. "Go out and see these things," Parks recalled Stryker saying, "the people, eat here, go to a theater, go to the department store and buy yourself a coat. You need a coat." Visiting Washington was devastating. Parks remembered that he was not allowed to eat at a hot dog stand with white people. He was not allowed to buy a camelhair coat in a department store. He was harassed for sitting with his fellow photographers in the building's cafeteria. "In a very short time," Parks wrote, "Washington was showing me its real character. It was a hate-drenched city, honoring my ignorance and smugly creating bad memories for me." [36]

Washington had opened Parks's eyes, but one picture in particular was to summarize his newfound feelings. While looking around in the building where the photographers worked, Parks found a black woman cleaning offices. He explained in his memoir that Stryker told him to interview the charwoman and that after talking with her, "I stood her up with her mop hanging down with the American flag hanging down Grant Wood style and did this marvelous portrait." He dubbed the portrait *American Gothic* (fig. 9.15). Like Dorothea Lange's *Migrant Mother,* this photograph has been frequently reproduced as the quintessential example of Parks's reform-oriented photography. According to Parks's captions and his memoir, the woman in *American Gothic* was Ella Watson and her government salary was $1,080 per year. A lynch mob had killed her father, her husband had been shot to death, and her daughter had given birth to two illegitimate children and then died. Gordon Parks described Ella Watson's life as "pitiful." Ella Watson and Washington convinced Parks of the power of the camera. "I had known poverty first hand," he wrote in a later memoir, "but there I learned how to fight its evil—along with the evil of racism—with a camera.[37]

Gordon Parks had found a framework to understand the meaning of his years working with the Historical Section, and it fit well with the general understanding of Stryker's project. Like most of the other photographers, Parks wanted to take pictures to stimulate social change. As we have seen, however, there were other goals of the Historical Section. Parks later admitted that he "overdid it" when making *American Gothic.* When he asked whether Stryker liked it, his boss "just smiled and shook his head." Parks told an interviewer in 1964 that Stryker quipped, "My God, this can't be published, but it's a start." But Parks also recalled that he "sneaked out and published it" in the progressive New York newspaper *PM.*[38]

Stryker probably was unenthusiastic about working with the young man from the Midwest whom he had not hired. Gordon Parks arrived in Washington in January 1942, a month after the Japanese bombed Pearl Harbor. America's entrance into the war had changed the whole nation, and for Stryker it meant he would be preoccupied for the rest of his tenure in the

9.15   Gordon Parks, Ella Watson posed as *American Gothic.*
Washington, D.C., August 1942 (LC-USF34-013407-C)

government with the changing mission of his project. Although Parks was enthusiastic about his fellowship, he had no training in art or photography. He made no pictures for the Historical Section until that summer.[39] In addition, Washington was a southern city, and Stryker knew it would be difficult for the darkroom technicians to accept a black professional. There would be social problems to cope with. From Stryker's perspective, the new photographer arrived at a bad time.

Gordon Parks remembered only the potential of the camera as a weapon to destroy racism, but in actuality he took as many pictures of satisfied and patriotic blacks as of dispossessed ones. Roy Stryker was trying to meet the needs of the Office of War Information for pictures of a strong America, and did not need more examples of urban black poverty. When Parks was in Washington, he made portraits of the baritone Paul Robeson and recorded commencement exercises at Howard University. In July 1942 he photographed patriotic black air raid wardens and cheerful-looking children happy to be living in a new government housing project in Anacostia. When he traveled to New York, he photographed Richard Wright, as well as Duke Ellington's band playing at the Hurricane Ballroom. His New England photographs taken around Memorial Day in 1943 include sturdy Italian and Portuguese-American fishermen and

9.16   Gordon Parks, Ella Watson sitting in front of her bedroom altar. Washington, D.C., August 1942 (LC-USF34-013443-C)

women welders.[40] While Gordon Parks was most proud of the pictures he made that visually criticized the patriotic hypocrisy of the country, Stryker must have been grateful to Parks for the intelligent pictures he made to support the war effort.

Parks never mentioned in his published memoirs that his picture of Ella Watson's "store-front church" was first published in *Negroes and the War* and was distributed by the Office of War Information to millions of African Americans. Parks did remember, however, that Stryker told him, "Keep working with her. Let's see what happens."[41] For almost a month Parks followed Ella Watson around. After photographing her at work, Parks went to the apartment where she lived with her adopted daughter and grandchildren. He also photographed her neighborhood and her church. There are at least ninety photographs of the world of Ella Watson. Parks and other historians have used only one, *American Gothic,* to evoke Ella Watson's grim world defined by a life of menial labor. Parks's other photographs of Watson, however, demonstrate that the woman lived in many worlds.

Let us push aside the photographer for a moment and concentrate on the religious world in which Ella Watson lived. Like many pious people, Ella Watson surrounded herself with images of many supernatural characters. She hung their pictures on walls and put their statues on dressers. Photographs of Ella Watson's dresser shrine show statues of St. Theresa of Lisieux, Our Lady of Lourdes, St. Joseph, St. Martin de Porres, St. Anthony, and Our Lady of the Immaculate Conception (fig. 9.16). Two votive candles, two small elephants, and two crucifixes also grace the altar. A rosary is draped over the mirror and a picture of the Sacred Heart hangs on the wall to the left. In other photographs, an open bible sits on the dresser, necessitating a rearrangement of her candles. Parks also photographed Watson reading her bible to the household. Parks might have introduced the bible in order to make Ella Watson's prayer life look more Protestant. In this way she fit better into the "Negro church." Or Ella Watson may have suggested the poses in order to show her own scriptural commitments.[42]

If Parks had photographed Ella Watson only at home, we might have assumed that this was another urban Catholic or perhaps an African American who had migrated from Catholic Maryland to work in the nation's growing capital. Ella Watson, however, took Gordon Parks to her church, and there he photographed rituals that established that she was not a Roman Catholic. Parks made pictures of churchgoers making the Sign of the Cross, genuflecting, and silently praying in front of a statue of St. Joseph (fig. 9.17). At the back of the church, under the word "CALVARY," is a shrine with a statue of St. Anthony of Padua, St. Theresa of Lisieux, and a crucifix. In another part of the church is a shrine to the Holy Sepulcher with a statue

9.17   Gordon Parks, women praying in front of a statue of the Immaculate Conception and St. Joseph. Washington, D.C., August 1942 (LC-USF34-013468-C)

of the body of Jesus laid out in the tomb of Joseph of Arimathea (fig. 9.18). In one particularly powerful photograph, a woman dressed in a white veil and robe prays with a rosary in her hand (fig. 9.19). Other people wear robes, and one man stands in a pool of water surrounded by roses (fig. 9.20). During his visit, Parks photographed members waiting in a line to be anointed with healing oil. He photographed Watson being touched on the forehead with blessed oil (fig. 9.21).[43]

Gordon Parks's captions provide the names of some members of Watson's church. The Rev. Vondell Gassaway is cited as the church's pastor. Gassaway had founded the church in 1928 and was its presiding archbishop. He led the church for thirty-six years until his death in 1964. The son of a minister and a native of Washington, Vondell Verbycke Gassaway named the church the Verbycke Spiritual Church. Gordon Parks called the church St. Martin's, but this was the school of metaphysical studies that Gassaway had established. St. Martin's Spiritual Center probably also met in the sanctuary. Although the congregation has changed its location and altered some of its practices since Parks took his photographs, it is still active.[44]

The Spiritual movement, of which Ella Watson's church was a part, thrived in urban black neighborhoods between 1920 and 1950. The origins of the Spiritual movement remain obscure, but historians believe that during the first quarter of the twentieth century it emerged first in Chicago and then in other cities north and south. Mother Leafy Anderson established a particularly vibrant community in the 1920s in New Orleans. St. Clair Drake and Horace Cayton wrote in *Black Metropolis* that in 1928 one out of every twenty churches in black Chicago was Spiritualist. By 1938 that number had increased to one in ten. The authors' description of Chicago's Spiritual churches fits the Verbycke Church. The Spiritual movement, they wrote, "borrows its hymns from the Baptists and Methodists, and appropriates altar, candles, and statues from the Catholics. It offers healing, advice and 'good luck' for a prayer and the price of a candle or holy flower. It provides colorful robes for its preachers and 'mediums,' but despite its name it rarely offers messages from the dead. . . . And most important, the Spiritualist church . . . has no unkind words for card-playing, dancing, policy, ward politics, or the 'sporting life.'"[45] Spiritual churches adapted well to life in the city.

Gordon Parks recorded a variety of modes of worship at Verbycke. Members alternated between quietly praying to the saints, experiencing ecstatic possession, and studying metaphysics. Although the cult of the saints was important at Verbycke, the church did not have a Catholic eucharistic celebration. Gordon Parks's captions indicate that he photographed the "annual flower bowl demonstration," but he does not explain the ritual. Members of Spiritual churches used the term *demonstration*. According to Naiom Davis, who was a member of the Verbycke Church in the 1940s, the flower bowl demonstration was made up of several parts. First members were anointed (fig. 9.20), and then they read from the Bible. After that they removed their shoes and stepped into a shallow pool of water surrounded by flowers. Parks commented in captions, "As in Moses' times," they take off their shoes because "they walk on holy ground." When all of the members had accomplished this, Reverend Gassaway stood

9.18 (facing page)   Gordon Parks, woman praying in front of shrine to the Holy Sepulcher, with photograph of the Rev. Vondell V. Gassaway standing among statues. Washington, D.C., August 1942 (LC-USF34-013497-C)

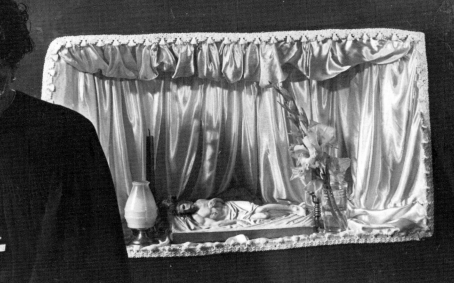

9.19   Gordon Parks, woman praying while holding a rosary. Washington, D.C., August 1942
(LC-USF34-013504-C)

9.20 (facing page)   Gordon Parks, Reverend Gassaway standing in a pool of water next to a
statue of the Virgin Mary. Washington, D.C., August 1942 (LC-USF34-013502-C)

in the water himself (fig. 9.19). According to Davis, Gassaway did not give out the roses, but Parks mentions in his captions that after members were anointed and prayed for, each was given a flower. Other historians have also mentioned this practice.[46]

At the "bless service" on Sunday, Gassaway delivered messages from the Spirit that typically related practical advice and gave comfort (fig. 9.22). Members sang many hymns. At times the highly emotional bless service would be so intense that the member would go into a trance. According to Davis, the woman in the photograph was her sister Bertha Todd, who later went on to be a preacher and minister. She carried her "love of wild dancing" into the church. At other times Gassaway prophesized and delivered more conventional sermons.[47]

Women were important actors within the church. Reverend Gassaway shared his power with Clara Smith, a senior member of the church who had similar liturgical and leadership authority. In many Spiritual churches the pastor and assistant pastors carry the title of archbishop or bishop, and this might explain the type of miter that Smith was wearing (see fig. 9.21). Other women were ministers, and they received spiritual messages, gave healings and prophecies, and taught classes in metaphysics. St. Martin's Spiritual Center provided training in mediumship, numerology, healing, positive thinking, and meditation techniques. Women who graduated from St. Martin's wore the mortarboards as symbols of their accomplishments. Ella Watson was probably a deaconess in her church, because she wears their characteristic white dress. At Verbycke, deaconesses assisted with the ritual activities of the church, looking after the altar and serving communion. Women "missionaries" visited the sick and helped the needy. Parks's photographs hint at Verbycke's diverse leadership structure that involved its women extensively and used clothing to signal various church roles.[48]

In his memoir *A Choice of Weapons,* Gordon Parks ends his reflections on meeting Ella Watson by quoting Roy Stryker. One late evening after Parks had laid out the results of his work, Stryker "admitted" that the new photographer was "learning." "You're showing you can involve yourself in other people. This woman has done you a great service. I hope you understand this." Parks writes, "I did understand." Ella Watson's image in *American Gothic* has been used as evidence of the evolving social consciousness of Gordon Parks, and in that way she did do him a "great service."[49] Her individuality was eclipsed in order that Gordon Parks's could be more developed. But he also did her a great service. Although he photographed only one Sunday in her church, his photographs provide the starting point for seeing Ella Watson as more than a cipher for American racism. The photographs preserve a sense of the importance of the Verbycke Spiritual Church for Ella Watson. They also help us understand why poor men and women living in cities went to church. Even if Parks did not understand what he was seeing, his courage in recording what he did makes it possible for us to remember the Verbycke Spiritual Church as an intense place of spiritual exchange.

African-American churches flourished in Chicago and Washington, D.C., because leaders and members responded in creative and flexible ways to changing spiritual and physical needs. While the FSA/OWI photographers and other historians have not taken seriously the importance of denominational differences, they have given us rare glimpses into black

9.21 (facing page)   Gordon Parks, Ella Watson being anointed by the Rev. Clara Smith. A second exposure shows Reverend Gassaway blessing another celebrant. Washington, D.C., August 1942 (LC-USF34-013491-C)

churches. What we can see underscores the eclectic, the "catholic" nature of city congregations. Migrants from the South entered cities filled with buildings that ranged from Catholic cathedrals to Jewish synagogues to storefront Spiritual churches. Ways of worship were manifold, and southern blacks were not limited by some essential notion of the character of their race to evangelical Protestantism. Once in the city, African Americans moved between denominations and religious traditions. Congregations gathered a diverse set of objects and images to put into their churches. Some churches mixed the everyday and sacred, while others followed established traditions of segregating the sacred from the profane. Rituals could be deliberate or they could be spontaneous. The photographs (enlivened by other historical documents) indicate that the Chicago School's belief in a fixed, tripartite class division reflected in religion is inadequate to describe congregational life. While class is not irrelevant to the story of city congregations, it has been overemphasized. The evidence from Chicago and Washington is less of rigid distinctions between upper and lower class churches than of movement and fluidity. The city was a place of experimentation where African Americans had the option of experiencing a variety of religious forms.

The FSA/OWI photographs also help us see how women and children were critical in creating city congregations. Women had roles in churches that frequently ignored the prescribed male-female hierarchical arrangement of the bourgeois family. In stark contrast with Richard Wright's conclusion that women were antimodern, many female churchgoers welded together technology and faith and used the combination to promote their own spiritual goals. Without denying the oppressive character of either church communities or life in racist America, the pictures provide us clues about how congregations cultivate the ritual lives of the poor. Whereas at work Ella Watson gave of her labor to white men, at church she received blessings from black women. Women exchanged their dreary housekeeping clothes for special white deaconess dresses. In church women were healed and shared in the healing of others. Congregational life was important enough to women that they expected their children to master ritual activities, and the FSA/OWI photographs indicate that many children complied.

It was the conviction of Roy Stryker and the photographers who worked with him that Americans could learn something about their fellow citizens by looking at their pictures. Furthermore, Stryker and his team believed that knowledge would eventually improve how Americans treated each other. While this humanist and reformist orientation reflects the optimism of another era, Stryker's intuition about the importance of photography was correct. Behind the FSA/OWI images, even the decidedly political ones produced for *12 Million Black Voices* and *Negroes and the War,* stand real people. While the illustrations in *12 Million Black Voices* try to convince us that the "Negro church" is otherworldly and therefore cannot survive in the "worldly" city, other historical evidence points in the opposite direction. Rather than experience a "death" on the city pavements, African-American religion was invigorated by its engagement with urban life in cities like Chicago and Washington. This picture of a vital and complicated Christianity comes much closer to accurately representing trends in modern religious culture than the vanishing faith imagined by modernists like Richard Wright and Edwin Rosskam.

9.22 (facing page)   Gordon Parks, Reverend Gassaway giving a blessing to church member. Washington, D.C., August 1942 (LC-USF34-013499-C)

10.1   Edwin Rosskam, priest at annual blessing of the shrimp fishing fleet. Barataria, Louisiana, August 1945 (Standard Oil of New Jersey Collection, University of Louisville Photographic Archives, neg. 28088)

10
Project's End

S tryker's hope that the Historical Section could be saved by providing pictures for the Office of War Information was short-lived. By early 1943 the pressures of war had made it next to impossible for the project to continue. Gas and rubber rationing had made the peripatetic life of the photographers unfeasible. Local officials, who always were suspicious of federal workers, now could cast their distrust of strangers in patriotic terms. As early as 1940 Marion Post wrote to Stryker, "Everyone is so hysterically war and fifth column minded. You'd be amazed. So suspicious. Even the little Cajun children in La. would run home or hide or run to get their father in the field, scared to death and saying I was a German spy with a machine gun." Police freely searched photographers' cars and asked "many irrelevant and sometimes personal and slightly impertinent questions." Congress was able to solidify its suspicions about New Deal experiments and refuse funding for projects not directly war related. Shortly before he quit, Stryker wrote to Dorothea Lange, "The whole trend in this town is now against the things which we were doing."[1]

The youth of many of the photographers, which had once been one of the strengths of the project, now meant that the men were being drafted into the military. Rather than wait to be inducted, Arthur Rothstein joined the Army Signal Corps, and Russell Lee signed up for officer training. Jack Delano fantasized that his flat feet might disqualify him from serving, but his draft notice arrived in August. He eventually served as a military photographer. John Collier, Jr., joined the merchant marines but then quit because the duty was making him deaf. Once the Historical Section's budget was slashed, Stryker had to let go most of those photographers who were still working. To his great frustration, they were then hired by the Overseas Operations Branch of the OWI to make pictures for propaganda. While Edwin Rosskam was too old to be drafted, Stryker was eventually able to secure deferments for John Vachon and Gordon Parks, and the three of them (and Rosskam's wife, Louise) went on to work with Stryker at Standard Oil.

Stryker might have been able to continue the project with a severely reduced budget, but he could not tolerate seeing the goals of the Historical Section caricatured by the propaganda arms of the government. Throughout his tenure as director of the project, Stryker had insisted that his photographers educate themselves about the particular economic problems of a specific geographic area. He sent them reading lists and expected them to make intelligent photographs. He encouraged his photographers to try to understand what they saw. Under the pressure of war, though, not only was "American background" transformed into sentimental and heroic propaganda, the new OWI men and women behind the camera had no training and no sensitivity toward what they were photographing. "Many second rate newspapermen," Stryker wrote Lange, "feel that slap-stick cheesecake is good enough to send overseas and to be used on the domestic scene." Stryker bristled at the fact that untrained amateurs were making poor-quality propaganda in the name of patriotism. Even as he watched his project dissolve, Stryker tried not to sound too pessimistic: "Let us all keep up our spirits," he wrote, "because we feel very certain that our idea will be picked up again before too long and we will be back working for the government."[2]

Private Citizens

After the war was over, neither Stryker nor any of the other photographers ever worked for the federal government again. Stryker's vision became fragmented and shaped by the demands of the private, commercial economy. Once he realized that the Historical Section had no future, Stryker became open to other possible avenues of employment. When he looked back twenty years later and described his move to Standard Oil to an interviewer, Stryker shaped and enlivened his narrative with biblical language. He recalled that a former mentor had arranged a meeting between the soon-to-be-unemployed photo director and the head of a large New York public relations firm. Stryker traveled from Washington and dined with the firm's head, Earl Newsom. After the meal, Newsom took Stryker to his office on Madison Avenue and the pair looked at the city from the twenty-second floor. Then Newsom, playing the role of the devil, offered Stryker the world: "Roy, wouldn't it be wonderful to be able to hire photographers, pay them a good salary, [and] send them around the world?" Stryker remembered replying with the appropriate retort, "Get thee behind me, Satan." As in the New Testament, the devil did not give up. The next day Newsom had Stryker to tea, dropping the hint, "Our big account is Standard Oil." Again Stryker rebuffed this temptation, recalling that as a boy his father believed that "there were great evils in the world: railroads, Wall Street, and the greatest of these three was Standard Oil." Stryker remembered reassuring himself, "I didn't think it altogether wise; I might have to meet my father in hell."[3]

The story ends in a suitably modern way. Returning to Washington, Stryker talked with friends and associates about the offer. Soon after, he finished up the process of transferring the Historical Section's photographs to the Library of Congress. Knowing that the file's future was safe, Stryker quit and joined Standard Oil. Stryker's narrative aptly summarizes his own relationship with Christianity. Stryker knew New Testament stories; his memories could be ordered and framed using biblical language. But Stryker acted as a secular man who would not place himself even metaphorically on the path of Jesus. The New Testament recounts that after being tempted in the wilderness, the Savior rejected the glories of the world and then was ministered to by angels. After his first refusal, however, Stryker reconsidered the glories of the world. Perhaps compromises could be made with the devil. Reality was a world where things changed and ideals had to be continually renegotiated.

Stryker and his family moved to New York City, and he began to hire back some of the men and women who had worked with him in Washington. Standard Oil proved to be a good employer. John Collier, John Vachon, Edwin and Louise Rosskam, Russell Lee, Jack Delano, and Gordon Parks all took pictures for Standard (see fig. 10.1). Other photographers who had worked with Stryker when the Historical Section was under the OWI — Arthur Siegel, Esther Bubley, Martha McMillan Roberts, and John Corsini — were freelancers. The Photo League photographers Sol Libsohn, Berenice Abbott, and Arnold Eagle also were lured into making pictures that showed the making and distribution of petroleum products. During Stryker's seven years in New York, he oversaw the creation of approximately seventy thousand images that demonstrated that "there's a drop of oil in everything."[4] When Standard Oil decided to terminate the project in the late forties, Stryker's career as "photo documentarian" was established. He went on to direct projects photographing social changes in Pittsburgh and the activities of Jones and Laughlin Steel Corporation. In his later years, Stryker lectured and consulted on photojournalism, retiring in the 1960s to his childhood home in western Colorado. He died in Grand Junction on September 27, 1975.

After the war, many of the men and women who took pictures for the Historical Section made names for themselves in photography. The changing nature of American politics, culture, and society, however, was to shape what they photographed. World War II evolved into the Cold War, and the effect on socially conscious photographers was chilling. The late forties and early fifties brought about a hostile environment for producing images that reflected the failure of the American dream and demanded social change. In 1947 President Harry Truman supported the creation of a Loyalty Review Board to make sure that federal employees and their families would have no connection to left-wing organizations, subversives, or communist associations. J. Edgar Hoover used the FBI to "wage a relentless war" against whomever was deemed to be a "security risk."[5] No cultural expression was considered "neutral." Art either supported democracy or it supported communism.

Modern art was particularly suspect; particularly modern art that sought to convey a "message." In 1947 the State Department organized a traveling exhibition to demonstrate to the world the importance the American government placed on culture as well as the excellence of contemporary art in the United States. The government bought three paintings by Ben Shahn, who had made photographs for Stryker in the 1930s. After attacks by Republicans and the press, the exhibition was halted, defined as "subversive" by the State Department; the art was sold by the very agency that had initially purchased it. When Truman saw one of the paintings, he exclaimed, "If that's art, I'm a Hottentot."[6]

Truman's comment can be dismissed as the opinion of the ignorant, but the dogged determination of certain congressmen to purify the nation of communism cannot be underestimated. Until he left the House of Representatives in 1957, Republican George A. Dondero used the floor of the Congress to attack artists, private art associations, galleries, and critics. Similar attacks on the movie industry prompted Hollywood to adopt loyalty oath programs and to blacklist those thought to be associated with communism. The art world, more decentralized and individualistic than the movie industry, responded in a variety of ways: Some private museums and associations protested. Artists like Jackson Pollock and critics like Clement Greenberg promoted the "apolitical" art of abstract expressionism. Ben Shahn continued to paint socially progressive art at his home in the Jersey Homesteads, now renamed Roosevelt.

Less well-funded and more politically liberal groups floundered. The Photo League, founded in 1936 by progressives who wanted to use photography in much the same way as Stryker did, was listed as a subversive organization in 1947. Two years later, the House Committee on Un-American Activities denounced the league's leaders as communists. A government informant had infiltrated the organization and "named names." In 1951 the Photo League disbanded, and many of its members moved away from social criticism and toward the production of visions of "interior, personal realms." In 1948 congressmen again questioned the merit of the "silly photos" that "clutter" the Library of Congress, but the pictures were preserved.[7]

While the federal government was targeting certain citizens as subversive, photographers found that the picture magazines *Look* and *Life* wanted to maintain the heroic and sentimental vision of America begun during the war years. Investigative photojournalism was not commercially viable in the fifties. Instead, photographs were assembled into such humanistic celebrations as Edward Steichen's "The Family of Man." Stryker's photographers found themselves on noncontroversial assignments. *Life* sent Gordon Parks to Europe in 1950 to photograph fashion models and actresses. In 1954 Dorothea Lange went to Utah with Ansel Adams, and *Life* published their pictures of self-sufficient Mormons and wide-open spaces. John Vachon had taken gritty photographs of life in Poland in 1946 for the newly constituted United Nations, but these were not published until 1995. In 1948 Vachon joined the staff of *Look* magazine and photographed celebrities under the direction of the former FSA/OWI photographer Arthur Rothstein.[8]

Rothstein remained at *Look* until its demise in 1970. He had no illusions about how commercial photography differed from Stryker's project. "Now this is an entirely different kind of photograph[y]," he told an interviewer in 1964. "Every picture that I take is taken with the idea that the picture is going to be printed somewhere. It's going to be printed on a page and it's going to reach a vast, tremendous audience." In contrast, when he had worked for the government, pictures "were not taken with the idea that they were going to be printed. They were taken as a historical record. The emphasis was on the quality of the photograph as a means of getting across information and at the same time preserving a certain amount of artistic interpretation." Rothstein realized that while Stryker had to defend the utilitarian nature of the project, the public consumption of the photographs was not the end. "The picture was the end," he explained, "once the picture got in the files, that was the end." At the height of *Look*'s popularity, eight million Americans purchased each issue of the magazine. As many as one in every five Americans skimmed through its pages. For commercial photographers after the war, "the photograph is just the means to the end. The end is the printed page."[9] A commercial, profit-making organization like *Look* or *Life* needed to sell magazines, so they tightly controlled what would be photographed and what would be published.

Arthur Rothstein is correct in emphasizing that the file was "an end in itself." Stryker gave to his photographers a considerable amount of freedom. For many years, the sheer number of the photographs they had produced made it difficult for people to use the file. Some of the negatives had been printed and were stored in filing cabinets at the Library of Congress, but other pictures had never been made available. The need to preserve the photographic negatives meant that they had to be carefully stored. While museum curators assembled selections from the file and scholars used FSA/OWI pictures in books, most Americans had no access to the images. Within the past few years, however, technology has revolutionized the accessibility of the OWI/FSA file of photographs. Now almost all of the negatives have been digitized and can be viewed online. One need only go to a public library and log on to the Library of Congress Web page to view this record of the past.[10] When Stryker left the government, a remarkable moment in the history of photography was over. But his goal of assembling an immense file of pictures of American life, paid for by the people and accessible to them for whatever use they desire, has been accomplished.

The Churched and the Unchurched

The very accessibility of these government photographs makes it all the more important that we set the images within their historical context. The FSA/OWI photographic vision was highly dependent on the needs of a federal government that sometimes recognized but sometimes ignored religious behaviors. While religion is as much about the extraordinary as about the ordinary, the photographs stressed the very ordinary, domesticated nature of religious life in America. Images of religion supported Stryker's underlying assumption of the dignity and reasonableness of the poor. Migrant laborers were not shiftless bums or potential revolutionaries but honest families down on their luck. Unlike commercial photographers like Margaret Bourke-White, who showed the highly emotional and potentially explosive character of faith, the FSA/OWI photographers concentrated on the stable nature of belief.

During the early years of the project, when the stress was on providing evidence to support New Deal reforms, religious practices were set among other cultural expressions. The photographers, however, were not merely government employees with cameras. They were artists with cameras. Photographers looked at religion differently from the writers, scholars, or journalists of the period. Rather than seeing faith expressed through words, they explored the ways that individuals and communities communicated with the supernatural through the buildings they constructed, the signs they painted, the sermon rhythms they moved to, and the graves they designed. Religious practices and spaces offered visually compelling and unique expressions of the creative spirit of the "common man," which were rendered with an eye toward abstract modernist and American regionalist styles. The photographers shared with believers a respect for the ways that space, form, color, movement, and texture could move one beyond the everyday nature of things. Consequently, the photographs act as a bridge between the churched and the unchurched.

The photographers understood religion as art, and Stryker understood religion as culture. Neither had sympathy for the religious impulse to transform individual and communal behavior. Stryker and his photographers were committed to the secular agenda of the New Deal and were pessimistic about alternative or competing visions. Given the fragility of the newborn semiwelfare state of the thirties, this is not surprising. There are no photographs of Father Coughlin or Gerald K. Smith, whose faith-based remedies to the Depression were perceived by many to constitute a fundamentally dangerous force in American politics. Even the conventional ways that religious people expressed concern about social welfare were either ignored or portrayed as hopelessly old-fashioned. While the beauty of religious performance and spaces may have drawn the photographers toward religious people, the file of photographs suggests that the unchurched were decidedly uncomfortable about the mixing of religion and reform.

This is not to say, however, that religion and reform were never pictured together. Key to understanding the FSA/OWI photographs is the recognition of the changing mission of Stryker's project. When the government needed evidence that the United States was strong enough to fight worldwide fascism, the photographers looked to religious communities to provide evidence of spiritual strength. In the later years of the project, religion played a more important role because it was set above other cultural expressions. President Roosevelt had declared that the nation would fight to preserve "freedom of religion," so faith entered into the realm of propaganda. Outsiders—Jews, Native Americans, Catholics—gained new relevancy as potential witnesses to the nation's commitment to religious freedom. Religious communities were pictured as mediating institutions that established and cultivated civic virtues. Even writers like Richard Wright, who held critical opinions of both the American government and religious people, used the FSA/OWI photographs to construct flat and ambivalent, rather than negative, stories of faith.

The photographers, however, were not above poking fun at what they saw as the odd ways that religion and culture interacted in America. They delighted in using juxtaposition to illustrate the mixing of the sacred and the profane across the country. Their visual jokes tell us that they were amused at the ways that religious people mixed the sacred with the profane. In Hobbs, New Mexico, Russell Lee set up a photograph in which signs for the movie *White Zombie* and "OIL LEASES" competed for attention with announcements for the town's churches (fig. 10.2). John Vachon photographed a traveling evangelist's truck in front of the

10.2   Russell Lee, signs outside town. Hobbs, New Mexico, March 1940 (LC-USF34-035815-D)

Washington Capitol building (fig. 10.3). His photograph contrasted the rambling jeremiad of doom and destruction with the quiet stability of national tradition. Such photographs illustrate the many places that the photographers were charmed, delighted, puzzled, and perhaps even put off by the integration of religion into everyday life.

The religious world that the photographers saw, first in the country and then in the city, was made up of Christians and Jews. In this way it reflected the personal background of Stryker and the photographers, who were familiar with Jewish and Christian communities even if they themselves were unchurched. During the thirties and forties, Muslims and Buddhists were too exotic to represent the "common man," and Native Americans were too controversial. But the Protestants, Catholics, and Jews pictured in the file are quite different from those described in other histories of the period. As unchurched outsiders, Stryker and the photographers turned away from conventional and middle-class religion, for which they had little respect. They were

looking for Christians and Jews who did not remind them of their own families. Since Stryker and the photographers were looking for places of religious creativity, vitality, and endurance among poor Americans, they did not produce pictures of the supposed "spiritual depression" of the period.[11] Rather they recorded many overlooked religious communities of the thirties and forties: French-Canadian Catholics in Maine; Amish in Pennsylvania; House of David Israelites in Benton Harbor, Michigan; black Episcopalians on Chicago's South Side; Utah Mormons; the Salvation Army in California.

These communities were all visually dynamic and socially alive during the dark days of the Depression, but when it came time to publish books with FSA/OWI photographs in them, such images were rarely used. Richard Wright was not alone in choosing stereotypical photographs of religious life for *12 Million Black Voices.* None of the authors of the period availed themselves of the diverse images of religious life that Stryker was compiling. Rather, pictures were chosen that supposedly were representative of religions in a particular area or which conveyed a particular feel about religions. A New England church bold against a wintry snow, an open bible on a pulpit, black faces excited about song, crosses in a graveyard—these familiar Christian themes reinforced the idea that Americans knew what religion was all about. Such images allowed middle-class, white, Protestant Americans to see themselves as the center of the story of religion in the United States.

A far more complicated picture of American religions arises out of the full file of photographs. The great gift of the FSA/OWI file is that it gives us a different way of looking at religion in the thirties and forties. The variety of photographs forces us to admit that there is no simple story embedded in the religious history of the American people. Faith does not float down from above but rather is entangled in families, leisure pursuits, class pretensions, aesthetic styles, and ethnic customs. When the visual record is supplemented with the written and oral record, we see the thirties and early forties as a dynamic period of religious history in the United States. Americans were on the move, spreading out from the South, traveling from the country to city, and even from city to the country. In these new places they both continued their religious traditions and expanded and diversified them.

Mass production and distribution made it easier to heighten the sensual dimensions of religion. At times, Christians and Jews rigorously maintained an established order of the material culture of their churches, synagogues, businesses, and homes. At other times, they mixed together sacred and commercial images, creating a hodgepodge of traditions and styles. While the photographers waited for churches to be emptied of people so that they could capture the structures' simple and authentic forms, people insisted on getting in the way. Religious sensibilities marked their routines. The pristine wooden church that Walker Evans and other scholars have used to symbolize the essence of American religion fails as an image of what turns out to be a preference for clutter by many Americans during the thirties and forties. Rather than being a time of retreat from the supernatural, the Depression years were a time when Americans intensely engaged the world beyond and integrated it into their everyday lives.

Because of the humanistic spirit of the FSA/OWI project, the photographs let us see how

10.3 (facing page)   John Vachon, truck of an itinerant preacher parked in front of the United States Capitol. Washington, D.C., July 1939 (LC-USF34-060110-D)

critical lay people were in defining religion in the thirties and forties. Although male clergy and theologians may have set certain standards of practice and belief, the energy of religious communities was cultivated by lay men, women, and children. Not only were religious spaces not empty or bare, they were filled with children learning Yiddish and Hebrew, altar boys, choirgirls, women preachers, Sunday school matrons, and teaching nuns. The FSA/OWI photographs also show people spilling out of their churches and synagogues and claiming even more space. They gathered on courthouse lawns to listen to preaching, they conducted processions in front of city row houses, they put up billboards that demanded the attention of motorists. These men, women, and children did not confine religion to the realm of thought but brazenly displayed their faith for all to see. Their use of material culture and their employment of modern techniques of communication enabled them to be cagey actors in a world increasingly defined by consumerism and technology.

The thirties and forties were a period of time when those once defined as religious outsiders by middle-class Protestants self-confidently asserted their presence. Roosevelt had appointed Catholics and Jews to positions in the New Deal, legitimizing their increasingly vigorous political power. The pressures of war rhetorically, if not in actuality, accorded religious minorities an honored place in the national story. Catholics, who had at one time symbolized intolerance and authoritarian foreign regimes, were pictured in the movies as stalwart defenders of individual conscience. Cities increasingly reflected the diversity of black spirituality, from the high-church liturgies of Catholics to the spontaneous outbursts of Pentecostals to the nationalistic claims of the followers of Marcus Garvey and Elijah Muhammad. The music of African Americans was danced to in nightclubs, listened to on the radio, and copied by white musicians. In the West, Mexican migrant laborers elaborated on their Catholic devotionalism, and Okies established their evangelical ways. Even a few Jews were secure in Yankee farm country.

Cultural leaders met the flourishing of such outsiders during the thirties and forties with a variety of silence, skepticism, and disdain. Protestant social scientists like Robert Lynd preferred to note the decline in liberal Protestantism rather than the rise of conservatives and Catholics. Rabbis in New York also perceived a "spiritual depression" that influenced synagogue attendance. Artists and intellectuals may have explored the "spiritual" in the "primitive," but most had little good to say about congregational life. Their fascination with empty churches echoes the modernist preference for authenticity, abstraction, simplicity, and rationality. Even in the forties, when religious communities were accorded more cultural worth, religious leaders could only act as accommodating partners with the state. "Freedom of religion" made for good war propaganda; it did not make for good welfare policy. Stryker and the photographers constructed a visual bridge between the churched and the unchurched, but they remained on their side of the divide. Their project thus leads us into the next century, when the United States continues to be split between those who communicate with the supernatural, those who do not, and those who take pictures of both.

Notes

1
Introducing Americans to America

1. Dorothea Lange, "The Assignment I'll Never Forget," *Popular Photography* 46 (February 1960), 126. To search the collection of FSA photographs by their catalogue numbers, see lcweb2.loc.gov/pp/fsaquery.html (accessed March 23, 2004). "What Does the 'New Deal' Mean to This Mother and Her Children?" *San Francisco News,* March 11, 1936. Lange actually made six negatives, one of which was not sent to Washington and remained in her private collection. It is now housed at the Oakland Art Museum.

2. For examples of how *Migrant Mother* has been used see Vicki Goldberg, *The Power of Photography: How Photographs Changed Our Lives* (New York: Abbeville, 1991), 138–141.

3. Library of Congress caption number LC-USF34-018216-E.

4. FSA/OWI images may be accessed via memory.loc.gov/ammem/fsahtml/fahome.html. The number 270,000 was cited by Roy Stryker in an interview by Richard K. Doud on June 13, 1964, Archive of American Art [hereafter abbreviated AAA], and is the number used in many reference works on the FSA/OWI file. There is no evidence, however, that Stryker kept a count of the number of negatives made, the number destroyed, or the number of prints made. The number 270,000 was probably a guess on Stryker's part. The caption lists compiled by the photographers show that both they and Stryker "killed" many negatives, which indicates that the number of pictures taken was far greater than the surviving file. Nancy Wood speculates that during the lifetime of the file Stryker punched holes in about 100,000 negatives. Stryker recalled that after he had arranged for the file's deposit at the Library of Congress in 1943 he "narrowed down" the number of negatives to 170,000, although neither he nor Wood gave an explanation for why the file was thinned. With the digitizing of the file, a more accurate number of the surviving negatives is now being assembled. The Library of Congress also has 1,600 color negatives taken during this project. See Roy Emerson Stryker and Nancy Wood, *In This Proud Land: America, 1935–1943, As Seen in the FSA Photographs* (Greenwich, CT: New York Graphic Society, 1973), 16.

5. Stryker and Wood, *In This Proud Land,* 8.

6. William Stott, *Documentary Expression and Thirties America* (Chicago: University of Chicago Press, 1973), 3.

7. Ann Wilkes Tucker et al., *This Was the Photo League: Compassion and the Camera from the Depression to the Cold War* (Chicago: Stephen Daiter Gallery, 2001), 9.

8. Jewish Photo League members include Alexander Alland, Arnold Eagle, Morris Huberland, Jack Manning, Walter Rosenblum, Paul Strand, and even Weegee (Arthur Fellig), as well as founders Sid Grossman and Sol Libsohn.

9. Stott, *Documentary Expression,* 103.

10. These numbers, taken from Guide to the Records of the Work Projects Administration (Record Group 69), are of the "photographic images" of the Federal Theater Project (69.5.4) and Records of the Federal Writers' Project (69.5.5); cited in the National Archives and Records Administration

online guide, www.archives.gov (accessed March 2003). The records and photographs are located in the College Park, Maryland, facility. Arnold Eagle was already photographing a Brooklyn Hasidic Jewish community when he became a Federal Art Project photographer and produced *Sabbath Studies* in 1937. Other New York projects included Bernice Abbot's "Changing New York" (1939), Helen Levitt's *Children of New York City at Play* (1935); Arnold Eagle and David Robbins's *One Third of a Nation* (1935); Sid Grossman's *Harlem* (1939); Andrew Herman's *Coney Island* (1939), and George Herlick's *City Scenes* (1937).

11. Roy Stryker Papers [hereafter abbreviated RSP], series 3, part A: scrapbook, 1936–1958.

12. Elizabeth McCausland, "Rural Life in America as the Camera Shows It," *Springfield Sunday Union and Republican,* September 11, 1938. Included in Printed matter, 1934–1962, series 2, part A: scrapbook, 1936–1958, RSP.

13. "A Miss Lowery," Roy E. Stryker to Marion Post, January 26, 1939, RSP; "easy on this," Roy E. Stryker to Marion Post, February 1, 1939, RSP. Marion Post married Lee Wolcott in 1941 and left the FSA shortly after the marriage. Under pressure from Wolcott, she insisted that Stryker change all of the photographs that she had taken to include her married name. F. Jack Hurley, *Marion Post Wolcott: A Photographic Journey* (Albuquerque: University of New Mexico Press, 1989), 8.

14. Marion Post to Roy E. Stryker [n.d., c. February 3, 1939], RSP.

15. Roy E. Stryker to Marion Post, February 10, 1939, RSP.

16. Dona Freeman, *100 Years, Montrose, Colorado* (n.p.: n.p., 1982), 60. Located at the Denver Public Library.

17. "Radical populist," Stryker and Wood, *In This Proud Land,* 10; "we all had," Jhan and June Robbins, "The Man Behind the Man Behind the Lens," *Minicam Photography,* November 1947, 146. This interview with Stryker has been widely quoted.

18. Roy Stryker, interview by Jack Hurley, July 27, 1967; typescript, Memphis State University Library, 3, cited in F. Jack Hurley, *Portrait of a Decade: Roy Stryker and the Development of Documentary Photography in the Thirties* (Baton Rouge: Louisiana State University Press, 1972), 8. Just who exactly George Collins was, or whether there were two George Collinses, is unclear. In a 1964

interview Stryker explains, "I had met a young minister at Illiff Seminary in Denver and he was a New Yorker. . . . I might digress just for a moment and bring in another name. At the Colorado School of Mines there was a man by the name of George Collins who represented four church boards. I was sore at the Army and resentful at the Army and he had—he introduced me to the New Republic, the Nation, Rauschenbusch, the very famous theolog[ian] from Rochester Seminary, a liberal, probably almost a Socialist. . . . And I had met this man from Illiff who needed, who would like to have some help in some boys' clubs he was running." The "Illiff Collins" gave a course in economics, and Stryker took it. "Anyway, I think it was a very important—meeting him was a very important—part of this, my life. It was the thing that turned me from my chemistry to the social sciences. So when the young theologian said, when you go back to New York City, why don't you contact Union Settlement which was a part of Union Seminary on the East Side, they might just have a place for you." Roy Stryker, interview by Richard Doud, June 13, 1964 [AAA]. In Jack Hurley's 1967 interview, Stryker says, "I met a very interesting young minister who was in seminary at Denver University and we remained good friends." At another point Stryker again separates "Mr. Collins" from "my minister" (4). Stryker's daughter Phyllis, however, remembers only one Collins, who was a long-time friend of the family's. On December 27, 1975, George ("Shorty") Collins wrote to Phyllis Stryker about the recent death of her father. The letter was written on stationery from Grace Baptist Church in San Jose, California, and lists George L. Collins as "College Chaplain." Current church administrators do not recall this former minister. Collins may have become an American Baptist, or he might have been a Baptist who attended a Methodist seminary. Phyllis Stryker Wilson, telephone interview with author, June 17, 1999.

19. William G. McLoughlin, *Revivals, Awakenings, and Reform: An Essay on Religion and Social Change in America* (Chicago: University of Chicago Press, 1978), 175. McLoughlin quotes Rauschenbusch but does not cite the source.

20. Wilson wrote me regarding this conversation: "I'm not sure I quoted Papa right but pondering it I think he said 'Cowpunchers didn't have religion

and didn't carry a toothbrush.' It is cowpunchers—
he didn't like being called a cowboy! You can quote
it if you want, but sort of hedge it—it was never
meant to be a serious comment, I'm sure." Phyllis
Stryker Wilson, letter to author, June 28, 1999.

21. Stryker, interview with Doud.

22. Beverly Brannan, director of the Prints and Photograph Division of the Library of Congress, speculates that those photographers were at least ethnically Jewish. Personal communication with author,
May 2, 2002.

23. Felix Adler, *An Ethical Philosophy of Life: Presented in Its Main Outlines* (New York: D. Apple-
ton, 1918), 353; Vicki Goldberg, *Margaret Bourke-
White: A Biography* (New York: Harper and Row,
1986), 5.

24. Professional activities, shooting scripts, series 2,
part C, subsection a, RSP. Also reproduced in
Stryker and Wood, *In This Proud Land*, 187.

25. "Stories of Groups of People," series 2, part C, section 1, RSP. It is unclear what this document is,
as there is no date on it. The list is called "Documentary Photography" and has "Vachon" penciled
across the top. Other lists of "stories" in the document include "Land Problem Stories," "Stories of
Places," "Stories of Activities," and "Stories of the
Cities."

26. See LC-USF34-051021-E.

27. Rex Tugwell, as quoted in Maren Stange, "'Symbols of Ideal Life': Technology, Mass Media, and
the FSA Photography Project," *Prospects* 11 (1986),
100.

28. Paul Rotha, *Documentary Film* (1935; rpt. New
York: Communication Arts Books, 1968), 153.

2
Enduring Faith

1. Dorothea Lange to Roy E. Stryker, March 12, 1937,
RSP. The word in brackets is illegible in the original.

2. For example, see, LC-USF34-016517-E, LC-
USF34-016520-E, LC-USF34-016546-E, and
caption of LC-USF34-016468-E.

3. All of these photographs are discussed later except
for the Blythe (LC-USF34-009754-C), Tranquillity (LC-USF34-018780-E), and Bakersfield (LC-
USF34-019050-E) churches.

4. Franklin D. Roosevelt, inaugural address, January 20, 1937.

5. Ronald Edsforth, *The New Deal: America's Response to the Great Depression* (Malden, MA: Black-
well, 2000), 20.

6. Ian Jeffrey, *Photography: A Concise History* (New
York: Oxford University Press, 1981), 65.

7. This paragraph is based on Peter B. Hales, *Silver Cities: The Photography of American Urbaniza-
tion, 1839–1915* (Philadelphia: Temple University
Press, 1984); quotation, 202.

8. James Guimond, *American Photography and the
American Dream* (Chapel Hill: University of North
Carolina Press, 1991), 63.

9. Milton Meltzer, *Dorothea Lange: A Photographer's
Life* (New York: Farrar Straus Giroux, 1978), 12,
52.

10. Dorothea Lange, oral history interview by Suzanne
Reiss, 1960–1961; reproduced in 1968 as "The
Making of a Documentary Photographer" and
available from the Regional Oral History Office,
Bancroft Library, University of California, Berke-
ley; quotations, 12–15. Cited in Judith Fryer Davi-
dov, "The Only Gentile Among the Jews: Dorothea
Lange's Documentary Photography," in *Women's
Camera Work: Self/Body/Other in American Visual
Culture* (Durham, NC: Duke University Press,
1998), 225.

11. James N. Gregory, *American Exodus: The Dust
Bowl Migration and Okie Culture in California*
(New York: Oxford University Press, 1989), 192.

12. John Steinbeck, *The Grapes of Wrath* (1939; rpt.
New York: Penguin, 1992), 27.

13. Dorothea Lange and Paul Schuster Taylor, *An
American Exodus: A Record of Human Erosion*
(1939; rpt. Paris: Jean Michel Place, 1999), 149.

14. For instance, see Arthur Rothstein's photograph
of baseball at the Tulare (California) migrant camp
in March 1940 (LC-USF34-024144-D) and of harvesting in a community garden at an FSA camp
in Robstown, Texas, in January 1942 (LC-USF34-
018385-E).

15. For an Arvin library photograph, see LC-USF34-
018568-D.

16. Arthur Rothstein, *Arthur Rothstein: Words and
Pictures* (New York: Amphoto, 1979), 7.

17. F. Jack Hurley, *Portrait of a Decade: Roy Stryker
and the Development of Documentary Photography
in the Thirties* (Baton Rouge: Louisiana State University Press), 17.

18. See Joseph F. Chorpenning, ed., *The Holy Family
as Prototype of the Civilization of Love: Images from*

the Viceregal Americas (Philadelphia: St. Joseph's University Press, 1996), 134, 215.

19. Not all of the photographs in the FSA/OWI file were made by photographers who were in the full-time employment of the Historical Section or who worked for Stryker for a long time. Theodor Jung and Paul Carter, for instance, worked for only one year between 1935 and 1936. Ben Shahn contributed photographs, but he was a part of the Special Skills Division of the Resettlement Administration. Louise Rosskam, the wife of Edwin Rosskam, one of Stryker's employees, also made photographs for the FSA/OWI file. Other photographers, who may have worked in the RA or FSA field offices, contributed prints. The FSA/OWI file also contains pictures made by OWI photographers after Stryker left government service. For a list of photographers see "Creator Index": memory .loc.gov/ammem/fsahtml/fsaauthindex1.html (accessed June 2002).

20. Constance B. Schulz, ed. *Michigan Remembered: Photographs from the Farm Security Administration and the Office of War Information, 1936–1943* (Detroit: Wayne State University Press, 2001), 228.

21. Lee visited Sinton, San Juan, Edinburg, Weslaco, Alamo, Robstown, and Combes in February 1939, San Antonio, El Indio, and La Pryor in March.

22. Matt S. Meier and Feliciano Ribera, *Mexican Americans, American Mexicans: From Conquistadors to Chicanos* (New York: Hill and Wang, 1993), 150.

23. Russell Lee to Roy E. Stryker, February 28, 1939, RSP. For malnutrition see LC-USF34-032376-D; skin disease (impetigo), LC-USF34-032362-D; tuberculosis, LC-USF34-032405-D, LC-USF34-032384-D, LC-USF34-032388-D; arthritis, LC-USF34-032349-D; gonorrhea, LC-USF34-032352-D.

24. LC-USF33-012100-M4.

25. Russell Lee uses the word *shrine* to describe these altars, but Mexicans would use the Spanish word *altarcito,* meaning "little altar." I have used *shrine* and *altar* interchangeably. My discussion of home altars is based on Kay Turner, *Beautiful Necessity: The Art and Meaning of Women's Altars* (New York: Thames and Hudson, 1999).

26. For Raymondville see LC-USF34-032214-D and LC-USF34-032186-D. For Sinton see LC-USF33-012032-M3, LC-USF34-032177-D, LC-USF34-032162-D, LC-USF34-032210-D, LC-USF34-032183-D, LC-USF34-032212-D, LC-USF34-032194-D, LC-USF34-032159-D, LC-USF34-032221-D.

27. I would like to thank Robert B. D. Hartman, the historian and archivist at Culver Military Academy, for sending me information about Russell Lee. This paragraph draws from Russell Lee's page in Culver's 1921 yearbook *Roll Call,* the 1919 Culver Military Academy catalog, and a YMCA guide from 1933.

28. F. Jack Hurley, *Russell Lee, Photographer* (Dobbs Ferry, NY: Morgan and Morgan, 1978), 11.

29. Rodolfo Acuña, *Occupied America: The Chicano's Struggle Toward Liberation* (San Francisco: Canfield, 1972), 164–167.

3
Churches Without People

1. Max Kozloff, "Signs of Light: Walker Evans' American Photographs," in *Lone Visions, Crowded Frames: Essays on Photography* (Albuquerque: University of New Mexico Press, 1994), 134.

2. From an unfinished letter dated February 1934 from Walker Evans to Ernestine Evans, reprinted in *Walker Evans at Work: 745 Photographs Together with Documents Selected from Letters, Memoranda, Interviews, Notes* (New York: Harper and Row, 1982), 112.

3. Accounts vary on when Evans left the permanent employment of the government. His biographer Belinda Rathbone gives the date as March 23, 1937, in *Walker Evans: A Biography* (Boston: Houghton Mifflin, 1995), 147, but other sources cite September. See Michael Brix and Birgit Mayer, eds., *Walker Evans, America* (New York: Rizzoli, 1991), 36. Evans took on temporary assignments with the Historical Section—for instance, photographing New York apartments in August 1938.

4. Jack Delano studied at the Pennsylvania Academy of Fine Arts in Philadelphia (1932–1937), Ben Shahn at the National Academy of Design, New York (1917–1922) and in Paris (1925); Arthur Siegel studied photography under László-Nagy at the Institute of Design, Chicago (1937–1938); Russell Lee studied at the San Francisco Art Institute (1929–1931); John Collier attended the California School of Fine Arts in San Francisco (1934). Roy Stryker, interview by Richard K. Doud for the Archives of American Art, October 17, 1963.

5. Ibid.

6. There is considerable debate over the definition of *religion* and thus of the connected terms *religions, religious, spiritual, spirituality, transcendent,* and *sacred.* Like the scholars Jonathan Z. Smith and Russell T. McCutcheon, I take a historical approach to the use of the term *religion.* I would modify Smith's concluding sentences regarding the history of the term to read: "'Religion' [or terms like *spirituality* or the *transcendent*] is not a native term; it is a term created by scholars [and artists and writers] for their intellectual purposes and therefore is theirs to define. It is a second-order, generic concept that plays the same role in establishing a disciplinary horizon that a concept of 'language' plays in linguistics or 'culture' plays in anthropology [or *art* in aesthetics]." See Mark C. Taylor, *Critical Terms for Religious Studies* (Chicago: University of Chicago Press, 1998), 269–284, especially 281–284. Likewise, Russell T. McCutcheon in *Manufacturing Religion: Discourse on Sui Generis Religion and the Politics of Nostalgia* (New York: Oxford University Press, 1997), 3, writes, "Simply put, the discourse on *sui generis* religion deemphasizes difference, history, and sociopolitical context in favor of abstract essences and homogeneity." My contribution in this debate is to explore the role of modernist photography in constructing a visual image of this sui generis religion.

7. James Agee and Walker Evans, *Let Us Now Praise Famous Men* (1939; rpt. New York: Houghton Mifflin, 1960), 38; italics Agee's.

8. Robert Hughes, *The Shock of the New* (New York: Knopf, 1981), 18. Hughes stresses that there is no simple relationship between abstract form and nature. It is the relationship between forms—a relative relationship which is always changing and which can be doubted—which is critical. Corbusier, *Towards a New Architecture,* trans. Frederick Etchells (London: J. Rodker, 1931), 29; Agee and Evans, *Let Us Now Praise Famous Men,* 38.

9. LC-USF34-018780-E.

10. Stryker interview with Doud, 1963.

11. It is unclear when the retouching took place. In 1936 Lange wrote that she wanted the negatives "of the mother and children. Pea pickers—of which I wrote. Miss Slackman said in her letter that you were making prints for me. Please [mister?] that idea is no good. This show is the most important photographic show we have. It tours the country.

It tours Europe. I couldn't afford to show prints, unsigned, which I have not even seen. I'll send the negatives right back." Stryker sent her the negatives, and she returned them. Dorothea Lange to Edwin Locke, September 10, 1936, RSP. F. Jack Hurley speculates in *Portrait of a Decade: Roy Stryker and the Development of Documentary Photography in the Thirties* (Baton Rouge: Louisiana State University Press, 1972), 142, that the erasure may have occurred as Lange was preparing the photograph for the 1939 publication of *American Exodus,* though she did not reprint it in the volume. James Curtis, *Mind's Eye, Mind's Truth: FSA Photography Reconsidered* (Philadelphia: Temple University Press, 1989), 67, says that it was when she was "preparing the print for permanent exhibition," but he does not specify an exhibition.

12. The published photograph was LC-USF34-004507-E. For a discussion of the controversy see Hurley, *Portrait of a Decade,* 86–94, and Curtis, *Mind's Eye, Mind's Truth,* 70–78.

13. John Vachon to Roy E. Stryker, April 19, 1940, RSP; Hurley, *Portrait of a Decade,* 156.

14. Cartier-Bresson described the "decisive moment" in photography as "the simultaneous recognition, in a fraction of a second, of the significance of an event as well as of a precise organization of forms which give that event its proper expression." Henri Cartier-Bresson, *The Decisive Moment,* trans. E. Tériade (New York: Simon and Schuster, 1952), no pagination.

15. Agee and Evans, *Let Us Now Praise Famous Men,* 39–40.

16. Ibid., 39.

17. Curtis, *Mind's Eye, Mind's Truth,* 35–44; LC-USF34-017306-C.

18. Walker Evans, *American Photographs,* with an essay by Lincoln Kirstein (1938; rpt. New York: Museum of Modern Art, 1988), 197; Walker Evans, "The Reappearance of Photography," *Hound and Horn* 4 (1931), 126–127.

19. Walker Evans to Ernestine Evans, February 1934, as published in *Walker Evans at Work,* with an essay by Jerry L. Thompson (New York: Harper and Row, 1982); Rathbone, *Walker Evans,* 11.

20. Carl Jung, "Das Seelenproblem des modernen Menschen," *Europäische Revue* 4 (1928), 700–715, trans. W. S. Dell and Cary F. Baynes as *Modern Man in Search of a Soul* (New York: Harcourt, Brace and World, 1933). For a discussion of modern art and

spirituality see Mark C. Taylor, *Disfiguring: Art, Architecture, Religion* (Chicago: University of Chicago Press, 1992), 98–142.

21. Miles Orvell, *The Real Thing: Imitation and Authenticity in American Culture, 1880–1940* (Chapel Hill: University of North Carolina Press, 1989), 290; Leslie Katz, "An Interview with Walker Evans, 1971," in Vicki Goldberg, ed., *Photography in Print* (New York: Simon and Schuster, 1981), 365 (rpt. from *Art and America,* March–April 1971).

22. Rathbone, *Walker Evans,* 111.

23. Michael Brix and Birgit Mayer, eds., *Walker Evans, America* (New York: Rizzoli, 1991), 15.

24. For instance, see Allen Trachtenberg's discussion in "From Image to Story: Reading the File," in Carl Fleischhauer and Beverly W. Brannan, eds., *Documenting America, 1935–1943* (Berkeley: University of California Press, 1988), 44–51, and Graham Clarke, *The Photograph* (New York: Oxford University Press, 1997), 154.

25. LC-USF342-001160-A.

26. Evans cites Strand's "Blind Woman" as prompting his own documentary style; see Katz, "Interview," 357.

27. Hughes, *The Shock of the New,* 32.

28. John Collier, Jr., and Malcolm Collier, *Visual Anthropology: Photography as a Research Method* (Albuquerque: University of New Mexico Press, 1986), xiii–xiv.

29. John Collier, *From Every Zenith: A Memoir and Some Essays on Life and Thought* (Denver: Sage, 1963), 165. There seems to be some confusion about when Collier took his sea voyage. This account is based on his father's memoirs and J. B. Colson et al., *Far from Main Street: Three Photographers in Depression-Era New Mexico* (Santa Fe: Museum of New Mexico Press, 1994), 11–12.

30. The term *Spanish New Mexican* has been widely used to describe residents of New Mexico who trace their ancestry back to colonial settlements. For a general survey see Nancie L. González, *The Spanish-Americans of New Mexico* (Albuquerque: University of New Mexico Press, 1967); for the 1940s, Ernest B. Fincher, *Spanish-Americans as a Political Factor in New Mexico, 1912–1950* (New York: Arno, 1974); and for contemporary usage, Joseph V. Metzgar, "The Ethnic Sensitivity of Spanish New Mexicans: A Survey and Analysis," *New Mexico Historical Review* 49 (1974), 49–73.

31. W. Jackson Rushing, *Native American Art and the New York Avant-Garde: A History of Cultural Primitivism* (Austin: University of Texas Press, 1995), 29.

32. The details of Collier's studio work in Taos are unknown. I have found only a brief mention in the John Collier, Jr., entry in Michéle Auer, ed., *Encyclopédie International des Photographes de 1839 à Nos Jours* (Hermance, Switzerland, 1985), n.p. Georgia O'Keeffe exhibited her paintings in New York at her husband Alfred Stieglitz's galleries, but her work was known in art circles. During the early thirties, such art museums as the Cleveland Museum and the Whitney had purchased her New Mexico paintings. Laurie Lisle, *Portrait of an Artist: A Biography of Georgia O'Keeffe* (Albuquerque: University of New Mexico Press, 1986), 197.

33. LC-USW3-017338-C, LC-USW3-017339-C.

34. George Kubler, *The Religious Architecture of New Mexico* (1940; rpt. Albuquerque: University of New Mexico Press, 1972), 104–105, and Marc Treib, *Sanctuaries of Spanish New Mexico* (Berkeley: University of California Press, 1993), 172–182. The parishioners of San José de Gracias de las Trampas in the 1960s were willing to have a road widened to enable them to travel more easily to Taos and Santa Fe even if it meant removing part of the churchyard. Like the congregation in Peñasco, some of the townspeople preferred convenience and comfort to historical beauty. The churchyard was "saved" by preservationists who secured its status as a National Landmark in 1967. Treib, *Sanctuaries of Spanish New Mexico,* 180.

35. Corbusier, *The City of To-morrow and Its Planning* (1924; London: Architectural Press, 1947), 23.

36. Steve Yates, "Cultural Landscapes: New Mexico, 1940–1943," *El Palacio* 96 (1991), 35.

37. Rushing, *Native American Art,* 117.

38. "Cure all," John Collier to Roy E. Stryker, Trampas, [1943], RSP; "primitive people," John Collier to Roy E. Stryker, Santa Fe, Monday, [1943], RSP; "shoot this town," John Collier to Roy E. Stryker, Trampas, [1943], RSP; "sheep stories," John Collier to Roy E. Stryker, [1943], RSP.

39. The political implications of representations of "the other" have been developed in Edward W. Said's *Orientalism* (New York: Random House, 1978), following from the work of Michel Foucault and Antonio Gramsci. Other scholars have developed similar themes in their fields, including James Clifford in *The Predicament of Culture: Twentieth-*

Century Ethnography, Literature, and Art (Cambridge: Harvard University Press, 1988); Trinh T. Minh-ha in *Woman, Native, Other: Writing, Post-coloniality, and Feminism* (Bloomington: Indiana University Press, 1989); and Marianna Torgovnick in *Gone Primitive: Savage Intellects, Modern Lives* (Chicago: University of Chicago Press, 1990) and *Primitive Passions: Men, Women, and the Quest for Ecstasy* (Chicago: University of Chicago Press, 1998).

40. *Official Guide Book of the New York World's Fair,* 1939, 102; *New York Times,* April 17, 1939.

41. "For those who worship," *New York Times,* May 14, 1939; "neither the building," *Official Guide Book,* 103; "here in the Temple" and "simple concepts," *New York Times,* May 1, 1939.

42. *New York Times,* July 4, 1939; *Time,* May 29, 1939, 47.

43. *New York Times,* February 10, 1939.

4
Another South

1. Irene Delano to Clara Dean "Toots" Wakeman, April 21, 1941. "Toots" was Stryker's secretary. Correspondence at times was addressed to her when it was meant for Stryker, especially if he was out of town.

2. As with all of the FSA/OWI photographs, I can only speculate about the order in which the pictures were taken. The lineup of deacons is LC-USF34-043954-D. The individual Delano refers to as a "Negro preacher" in photograph LC-USF34-043918-D is the same man posing in photograph LC-USF34-043915-D, which is uncaptioned. This man is also standing in the middle of the lineup captioned, "the preacher and the deacons of a Negro church," fourth from the right.

3. Walker Evans visited the South in 1935 and met his future lover Jane Smith in New Orleans, but I know of no other FSA photographer who traveled in the South before working for the government.

4. Susan Sontag, *On Photography* (New York: Doubleday, 1973), 109, 112.

5. Willa Cather, Prefatory Note to *Not Under Forty* (1936; rpt. Lincoln: University of Nebraska Press, 1988), v. Dividing America geographically or temporally into binaries is a popular activity for writers. The journalist David Brooks provides a recent example in an essay that explores "red" (rural, religious, Republican) and "blue" (urban, secular, Democratic) America. See "One Nation, Slightly Divisible," *Atlantic,* December 2001.

6. Roderick Nash, *The Nervous Generation: American Thought, 1910–1930* (Chicago: Rand McNally, 1970).

7. Kenneth K. Bailey, *Southern White Protestantism in the Twentieth Century* (New York: Harper and Row, 1964), 97.

8. Erskine Caldwell, *Tobacco Road* (1932; rpt. Athens: University of Georgia Press, 1995), 44, 104.

9. See James J. Thompson, Jr., "Erskine Caldwell and Southern Religion," in Robert L. McDonald, ed., *The Critical Response to Erskine Caldwell* (Westport, CT: Greenwood, 1997), 268–278; orig. pub. in *Southern Humanities Review* 5 (Winter 1971), 33–44. Caldwell was fascinated by religion, and his memoir, *Deep South: Memory and Observation* (New York: Weybright and Talley, 1968), is filled with observations on southern faith. The first part was initially published in England under the title "In the Shadow the Steeple."

10. Margaret Marshall, "Their Faces," *Nation* 145 (4 December 1937), 622.

11. Erskine Caldwell and Margaret Bourke-White, *You Have Seen Their Faces* (1937; rpt. Athens: University of Georgia Press, 1995), 39, 40.

12. Robert DeMott, Introduction to John Steinbeck, *The Grapes of Wrath* (1939; rpt. New York: Penguin, 1992), xix–xx. The Joads' farm was set near Sallisaw in the eastern part of Oklahoma, where residents participated in southern culture (for example, evangelical Protestantism) and economy (for example, raising cotton). They traveled west along U.S. Route 66. While the western part of the state is more ambiguous in terms of regional identity, Californian growers understood all Dust Bowl migrants like the Joads as "southerners." The FSA photographers often used the description "southwesterners" to more precisely pinpoint where the migrants came from, although nowadays this term more frequently refers to someone from New Mexico or Arizona rather than from Oklahoma and Arkansas.

13. Steinbeck, *Grapes of Wrath,* 29, 127. See also 233. Steinbeck casts women in the role of the overly pious who have neither the humanistic orientation of Jim Casy nor the practical religious wisdom of Ma Joad. See the exchange between Ma Joad and Holiness women concerning prayers for

the dying Granma (286–290); the warning of "the brown woman" (Mis' Lisbeth Sandry) about Rose of Sharon's unborn child (420–425); and Sandry's condemnation of dancing (437–439).

14. W. J. Cash, *The Mind of the South* (New York: Knopf, 1941), 56.

15. Church exteriors devoid of congregations include those taken by Ben Shahn in Louisiana in October 1935 and by Marion Post in the vicinity of Summerville, South Carolina, in December 1938; Homestead, Florida, in January 1939; and Rodney, Mississippi, in June 1939. Walker Evans photographed in various southern states in 1936; Jack Delano worked in Cedar Grove, North Carolina, in May 1940 and Greene County, Georgia, in May 1941; Dorothea Lange in Leland, Mississippi, in June or July 1937; Russell Lee in Arkansas in September 1938, Cruger, Mississippi, in September 1938, and Krote Springs, Louisiana, in October 1938; and Carl Mydans in Charleston, South Carolina, in June 1936.

16. Evans does not name the church in his captions, but another artist who grew up in Hale County, William Christenberry, connected Evans's photograph with a real congregation. Christenberry photographed the church in 1971 and 1983 and built a sculpture of it in 1974–1975. See William Christenberry, *Southern Photographs* (Millerton, NY: Aperture, 1983), 21, 41; also Thomas Southall, *Of Time and Place: Walker Evans and William Christenberry* (San Francisco: Friends of Photography, 1990). Southall points out that when the congregation decided to expand the church by building a porch entrance, they removed its twin towers (30).

Marion Post took pictures of three churches in Rodney. An additional one not mentioned here was the Rodney Presbyterian Church, built of brick and dedicated in 1832. Rodney was built in the 1830s as a Mississippi River port town. It thrived until the 1840s, when the river changed course and left the town without a viable port. By 1933 the population had diminished to less than one hundred. Rodney was probably thought of as a ghost town when Marion Post photographed there in 1940, and her other pictures of the town show no life. Eudora Welty also photographed in Rodney in the late 1930s, perhaps during her travels as a WPA worker. Three of the town's churches are reprinted in *Country Churchyards* (Jackson: University of Mississippi Press, 2000). In 1984 Sacred Heart Church was moved from Rodney to Grand Gulf, Mississippi. www.grandgulfpark.state.ms.us /grandgulfpark.html and www.rootsweb.com/ms jeffe2/rodney.htm (accessed November 2, 2001).

17. The following discussion of Wheeley's church is based on Dorothea Lange's general caption no. 23 (Supplementary reference file lot 1496) and caption no. 24 (Supplementary reference file lot 1498). The report implies that Lange was not alone, but I do not know who accompanied her so I have referred only to her in this discussion. Queen's photographs are LC-USF34-019917-C through 019919-C.

18. This discussion of the history of Wheeley's church comes from Ron Boswell, *The Blessing of Beulah* (Roxboro, NC: Beulah Baptist Association, 1984), 18–71.

19. Paul Harvey, *Redeeming the South: Religious Cultures and Racial Identities Among Southern Baptists, 1865–1925* (Chapel Hill: University of North Carolina Press, 1997), 80.

20. Cash, *Mind of the South*, 136.

21. The series of quotations is from Marion Post to Clara Dean "Toots" Wakeman, August 16, 1940.

22. Marion Post's photographs of St. Thomas's Catholic Church, near Bardstown, Kentucky, include pictures of church and rectory in addition to the dinner preparations. Photograph LC-USF33-030987-M4 is a sign advertising the picnic and mentioning the price. Post also photographed St. Joseph's Catholic Church in Bardstown, a historic church built between 1816 and 1819. See LC-USF34-055223-D.

23. Marion Post Wolcott's daughter, Linda Wolcott-Moore, does not know which church her mother attended as a child, which speaks to the weakness of its influence on Marion Post's life. Email from Linda Wolcott-Moore, March 20, 2001. "Marched to church," F. Jack Hurley, *Marion Post Wolcott: A Photographic Journey* (Albuquerque: University of New Mexico Press, 1989), 6. "Progressive atmosphere," biographical sketch of Marion Post Wolcott by her daughter, Linda Wolcott-Moore, www.people.virginia.edu/bhs2u/mpw/mpw-bio .html (page now inactive, accessed May 13, 2002).

24. I would like to thank Diane Tackett for responding to my email and enabling me to contact her father-in-law, Elijah Tackett. Elijah and his wife, Nelly, shared with me their reflections on the Primitive Baptists of Morehouse, and to them I offer my grati-

tude. I also would like to thank Samantha Davis for her ideas on the Poplar Grove Church and Triplett Creek.

25. As described in James L. Peacock and Ruel W. Tyson, Jr., *Pilgrims of Paradox: Calvinism and Experience Among the Primitive Baptists of the Blue Ridge* (Washington, DC: Smithsonian Institution, 1989), 20–21.

26. See photographs LC-USF33-031003-M4, LC-USF33-031003-M1, LC-USF33-031002-M4, LC-USF33-031002-M3, LC-USF33-031040-M2, LC-USF33-031075-M2, LC-USF34-055311-D, LC-USF34-055310-D, LC-USF34-055315-D.

27. Samuel S. Hill, "Southern Religion and the Southern Religious," in John B. Boles, ed., *Autobiographical Reflections on Southern Religious History* (Athens: University of Georgia Press, 2001), 14.

28. I would like to thank Susan Brown and her staff at the Campton County Courthouse, who graciously shared their knowledge of their town's history and architecture. It was they who told me that the pews came from the courthouse and referred me to ninety-three-year-old Bertie Center, who vividly remembered what life was like in 1940. I especially want to acknowledge Ms. Center's graciousness. On courthouse lawns see Christine Leigh Heyrman, *Southern Cross: The Beginnings of the Bible Belt* (New York: Knopf, 1998), 239.

29. Marion Post [Wolcott], Durham, North Carolina, November(?) 1939, LC-USF33-030741-M1 through M5; Ben Shahn, Nashville, Tennessee, September 1935, LC-USF33-006103-M1 through M5; Russell Lee, Tahlequah, Oklahoma, July 1939, LC-USF33-012336-M4, LC-USF33-012336-M5.

30. See caption of LC-USF33-011884-M3.

31. See the series of photographs accompanying LC-USF33-011703-M4. Lee may have been coming from the festival, as the ordering is unclear. Quotation listed on LC-USF33-011702-M1 through M5.

32. Jack Delano, June 1941, Greensboro, Georgia, "Every Eye Shall . . ." LC-USF33-020960-M3 and "Watch! For Ye . . ." LC-USF33-020960-M4; Marion Post [Wolcott], December 1940, Augusta, Georgia, "Unto You a Son . . ." LC-USF34-056457-D and "War Brings Death . . ." LC-USF34-056457-D; Marion Post [Wolcott], December 1940, Augusta, Georgia, "God Will Judge Your Thoughts 'The Thought of Foolishness Is Sin' What Wilt Thy Judgment Be?" LC-USF34-6056454-D; Marion Post [Wolcott], May 1939,

[no name], Georgia, "God Is Not Mocked . . ." LC-USF34-051361-D; Marion Post [Wolcott], [?] March 1939, [no name], Alabama, "Hark! The Voice . . ." LC-USF34-051806-D; Marion Post [Wolcott], December 1940, Augusta, Georgia, "Whosoever Will Be . . ." LC-USF33-030409-M3.

33. LC-USF34-016317-E.

34. Arthur F. Raper, *Tenants of the Almighty* (New York: Macmillan, 1943), 336, 337.

35. Jack Delano to Roy E. Stryker, May 16, 1941, RSP.

5
Christian Charity

1. John Vachon to Roy E. Stryker, April 19, 1940, RSP, and rpt. in Miles Orvell, *John Vachon's America* (Berkeley: University of California Press, 2003), 295.

2. Roy E. Stryker to John Vachon, April 23, 1940, RSP, and rpt. in Orvell, *John Vachon's America*, 297.

3. Robert L. Reid, *Picturing Minnesota, 1936–1943: Photographs from the Farm Security Administration* (St. Paul: Minnesota Historical Society Press, 1989), 3; Orvell, *John Vachon's America*, 6–11.

4. Stryker sent Vachon shooting scripts that April that included both small-town activities ("barber shops and their habitues") and farming ("unplowed land, the stubble showing ragged"); Orvell, *John Vachon's America*, 287–290. There is no mention of religion in those scripts, but an undated script on the "American Small Town" (291–293) includes Stryker's understanding of the importance of churchgoing to rural communities. Vachon, however, found something very different in the urban religion of Dubuque. "All inconsequential," John Vachon to Penny Vachon, April 18, 1940; rpt. in Orvell, *John Vachon's America*, 157.

5. John Vachon to Penny Vachon, April 18, 1940; rpt. in Orvell, *John Vachon's America*, 158.

6. Photographs not shown in this chapter: sign, LC-USF33-001709-M4; waiting to be fumigated, LC-USF34-060586-D; in bed, LC-USF34-060587-D; children with buckets, LC-USF34-060600-D, LC-USF34-060603-D, LC-USF34-060604-D.

7. Orvell, *John Vachon's America*, 270, 269.

8. Photographs include Salvation Army, LC-USF34-062724-D, LC-USF34-062720-D, LC-USF34-062719-D, LC-USF34-062707-D; Helping Hand, LC-USF34-062556-D,   LC-USF34-062582-D,

LC-USF34-062688-D,   LC-USF34-062514-D;
face of pianists, LC-USF34-062642-D, LC-
USF34-062675-D.

9. Arthur Rothstein first photographed Irwinville tenant farmers and their ramshackle houses in 1935 before their relocation; see, for instance, LC-USF34-
000432-D. Vachon returned in May of 1938 and
using a 35 mm camera took many pictures of the
FSA camp; see LC-USF33-001133-M1 through
001180-M3. Lange's photographs of the Tulare
FSA camp include LC-USF34-019577-E through
019599-E. Rothstein's of Sinton are LC-USF33-
003627-M1 through 003643-M3; Post's tenant
purchase homes in Isola are LC-USF34-052438-D
through 052443-D.

10. Fields, cabins, and farmers, LC-USF34-017349-
C, LC-USF34-017356-C, LC-USF34-017497-E;
poultry unit, LC-USF34-017366-C; community
house, LC-USF34-017484-E; vegetable garden,
LC-USF34-017354-C; evicted boy, LC-USF34-
017338-C. Sherwood Eddy and Kirby Page, *Creative Pioneers* (New York: Associated Press, 1937),
67. See also Sherwood Eddy, "The Delta Cooperative's First Year," *Christian Century* 54 (February 3, 1937), 139–140; Sherwood Eddy, "The
Future of the Sharecroppers," *Christian Century*
54 (December 12, 1937), 1390–1392; Reinhold
Niebuhr, "Meditations from Mississippi," *Christian Century* 54 (February 10, 1937), 183–184. I
would like to thank Peter Slade for this observation
about the Delta Cooperative.

11. June Hopkins, *Harry Hopkins: Sudden Hero,
Brash Reformer* (New York: St. Martin's, 1999), 7,
13.

12. Other New Dealers who had graduated from Grinnell include Florence Stewart Kerr and Hallie Fer-
guson Flanagan, who worked in the WPA Federal Theater Project, and Chester Davis and Paul
Appleby, who worked in the Department of Agriculture.

13. Hopkins, *Harry Hopkins,* 35.

14. Quoted ibid., 51.

15. Michael B. Katz, *In the Shadow of the Poorhouse:
A Social History of Welfare in America* (New York:
Basic, 1986), 132.

16. On the struggles between Catholic charities and
local authorities in New York City, see Hopkins,
Harry Hopkins, 70–89, and Dorothy M. Brown
and Elizabeth McKeown, *The Poor Belong to Us:
Catholic Charities and American Welfare* (Cambridge: Harvard University Press, 1997), 13–50.

17. Hopkins, *Harry Hopkins,* 51.

18. Felix Adler, "Address on the Occasion of the Fifty-
Fifth Anniversary of the Founding of the Ethical Movement," May 10, 1931; www.aeu.org/adler4
.html (accessed May 1, 2003).

19. Katz, *In the Shadow of the Poorhouse,* 208.

20. Ronald Edsforth, *The New Deal: America's Response to the Great Depression* (Malden, MA: Black-
well, 2000), 87.

21. "Federal Emergency Relief Administration," in
James S. Olson, ed., *Historical Dictionary of the
New Deal* (Westport, CT: Greenwood, 1985), 177.

22. Hopkins, *Harry Hopkins,* 166.

23. Brown and McKeown, *The Poor Belong to Us,* 164–
170.

24. Norris Magnuson, *Salvation in the Slums: Evangelical Social Work, 1865–1920* (Metuchen, NJ:
Scarecrow, 1977), 56.

25. Harvie M. Conn, *The American City and the Evangelical Church* (Grand Rapids, MI: Baker, 1994),
62.

26. www.dbqunitedway.org/history.html   (accessed
April 22, 2003). I would like to thank Kathy Gra-
tace of United Way Services of Dubuque for enabling me to make contact with the Dubuque Rescue Mission, which is still responding to urban
poverty. Its current executive director, Murray Phil-
lips, graciously recounted the mission's history and
sent me information on William Masters. In addition to housing homeless men, as it did in 1940, the
mission now manages a thrift store, provides individual meals, and organizes a medical clinic for the
uninsured. The DRM is funded by local Protestant
and Catholic churches, which supply volunteers
to work with its clients. It now has an ecumenical
Christian orientation. Michael D. Gibson, director
of the Center for Dubuque History, also sent me
materials that set the DRM in historic context.

27. Magnuson, *Salvation in the Slums,* 138. I would
like to thank the historian Lillian Taiz and Susan
Mitchem, director of the Salvation Army National
Archives, for helping me understand this process.
See especially Lillian Taiz, *Hallelujah Lads and
Lasses: Remaking the Salvation Army in America,
1880–1930* (Chapel Hill: University of North Caro-
lina Press, 2001).

28. In an essay on Lange's Salvation Army photographs
Carl Fleischhauer and Beverly W. Brannan comment, "On Palm Sunday weekend Lange documented the first of two regular morning services at
Salvation Army headquarters and then accompa-

nied the group to an open-air meeting where they sought to attract newcomers." "Salvation Army," in *Documenting America, 1935–1943* (Berkeley: University of California Press, 1988), 161. Fleischhauer and Brannan then ordered Lange's photographs from inside the Corps to outside on the street. Common Salvation Army practice would have been just the opposite. The order of the captions in the caption file is probably not the order in which the pictures were shot.

29. For further evidence that Dorothea Lange frequently overlooked the probable "reality" of a place in order to visually support reformist ideas, see James R. Swensen, "Dorothea Lange's Portrait of Utah's Great Depression," *Utah Historical Quarterly* 70 (Winter 2002), 39–62.

30. Diane Winston, *Red-Hot and Righteous: The Urban Religion of the Salvation Army* (Cambridge: Harvard University Press, 1999), 192–213.

31. John Steinbeck, *The Grapes of Wrath* (1939; rpt. New York: Viking Penguin, 1992), 128.

32. Ibid., 429–432.

6
New Mexico's Patriots

1. "This is my home," John Collier, Jr., to Roy E. Stryker, January 13, 1943, RSP; "Peñasco," John Collier, Jr., to Roy E. Stryker, [no date,] Santa Fe, Monday, 1943, RSP.

2. John Collier, Jr., to Roy E. Stryker, [no date,] Peñasco, 1943, RSP.

3. Roy E. Stryker to Jack Delano, September 12, 1940, RSP.

4. Brett Gary defines propaganda as "the organized manipulation of key cultural symbols and images (and biases) for the purposes of persuading a mass audience to take a position, or move to action, or remain inactive *on a controversial matter.*" *The Nervous Liberals: Propaganda Anxieties from World War I to the Cold War* (New York: Columbia University Press, 1999), 8 (italics in original).

5. "Americans," Barbara Dianne Savage, *Broadcasting Freedom: Radio, War, and the Politics of Race, 1938–1948* (Chapel Hill: University of North Carolina Press, 1999), 36; "without precedent," Gary Gerstle, *American Crucible: Race and Nation in the Twentieth Century* (Princeton: Princeton University Press, 2001), 195.

6. [Clara Wakeman] to Russell Lee, August 10, 1940, RSP.

7. Roy E. Stryker to Russell Lee, November 3, 1939, RSP. On October 23, 1939, Stryker sent a memo about possible "picture stories" to be distributed in Latin America to Earl Bressman, an adviser to the secretary of agriculture. The correspondence indicated that some photo-essays were eventually placed in newspapers.

The use of FSA/OWI photographs in Latin America was also mentioned in a letter from Albert Bailey to Roy E. Stryker dated March 1, 1941, RSP. Bailey explained that the YMCA, through its "Good Neighbor Forum," was about to publish for the Latin American market a book (with, it is implied, some FSA/OWI pictures) on everyday life in the United States. "This enterprise," Bailey wrote, "springs from the conviction that permanent good neighbor relations must be based on knowledge and mutual understanding." The picture book was to contain eighteen chapters, including one on religion.

8. Russell Lee to Roy E. Stryker, July 13, 1940, RSP.

9. Franklin Roosevelt, State of the Union Address, January 6, 1941; see also Robert E. Sherwood, *Roosevelt and Hopkins: An Intimate History* (New York: Harper, 1948), 361–362, quoting a Hopkins memo to Roosevelt of December 27, 1941, reprinted on 448. According to Sherwood, the idea of the Four Freedoms was Roosevelt's. "Roosevelt had mentioned them at a press conference six months previously when asked a question about his long-term peace objective. There were then five freedoms—two of them coming under the heading of 'Freedom of Speech.' Roosevelt had no name in mind for the Third Freedom, though he was clear about its social import, and Richard L. Harkness of the *Philadelphia Inquirer* suggested it be called, 'Freedom From Want'" (231).

10. United States Treasury Department, *Our War . . . Our Victory* (Washington, DC: United States Government Printing Office, 1942), 12.

11. United States Office of War Information, *U.S.A.* (Washington, DC: United States Government Printing Office, nd), np. Filed in RSP, series 3, part B, publications, 1934–1962.

12. The ethnic and religious photographs taken in the early forties are quite extensive and best accessed through a keyword search at the online FSA/OWI archive (memory.loc.gov/ammem/fsaquery.html) that includes the creator of the photograph and the general subject—for instance, "Delano Jones Greene" or "Collins Mennonite Lititz."

13. Jack Hurley, *Portrait of a Decade: Roy Stryker and the Development of Documentary Photography in the Thirties* (Baton Rouge: Louisiana State University Press, 1972), 164, quoting an editorial from the Memphis, TN, *Commercial Appeal*, May 25, 1943. Budget cuts: ibid., 162.

14. Roy E. Stryker, shooting script, February 19, 1942, RSP, series 2, part C, section 3, subsection A.

15. "New Mexico Winter," no date, series 2, part C, section 3, subsection C; Franklin Roosevelt, "The Arsenal of Democracy," fireside chat delivered December 29, 1940, www.tamu.edu/comm/pres/speeches/fdrarsenal.html (accessed June 2002).

16. "Indian youth," "New Mexico Winter" letter; "Your errant photographer," John Collier to Roy E. Stryker, [no date,] Santa Fe, Monday, 1943, RSP; "I was opposed," Roy E. Stryker to John Collier, February 2, 1943, RSP.

17. "Portrait of America," no. 38, is included in typescript form in the FSA Supplementary Files (reel 16, reference to lot 871) at the Library of Congress. I have been unable to locate the finished pamphlet, although the manuscript contains the notice: "Approved by the Appropriate U.S. Authority."

18. Sidney Baldwin, *Poverty and Politics: The Rise and Decline of the Farm Security Administration* (Chapel Hill: University of North Carolina Press, 1968), 209, citing John Collier to Roy E. Stryker, [no date,] Santa Fe, Monday, 1943, RSP. See also Michael R. Grey, *New Deal Medicine: The Rural Health Programs of the Farm Security Administration* (Baltimore: Johns Hopkins University Press, 1999), 114–119.

19. "My transportation problem," John Collier, Jr., to Roy E. Stryker, January 3, 1943, RSP. This interpretation differs from that of Nancy C. Wood in *Heartland New Mexico: Photographs from the Farm Security Administration, 1935–1943* (Albuquerque: University of New Mexico Press, 1989). Wood, drawing from an interview with Father Cassidy in 1987, concludes that his community organizing actually caused his eventual removal from the parish. Wood explains that the pamphlet describing Cassidy's work in Las Trampas eventually was sent to Latin America, where bishops considered the brochure "communist propaganda." The archbishop of Lima, Peru, complained to the Vatican, which contacted the apostolic delegate in Washington; the delegate pressured the archbishop of Santa Fe to remove Father Cassidy merely seven months after his assignment to Peñasco (86–87). While there is no question that Latin American bishops might have been sensitive to progressive priests and American propaganda, it is doubtful that a small pamphlet would have motivated such action against a specific foreign priest. It is even more doubtful that the pamphlet could have been produced in Washington, distributed in Peru, discovered by the clergy, and complaints successfully heard in the Vatican and then passed on to New Mexico in the short span between when the photographs were taken, in January and February, and March 2, when Father Cassidy says he was removed. There is no indication in the archdiocesan archives of Father Cassidy's problems or hasty transfer. More likely he was moved because he was merely a new assistant pastor who would have been considered to be very "mobile" and transferred whenever the archbishop felt a young priest was needed in another parish.

20. C. Stewart Doty, *Acadian Hard Times: The Farm Security Administration in Maine's St. John Valley, 1940–1943* (Orono: University of Maine Press, 1991), 57–60. Collier mentions in an undated letter [1943, Peñasco] to Roy Stryker that he planned to do the story of the priests and community in New Mexico "much in the same way as the Maine story, a day with a family." Two papal encyclicals stimulated Catholic social reform during this period: *Rerum Novarum* (1891) and *Quadragesimo Anno* (1931). *Rerum Novarum*, promulgated by Pope Leo XIII in response to Marxism, upheld private property as a natural right while insisting that the state should be called up to safeguard the rights of workers. It argued that workers should have a living wage but that class warfare was not inevitable. To commemorate the fortieth anniversary of *Rerum Novarum*, Pope Pius XI issued *Quadragesimo Anno*, which continued to develop a middle ground between socialism and capitalism. Twelve years earlier American bishops had produced the "Bishops' Program for Social Reconstruction," and the National Catholic Welfare Conference established the Social Action Department to conduct studies and implement the teachings of *Rerum Novarum*. Father John Ryan, who later was influential in Roosevelt's New Deal, was placed at the department's head. In general, progressive Catholic reform argued for a minimum wage, regulation of monopolies, unemployment insurance,

workers' compensation, the right to unionize and strike, the eight-hour day, child labor laws, democratization of industrial management, and a host of other legislative initiatives designed to protect the workers and the poor. See George Q. Flynn, *American Catholics and the Roosevelt Presidency, 1932–1936* (Lexington: University of Kentucky Press, 1968); Joseph M. McShane, *"Sufficiently Radical": Catholicism, Progressivism, and the Bishops' Program of 1919* (Washington, DC: Catholic University of America Press, 1986); and Michael J. Baxter, "Notes on Catholic Americanism and Catholic Radicalism: Toward a Counter-Tradition of Catholic Social Ethics," in Sandra Yocum Mize and William Portier, *American Catholic Traditions: Resources for Renewal* (Maryknoll, NY: Orbis, 1997), 53–76.

21. "Portrait of America." For an example of a descriptive caption, see LC-USW3-017399-C. At fireside, LC-USW3-015118-E; woodcarving, LC-USW3-017370-C, LC-USW3-017369-C.

22. Ronald H. Carpenter, *Father Charles E. Coughlin: Surrogate Spokesman for the Disaffected* (Westport, CT: Greenwood, 1998), 38, 122–123; see also Donald Warren, *Radio Priest: Charles Coughlin, the Father of Hate Radio* (New York: Free Press, 1996), 244.

23. Carpenter, *Father Charles E. Coughlin,* 124.

24. On censorship see George H. Roeder, Jr., *The Censored War: American Visual Experience During World War Two* (New Haven: Yale University Press, 1993); Coughlin's comments on the "great betrayer" at the Union Party's 1936 nominating conference in Cleveland is cited in Warren, *Radio Priest,* 89.

25. LC-USW3-017330-C.

26. Patrick Smith to Augustine Danglmayer, October 26, 1942, Archives of the Diocese of Santa Fe. On religious diversity in New Mexico see Ferenc M. Szasz and Richard W. Etulain, *Religion in Modern New Mexico* (Albuquerque: University of New Mexico Press, 1997), and Daniel Richard Carnett, *Contending for the Faith: Southern Baptists in New Mexico, 1938–1995* (Albuquerque: University of New Mexico Press, 2002).

27. Quoted in Doug McClelland, *Forties Film Talk: Oral Histories of Hollywood, with 120 Lobby Posters* (Jefferson, NC: McFarland, 1992), 407.

28. Mary Gordon, "Father Chuck: A Reading of *Going My Way* and the *Bells of St. Mary's,* or Why Priests Made Us Crazy," in Thomas J. Ferraro, ed., *Catholic Lives, Contemporary America* (Durham: Duke University Press, 1997), 68.

29. Frank Walsh, *Sin and Censorship: The Catholic Church and the Motion Picture Industry* (New Haven: Yale University Press, 1996), 215.

30. For a thorough discussion of anti-Catholicism among intellectuals in the postwar years, see John T. McGreevy, "Thinking on One's Own: Catholicism in the American Intellectual Imagination, 1928–1960," *Journal of American History* 84 (June 1997), 97–131.

31. Walsh, *Sin and Censorship,* 228. "UnCatholic throughout" quoted ibid., 229.

7
Farming Jews

1. "Fed up with the rain," Jack Delano to Roy E. Stryker, November 12, 1940, RSP; "part-time farmer," Jack Delano to Roy E. Stryker, November 6, 1940, RSP; "social agitators," "Justification of Special Project to Extend Assistance to Rural Part-Time Farmers in New England Industrial Area, Especially Massachusetts, Connecticut, and Rhode Island," supplemental file for lot 1260, reel 17. Stryker's often cited comment to Delano to "emphasize the idea of abundance" comes from this New England trip.

2. On the history of Colchester see Alexander Feinsilver and Lillian Feinsilver, "Colchester's Yankee Jews," *Commentary,* July 1955, 64–70; Seymour S. Weisman, *The Jewish Community of Colchester, Connecticut* (West Palm Beach, FL: Hadeira, 1995).

3. Stephen Schwartz, interviewed by Chris Bailey on February 26, 1986, oral history collected by the Jewish Historical Society of Greater Hartford (JHSGH). Janice P. Cunningham and David F. Ransom, *Back to the Land: Jewish Farms and Resorts in Connecticut, 1890–1945* (Hartford: Connecticut Historical Commission, 1998), 20.

4. Bernard (Bernie) Goldberg, interviewed by John Sutherland on January 29, 1986, and February 10, 1986 (JHSGH). Charles S. Bernheimer, *The Russian Jew in the United States* (Philadelphia: John C. Winston, 1905), 388. The estimate of one thousand families was based on a report prepared in 1927, Works Projects Administration Records, box 68 "Jews," Connecticut State Library. I'd like to

thank Peter Gardella for finding this information. As for the rest of the nation, Henry L. Feingold writes, "By 1931 the minuscule Jewish agricultural sector had grown to 16,000 families. The retaining of potential farmers was supported by the Jewish Agricultural Society, which lent $6.5 million for that purpose in 1930 alone." *A Time for Searching: Entering the Mainstream, 1920–1945* (Baltimore: Johns Hopkins University Press, 1992), 151.

5. Deborah Dash Moore, *To the Golden Cities: Pursuing the American Jewish Dream in Miami and L.A.* (New York: Free Press, 1994), 4. Bureau of the Census, vol. 2, part 1, *Religious Bodies: 1936* (Washington, DC: U.S. Government Printing Office, 1941), 756. Farming colonies of Eastern European Jews supported by Jewish philanthropists and charitable organizations were founded in the United States, Argentina, and Palestine. Communities were established in Sicily Island, Louisiana (1881); Cremieux, South Dakota (1882); New Odessa, Oregon (1883); Beersheba, Kansas (1882); Clarion, Utah (1911); and Alliance, Carmel, and Rosenhayn, New Jersey (all 1882). They tended to be short-lived; only the New Jersey colonies persisted for more than one decade. See Ellen Eisenberg, *Jewish Agricultural Colonies in New Jersey, 1882–1920* (Syracuse: Syracuse University Press, 1995), xviii.

6. While I only know of one photograph from this series that was used during the war for propaganda, there is evidence that the Historical Division may have been preparing the prints for publication during the war years. Several of the photographic negatives have cropping lines drawn across them, indicating their preparation for printing.

7. Max Kozloff, "Jewish Sensibility and the Photography of New York," in *New York: Capital of Photography* (New Haven: Yale University Press, 2002), 71, 75.

8. History of Roosevelt, New Jersey, in the Borough of Roosevelt Historical Collection, manuscript collection 1060, Special Collections and University Archives, Rutgers University, www.libraries.rutgers.edu/rul/libs/scua/roosevelt/rstory.shtml (accessed July 2, 1999). See also Jersey Homesteads, supplemental reference file, lot 1214. FSA photographer Marjory Collins photographed Jews in New York City in August 1942 as a part of her series on ethnic New York.

9. LC-USF34-009177-E, June 1936.

10. Jack Delano, *Photographic Memories* (Washington,

DC: Smithsonian Institution, 1997): "sorry," 29; "to do justice," 56; "too cool," 28; "favorite subjects," 56.

11. Ibid., 1.

12. Ibid., 21.

13. Jack Delano to Roy E. Stryker, November 6, 1940, RSP.

14. "Spent his days reading," Alberta Eiseman and Herbert F. Janick, *In Touch with the Land: Images of Connecticut Farm Life, 1937–1985* (Hartford: Connecticut State Library, 1985), np; Delano, *Photographic Memories*, 59.

15. Jack Delano to Roy E. Stryker, November 6, 1940, RSP.

16. I would like to thank the following citizens of Colchester for identifying people in the FSA photographs and providing me a glimpse into their town's past: Arthur and Nathan Liverant, Faye Zupnick, Molly Aom, Bob Goldberg, Morris and Pearl Epstein, David Levine, and Ruth and David Adler.

17. "The pix you sent," J. B. Colson, "The Art of the Human Document: Russell Lee in New Mexico," in Colson et al., *Far from Main Street: Three Photographers in Depression-Era New Mexico* (Santa Fe: Museum of New Mexico Press, 1994), 7, citing correspondence from September 27, 1940; "bunch of sociologists," quoted in Roy Emerson Stryker and Nancy Wood, *In This Proud Land: America, 1935–1943, As Seen in the FSA Photographs* (Greenwich, CT: New York Graphic Society, 1973), 8. Ansel Adams to W. W. Alexander with carbon copy to Roy E. Stryker, April 23, 1940, LOC exhibits, reel 3. The distance between the men is reflected in the fact that Adams sent the original request to Stryker's boss, Will Alexander, head of the FSA, and sent only a carbon copy of the letter to Stryker. On Rosskam choosing images see Gary D. Saretzky, "Documenting Diversity: Edwin Rosskam and the Photo Book, 1940–1941," *Photo Review* 23 (Summer 2000), 10–11.

18. Arthur Zupnick interviewed by Chris Bailey, February 19, 1986, JHSGH. Faye Zupnick interviewed by Colleen McDannell, February 22, 1999.

19. Ruth Adler and David Adler interviewed by John Sutherland, February 14, 1986, JHSGH.

20. Beatrice Abrams interviewed by Ethel Clamon, January 2, 1986, JHSGH.

21. Jack Delano to Roy E. Stryker, November 12, 1940, RSP.

22. *1898–1998, Congregation Ahavath Achim* (cente-

nary history), printed August 22, 1998, n.p., JHSGH.

23. By the 1930s Yiddish in Colchester was dying out. Beatrice Abrams had to learn it from a tutor. Rachel Himmelstein spoke Yiddish to her parents but spoke English to her siblings. Ruth and David Adler also remembered speaking Yiddish at home but English with their siblings. There is no evidence in the oral histories that this change was regretted. On Hebrew schools see Barry Chazan, "Education in the Synagogue: The Transformation of the Supplementary School," in Jack Wertheimer, ed., *The American Synagogue: A Sanctuary Transformed* (Cambridge: Cambridge University Press, 1987), 171–172; "read Hebrew," Rachel Himmelstein interviewed by John Sutherland, on February 14, 1986, JHSGH; on the 1929 study see Beth S. Wenger, *New York Jews and the Great Depression: Uncertain Promise* (New Haven: Yale University Press, 1996), 184, citing Uriah Zevi Engelman, "The Jewish Synagogue in the United States," *American Journal of Sociology* 41 (1935–1936), 44.

24. I would like to thank Harris Lenowitz for reading the Hebrew and Yiddish texts for me.

25. "The Jews: Again the Wandering Children of Israel Are on the Move in Hostile Europe," *Life*, April 18, 1938, 46–55; *The American Jewish Yearbook, 5701* (Philadelphia: Jewish Publication Society, 1940), 332–408; Lublin mentioned on 375.

26. Wenger, *New York Jews and the Great Depression,* 183.

27. Zion Hall, which Delano did not photograph, was a one-story, brown-shingled building containing a small auditorium and stage, a classroom and in the basement a mikvah, and several baths. According to Bernie Goldberg, in addition to the steam baths and mikvah, there were fifteen or so bathtubs. "You know," he explained, "in a country town not everybody had running water or a bathtub in the house." The facilities of Zion Hall expanded and changed after the war, but during the thirties it was a no-frills place for education, health, and sociability. Bernard (Bernie) Goldberg, interviewed January 29 and February 10, 1986, JHSGH. Colchester's Zionist orientation is also mentioned by the local historian Seymour Weisman, who noted that Henrietta Szold visited in 1922 and set up the Hadassah chapter. Weisman, *Jewish Community of Colchester,* 30.

28. Edward Scott, interview summary by David Schulinder, n.d. (circa February 1986), JHSGH.

29. Weisman, *Jewish Community of Colchester,* 30.

30. "Spiritual depression," Wenger, *New York Jews and the Great Depression,* 167; David Kaufman, *Shul with a Pool: The "Synagogue-Center" in American Jewish History* (Hanover, NH: University Press of New England, 1999).

31. Wenger, *New York Jews and the Great Depression,* 195.

32. Bernard Goldberg interview.

33. See Joseph Brandes, *Immigrants to Freedom: Jewish Communities in Rural New Jersey Since 1882* (Philadelphia: University of Pennsylvania Press, 1971), 209–231.

8
The Negro Church

1. This background information was taken from the Chicago *Defender,* April 12 and 19, 1941.

2. This narrative was constructed from internal evidence in the photographs and from church traditions on the South Side. The movement between churches will be discussed further in the next chapter.

3. Richard Wright interviewed by Edwin Seaver for a radio broadcast on December 23, 1941, rpt. in Keneth Kinnamon and Michel Fabre, eds., *Conversations with Richard Wright* (Jackson: University Press of Mississippi, 1993), 43.

4. Richard Wright, photo direction by Edwin Rosskam, *12 Million Black Voices* (1941; rpt. New York: Thunder's Mouth, 1995), xix. All further references are to this edition and are cited parenthetically in the text.

5. I have counted only photographs that show religious practices, not pictures of churches (115) or nonreligious activities taking place in church (66).

6. Reviewers in the forties refer to the illustrations as being taken either by "the FSA photographers" or by Edwin Rosskam. In the most recent biography of Richard Wright, Hazel Rowley confuses the FSA with the WPA, typically referring to Rosskam as a WPA photographer rather than an FSA photoeditor. She does give correct attribution in her endnotes. *Richard Wright: The Life and Times* (New York: Henry Holt, 2001), 236, 249, 557 note 2. In his 1988 introduction to a recent reprint of *12 Million Black Voices,* the novelist David

Bradley incorrectly notes that the photographs were from the "archives of the Farm Credit Administration" (xiv) but later refers to them as the FSA photographs (xvi). Wright's friend and biographer, Michel Faber, writes that all of the photographs in *12MBV* were "taken by Rosskam" except for one that Richard Wright himself took. *The Unfinished Quest of Richard Wright* (New York: William Morrow, 1973), 234. Miles Orvell in *American Photography* (Oxford: Oxford University Press, 2003) writes that the photographs were "largely from the files of the FSA by Edwin Rosskam" (119). In actuality, Rosskam took only five of the photographs. A few photographs were from the Associated Press and United Press International services. Wright's photograph was lost (as was one by Louise Rosskam) and did not appear in later reprints. Nicolas Natanson in *The Black Image in the New Deal: The Politics of FSA Photography* (Knoxville: University of Tennessee Press, 1992) pays close attention to the photographs but continues the attribution errors of Rosskam and Lee regarding the churches they visited; see my discussion in the next chapter.

A few articles consider the photographs and the text; see James Goodwin, "The Depression Era in Black and White: Four American Photo-Texts," *Criticism* 40 (1998), 273–308, with focus on *12MBV* at 281–287; David G. Nicholls, "The Folk, the Race, and Class Consciousness: Richard Wright's *12 Million Black Voices*," in *Conjuring the Folk: Forms of Modernity in African America* (Ann Arbor: University of Michigan Press, 2000), 113–129; and an unpublished essay by Maren Stange presented at the 2000 ASA meeting, "'Not What We Seem': Image and Text in *12 Million Black Voices*."

7. Benjamin E. Mays, *The Negro's God as Reflected in His Literature* (1938; rpt. New York: Atheneum, 1968), 189–244, citing Countee Cullen, "Black Christ" (1929); Nella Larsen, *Quicksand* (1928); Langston Hughes, "Good-bye Christ" (1932), reprinted in Mays, *Negro's God,* 227, 224, 238.

8. This biographical summary is compiled from an interview of Edwin and Louise Rosskam by Richard Doud on August 3, 1965, American Archives of Art; and an interview of Louise Rosskam by Gary Saretzky on March 24, 2000, Oral History of Monmouth [New Jersey] County. Available at www.visitmonmouth.com/oralhistory/bios/Ross kamLouise.htm (accessed October 1, 2002). Roy Stryker hired Edwin Rosskam to photograph for his Standard Oil project, and some biographical materials are in the archives of the University of Louisville. See Employment Records, Personnel Correspondence, box 3, folder 14.

9. "I was not a painter," Rosskam interview with Doud; "walked off," Rosskam interview with Saretzky.

10. Rosskam interview with Saretzky.

11. Ibid.

12. Edwin Rosskam, *Roosevelt, New Jersey: Big Dreams in a Small Town and What Time Did to Them* (New York: Grossman, 1972), 103–106.

13. These include Edwin Rosskam with an introduction by William Saroyan, *San Francisco, West Coast Metropolis* (1939); Edwin Rosskam and Ruby A. Black with an introduction by Eleanor Roosevelt, *Washington: Nerve Center* (1939); Sherwood Anderson with photographs by Farm Security Photographers, *Home Town* (1940); Oliver La Farge with photographs by Helen M. Post, *As Long as the Grass Shall Grow: Indians Today* (1940); and Wright and Rosskam's *12 Million Black Voices* (1941).

14. "I had no knowledge," Rosskam interview with Doud; "I told him," Richard Wright interview with Seaver in Kinnamon and Fabre, *Conversations*, 44; "it is one," ibid., 43.

There is some controversy about who first had the idea for the book. According to the biographer Margaret Walker, "Wright told his friends in Chicago that he had been commissioned to write *Twelve Million Black Voices*, and that some of the pictures would come from the Farm Administration files, and that additional pictures would be taken by a young Jewish photographer, Edwin Rosskam." *Richard Wright: Daemonic Genius* (New York: Warner, 1988), 171. On the other hand, the biographer Michel Fabre implies in *Unfinished Quest* that the idea was Rosskam's: "Wright had just decided to go ahead with the stage adaptation of *Native Son* when he also agreed to write the text for an illustrated book on black Americans that Edwin Rosskam, a former photographer for the Farm Security Administration, was preparing for the Viking Press" (232). Hazel Rowley in *Richard Wright* also agrees that "Edwin Rosskam approached [Wright]" (236).

15. Clara Dean Wakeham to Jack Delano, April 3, 1941,

RSP. Clara "Toots" Wakeham, Stryker's administrative assistant, often wrote to the photographers echoing Stryker's sentiments.

16. Richard Wright had not been active in the Communist Party since 1936 but still was an official member until 1942.

17. Gunnar Myrdal, *An American Dilemma: The Negro Problem and Modern Democracy* (New York: Harper and Brothers, 1944).

18. *New Yorker,* November 15, 1941; George Streator, Review of *12 Million Black Voices, Commonweal,* November 28, 1941. For an opposing Catholic view see Euphemia Wyatt, *Catholic World* 153 (May 1942), 217–218. On Wright's role in the Communist Party see Addison Gayle, *Richard Wright: Ordeal of a Native Son* (Garden City, NY: Doubleday, 1980), 139. Stange, "'Not What We Seem,'" mentions an offer by *The New Masses,* but her reference does not substantiate her claim. Wright did, however, write for this Communist Party publication.

19. FWP materials on Chicago are available at the Illinois State Historical Library in Springfield. If we include African-American churches in north and west Chicago, the number climbs to 458. I found one summary of All Nations Penecostal [*sic*] Church that was signed by an "R. Wright" as "editor" and dated during the period that Richard Wright was working for the FWP. See Federal Writers' Project, box 187, Negro material 661 (churches).

20. St. Clair Drake and Horace R. Cayton, *Black Metropolis: A Study of Negro Life in a Northern City* (1945; rpt. Chicago: University of Chicago Press, 1993), xvii. See also Horace R. Cayton, *Long Old Road* (New York: Trident, 1965), 237–250.

21. Martin Bulmer, *Chicago School of Sociology* (Chicago: University of Chicago Press), 6. On Richard Wright's connection to the Chicago School see Carla Cappetti, *Writing Chicago: Modernism, Ethnography, and the Novel* (New York: Columbia University Press, 1993), and Carla Cappetti, "Sociology of an Existence: Richard Wright and the Chicago School," in Robert J. Butler, ed., *The Critical Response to Richard Wright* (Westport, CT: Greenwood, 1995), 84–87.

22. Drake and Cayton, *Black Metropolis,* 388, 382.

23. Ibid., 614; see 537–540 for the upper class, 670–688 for the middle class, and 636–657 for the lower class.

24. Supplemental reference files for lot 241, reel 14, LOC. While the "Negro Church" file does not mention Rosskam as its author, it follows the pattern in the Historical Section of photographers writing supplemental notes to explain a series of photographs they had taken. A selection from this document is reprinted in Maren Stange, *Bronzeville: Black Chicago in Pictures, 1941–1943* (New York: New Press, 2003), 151–152. Stange cites Rosskam as its author.

25. Ibid.

26. Richard Wright, *Black Boy* (1944; rpt. New York: HarperCollins, 1993), 59, 112, 136. All further references are to this edition and are cited parenthetically in the text. While all biographers note the importance of the Seventh-day Adventist Church in Wright's life, literary critics have glossed over the unique history and theology of the SDA. Following Wright's lead, they discuss his participation in a generic "Negro Church" with seemingly no distinctive theology or history. A recent example is Tara T. Green, who mistakenly refers to the SDA prophet Ellen White as "Ella White." See "'That Preacher's Going to Eat All the Chicken': Power and Religion in Richard Wright," Ph.D. diss., Louisiana State University, 2000, 10. Richard Wright's mother, Ella, might have been named after Ellen White. On the radio see Walker, *Richard Wright,* 33; on working see Fabre, *Unfinished Quest,* 32.

27. Rosskam chose to illustrate black concern for education with a photo from Gees Bend, Alabama, where school is being conducted in a church. Over the head of the teacher are the words "One Lord, One Faith, and One Baptism." LC-USF34-025348-D.

28. Jack Delano, Greene County, Georgia, 1941, LC-USF34-044610-D. Rosskam may have merely forgotten to check the caption list to see how Delano described the scene, although he did note the state correctly in the picture credits. The original photographer's captions were separate from the photographic negatives and prints, although eventually many negatives were printed, glued on mounting board, and the photographer's captions included at the top. On altering, see Natanson, *Black Image in the New Deal,* 250–253.

29. LC-USF34-038779-D.

30. Drake and Cayton, *Black Metropolis,* 620.

31. John M. Reilly, "Richard Wright Preaches the Nation *12 Million Black Voices,*" *Black American Lit-*

erature Forum 16 (1982), 117. Reilly sees Wright's whole book as a sermon, and, as do many literary critics, he overgeneralizes about black religious practices. Wright does not start with a biblical proof text, which is critical in defining an evangelical sermon. Nor does his text clearly articulate a basic point. Typically sermons in the African-American tradition are made up of a series of short, repeated observations that culminate in a burst of verbal enthusiasm. Although one could imagine that the reader provides a silent "amen, brother" response to the call of Wright the preacher, the text does not easily translate into a verbal performance. What the "preacher of long ago" is sharing is less a preached sermon than a visionary revelation.

32. These quotations come from the online version of the *Story of Redemption,* www.preparingforeternity .com (accessed February 1, 2003), also published as *The Story of Redemption: A Concise Presentation of the Conflict of the Ages Drawn from the Earlier Writings of Ellen G. White* (Washington, DC: Review and Herald, 1944). The story of the Fallen Angels was first presented in an ancient Jewish source, the Book of Enoch, which survived in Christian Ethiopia but did not become a part of the biblical canon. It may be the source for Gen 6:1–4. In spite of its noncanonical status, it became a popular Christian story and was retold by John Milton in *Paradise Lost* (book 5). Skeptics believe that Ellen White merely plagiarized Milton; see Walter Rea, *The White Lie* (Turlock, CA: M & R, 1982).

33. Drake and Cayton, *Black Metropolis,* 619.

34. Ellen G. White, *The Great Controversy Between Christ and Satan* (1888; rpt. Omaha, NE: Pacific Press, 1950), 678.

35. Many African Americans thought that the Great Migration was of "providential import" (6). See Milton C. Sernett, *Bound for the Promised Land: African American Religion and the Great Migration* (Durham, NC: Duke University Press, 1997).

36. This photograph was included in the first edition of *12 Million Black Voices,* but in later editions a different one (LC-USF34-038827-D) was substituted. It is unknown why this photograph was exchanged for one that included only the young people standing on the church steps, although visually it is better composed.

37. Steelworker, LC-USF34-026502-D. The character of Reverend Taylor in "Fire and Cloud" (1938) successfully moves from being an otherworldly preacher to being a leader of his people, but only when he adopts a humanist orientation. Richard Wright, "Fire and Cloud," in Martha Foley, ed., *200 Years of Great American Short Stories* (New York: Galahad, 1975), 598–642. On the image of the worker see Barbara Melosh, *Engendering Culture: Manhood and Womanhood in New Deal Public Art* (Washington, DC: Smithsonian Institution Press, 1991).

38. This discussion of *Negroes and the War* is drawn from Barbara Dianne Savage, *Broadcasting Freedom: Radio, War, and the Politics of Race* (Chapel Hill: University of North Carolina Press, 1999), 124–135.

39. Ibid., 132, and 130, quoting an OWI official.

40. For example, medical personnel, LC-USW3-000534-D; musician with family, LC-USW3-001524-D; jazz musicians, LC-USW3-001533-D, LC-USW3-001529-D; Ida B. Wells housing, LC-USW3-000566-D, LC-USW3-000282-D, LC-USW3-000805-D, LC-USW3-000293-D, LC-USW3-000278-D.

41. In most cases these photographs do not show the struggles that black families endured in order to afford the art classes or the humiliations they had to bear in order to achieve an education. The exception was Arthur Siegel's 1942 series of photographs of the riots surrounding the Sojourner Truth Housing Project in February. Siegel was a Detroit-based photography teacher and photojournalist working on assignment for *Life* magazine. He sent Stryker pictures of a race riot that occurred over the delays at a public housing project, including one showing a sign festooned with American flags that read, "WE WANT WHITE TENANTS IN OUR WHITE COMMUNITY." LC-USW3-016549-C.

9
City Congregations

1. Russell Lee to Roy E. Stryker, Friday night [April 1941], RSP.

2. Nicholas Natanson, *The Black Image in the New Deal: The Politics of FSA Photography* (Knoxville: University of Tennessee Press, 1992), 167; Robert L. Reid and Larry A. Viskochil, eds., *Chicago and Downstate: Illinois as Seen by the Farm Security Administration Photographers, 1936–1943* (Urbana: University of Illinois Press, 1989), 144–145.

3. I would like to thank for their October 13, 1998, interviews Juanita Ridgner-Horace, Hope Horace-Logwood, and the Rev. Sidney Logwood, as well

as Pastor France Davis of Salt Lake City for giving me these important contacts.

4. The field reports filed by FWP employees are located at the Illinois State Historical Library, Springfield, hereafter ISHL. I would like to thank manuscript librarian John M. Stassi for his help in locating these resources.

5. Robert S. Lynd and Helen Merrell Lynd, *Middletown in Transition: A Study in Cultural Conflicts* (New York: Harcourt, Brace, 1937), 301.

6. The number of Church of God churches in Chicago was counted from the list of "Negro Churches 1938," Federal Writers' Project in Illinois [hereafter FWPI], box 187, ISHL.

7. Natanson, *Black Image in the New Deal*, 167.

8. Edward Rembert, Interview no. 1, October 3, 1938, FWPI, box 185, ISHL. See also report from October 17, 1938, in same box.

9. Edward Rembert, Interview no. 13, October 24, 1938, FWPI, box 185, ISHL.

10. Ibid.

11. Colleen McDannell, *Material Christianity: Religion and Popular Culture in America* (New Haven: Yale University Press, 1995), 229–246.

12. "Ecce Homo," LC-USF34-044851-D. The woman also had a large parlor organ and a print of the Young Samuel by Sir Joshua Reynolds. This photograph is reprinted and discussed in *Material Christianity*, xii–1. Jack Delano, Woodville, Green County, Georgia, October 1941, took the photograph of a crucifix in the Baptist church, LC-USF34-046144-D. On religion and race movies see "'Saturday Sinners and Sunday Saints': The Nightclub as Moral Menace in 1940s Race Movies," in John M. Giggie and Diane Winston, eds., *Faith in the Market: Religion and the Rise of Urban Commercial Culture* (New Brunswick, NJ: Rutgers University Press, 2002), 155–176, and Judith Weisenfeld, *And Hollywood Be Thy Name: African-American Religion in American Film, 1929–1950* (Berkeley: University of California Press, forthcoming).

13. The first hymn written in English for public worship, by Isaac Watts in 1688, includes blood imagery: "Thou hast redeemed our souls with blood,/ Hast set the prisoner free;/Hast made us kings and priests to God,/And we shall reign with Thee." The first four lines of a hymn by William Cowper (1731–1800) are: "There is a fountain fill'd with blood/Drawn from Emmanuel's veins;/ And sinners, plunged beneath that flood,/ Lose all their guilty stains." In addition to trusting in the "precious blood," Fanny Crosby (1820–1915) wrote in "The Cleansing Fountain" that "From Calv'ry's cross, where Jesus died/In sorrow, pain, and woe;/Burst forth the wondrous crimson tide/ That cleanseth white as snow, That cleanseth white as snow!"

14. Richard Wright, photo direction by Edwin Rosskam, *12 Million Black Voices* (1941; rpt. New York: Thunder's Mouth, 1995), 135.

15. St. Clair Drake and Horace R. Cayton, *Black Metropolis: A Study of Negro Life in a Northern City* (1945; rpt. Chicago: University of Chicago Press, 1993), 601. For a close-up of the crutches see LC-USF34-38768-D. On All Nations Pentecostal see Wallace Best, "Passionately Human, No Less Divine: Racial Ideology and Religious Culture in the Black Churches of Chicago, 1915–1963," Ph.D. diss., Northwestern University, 2000. The 1936 report is by H. Bratton, n.d., and the summary is stamped with a routing form that lists as editor R. Wright and the date as April 26, 1936, when Richard Wright was working for the agency. Cassel C. Gross, "Church of All Nations Pentecostal," July 18, 1940, box 186, ISHL. On the funeral see [Chicago] *Defender,* June 18, 1952. I'd like to thank Wallace Best for all of his help in researching the biography of Lucy Smith.

16. Alvin Cannon, October 23, 1938, FWPI, box 185, ISHL.

17. Drum set, LC-USF34-038785-D, LC-USF34-038746-D. On Smith's reflections on fascism see Wallace Best, "Lucy Smith," in Colleen McDannell, ed., *The Religions of the United States in Practice* (Princeton: University of Princeton Press, 2001), 11–22.

18. Cassel C. Gross, July 18, 1940, FWPI, box 186, ISHL; [Robert Lucas?], "General Survey," FWPI, box 186, ISHL. The "General Survey" describes Smith as "a large woman; about 5 feet 7 inches tall and weighs about 250 pounds. She has smooth, dark brown skin and rather short hair, slightly gray, brushed straight back. Her hands and feet seem remarkably small for a person her size." Alvin Cannon on October 18 described her as weighing 350 pounds and having "large but weary looking feet."

19. Robert Lucas, October 26, 1938, FWPI, box 185, ISHL.

20. Rosskam writes in a supplemental reference file to the Chicago pictures, "These pictures were taken on Easter Sunday. Their subject matter varies from

the Easter parade outside a Congregational Church . . . to the crowd outside a Negro moving picture theater at matinee time. What the pictures cannot convey is the rainbow of color in both men's and women's clothing." In fact, the photographs were of an Episcopal church. Rosskam continues, "On days such as Easter Sunday Negro 'Society' parades as White 'Society.' . . . Negro 'Society' is an exact replica of white 'Society' on a lower income level. Imitative of its white example, Negro 'Society' is, if anything, more restrictive and more proper." "Holiday," supplemental reference files, lot 241, LOC. Delano's photographs of St. Edmund's are interspersed between LC-USW3-000821-D and LC-USW3-000838-D.

21. "History of the Church of St. Edmund," n.p., files of St. Edmund's Episcopal Church, Chicago. The spelling of the name of Father Martin's church varies. In 1937 Hortense Bratton referred to the church as "St. Edmunds Episcopal Church," and "Edmunds" was repeated in an undated list of churches by Henry N. Bacon, who writes that it was "named after the English martyr." Federal Writers' Project, box 187, folder "Negro Material, Churches." Russell Lee and Edwin Rosskam merely refer to it as "an Episcopal church," but Jack Delano follows the FWP report and calls it St. Edmunds. The parish history, however, is entitled "History of the Church of St. Edmund" and refers to St. Edmund as a king and martyr. St. Edmund (841–869) was a king of East Anglia who was killed by the Vikings and whose remains were eventually moved to Bedricsworth, later renamed Bury St. Edmunds. The history and parishioners refer to the church as "St. Edmund's" or "St. Edmund's church."

22. On religion and "changing" urban neighborhoods see John T. McGreevy, *Parish Boundaries: The Catholic Encounter with Race in the Twentieth-Century Urban North* (Chicago: University of Chicago Press, 1996); Gerald Gamm, *Urban Exodus: Why the Jews Left Boston and the Catholics Stayed* (Cambridge: Harvard University Press, 1999). By 1930 Pilgrim Baptist was the third-largest church in the National Baptist Convention and one of the ten largest churches (for blacks or whites) in the United States. The sanctuary held 2,500 people and was filled to overflowing two and three times each Sunday. Pilgrim Baptist's pastor, J. C. Austin, played an important role in local politics. See Randall Burkett, "The Baptist Church Years of Crisis: J. C.

Austin and Pilgrim Baptist Church, 1926–1950," in Timothy E. Fulop and Albert J. Raboteau, eds., *African American Religion: Interpretive Essays in History and Culture* (New York: Routledge, 1997). See LC-USF33-013000-M1 through M3, LC-USF34-038602-D, LC-USF34-038603-D.

23. On membership, Henry N. Bacon, "Churches," n.d., FWPI, box 187, ISHL. On the funeral, Hortense Bratton, March 3, 1937, FWPI, box 187, folder "Negro Material, Churches," ISHL.

24. The Easter pictures span from LC-USF33-013013-M1 through 013017-M2. I would like to thank Reverend Tolliver, Jess Brodnax, and the parishioners of St. Edmund's (especially Mrs. June Finch), interviewed in October 1998, for helping me prepare this section.

25. "History of the Church of St. Edmund."

26. St. Edmund's has received more than $42 million to renovate and construct 395 apartments in thirteen buildings and has built a home for senior citizens. In May 2002 it had plans to build 69 new apartments and to transform a former public-housing low-rise into a mixed-income community, projects estimated to cost $21 million. Its priest, Richard Tolliver, also coordinates grassroots resistance to drug dealing in addition to running a church and school. Mark Sappenfield, "A Home of One's Own," *Christian Science Monitor,* May 23, 2002.

27. Bureau of the Census, *Census of Religious Bodies* (Washington, DC: U.S. Government Printing Office, 1939–1940), 441; President's Research Committee on Social Trends, *Recent Social Trends in the United States* (New York: McGraw-Hill, 1933), 1021.

28. In addition to Rosskam and Lee's recessional photographs where boys are prominently figured, Jack Delano photographed their apparent ease in wearing their clerical garbs; see LC-USW3-000821-D, LC-USW3-000824-D, LC-USW3-000836-D, LC-USW3-000838-D.

29. LC-USF34-038782-D,   LC-USF34-038823-D, LC-USF34-038743-D, LC-USF34-038805-D.

30. Alvin N. Cannon, December 11, 1938, FWPI, box 185, ISHL.

31. These statistics are gathered from *Census of Religious Bodies,* vol. 2.

32. Statistics come from the annual reports gathered by the Archdiocese of Chicago and located at the Chicago Archdiocesan Archives. Whereas the numbers of baptisms are probably accurate because of

the paperwork needed to conduct the sacrament, the number of families and "souls" are rough estimates by the parish pastor. The captions of Jack Delano's photographs cite church membership of Corpus Christi Roman Catholic Church as "over 2,000." Although there still needs to be more information compiled on African-American Catholics during the 1930s and 1940s, a similar growth took place in Cleveland; Washington, D.C.; Richmond, Virginia; and Newark, New Jersey. See Dorothy Ann Blatnica, *At the Altar of Their God: African American Catholics in Cleveland, 1922–1961* (New York: Garland, 1995), 65–69; Morris J. Mac-Gregor, *The Emergence of a Black Catholic Community: St. Augustine's in Washington* (Washington, DC: Catholic University of America Press, 1999), 271; Gerald P. Fogarty, *Commonwealth Catholicism: A History of the Catholic Church in Virginia* (Notre Dame, IN: University of Notre Dame Press, 2001), 497–499; Mary A. Ward, *A Mission For Justice: The History of the First African American Catholic Church in Newark, New Jersey* (Knoxville: University of Tennessee Press, 2002), 71. Diana L. Hayes and Cyprian Davis, in *Taking Down Our Harps: Black Catholics in the United States* (Maryknoll, NY: Orbis, 1998), estimate that in 1930 out of a total African-American population of 11 million there were 200,000 Catholics. This number had increased to 300,000 ten years later, out of a total population of 12 million (39). For the importance of parochial schools see Nancy M. Davis, "Finding Voice: Revisiting Race and American Catholicism in Detroit," *American Catholic Studies,* Fall 2003, 46–50.

33. Unpublished typescript, written by Sisters of Saint Francis, December 20, 1934, files of Corpus Christi Roman Catholic Church, Chicago.

34. Reid and Viskochil, *Chicago and Downstate,* 147. For other pictures of Vincent Smith see LC-USW3-000136-D, LC-USW3-000137-D, LC-USW3-000141-D, LC-USW3-000125-D, LC-USW3-000126-D, LC-USW3-000129-D, LC-USW3-000133-D, LC-USW3-000134-D, LC-USW3-000132-D.

35. I would like to thank Gerald F. Garry, S.V.D., archivist for the Divine Word Fathers, for sending me this biographical information on Father Vincent Smith. Vincent Smith took the name Simon when he entered the Trappist monastery.

36. "Go out . . . a coat," Gordon Parks, *A Choice of Weapons* (Harper and Row, 1966), 220–252. "In a very short time," Gordon Parks, *Voices in the Mirror* (New York: Doubleday, 1990), 81.

37. "I stood her up," Gordon Parks interview by Richard Doud, December 30, 1964, AAA; "pitiful," Parks, *A Choice of Weapons,* 230; "had known poverty," Gordon Parks, *To Smile in Autumn: A Memoir* (New York: Norton, 1979), 124. *American Gothic* has been published often without other Parks FSA/OWI photographs; see Parks, *To Smile in Autumn,* first photo insert; Gordon Parks, *Half Past Autumn: A Retrospective* (Boston: Little, Brown, 1997), 33; Gordon Parks, *Voices in the Mirror,* 176; Skip Berry, *Gordon Parks: Photographer* (New York: Chelsea House, 1991), 19; Leah Bendavid-Val, *Propaganda and Dreams: Photographing the 1930s in the USSR and the U.S.* (Zurich: Stemmle, 1999), 152; F. Jack Hurley, *Portrait of a Decade: Roy Stryker and the Development of Documentary Photography in the Thirties* (Baton Rouge: Louisiana State University Press, 1972), 159; Carl Fleischhauer and Beverly Brannan, eds., *Documenting America, 1935–1943* (Berkeley: University of California Press, 1988), 235; Lawrence W. Levine, *The Unpredictable Past: Explorations in American Cultural History* (New York: Oxford University Press, 1993), 308; Deedee Moore, "Shooting Straight: The Many Worlds of Gordon Parks," *Smithsonian* 20 (April 1989), 68; "End Papers," *Chronicle of Higher Education,* January 10, 1990, 84; Natalie Hopkinson, "Photos Put Under Skeptical Lens," *Washington Post,* January 6, 2002; Miles Orvell, *American Photography* (Oxford: Oxford University Press, 2003), 119.

38. "Overdid it . . . just smiled," Parks, *A Choice of Weapons,* 231. In his 1964 interview with Richard Doud, Parks cryptically explained, "I sneaked out and published it in an old paper that used to be in Brooklyn. It was published in Brooklyn, you probably remember, what was it called? I forget, a Marshall Field paper, do you remember that one?" Doud does not, but *PM* was published from 1940 through 1948 in Brooklyn, financed by the millionaire Marshall Field and was noted for its photo illustrations. See Paul Milkman, *PM: A New Deal in Journalism, 1940–1948* (New Brunswick, NJ: Rutgers University Press, 1997).

39. "Arriving in January," Parks, *Voices in the Mirror,* 81. According to the Parks-Doud interview, Parks arrived in Washington with only a rudimentary understanding of photography. He had only purchased his first camera in 1937 and sold a few fash-

ion photographs. I have found no photographs in the FSA/OWI file before June, but there is no account in Gordon Parks's memoirs of what he was doing from January through June.

40. Robeson, LC-USF34-013361-C through 013365-C; Howard, LC-USF34-013320-C through 013327-C; air raid wardens, LC-USF34-013389-C through 013398-C; Anacostia, LC-USF34-013369-C, LC-USF34-013371-C, LC-USF34-013374-C, LC-USF34-013381-C; Ellington, LC-USW3-023912-C through 023983-D; fisherman, LC-USW3-030304-C; welders, LC-USW3-034283-C.

41. Gordon Parks, *A Choice of Weapons,* 231. In his 1964 interview, Parks mentions that Jack Delano was in Chicago making photographs of the South Side and that he saw some of Parks's photographs. Delano suggested that if Parks got the Rosenwald Fellowship, "they would be happy to have me down with the FSA." Delano took Parks with him on some of his Chicago assignments and probably included Parks in a photograph of a painting class; see LC-USW3-000702-D.

42. For the open bible see LC-USF34-013444-C, LC-USF34-013445-C. Other photographs of the altar without the bible include LC-USF34-013431-C, LC-USF34-013430-C. For Watson reading the bible see LC-USF34-013425-C.

43. Other statues, LC-USF34-013464-C; LC-USF34-013465-C; Calvary, LC-USF34-013493-C; healing, LC-USF34-013500-C, LC-USF34-013503-C.

44. Obituary of Vondell Gassaway in *Afro American,* November 21, 1964, clipping file of the Washington Public Library. The thirties and forties were a time of membership growth for Ella Watson's church. By 1954 the expanding congregation had sold the storefront church that Parks photographed and moved into a former Syrian Orthodox church. When Reverend Gassaway died ten years later, the leadership of the church was taken over by his close friend Jessie Marsh, the Mother of the Church. In 1974 the federal government's downtown expansion forced the church to relocate, and the congregation bought a building in northeast Washington. Jessie Marsh's nephew, Osirus Marsh, was the pastor of the church in 2000. This resilient congregation comprises approximately eighty members, including many relatives of Jessie Marsh. Genola Williams, the church's secretary, calls Verbycke a

"family church." The congregation now stresses the biblical orientation of their practices and no longer maintains the Catholic material culture of the forties. Members do, however, continue to make the Sign of the Cross and sing from a Catholic hymnal. I would like to thank the church members for their information, interviewed July 1999.

45. Drake and Cayton, *Black Metropolis,* 642.

46. Anointing, LC-USF34-013492-C, 013496-C, LC-USF34-013494-C; waiting shoeless, LC-USF34-013500-C, and close-up of feet, LC-USF34-013501-C, LC-USF34-013503-C (with explanatory caption); Gassaway in water, LC-USF34-013495-C, LC-USF34-013498-C. On demonstrations and the roles of flowers see Hans A. Baer, *The Black Spiritual Movement: A Religious Response to Racism* (Knoxville: University of Tennessee Press, 1984), 73–75; Cayton and Drake, *Black Metropolis,* 642. I would like to thank Archbishop Naiom Davis, who at ninety-five still had crisp memories of these rituals. Interviewed July 1999.

47. See Baer, *The Black Spiritual Movement,* 69. Gassaway preaching, LC-USF34-013384-C, LC-USF34-013461-C.

48. For a clear example of women wearing mortarboards see LC-USF34-013462-C. Watson's dress, LC-USF34-013500-C.

49. Gordon Parks, *A Choice of Weapons,* 231.

10
Project's End

1. "Everyone is so," Marion Post to Roy E. Stryker, July 28, 1940, RSP; "whole trend," Roy E. Stryker to Dorothea Lange, September 16, 1943, RSP.

2. Stryker to Lange, September 16, 1943. Stryker's comment probably was directed against Tom Sears, the director of the office of the picture division of the OWI located in New York City. Sears had worked for the Associated Press, which had competed with the FSA to produce pictures for America's media. Stryker was convinced that Sears was out not only to end the project but to destroy the file itself. See F. Jack Hurley, *Portrait of a Decade: Roy Stryker and the Development of Documentary Photography in the Thirties* (Baton Rouge: Louisiana State University Press, 1972), 168.

3. Roy E. Stryker, interview by Richard Doud, 1964. Standard Oil was looking to improve its image be-

cause it had a long-standing agreement with the German chemical company I. G. Farben not to pursue research on synthetic rubber—which proved to be almost treasonable when sources of natural rubber came under the control of the Japanese during World War II. A trial ensued. After five months of proceedings the company was cleared of wrongdoing, but by 1942 Standard Oil stood in the minds of the public near the bottom of American industrial companies. See James C. Anderson, *Roy Stryker: The Humane Propagandist* (Louisville: Photographic Archives of the University of Louisville, 1977), 9. The story of Jesus being tempted by the devil with the glories of the world is recounted in Mt 4:1–11, Lk 4:1–3, and Mk 1:12–14.

4. Stryker interview with Doud. On the Standard Oil photographs see www.louisville.edu/library/ekstrom/special/stryker/stryker.html (accessed February 2003).

5. Lili Corbus Bezner, *Photography and Politics in America: From the New Deal into the Cold War* (Baltimore: Johns Hopkins University Press, 1999), 17.

6. Howard Greenfeld, *Ben Shahn: An Artist's Life* (New York: Random House, 1998), 235. See also Frances K. Pohl, *Ben Shahn: New Deal Artist in a Cold War Climate, 1947–1954* (Austin: University of Texas Press, 1989).

7. Bezner, *Photography and Politics in America,* 71. On later criticism of the file see clippings contained in the Roy Stryker Papers: series 3, part A, scrapbook, 1936–1958, RSP.

8. On picture magazines see Wendy Kozol, *Life's America: Family and Nation in Postwar Photojournalism* (Philadelphia: Temple University Press, 1994); on exhibitions see Eric J. Sandeen, *Picturing an Exhibition: The Family of Man and 1950s America* (Albuquerque: University of New Mexico Press, 1995); John Vachon, *Poland, 1946: The Photographs and Letters of John Vachon,* ed. Ann Vachon (Washington, DC: Smithsonian Institution Press, 1995).

9. Arthur Rothstein, interview by Richard Doud, May 25, 1964, AAA.

10. See international.loc.gov/ammem/fsahtml/fahome.html (accessed on May 1, 2003).

11. Robert T. Handy, "The American Religious Depression, 1925–1935," *Church History* 24 (1960), 3–16. Handy partially based his conclusions on the work of the sociologist Robert Lynd, whom Stryker also consulted. Lynd had a particularly pessimistic evaluation of the state of twentieth-century religion; see Richard Wightman Fox, "Epitaph for Middletown: Robert S. Lynd and the Analysis of Consumer Culture," in Richard Wightman Fox and T. J. Jackson Lears, eds., *The Culture of Consumption: Critical Essays in American History, 1880–1980* (New York: Pantheon, 1983). Although Handy's work was influential during the sixties and seventies, it has increasingly been criticized. See Joel A. Carpenter, "Fundamentalist Institutions and the Rise of Evangelical Protestantism, 1929–1942," *Church History* 9 (1980), 62–75.

Acknowledgments

When I began working with Farm Security Administration photographs, I had to travel to Washington, D.C., to work with the prints and the microfilmed lots of pictures. It was a slow process, looking through the filing cabinets and scrolling through microfilm at the Library of Congress. The staff of the Prints and Photograph Division made all those trips worthwhile. In particular, I would like to thank Beverly Brannan, the curator of photography, who shared her expertise on Roy Stryker and his team, and Mary Ison, who got me prints when all else failed. Now most of the FSA/OWI negatives are online, and anyone can search them using keywords. This digitizing not only made my work much easier, it has opened up the file for wider use by the general public. I am thankful that the federal government—at least this time—has spent my tax money in such a wise way. Without the groundbreaking books of Jack Hurley and James Curtis this one would not be possible. Both scholars of the FSA/OWI project helped during the conceptualizing and writing of *Picturing Faith*. Jack Hurley's perceptive suggestions on improving the final manuscript saved me from making several incorrect conclusions.

Getting to Washington and to the places where the photographers traveled was made possible by a grant from the Lilly Endowment. Lilly funded the Material History of American Religion Project, which supported three years of research and scholarly conversation. Under the direction of James Hudnut-Beumler, I was able to discuss my work with Marie Griffith, Bob Orsi, Dan Sack, Leigh Schmidt, David Watt, Judith Weisenfeld, and Diane Winston.

When Dan first called me about the project, I was heavy with child, confined to bed, and wondering whether I could survive motherhood. All I could manage to promise was a short book with some pictures. With the group's critical comments, however, I eventually understood the potential of the photographs for rethinking American religions during the interwar years.

A special thank you goes to Jim Hudnut-Beumler, who permitted me to use project funds to curate an exhibition of forty-five of the FSA/OWI religious photographs. Gary Wickard, one of our history graduate students, was invaluable in the design and construction of the exhibition. Now in its fourth year, the exhibition has traveled to twenty-five colleges and museums in the United States and Europe. I mounted a smaller exhibition of photographs of southern religion at Emory University in Atlanta. Given how difficult it is to secure funding for such exhibitions, I want to thank all of those who have hosted both the photographs and their curator. As I lectured on the exhibition, audiences raised questions that forced me to clearly articulate the relationship between visual culture, religion, and history.

The pictures led me across the United States, where I worked in regional archives and interviewed people who attended the photographed churches and synagogues. A John Simon Guggenheim Memorial Foundation Fellowship made all of this possible. "Being there" was a vital part of the project, and I was continually struck by the hospitality of community people, librarians, archivists, religious leaders, and scholars. I have tried to acknowledge each of you in the notes, but if I have missed someone, please forgive my omission. Likewise, I relied on the special expertise of my friends who read individual chapters with their red pens in hand. Thank you: Dianne Ashton, Wallace Best, Jim Fisher, Peter Gardella, Bob Goldberg, Linda Gordon, Paul Harvey, David Igler, Gary Laderman, Harris Lenowitz, Shannon Miller, Vanessa Ochs, Roger Payne, Steve Prothero, and Kathryn Stockton. Will Gravely not only read the chapter on the South, he let me stay in his wonderful house in Liberty, South Carolina. Julie Ingersoll and Paul Croce also let me lounge about in their cozy homes in Florida. Lillian Wondrack fed me in Connecticut. Such hospitality throughout the country enabled me to get a sense of what the FSA/OWI photographers experienced in their peregrinations.

Back in Utah there were many supporters. Margaret Toscano's warm friendship carried me through the whole project. She reassured me that if she could raise four daughters while teaching and writing, surely I could manage one. I do not know how Margaret found the time to carefully read the entire manuscript, but I am glad that she did. A University of Utah Research Committee Grant funded travel to Chicago and to Washington, D.C. Holly Campbell at the Tanner Humanities Center graciously let me transform their meeting room into an art gallery for the first exposure of the *Picturing Faith* exhibition. As I completed the project, funding from the Humanities Center enabled our Religious Studies Research Interest Group to hear about the book over takeout Indian curry. The University of Utah Undergraduate Research Opportunities Program funded students who worked both on the exhibition and on the book. Bryan Olsen, Julieanne Sabula, and Meg Spencer not only were efficient and insightful; they always were cheerful, even on the gloomy days. Reid Sondrup in the Multimedia Center found obscure videos from the thirties, and Roger Newbold made slides and photographs. Given how overburdened our staff is in these days of university budget cuts, I want to acknowledge their care and attention.

The origin of this project occurred with the origin of Brigit Hurdle McDannell. Now a third-grader, she is just exploring the joys and tribulations of reading and writing. While words are grand, she and I share a preference for pictures, an inclination I hope she never loses. I have dedicated this book to Brigit's favorite playmates—my parents, Kenneth and Margaret Mary McDannell. They lived through both the Great Depression and World War II, and it is their generation that this book is about. As my mother read through and corrected my drafts, I was often encouraged by her comment, "I remember this." I truly appreciate the love and sacrifices of both generations of McDannells.

After I finish each book, I swear I will never write another one. And after each such pledge, John Hurdle rolls his eyes and wags his head. He realizes that he will never be free from book conversations or reading endless manuscript drafts. After thirty years of marriage and an even longer friendship, there is not much that he hasn't done to foster my creativity and independence. In my first book, I explained that I would be "forever in his debt." Friends warned me that publishing such sentiments might be risky given the fragility of modern romance. I continue to stand by that declaration. Here is yet another book that would not have existed without your love.

Index

Note: Illustrations are indicated by **bold face** type.